The Dolphin Writer, Book Two

The Dolphin Writer, Book Two
Composing Paragraphs and Crafting Essays

HOUGHTON MIFFLIN COMPANY   **Boston**   **New York**

Executive Publisher: Patricia Coryell
Editor-in-Chief: Carrie Brandon
Sponsoring Editor: Joann Kozyrev
Senior Marketing Manager: Tom Ziolkowski
Senior Development Editor: Judith Fifer
Project Editor: Shelley Dickerson
Art and Design Manager: Jill Haber
Cover Design Manager: Anne S. Katzeff
Senior Photo Editor: Jennifer Meyer Dare
Senior Composition Buyer: Chuck Dutton
New Title Project Manager: James Lonergan
Editorial Assistant: Daisuke Yasutake
Marketing Assistant: Bettina Chiu
Editorial Assistant: Anthony D'Aries

Cover image: Lisa Kreick—Ocean Eyes Photography; www.oceaneyesphotography.com

Printed in the U.S.A.

Library of Congress Control Number: 2007931652

Instructor's Annotated Edition ISBN 10: 0-618-37914-2
Instructor's Annotated Edition ISBN 13: 978-0-618-37914-9
For ordering, use student text ISBNs
Student Edition ISBN 10: 0-618-37911-8
Student Edition ISBN 13: 978-0-618-37911-8

4 5 6 7 8 9–DOC–11 10

Brief Contents

Part I THE WRITING PROCESS

Chapter 1 Improving Writing and Thinking   1
Chapter 2 Prewriting   18
Chapter 3 Organizing and Outlining   35
Chapter 4 Writing a Paragraph   53
Chapter 5 Revising   75
Chapter 6 Proofreading, Editing, and Preparing a Final Draft   94
Chapter 7 Writing the Essay   125

Part II DEVELOPING PARAGRAPHS AND ESSAYS WITH THE RHETORICAL MODES

Chapter 8 The Reading/Writing Connection   158
Chapter 9 Narration   193
Chapter 10 Description   209
Chapter 11 Process   227
Chapter 12 Illustration   242
Chapter 13 Classification   256
Chapter 14 Division   271
Chapter 15 Comparison/Contrast   286
Chapter 16 Cause/Effect   305
Chapter 17 Definition   320
Chapter 18 Argument   335
Chapter 19 Combining Modes of Development   355

Part III READING SELECTIONS   370

Part IV HANDBOOK WITH EXERCISES   417

Additional Practice for Multilingual Writers   544
Index   554
Rhetorical Index   568

Table of Contents

Preface   xviii

Part I   THE WRITING PROCESS

CHAPTER 1   IMPROVING WRITING AND THINKING   1

Goals for Chapter 1   1

Expectations and Attitudes   2

Writing as Opportunity   4

The Opportunity to Express Yourself   4

The Opportunity to Expand Your Own Understanding   5

The Opportunity to Improve Crucial Thinking Skills   5

The Opportunities Before You Now   6

The Opportunity to Increase Your Knowledge About Writing   6

The Opportunity to Practice and Gain Valuable Feedback   7

   Student Jamie Stevenson, "Let Students Have Cell Phones"   8

The Opportunity to Learn from Others' Writings   11

   Russell Baker, "Learning to Write"   11

   from Anne Lamott, Bird By Bird   14

Writing Opportunities   16

Chapter 1 Review   16

Web Work   17

CHAPTER 2   PREWRITING   18

Goals for Chapter 2   18

The Writing Process   18

Prewriting   19

WRITING FOR SUCCESS: *Using Prewriting Techniques*   21

Talking   21

Freewriting   22

Brainstorming   24

Clustering   25

Asking Questions   27

Focus on Research: Using Questions   28

Topic to Main Idea   **29**

Prewriting to Main Idea: A Student Demonstration   **31**

Chapter 2 Review   33

Web Work   34

CHAPTER 3 ORGANIZING AND OUTLINING   **35**

Goals for Chapter 3   35

Organizing   **35**

Determining a Framework   36

Natural Versus Logical Organization   42

Outlining   **44**

Myths About Outlining   44

WRITING FOR SUCCESS: *Outlining and PowerPoint Presentations*   45

Formal Outlines   46

Focus on Research: Using an Outline to Identify Needed Information   47

Informal Outlines   48

Organizing and Outlining: A Student Demonstration   **49**

Chapter 3 Review   51

Web Work   52

CHAPTER 4 WRITING A PARAGRAPH   **53**

Goals for Chapter 4   53

The Paragraph and Its Purpose   **53**

The Topic Sentence   54

The Body   61

A Step-by-Step Guide to Composing a Paragraph   **62**

Step One: Transform Your Main Idea into a Topic Sentence   62

Step Two: Reevaluate Your Outline and Consider Common Strategies for Organizing Ideas   64

Step Three: Using Your Outline as a Guide, Compose with Layers of Development and Transitional Expressions   67

Carol Kanar, "Be Proactive About Studying," *from* The Confident Student   69

Some Helpful Tips for Composition   **70**

WRITING FOR SUCCESS: *Advantages and Disadvantages of Composing on a Computer*   71

Writing a Paragraph: A Student Demonstration 71

Chapter 4 Review 73

Web Work 74

CHAPTER 5 REVISING 75

Goals for Chapter 5 75

Revising Versus Editing 75

Revising for Completeness 76

Revising for Cohesiveness 79

Revising for Coherence 81

Organization and Transitions 81

Repetition of Key Words and Ideas 84

Two Important Revision Tips 85

WRITING FOR SUCCESS: *Qualities of a Good Peer Reviewer* 88

Revising a Paragraph: A Student Demonstration 88

Chapter 5 Review 92

Web Work 93

CHAPTER 6 PROOFREADING, EDITING, AND PREPARING A FINAL DRAFT 94

Goals for Chapter 6 94

Editing to Improve Style 94

Sentence Length 95

Techniques for Combining Sentences 95

Sentence Types 97

Diction 98

Eliminating Wordiness 103

Editing to Correct Major Sentence Errors 106

Sentence Fragments 106

Comma Splices and Run-on Sentences 108

WRITING FOR SUCCESS: *Careful Use of Computer Checks* 110

Misplaced or Dangling Modifiers 110

Faulty Parallelism 112

Editing Errors in Grammar and Mechanics 113

Editing Spelling Errors 115

from William M. Pride et al., Business 116

Preparing the Final Draft 116

Editing a Paragraph: A Student Demonstration   118
Student Maya Johnson, "Three Tools for Student Success"   120

Chapter 6 Review   122

Web Work   124

CHAPTER 7 WRITING THE ESSAY   125

Goals for Chapter 7   125

The Essay and Its Parts   125
The Introduction   128
The Body   135
The Conclusion   137

Steps in Writing an Essay: A Student Demonstration   138
Prewriting   139
Organizing and Outlining   140
Writing a Draft   141

WRITING FOR SUCCESS: *Beyond College Essays*   146

Revising   146

Proofreading, Editing, and Preparing the Final Draft   152

Chapter 7 Review   156

Web Work   157

Part II DEVELOPING PARAGRAPHS AND ESSAYS WITH THE RHETORICAL MODES

CHAPTER 8 THE READING/WRITING CONNECTION   158

Goals for Chapter 8   158

Reading for Ideas   158
Robert Lipsyte, "What Makes a True Sports Hero?"   159
Abraham Verghese, "Pain Gains"   161

Reading for Learning and Critical Thinking   165
Michael Barone, "A Tale of Two Nations"   165

Reading to Improve Writing Skills   168
Steve Salerno, "Not All in the Family"   168

Active Reading   171
Preview the Text   172
Formulate Questions and Read for Answers   173
Underline and Highlight Key Words and Phrases   173
Take Notes on the Text   174
John Merline, "Can E-Mail Be Saved from 'Spam'?"   175

Critical Reading   180
 Lawrence W. Reed, "Encourage Organ Donors with a Little
  Quid Pro Quo"   182
 Nick Jans, "Student Problems Begin at Home"   184

Keeping a Reading Journal   187
 Anne Becker, "Parenting for the Long Haul"   188
Focus on Research: An Introduction to Research   191

Chapter 8 Review   192
Web Work   192

CHAPTER 9 NARRATION   193
 Goals for Chapter 9   193

Writing a Narrative Paragraph   193
Determining a Main Idea and Writing a Topic Sentence   193
Selecting the Right Details for a Narrative   195
Organizing Details and Using Transitions   196

Using Vivid Language   199
Specific Words   199
Factual and Sensory Details   199
Action-Oriented Verbs   199

Writing Longer Narratives and Narrative Essays   200
 Carmen Machin, "The Deli"   200

Focus on Research: Conducting Library Research   202
 Maya Angelou, "A Thanksgiving Feast in Aburi" *from* All God's Children
  Need Traveling Shoes   203

IN SUMMARY: *Steps in Writing Narratives*   205
Chapter 9 Review   206

Topic Ideas for Narratives   207
Web Work   208

CHAPTER 10 DESCRIPTION   209
 Goals for Chapter 10   209

Writing a Descriptive Paragraph   209
Prewriting   209
Determining a Main Idea and Writing a Topic Sentence   210
Selecting the Right Details for a Description   212
Organizing Details and Using Transitions   213

Using Vivid Language   215

Writing Longer Descriptions and Descriptive Essays   219
The National Park Service, "Maya Ying Lin's Design Submission to the
Vietnam Veterans Memorial Competition"   219

Focus on Research: Internet Sources   221
Oliver Mackson, "As Eyes Pan Ground Zero, Words Fail"   221

IN SUMMARY: *Steps in Writing Descriptions*   224
Chapter 10 Review   224

Topic Ideas for Descriptions   225
Web Work   226

CHAPTER 11 PROCESS   227
Goals for Chapter 11   227

Writing a Process Paragraph   229
Determining a Main Idea and Writing a Topic Sentence   229
Organizing Details and Using Transitions   230
Developing a Process Paragraph   233

Writing Longer Process Passages and Process Essays   234
from Winston Fletcher, "It's Time to Make Up Your Mind"   234

Focus on Research: Nonprint Sources   236
from Garrison Keillor, "How to Write a Personal Letter"   236

IN SUMMARY: *Steps in Writing Process*   239
Chapter 11 Review   239

Topic Ideas for Process   240
Web Work   241

CHAPTER 12 ILLUSTRATION   242
Goals for Chapter 12   242

Writing an Illustration Paragraph   243
Determining a Main Idea and Writing a Topic Sentence   244
Selecting Relevant Examples   244
Including Adequate Examples   246
Organizing Details and Using Transitions   246
Developing an Illustration Paragraph   249
Focus on Research: Evaluating the Credibility of Sources   249

Writing Longer Illustration Passages and Illustration Essays   250
John Leo, "Taking It Off the Streets"   251

IN SUMMARY: *Steps in Writing Illustration*   253

Chapter 12 Review   254

Topic Ideas for Illustrations   **255**
Web Work   255

CHAPTER 13 CLASSIFICATION   **256**
Goals for Chapter 13   256

Writing a Classification Paragraph   **257**
Applying an Organizing Principle, Determining a Main Idea, and
    Writing a Topic Sentence   257
Organizing Details and Using Transitions   259
Developing a Classification Paragraph   261
Focus on Research: Writing a Summary   262

**Writing Longer Classification Passages and
Classification Essays**   **262**
    William Pride and O.C. Ferrell, "Consumer Products,"
        from Marketing   262
    Robert J. Trotter, "How Do I Love Thee?"   264

IN SUMMARY: *Steps in Writing Classification*   268
Chapter 13 Review   269

Topic Ideas for Classification   **269**
Web Work   270

CHAPTER 14 DIVISION   **271**
Goals for Chapter 14   271

Writing a Division Paragraph   **272**
Determining the Parts and the Main Idea and Writing
    a Topic Sentence   273
Organizing the Parts and Using Transitions   274
Developing the Parts in a Division Paragraph   277

Writing Longer Division Passages and Division Essays   **277**
    U.S. Environmental Protection Agency, "Municipal Solid Waste
        in the United States"   277

Focus on Research: Note-Taking Methods   280
    John Leo, "The Good-News Generation"   281

IN SUMMARY: *Steps in Writing Division*   283
Chapter 14 Review   284

Topic Ideas for Division   **284**
Web Work   285

CHAPTER 15   COMPARISON/CONTRAST   286
Goals for Chapter 15   286

Writing a Comparison/Contrast Paragraph   288
Determining the Points of Comparison and the Main Idea
  and Writing a Topic Sentence   288
Organizing Points of Comparison and Using Transitions   290
Developing the Points in a Comparison/Contrast Paragraph   293

**Writing Longer Comparison/Contrast Passages and
Comparison/Contrast Essays**   294
  Axel Boldt, "A Subjective Comparison of Germany
  and the United States"   294

Focus on Research: *Writing a First Draft Using Outline and Notes*   295
  from John Gray, "Mr. Fix-It and the Home-Improvement
  Committee"   296

IN SUMMARY: *Steps in Writing Comparison/Contrast*   302
Chapter 15 Review   303

Topic Ideas for Comparison/Contrast   303
Web Work   304

CHAPTER 16   CAUSE/EFFECT   305
Goals for Chapter 16   305

Writing a Cause/Effect Paragraph   306
Generating Ideas, Determining the Main Idea, and
  Writing a Topic Sentence   306
Organizing Causes and/or Effects and Using Transitions   310
Developing the Points in a Cause/Effect Paragraph   312

**Writing Longer Cause/Effect Passages and
Cause/Effect Essays**   312
  from Marie Cocco, "Work Ethic Has Led to Overwork"   312
  Mortimer B. Zuckerman, "Our Energy Conundrum"   314

Focus on Research: What Is Plagiarism?   315

IN SUMMARY: *Steps in Writing Cause-Effect*   317
Chapter 16 Review   318

Topic Ideas for Cause/Effect   318
Web Work   319

CHAPTER 17 DEFINITION   320

Goals for Chapter 17   320

Writing a Definition Paragraph   321
Determining a Topic Sentence   321
Generating Ideas   322
Organizing a Definition Paragraph and Using Transitions   325
Developing the Details in a Definition Paragraph   327

Writing Longer Definition Passages and Definition Essays   327
  George Roche, "A World Without Heroes"   327
  from Constitutional Rights Foundation, "What Is Terrorism?"   328

Focus on Research: Integrating Source Material   329

IN SUMMARY: *Steps in Writing Definition*   332

Chapter 17 Review   333

Topic Ideas for Definition   333
Web Work   334

CHAPTER 18 ARGUMENT   335

Goals for Chapter 18   335

Writing an Argument Paragraph   336
Thinking About Your Audience   336
Determining Your Topic Sentence, Relevant Reasons,
  and Opposing Arguments   338
Organizing an Argument Paragraph and Using Transitions   343
Developing Your Reasons with Evidence   345

Writing Longer Arguments and Argument Essays   346

Focus on Research: Documenting Sources   348
  from Lou Dobbs, "To Reach for the Stars"   349

IN SUMMARY: *Steps in Writing Argument*   351

Chapter 18 Review   352

Topic Ideas for Argument   353
Web Work   354

CHAPTER 19 COMBINING MODES OF DEVELOPMENT   355

Goals for Chapter 19   355

Some Common Combinations   356

Writing a Paragraph Using a Combination of Modes   357
Evaluating Your Topic Sentence and Selecting
   Appropriate Modes   357
Organizing a Combination Paragraph and Using Transitions   359
Developing the Details in a Combination Paragraph   361

Combining Modes in Longer Passages and Essays   362
from William McKibben, "The End of Nature"   362
Helen Keller, "Three Days to See"   363

Focus on Research: Preparing the Works Cited List   363

IN SUMMARY: *Steps in Combining Modes*   367

Chapter 19 Review   368

Topic Ideas for Combining Modes   369
Web Work   369

Part III READING SELECTIONS

Each selection is followed by Vocabulary, Checking Comprehension,
Mode and Skill Check, and Questions for Discussion and Writing.

Amy Tan, "Mother Tongue"   370

Dave Barry, "Winning the War
   on Drugs"   376

Whitney Matheson, "What's the Matter
   with Moviegoers?"   381

Nancy Gibbs, "And on the Seventh Day
   We Rested?"   385

Leonard Pitts Jr., "At Large: Giving
   Teachers Guns a Simple but
   Stupid Idea"   389

Ian Urbina, "No Need to Stew: A Few Tips
   to Cope with Life's Annoyances"   394

Lenore Skenazy, "'Like,' Like,
   Covers It All"   399

Connie Schultz, "Most Divorced Dads
   Deserve to See Their Kids"   403

Ana Veciana-Suarez, "Don't LOL, but
   Texting Turns Me Off"   408

Marc Gellman, "The Deeper Truth of
   Good and Evil"   412

Part IV HANDBOOK WITH EXERCISES   417

Parts of Speech   417
Nouns   417
Pronouns   419
Adjectives   421
Verbs   423
Adverbs   424
Prepositions   426
Conjunctions   427
Interjections   429

The Basic Sentence   430

Subjects   430
Other Elements of Simple Sentences   435
Avoiding Sentence Fragments   440
Verbs   441
Modifiers: Adjectives, Adverbs, and Prepositional Phrases   457
Subject-Verb Agreement   469
Pronouns and Pronoun Agreement   478

Coordination   487

The Compound Sentence   487
Three Kinds of Compound Sentences   488
Distinguishing Compound Elements from
   Compound Sentences   494
Avoiding Comma Splices and Run-ons in Compound Sentences   495

Subordination   498

The Complex Sentence   498
Dependent Clauses   498
Relative Clauses   502
Avoiding Sentence Fragments   505

Parallelism   508

Parallel Words   508
Parallel Phrases   509
Parallel Clauses   510

Combining Sentences   514

Use a Compound Subject or Compound Verb   515
Use a Dependent Clause   516
Use a Relative Clause   518
Use an Appositive   519
Use a Prepositional Phrase   520
Use a Participle (-*ed* or –*ing*) Phrase   522

Mechanics   523

Punctuation   523
Capitalization   529

Spelling   532

The Importance of Correct Spelling   532
Abbreviations   541

Additional Practice for Multilingual Writers   544

Index   554

Rhetorical Index   568

Preface

The Dolphin Writer

The Dolphin Writer is a three volume series that focuses on writing sentences to paragraphs (Book One), paragraphs to essays (Book Two), and essays (Book Three) in an easy-to-understand and affordable format. Each volume of the Dolphin Writer presents students with comprehensive yet approachable coverage of the writing process, from prewriting through peer evaluation through revision and preparation of the final paper. Book One includes complete coverage of sentence-to-paragraph issues such as grammar, mechanics, and usage, while Books Two and Three include a brief Handbook that contains this basic coverage. Each volume includes a readings section with ten level-appropriate readings.

The Dolphin Writer — Book Two

Key features of this volume include:

- the same topics and content as do other comparable textbooks, but for a price that is more than a third less than that of similar books

- careful step-by-step explanations of each part of the writing process along with many student models; each of the Writing Process chapters includes a "Student Demonstration" of the process, as well as many shorter student samples throughout the chapter

- a multitude of practice exercises that permit students to practice each new concept; half of the practice exercises are self-tests, with suggested answers listed in the back of the book

- carefully-selected photos and other illustrations that enhance student understanding of the text and help students learn to understand and interpret visuals

- a focus on student success in all areas of reading, writing, and studying, with Writing for Success boxes that suggest ways to organize, manage, or implement techniques, including how to use a computer to assist in the writing process

- Web Work boxes at the end of each chapter provide suggestions for sites that provide additional help, exercises, or suggestions for further exploration

- definitions of difficult words as well as allusions in many of the examples, exercises, and readings appear as footnotes so that students don't have to look them up

- chapter pedagogy supports students in anticipating, learning, and reviewing key concepts, as well as providing suggestions for discussion and writing practice

- an ESL appendix focuses on areas of difficulty for multilingual students or students who need additional practice in standard English

- a grammar handbook with practice exercises, to help students review grammar principles and obtain practice with problem areas

- a student website that includes numerous grammar practice exercises and live links to additional practice sites

Organization of the Text

Part I: The Writing Process covers the stages of writing, from prewriting through organizing and outlining, drafting, revising, and editing and preparing a final draft. The introductory chapter, Improving Writing and Thinking, addresses student attitudes and expectations about writing and encourages students to continue to improve their thinking, reading, and writing skills.

Part II: Developing Paragraphs and Essays with the Rhetorical Modes uses the modes as a stepping-stone to organizing and improving writing. An introductory chapter (Chapter 8) discusses the connection between reading and writing. Separate chapters present narration, description, process, illustration, classification, division, comparison/contrast, cause/effect, definition, and a chapter on argument. The last chapter in the Part addresses how these patterns may be combined.

Part III: Reading Selections includes high-interest readings from authors such as Amy Tan, Ana Veciana-Suarez, and humorist Dave Barry. The reading selections were carefully selected for reading level, relevance to students' lives, diversity of authorship and subject matter, and applicability to the modes and concepts introduced in this text.

Pedagogy following each reading includes Vocabulary, Checking Comprehension, and Mode and Skill Check questions, as well as Questions for Discussion and Writing.

Part IV: Handbook with Exercises provides a review of grammar, punctuation, and mechanics that students can use to review and work on troublesome areas. The Handbook incorporates many practice exercises; additional interactive practice exercises that provide immediate feedback are available on the student website.

The final sections at the back of the book include an appendix for multilingual writers that provides special focus and practice on ESL issues, an Index, and Rhetorical Index.

Ancillaries

For instructors

An instructor's website for this volume provides sample syllabi, additional writing topic suggestions, and quizzes on chapter content.

WriteSpace for Developmental English, Houghton Mifflin's Blackboard-enabled content management system, allows an instructor to create a customized course with additional online components for students, a customized gradebook, and HM Assess, a diagnostic tool that evaluates student problem areas and provides a customized study path for that student. Instructors can also utilize Re:Mark, for online paper review and marking, and Peer Re:Mark, which allows students to review and comment on each other's papers.

For students

A student website provides a total of 650 interactive grammar exercises that provide instant feedback and direct students back to the appropriate text section for further study; and links to websites with further information and practice opportunities.

Acknowledgments

Special thanks are owed to the reviewers of this series:

Sydney Bartman of *Mount San Antonio College*

Kathleen Beauchene of *Community College of Rhode Island*

Dawn L. Brickey of *Charleston Southern University*

Carol Ann Britt of *San Antonio College*

James W. Cornish of *McLennan Community College*

Ned Cummings of *Bryant & Stratton College*

Joli J. Dusk of *Lurleen B. Wallace Community College*

Donna Eisenstat of *West Virginia University Institute of Technology*

Grushenka Engelbrecht-Castanon of *Northwest College*

Matt Fox of *Monroe Community College*

Hank Galmish of *Green River Community College*

Mary Gross of *MiraCosta College*

Aileen Gum of *San Diego*

Community College District

Toni Holloway of *Mountain View College*

Teresa S. Irvin of *Columbus State University*

Lilia A. Joy of *Henderson Community College*

Patsy Krech of *The University of Memphis*

Steven Lacek of *Southern West Virginia Community and Technical College*

Jill A. Lahnstein of *Cape Fear Community College*

James Landers of *Community College of Philadelphia*

Catherine A. Lutz of *Texas A&M? Kingsville*

Patricia Maddox of *Amarillo College*

Teri Maddox of *Jackson State Community College*

Lisa Maggard of *Hazard Community & Technical College*

Patricia A. Malinowski of *Finger Lakes Community College*

Eugene Marino of *Monroe Community College*

Patricia McGraw of *Cape Cod Community College*

Carol Miter of *Riverside Community College, Norco Campus*

Theresa Mohamed of *Onondaga Community College*

Barbara E. Nixon of *Salem Community College*

Peggy Roche of *Community College of Allegheny County*

Sara Safdie of *Bellevue Community College*

James Scannell McCormick of *Rochester Community and Technical College*

Midge L. Shaw of *Rogue Community College*

Linda Spoelman of *Grand Rapids Community College*

Deborah Stallings of *Hinds Community College*

Karen Supak of *Western New Mexico University*

Linda Marianne Taylor of *Tri-County Technical College*

Dennielle True of *Manatee Community College*

Margaret Waguespcak of *Amarillo College*

Cody Yeager of *Central Oregon Community College*

Dana Zimbleman of *Jefferson College*

Improving Writing and Thinking

> **GOALS FOR CHAPTER 1**

▶ Explain why developing good writing skills is important.

▶ Explain how expectations about writing affect attitudes about writing.

▶ Explain the three opportunities writing provides.

▶ Explain the three opportunities offered to you by this textbook, this course, your instructor, and your classmates.

You have probably already written quite a few papers, letters, e-mail messages, and other documents. When you have to write something, do you enjoy it? Why or why not?

If you are like many people, you probably answered that you dislike writing. You might find writing distasteful because it is always so difficult, because you struggle with it, and/or because your previous efforts have been unrewarding in terms of grades or feedback from others.

Yet you know by now that you have to write. You will have to write papers such as essays and research papers in your academic courses. You will have to write documents such as reports, memorandums, and letters as part of your professional responsibilities. And you will have to write letters, notes, and other documents in your personal life. Furthermore, your success in all of these areas will depend, in part, on your writing skills. As a matter of fact, there will be times in your life when others—such as your instructors, your supervisors, and your future customers or clients—will judge you and either reward you or hinder your progress based on your writing skills alone.

1

EXERCISE 1.1

In the blanks provided, list all of the benefits you will gain now and in the future by improving your writing skills.

1. _____

2. _____

3. _____

4. _____

5. _____

Now that you have been reminded about how important good writing skills can be, you might be ready to commit to improving yours. So where do you begin? This book covers various tools and techniques that are available to make both the writing process and your finished products better. Therefore, as you complete the activities and assignments in each chapter and share your results with your instructor and fellow students, you will be working on strengthening your writing skills. However, to get the most out of this course and this text, consider preparing yourself mentally to succeed by taking some time to examine your expectations, your attitudes, and the many opportunities that lie before you.

Expectations and Attitudes

We have expectations about writing, and these expectations influence how we feel about writing and about ourselves as writers. Many people hold two expectations in particular about writing, and these expectations eventually lead them to form negative attitudes. The first one is *Writing must be easy for everyone but me*. The second one is *Writing should be perfect the first time*.

If you hold the first expectation (*writing is easy for everyone but me*) or its variation (*writing is hard for everyone but the lucky, chosen few*), you probably feel frustrated, angry, or upset every time you write. But your belief that everyone but you must sail through a writing project is needlessly creating negative feelings about writing. Actually, writing is challenging for everyone. Just think about all of the complex mental tasks you must perform as you write. You must remember information and recall your own memories of people and events. You must form generalizations. You must synthesize ideas. You must analyze information. You must think creatively. You must apply logical reasoning. You must organize concepts. You must think of the words that most accurately communicate your thoughts and feelings. And you usually perform most or all of these tasks to write just one brief paper! Any activity that requires this many different kinds of thinking is challenging. Even experienced professional writers have to work to get it all right.

So consider adopting a more realistic expectation about writing. More specifically, *expect* writing to require thought, effort, and time. Then, when it demands all of those things from you, you may be less likely to feel overwhelmed.

Now that you have had the opportunity to revise your first expectation about writing, you will probably notice the flaw in the second expectation (*writing should be perfect the first time*). Because writing is a complex mental activity, chances are good that it will *rarely* turn out right the first time. Instead, writers should expect to have to experiment and rewrite. If you expect your writing to be perfect from the beginning, then you will be frustrated and disappointed again and again.

Finally, do not underestimate the toll that a generally negative attitude about writing can take on you. Have you ever heard of the term *self-fulfilling prophecy*? In terms of writing, it means that if you are in the habit of telling yourself and/or others that you are a bad writer, that you do not understand writing, or that you will never get it, then you are creating mental barriers to improving your skills. Even worse, other people will begin to believe those things about you, too! Instead, eliminate self-defeating thoughts from your mind and start telling yourself that you can—and will—learn to write better.

EXERCISE 1.2

Complete the three following statements by filling in the blanks provided with three *positive* statements about yourself as a writer, your goals for yourself as a writer, and/or your current writing abilities.

1. I am _____.

2. I am _____.

3. I am _____.

Writing as Opportunity

After you resolve to banish inaccurate expectations and negative attitudes from your thoughts, you can begin to see that writing offers you several important opportunities.

The Opportunity to Express Yourself

All humans like to express themselves. You probably like to discuss your ideas, beliefs, and feelings with friends or family members. You may like to express yourself creatively, perhaps by playing music, dancing, painting, or even writing poetry or stories. Writing is yet another tool for self-expression. Even the academic papers you write give you a chance to share with others your thoughts about important subjects. So instead of viewing writing as a punishment, begin to look at it as another opportunity for telling others what you think and feel.

EXERCISE 1.3

On the following blanks, write whatever comes into your head about something that inspires strong feelings in you. For instance, it could be the treatment of animals, your faith or spirituality, your favorite movie, or your educational goals. Take note of how freely your ideas and words come when you write about something about which you feel passionately.

_____

_____

_____

_____

_____

_____

_____

_____

_____

The Opportunity to Expand Your Own Understanding

Have you ever noticed that your thoughts and feelings always become clearer to you when you talk about them with others or write them down? This result happens because talking and writing require you to find words to express ideas that tend to be vague and half formed before you try to communicate them. The act of finding language to share your thoughts helps you clarify in your own mind what you think and believe. Therefore, writing is a valuable tool for increasing your understanding of your own ideas.

Writing is also a valuable tool for learning. When you write, you must think extensively about your subject. This lengthier, deeper, and more intense thought often leads to new insights and discoveries about the topic; as a matter of fact, when you write, you are likely to make new connections that you might not have made if you had not written about the subject. Thus, writing leads you to expand your knowledge and understanding of your subject matter.

EXERCISE 1.4

On the following blanks, write down three subjects you would like to learn more about. The next time an instructor gives you a choice of topics for a writing assignment, consider choosing one of the topics in this list. You might also begin writing about one or more of these topics in a journal rather than waiting for an assignment.

1. _____

2. _____

3. _____

The Opportunity to Improve Crucial Thinking Skills

As mentioned previously, writing requires many different kinds of thinking skills, including logical reasoning, analysis, synthesis, creativity, and organization. These are the same thinking skills you will need in many different areas of your academic, professional, and personal lives. Think of each new writing assignment as an opportunity to develop and strengthen the crucial thinking skills that will help you succeed in life.

On the following blanks, list two writing assignments that you have to complete in the near future. They could be academic, professional, or personal writing tasks. Beside each assignment, write down what you believe you will need to do in order to complete it.

1. _____

_____

2. _____

_____

The Opportunities Before You Now

Now that you have begun to think of writing itself as an opportunity, consider next the opportunities that lie before you as you begin this course. Specifically, this course, this textbook, this instructor, and these classmates offer you a number of valuable opportunities to develop your writing skills.

The Opportunity to Increase Your Knowledge About Writing

If writing has always been difficult or unrewarding for you, then you probably need to increase your knowledge about the process of writing and the essential features of a successful finished product. This course, this book, and your instructor's expertise can help you learn more about what you need to do to become a better writer. So view this course as an opportunity to expand valuable knowledge.

The goal of this text is to help you improve your writing skills by increasing your understanding of *what* you are doing and *how* you are doing it. Thus, Part I covers the writing process, describing steps you can follow and techniques you can use to discover, organize, and find the right words to express your ideas. Part II shows you different methods you can use to develop your ideas so that you can communicate more effectively with your readers. Part III provides you with reading selections to study and learn from, and Part IV offers a convenient grammar handbook to answer your questions about grammar and punctuation.

Place a check mark on the blank beside every aspect of your writing that you would like to improve. Then, for each checked item, fill in the chapter number(s) or part of this book that contains information about those topics. Use this book's table of contents and index to help you identify chapter and part numbers.

_____ Overcoming writer's block (Chapter __)

_____ Finding topics and ideas to write about (Chapter __)

_____ Figuring out how to organize or determine the right order for ideas (Chapter __)

_____ Writing clear sentences (Part __)

_____ Spelling words correctly (Part __)

_____ Making sentences grammatically correct (Part __)

_____ Knowing where to put commas, semicolons, and other punctuation marks (Part __)

_____ Developing or explaining ideas (Chapters _____)

_____ Knowing where to find information, or research (Chapters ____)

_____ Other: _____ (Chapter(s) __)

The Opportunity to Practice and Gain Valuable Feedback

In addition to increasing your knowledge about the processes and features of good writing, you must also practice writing if you are going to improve your writing skills. This textbook includes numerous writing assignments, and this course offers valuable opportunities to get feedback on what you write from your instructor and perhaps even from your classmates. The comments and suggestions you get from others will help you identify your strengths as a writer, as well as areas that need improvement. Thus, you will have many chances to discover what works and what does not work and to make adjustments accordingly the next time you write.

So get in the habit of carefully considering the feedback you get from your instructor and from your peers. Instead of putting a graded paper away right after you receive it, spend some time really trying to understand the instructor's suggestions for improvement. Formulate a plan for correcting the weak areas he or she identifies so that you will not repeat the same mistakes in your next paper. For example, if your paper contains apostrophe errors, resolve to study the rules for apostrophes. If your instructor points out organizational problems, review the chapter about organizing ideas. If you do not understand a teacher's comment or suggestion, make an appointment with him or her to ask questions and get some advice about how you can improve the next time.

 **EXERCISE 1.7**

The following paper was written by a student who was assigned to argue in favor of something. This student wrote the paper and submitted it, and then his instructor graded the paper, adding comments and suggestions in handwriting. Read over this graded paper and the teacher's comments, and answer the questions that follow.

Let Students Have Cell Phones

By Jamie Stevenson

effective intro   Just about everyone has a cell phone nowa-

days. Even teenagers and older kids are carry-

ing them around. But many schools have

banned students from having a cell phone on

campus. They say it is disruptive. But cell

phones do not have to be disruptive. They are

missing comma
necessary in modern times and students

clear thesis   should be allowed to have them at school.

noun-pronoun agreement
A student needs a cell phones for their

fragment
own safety. And in case of emergencies. If

give examples
there is a problem at school, students   *add specific details*

should be able to call someone for help.

Parents should be able to contact their child

give examples

in the event of an emergency to make sure

noun-pronoun agreement   *sp*

they are alright.

add transitions between paragraphs

sp

Cell phones are convenent, too. Modern

families lead busy, complex lives, and every

family member can be going in a different di-

rection at the same time. Parents need to be

able to keep in touch with their children. They

sp

need the convenence of calling on a cell phone   *develop with more specific details*

give examples

to confirm or change plans. They should not

have to rely on others to get messages to

their children. Instead, they should be able to

call them directly.

effective supporting points and organization

Schools say cell phones interrupt

classes and students will use them to chat

with their friends when they should be concen-

trating on learning. But disruptions can be

pronoun agreement

handled by requiring everyone to turn off their   *develop with more details*

cell phone when class begins. In between

classes students can check their cell phones

for missed calls and messages.

So I think it is unreasonable to deprive stu-

sp

dents of their cell phones while their on cam-

run-on sentence

pus. Cell phones are a fact of life students

need them, too.

1. What is one thing the instructor praised about this paper?

   _____

2. What grammar or punctuation concepts does the writer need to learn more about?

   _____

   _____

3. What is the instructor's advice about all three of the writer's body paragraphs?

   _____

4. Where in this book could this student go for more instruction in each of the following? Write the chapter number(s) in the blanks provided.

   Developing ideas with specific details (Chapters _____)
   Using transitions (Chapters _____)
   Sentence fragments (Part ___)
   Pronoun agreement (Part ___)
   Commas (Part ___)
   Run-on sentences (Part ___)
   Spelling (Part ___)

EXERCISE 1.8

Find one of your graded papers from another class. Read the instructor's comments and suggestions. Then fill in the following blanks.

Three of my strengths seem to be

   1. _____

   2. _____

   3. _____

Three areas in which I need to improve are

   1. _____

   2. _____

   3. _____

Comments or suggestions that I do not understand are

   _____

   _____

The Opportunity to Learn from Others' Writings

So far, you have learned that improving writing skills involves increasing your knowledge about writing, practicing, and learning from the feedback you get. A third way to improve your writing skills is to read and study the writing of others. This text includes both professional selections and student writing as examples and as the basis of exercises. You will learn many different techniques and writing concepts by determining what worked (and what did not work) in the writing of others. In addition, this course may offer you opportunities to read your class-mates' writing, which will provide you with even more examples for study.

EXERCISE 1.9

The following excerpt comes from *Growing Up* by Pulitzer Prize–winning author Russell Baker. Read this excerpt, and then answer the questions by writing your responses on the blanks provided.

Learning to Write

Russell Baker

1 When our class was assigned to Mr. Fleagle for third-year English I anticipated another grim year in that dreariest of subjects. Mr. Fleagle was notorious[1] among City students for dullness and inability to inspire. He was said to be stuffy, dull, and hopelessly out of date. To me he looked to be sixty or seventy and prim[2] to a fault. He wore primly severe eyeglasses, his wavy hair was primly cut and primly combed. He wore prim vested suits with neckties blocked primly against the collar buttons of his primly starched white shirts. He had a primly pointed jaw, a primly straight nose, and a prim manner of speaking that was so correct, so gentlemanly, that he seemed a comic antique.

2 I anticipated a listless[3], unfruitful[4] year with Mr. Fleagle and for a long time was not disappointed. We read *Macbeth*[5]. Mr. Fleagle loved *Macbeth* and wanted us to love it, too, but he lacked the gift of infecting others with his own passion. He tried to convey the murderous ferocity[6] of Lady Macbeth one day by reading aloud the passage that concludes

> . . . I have given suck, and know
> How tender 'tis to love the babe that milks me.
> I would, while it was smiling in my face,
> Have plucked my nipple from his boneless gums . . .

1. **notorious:** known widely and unfavorably
2. **prim:** excessively precise and proper
3. **listless:** lacking energy
4. **unfruitful:** not productive
5. *Macbeth*: a play by William Shakespeare
6. **ferocity:** fierceness

The idea of prim Mr. Fleagle plucking his nipple from boneless gums was too much for the class. We burst into gasps of irrepressible[1] snickering[2]. Mr. Fleagle stopped.

3   "There is nothing funny, boys, about giving suck to a babe. It is the—the very essence of motherhood, don't you see."

4   He constantly sprinkled his sentences with "don't you see." It wasn't a question but an exclamation of mild surprise at our ignorance. "Your pronoun needs an antecedent[3], don't you see," he would say, very primly. "The purpose of the Porter's scene, boys, is to provide some comic relief from the horror, don't you see."

5   Late in the year, we tackled the informal essay. "The essay, don't you see, is the . . ." My mind went numb. Of all forms of writing, none seemed so boring as the essay. Naturally we would have to write informal essays. Mr. Fleagle distributed a homework sheet offering us a choice of topics. None was quite so simpleminded as "What I Did on My Summer Vacation," but most seemed to be almost as dull. I took the list home and dawdled[4] until the night before the essay was due. Sprawled on the sofa, I finally faced up to the grim task, took the list out of my notebook, and scanned it. The topic on which my eye stopped was "The Art of Eating Spaghetti."

6   This title produced an extraordinary sequence of mental images. Surging up out of the depths of memory came a vivid recollection of a night in Belleville when all of us were seated around the supper table—Uncle Allen, my mother, Uncle Charlie, Doris, Uncle Hal—and Aunt Pat served spaghetti for supper. Spaghetti was an erotic treat in those days. Neither Doris nor I had ever eaten spaghetti, and none of the adults had enough experience to be good at it. All the good humor of Uncle Allen's house reawoke in my mind as I recalled the laughing arguments we had that night about the socially respectable method for moving spaghetti from plate to mouth.

7   Suddenly, I wanted to write about that, about the warmth and good feeling of it, but I wanted to put it down simply for my own joy, not for Mr. Fleagle. It was a moment I wanted to recapture and hold for myself. I wanted to relive the pleasure of an evening at New Street. To write it as I wanted, however, would violate all the rules of formal composition I'd learned in school, and Mr. Fleagle would surely give it a failing grade. Never mind. I would write something else for Mr. Fleagle after I had written this thing for myself.

8   When I finished it the night was half gone and there was no time left to compose a proper, respectable essay for Mr. Fleagle. There was no choice next

---

1. **irrepressible:** difficult to control or restrain
2. **snickering:** stifled laughter

3. **antecedent:** word to which the pronoun refers
4. **dawdled:** wasted time

morning but to turn in my private reminiscence[1] of Belleville. Two days passed before Mr. Fleagle returned the graded papers, and he returned everyone's but mine. I was bracing[2] myself for a command to report to Mr. Fleagle immediately after school for discipline when I saw him lift my paper from his desk and rap for the class's attention.

9   "Now, boys," he said, "I want to read you an essay. This is titled 'The Art of Eating Spaghetti.'"

10   And he started to read. My words! He was reading *my words* out loud to the entire class. What's more, the entire class was listening. Listening attentively. Then somebody laughed, then the entire class was laughing, and not in contempt and ridicule, but with an openhearted enjoyment. Even Mr. Fleagle stopped two or three times to repress a small prim smile.

11   I did my best to avoid showing pleasure, but what I was feeling was pure ecstasy[3] at this startling demonstration that my words had the power to make people laugh. In the eleventh grade, at the eleventh hour as it were, I had discovered a calling. It was the happiest moment of my entire school career. When Mr. Fleagle finished he put the final seal on my happiness by saying, "Now that, boys, is an essay, don't you see. It's—don't you see—it's of the very essence of the essay, don't you see. Congratulations, Mr. Baker."*

1. Were you, like Russell Baker, ever unexpectedly inspired by one of your past teachers? Describe this instructor, and explain how he or she inspired you.

_____

_____

_____

2. Russell Baker tells us that he wanted to write about eating spaghetti "simply for my own joy" (paragraph 6). Have you ever wanted to write about a subject for your own joy? What was that subject? Did you write about it?

_____

_____

_____

3. How do Russell Baker's classmates and teacher respond to the reading of his essay "The Art of Eating Spaghetti"? What impact does this response have upon Russell Baker?

_____

_____

1. **reminiscence:** remembrance of an event

2. **bracing:** preparing for an impact

3. **ecstasy:** intense joy

*Source: Russell Baker, "Learning to Write," from *Growing Up*, 1982 (a Plume title). Reprinted by permission of Don Congdon Associates, Inc. Copyright © 1982 by Russell Baker.

4. Baker writes that he was feeling "pure ecstasy" when he realized that "my words had the power to make people laugh" (paragraph 11). Think of something you have written in the past that inspired some emotion (such as anger, sorrow, or amusement) in someone else. What was the situation? What did you write? What was the emotion you provoked? And how did you feel about the response you received?

_____

_____

_____

5. In your opinion, what was the most interesting part of this excerpt? Why was it interesting to you? Try to determine _how_ Baker made that part interesting.

_____

_____

_____

✶ EXERCISE 1.10

In this excerpt from her book _Bird by Bird,_ author Anne Lamott talks about what she tells her students on the last day of writing class. Read this excerpt, and then answer the questions by writing your responses on the blanks provided.

1 There are so many things I want to tell my students in our last class, so many things I want to remind them of. Write about your childhoods, I tell them for the umpteenth time. Write about that time in your life when you were so intensely interested in the world, when your powers of observation were at their most acute[1], when you felt things so deeply. Exploring and understanding your childhood will give you the ability to empathize[2], and that understanding and empathy will teach you to write with intelligence and insight and compassion.

2   Becoming a writer is about becoming conscious. When you're conscious and writing from a place of insight and simplicity and real caring about the truth, you have the ability to throw the lights on for your reader. He or she will recognize his or her life and truth in what you say, in the pictures you have painted, and this decreases the terrible sense of isolation that we have all had too much of.

3   Try to write in a directly emotional way, instead of being too subtle[3] or oblique[4]. Don't be afraid of your material or your past. Be afraid of wasting any

1. **acute:** sharp or sensitive
2. **empathize:** understand someone else's feelings
3. **subtle:** difficult to detect
4. **oblique:** indirect

more time obsessing about how you look and how people see you. Be afraid of not getting your writing done.

4   If something inside you is real, we will probably find it interesting, and it will probably be universal. So you must risk placing real emotion at the center of your work. Write straight into the emotional center of things. Write toward vulnerability[1]. Don't worry about appearing sentimental. Worry about being unavailable; worry about being absent or fraudulent[2]. Risk being unliked. Tell the truth as you understand it. If you're a writer, you have a moral obligation to do this. And it is a revolutionary act—truth is always subversive[3].*

1. Do you think that the advice Anne Lamott gives applies to all of the different kinds of writing you will be asked to do or want to do in your life? If not, what types of writing are exempt from this advice, and why?

      _____

      _____

      _____

2. Why do you think Anne Lamott spends so much time talking about "truth" in writing? Why do you think she finds truth to be so important in writing?

      _____

      _____

      _____

3. What is one piece of advice that you will take from this selection? Why?

      _____

      _____

      _____

4. What kind of writer do you think Anne Lamott is—a technical writer, a fiction writer, a textbook writer? What information leads you to this conclusion? What kind of students do you think are enrolled in her class, and why would they take her class?

      _____

      _____

      _____

1. **vulnerability:** openness to criticism or attack
2. **fraudulent:** dishonest; deceitful
3. **subversive:** intending to weaken or destroy something established

*Source: From *Bird by Bird* by Anne Lamott, copyright © 1994 by Anne Lamott. Used by permission of Pantheon Books, a division of Random House, Inc.

WRITING OPPORTUNITIES

1. Write about how you complete a writing assignment. When do you actually start? What do you do first? What part of the process is usually easy for you? What part is most difficult?

2. Russell Baker says that he realized his writing had the power to make people laugh. What other kinds of power do writers have? Illustrate your ideas with examples of writing from your own experience, and explain the kind of power these writings demonstrate.

3. Respond to the statement "Becoming a writer is about becoming conscious." What does that mean, if anything, to you? How will you be "conscious" in your writing?

4. Think about what you have learned in this chapter. How will you transfer these new ideas or apply this advice to your own writing?

CHAPTER 1 REVIEW

Fill in the blanks in each of the following statements.

1. A person's _____ about writing influence his or her attitudes about writing.

2. One incorrect expectation about writing is "Writing must be _____ for everyone but me."

3. Another incorrect expectation about writing is "Writing should be _____ the first time."

4. Writing is challenging because it requires many different complex _____ tasks.

5. Writers should expect to have to experiment and _____.

6. Writing offers you the opportunity to _____ yourself.

7. Writing offers you the opportunity to expand your _____ of topics and your thoughts about those topics.

8. Writing offers you the opportunity to improve many different _____ skills, such as logical reasoning, synthesis, and analysis.

9. This text will help you improve your writing skills by helping you increase your _____ about writing.

10. To improve your writing, you must _____ and get _____ from others, such as your instructor and classmates.

11. To improve your own writing, you must _____ and study the writing of others.

WebWork

Access and explore the Web site *Journal for You* by typing "Journal for You" into an online search engine. Then answer the following questions.

1. According to this Web site, what are some of the benefits of writing in a journal?

_____

_____

_____

2. What have been your experiences with writing in a journal or diary? Do you think that you might benefit from recording your thoughts and feelings in a journal? How?

_____

_____

_____

3. Novelist Anita Brookner said, "You never know what you will learn till you start writing. Then you discover truths you never knew existed." Illustrate this statement by relating an experience from your own life.

_____

_____

_____

Online Study Center   For additional information and practice, go to the Houghton Mifflin Online Study Center for this book, at **http://www.college .hmco.com/pic/dolphinwritertwo**.

2

Prewriting

GOALS FOR CHAPTER 2

▶ List the five steps of the writing process, and describe the major task of each one.

▶ Use various prewriting techniques to generate ideas.

▶ Define the term *main idea*, and list the two components of a main idea.

▶ Explain the two characteristics of an effective main idea statement.

▶ Explain how audience and purpose affect the main idea statement.

The Writing Process

In Chapter 1 of this book, you learned that writing is a complex activity because it requires a variety of different mental skills. Fortunately, though, these different kinds of thinking tasks do not have to occur at the same time. Instead, you can separate them into different steps or stages of a larger process. As a matter of fact, writing can be viewed as a series of five main steps, each of which focuses on a particular kind of thinking:

Step 1: Prewriting. Discover your topic and generate ideas about it.

Step 2: Organizing and Outlining. Use logic to determine the order in which you should present ideas and create a plan for your paper.

Step 3: Writing. Using your outline as a guide, write the sentences and paragraphs that clearly state and develop your ideas.

Step 4: Revising. Reevaluate your paper's organization and development of ideas, and make the necessary improvements.

Step 5: Editing and Preparing the Final Draft. Correct grammatical, punctuation, and spelling errors, and generate a final copy that is ready to be submitted.

Chances are good that as you write, you are already completing all or most of these steps to some extent. However, you may not be devoting enough time and effort to each one, or you may be trying to complete two or more of the steps at the same time. For example, you might be attempting to think of and organize your thoughts *as* you are actually writing a draft, or you may be trying to write, revise, and edit simultaneously.

If you are neglecting or combining the steps, though, you are probably making the writing process more difficult, more time-consuming, and less rewarding for yourself. Because each of the steps requires a different kind of thinking, eliminating a step (such as organizing) or trying to complete it along with another step makes the whole process more difficult. When you are completing the various mental challenges simultaneously, you also slow yourself down, so the whole process takes more time. What is more, you reduce the overall quality of your writing when you do not give adequate attention to each separate stage.

Therefore, to make the writing process easier, faster, and more rewarding, always complete all of the five stages, and complete each one of them separately. While you work, return to previous stages as necessary. For example, if you realize during the revision stage that you have not fully developed one of your points, return to the prewriting stage to generate more ideas. If during the revision stage you think of another great point that you left out, go back to the organization stage to decide where to insert it. Then go back to the writing stage to actually compose the additional paragraphs.

The remainder of this chapter focuses on prewriting, the first stage in the writing process. Chapter 3 covers organizing and outlining. Chapter 4 shows you how to make the actual composition of the paper go more smoothly. Chapter 5 focuses on revising, and Chapter 6 discusses the procedures to follow to edit and prepare the final draft.

Prewriting

In Chapter 1 of this book, you were reminded that everyone has important ideas, thoughts, feelings, and beliefs about the world we live in. In other words, everyone has something significant to say. You may not agree, of course, if you tend to experience *writer's block*, the state of being unable to think of ideas whenever you sit down to write. It is indeed frustrating to be faced with a blank sheet of paper or a blank computer screen and be unable to think of anything to say. You can use certain techniques to help yourself get started and to begin coaxing those ideas out from where they are hiding. These techniques are known as **prewriting,** and this chapter will introduce you to several of them.

First, consider all of the benefits of prewriting. Prewriting is an important tool for writers because it has four uses:

1. **Prewriting can help you find a topic to write about.** On those occasions when you can write your paper about a topic of your own choice, prewriting can help you think of one.

2. **Prewriting can help you narrow a topic or find some interesting aspect of it.** When your topic is assigned, as it often is in academic courses, you may need to narrow it down. Even in a longer research paper, you could not do justice to a big subject such as the Civil War or abnormal psychology. You need to find a more specific aspect on which to focus, and prewriting can help you narrow, or limit, your topic to one that is more manageable for the assignment. In addition, prewriting can help you discover an aspect of the topic that is interesting to you. When you write about a topic that interests you, you will be more enthusiastic about the paper. As a result, you will be more likely to write a better paper.

3. **Prewriting can help you remember or discover what you already know about a topic.** Not only can you prewrite to discover a topic, but you can also prewrite to find out what you know about a topic. You probably have some knowledge or thoughts about most topics, and prewriting can help you unlock this information from where it is stored in your mind. At the same time, prewriting allows you to get a better understanding of what you do *not* know about a topic. Then you can determine what you will need to find out—through reading and research—before you begin to write.

4. **Prewriting can help you decide what you want to say about your topic.** Once you have decided on a topic and explored what you know about it, you can use prewriting techniques to help you formulate the idea or opinion you want to express about that topic. In addition, you can use prewriting as a tool to help you begin to sort through your thoughts about the topic so that you can determine which of those thoughts you want to include in your paper.

As you can see, prewriting is a valuable step in the writing process. It breaks through writer's block, getting the ideas flowing and helping you find a starting point. As a result, it reduces the anxiety and frustration that you might have felt in the past as you began writing.

WRITING FOR SUCCESS

Using Prewriting Techniques

Prewriting is useful for generating ideas prior to writing. In addition, it can be an effective method for preparing your mind to concentrate on tasks other than writing. Prewriting is a useful technique for clearing your mind of distracting thoughts. You might try freewriting for ten minutes before a test, for instance. Devote your full attention to whatever worries, plans, daydreams, or other thoughts might be on your mind. The act of writing about them will sweep them away temporarily, allowing you to concentrate on the test more easily. You can try this prior to any activity that requires your attention and concentration. You can also use prewriting techniques to help you solve personal or work-related problems. Try talking or brainstorming, for example, to generate some possible solutions.

The next section of this chapter covers five effective prewriting techniques you can use to help yourself get started.

Talking

Have you ever noticed that after you talk about a subject with someone for the first time, you understand more clearly what you yourself think about that topic? Even if you have given a considerable amount of thought to a subject, your ideas about it can tend to remain vague and half formed until you try to find the words to express them. The act of putting your ideas and feelings into language helps to make them clearer. Remember, when you discuss a subject with someone else (which requires using language), you understand it better.

The next time you need to generate ideas for a paper, try having an oral or written conversation (in person, via e-mail, or in an Internet chat room) with a fellow student, friend, relative, or coworker. Tell the other person what you know or what you think about the topic, and use the discussion as an opportunity to learn more. Afterward, you might want to jot your ideas down on paper using one of the other prewriting techniques discussed in this chapter.

EXERCISE 2.1   **Using Talk to Generate Ideas**

With one of your classmates, have a five- to ten-minute conversation about a current event or story in the news that neither of you has ever discussed or written about. Then write your answers to the following questions on the blanks provided.

1. What topic did you and your classmate discuss?

_____

_____

2. During this conversation, what did you realize that you know or believe about the topic?

_____

_____

_____

3. What did you learn about the topic from your classmate?

_____

_____

_____

Freewriting

A second effective prewriting technique is **freewriting**. The goal of freewriting is to generate ideas by recording, as quickly as you can, the flow of thoughts going through your mind. You simply consider the topic and write down what you are thinking about that topic. At this stage, though, you do not censor or reject any thoughts, nor do you try to organize them. You do not bother to cross out or correct anything—that comes later. You also do not pause to think about where to place a comma or to determine exactly the right word. In fact, you do not pause at all; instead, you write nonstop, and if you run out of ideas, you continue writing something, such as "my mind is blank my mind is blank my mind is blank…" until another thought comes to mind. Then you record that thought. Do not worry about neatness because freewriting is for your eyes only; it is a tool for the writer to get some ideas flowing, and readers do not see it.

When one student considered the topic "underage drinking," she generated the following freewriting:

Underage Drinking

Underage drinking has been a problem for a long time. I think I heard that about three-quarters of all high school students have tried alcohol by the time they graduate and for both h.s. and college students fake i.d.s are too easy to get—several of my friends have one and they use them at bars and in convenence stores to buy beer. So I think that business owners should be more skeptical when young people come in, even if they have an i.d. because they drink and get into auto accidents, one girl at our school was driving while drunk and rolled her car which killed her and the other person with her. It was very sad but it seems as though you can't be a member of the cool crowd if your not drinking The commercials on TV are partly to blame because they perpetrate the idea that drinking is fun and sexy. Its hard to resist those messages especially when everyone else is doing it.

You probably noticed as you read this freewriting that it contains errors such as misspellings and missing punctuation. That is fine, however, because the point of freewriting is to explore thoughts without worrying about the mechanics of writing. By completing this freewriting about underage drinking, this student touched on several different causes of the problem, and she is well on her way to creating an essay that will examine the reasons why underage drinking is so prevalent.

Freewriting is also useful for finding a topic to write about and for narrowing a topic. If you are in search of a topic to write about, you can freewrite about "things that anger me" or "topics that interest me." Once you have generated several topic possibilities, pick one or two of the most promising and freewrite about each of them. Similarly, if you need to narrow a broad topic, freewrite about different aspects of it in order to find one that interests you.

When you freewrite, you may want to time yourself. In other words, set a timer for ten minutes, and do not stop writing until the timer goes off. Doing so will encourage you to write longer than you might ordinarily write, helping you generate more ideas.

Choose one of the topics from the following list and freewrite about that topic for at least ten minutes.

    My goals   Celebrities   Romance   Relaxation

Brainstorming

Whereas freewriting involves recording ideas in the form of sentences, **brainstorming** involves writing down just the words and phrases that spring to mind when you think about a subject. You can write these words and phrases in rows and columns, or you can just write them all over the page. For example, when one student was asked to brainstorm about the topic of stress, here is what he wrote:

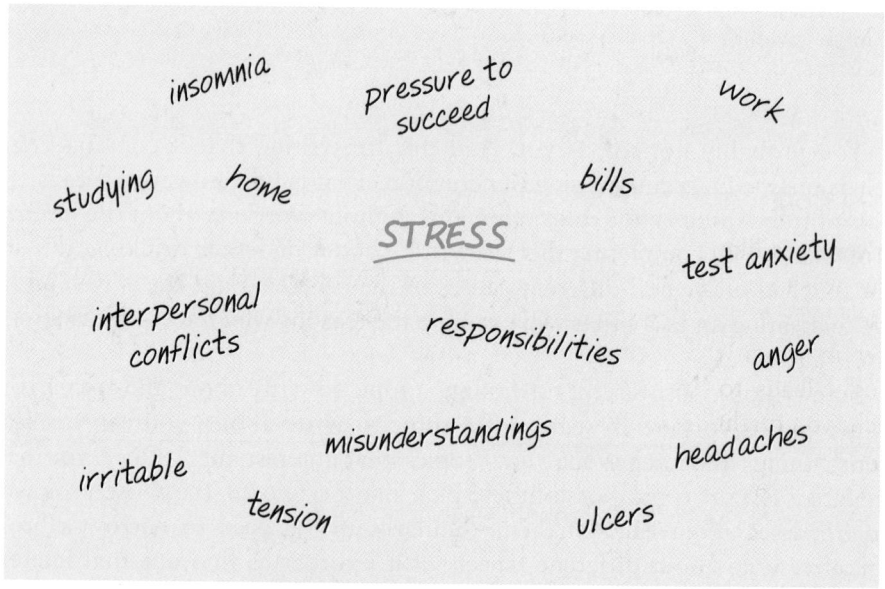

Figure 2.1 An Example of Brainstorming

    Like freewriting, brainstorming is most effective when you decide to spend a certain minimum amount of time—such as ten minutes—generating all the ideas you can. Do not pause to evaluate the worth of an idea, and do not censor any ideas. Later, you will go back and reconsider the value of each idea, but while you brainstorm, you simply write them all down. Just focus on the topic and record everything that pops into your head as quickly as possible. Because brainstorming is a tool for only you, the writer, do not worry about spelling, organization, or neat penmanship, for no one else needs to see it.

Brainstorming can be useful for finding a subject to write about. For example, you could write down "things that make me angry" in the middle of a piece of paper and then fill up the page with your pet peeves. In addition, brainstorming is an effective tool for narrowing a subject. Write down your broad subject, and then record all of the specific aspects that occur to you. If you already have a topic, you can use brainstorming to generate ideas about it. For instance, you might write down "reasons why students choose community colleges over universities" and then fill up the page with all of the reasons you can think of.

EXERCISE 2.3   **Using Brainstorming to Generate Ideas**

Select one of the topics from the following list and brainstorm for at least ten minutes about that topic.

My hobby   College life   Fame   E-mail

Clustering

Clustering is like brainstorming in that you write down words or phrases that occur to you when you think about a topic. However, when you cluster, you loosely group ideas as chains of thought, recording them on the page in the order in which they occur to you. Clustering is based on the idea that one thought leads to another. If you were to create a cluster of ideas about the beach, you might begin by jotting down one particular train of thought:

BEACH
  \ *sand*
    \ *sandcastles*
      \ *children*
        \ *buckets and pails*

Then you would add another thought chain:

You exhaust one train of thought before beginning another one, continuing to add new clusters branching out from the main topic until you cannot think of any more ideas.

Clustering can be especially useful for generating descriptive details about a subject. You can guide yourself toward coming up with information related to each of the five different senses by focusing each train of thought on a particular kind of detail:

You would complete this cluster by creating a thought chain for each of the other four senses.

 **EXERCISE 2.4**   **Using Clustering to Generate Ideas**

Select one of the topics from the following list and create a cluster of ideas that contains at least six different branches.

My classroom   My favorite meal   An award I received   A person I love

EXERCISE 2.5   **Creating a Cluster of Ideas from a Photograph**

Study the photograph below. Create a cluster of ideas based on this image.

Source: © Ana Abejon/Istockphoto

Asking Questions

A fifth way to generate ideas is by asking—and then finding answers to—questions about your topic. The best place to start is by posing the six questions (*Who? What? When? Where? Why?* and *How?*) that journalists ask when they are collecting information for a news story. These questions will help you narrow a broad topic down. For example, a student who was assigned to write a paper about modern zoos wrote the following questions:

Zoos

Who works in a zoo today?
What are modern zoos like?
What distinguishes modern zoos from zoos of the past?
What are the goals of the modern zoo?
When did zoos begin to evolve?
Where are today's state-of-the-art zoos?
Why have zoos changed?
How do zoos function?
How do zoo employees care for so many different animals?

These questions allowed the student to see the different aspects of the topic on which she could focus, and they helped her discover that she was most interested in concentrating on the goals of modern zoos. So she created a new round of questions about that more specific topic:

Goals of Modern Zoos

Who are the people who formulated the goals of modern zoos?
What are these goals?
When did these goals begin to change?
Where are the zoos that illustrate these new goals?
Why have these goals changed?
How do the goals of today's zoos differ from the goals of zoos in the past?

The student can now choose the questions that interest her most and then use one of the other prewriting techniques—such as freewriting or brainstorming—to identify the answers to these questions. In answer to the question *What are the goals of modern zoos?* she decided to use brainstorming:

What Are the Goals of Modern Zoos?

education
entertainment
conservation

FOCUS ON RESEARCH

Using Questions

Prewriting not only helps you discover what you already know about a topic but also reveals what you do *not* know. When you realize what you do not know, you can make a list of facts and other information that you will need to find for your paragraph or essay. The questions method, in particular, will reveal gaps in your knowledge. Look, for example, at the questions about zoos on page 27. The student who created these questions may be able to provide some of the answers to them, but she will probably need to do some research to find the answers to others. Asking these questions can lead her to create a "shopping list" of the details and information she needs, and she can then use this list as a guide when she goes to the library or to the computer to begin her research.

EXERCISE 2.6   **Asking Questions to Generate Ideas**

Select one of the topics from the following list and generate *Who? What? When? Where? Why?* and *How?* questions for that topic.

Exercise
Dating
Owning a pet
Parenting
Television
Education
Racism

Now that you have practiced five different prewriting techniques, you may have found that one of the methods seems particularly effective for you. You should use that method to generate ideas for your papers. However, be aware that different techniques may be more suitable for different kinds of topics. For example, if your paper will be in the form of a personal story from your experience, freewriting might be the best way to begin to remember the details, whereas the question method might yield more ideas for a paper about a World War I battle. Therefore, you might want to consider using at least two different prewriting techniques each time you need to generate ideas. Using a combination of methods may yield the best, most comprehensive results.

Topic to Main Idea

At the beginning of this chapter, you learned that one use for prewriting is discovering what you want to say about a topic. After you decide on a topic and explore your ideas about that topic, the next step in the process is determining your **main idea,** the point that you want to make. In order to write a coherent paragraph or essay, you must begin with a very clear understanding of this main idea, so it is important to spend some time working on it until it expresses exactly what you want to communicate.

A main idea has two components. It includes, first of all, your topic. Usually, your main idea statement will begin with this topic. Then the main idea statement goes on to state the point you want to make about the topic. Here, for example, are different main idea statements:

Topic	*Point*
Dating	has changed significantly over the last twenty-five years.

Topic	*Point*
Breakfast	is the most important meal of the day.

Topic	*Point*
Wind	is a valuable alternative energy source.

Remember that a topic alone cannot be a main idea. The main idea includes both the topic and what you want to say about that topic:

Topic: Sleep
Main Idea: Adequate sleep is important to good health.

Topic: Tiger Woods
Main Idea: Tiger Woods is today's most talented professional golfer.

Topic: Drunk-driving laws
Main Idea: Drunk-driving laws must be made even stricter.

EXERCISE 2.7   **Writing Main Idea Statements**

Complete each of the following main idea statements by adding a point about each topic.

1. Compact discs _____.

2. Television talk-show hosts _____.

3. Today's college students _____.

4. My best friend _____.

5. Taking tests _____.

6. Working out _____.

7. Cigarettes _____.

8. Pets _____.

9. A happy marriage _____.

10. Eating healthy _____.

 Prewriting to Main Idea: A Student Demonstration

For a demonstration of the writing process, you will follow the process that a student named Maya went through in order to write a paragraph for her English class. In this chapter, you will see how Maya began with prewriting, generated ideas, and decided on her main idea. Chapters 3–6 explain the process she went through to complete each of the other four steps.

Maya's instructor assigned the class the task of writing a paragraph about student success. Maya decided to brainstorm about the topic first. She came up with the following ideas:

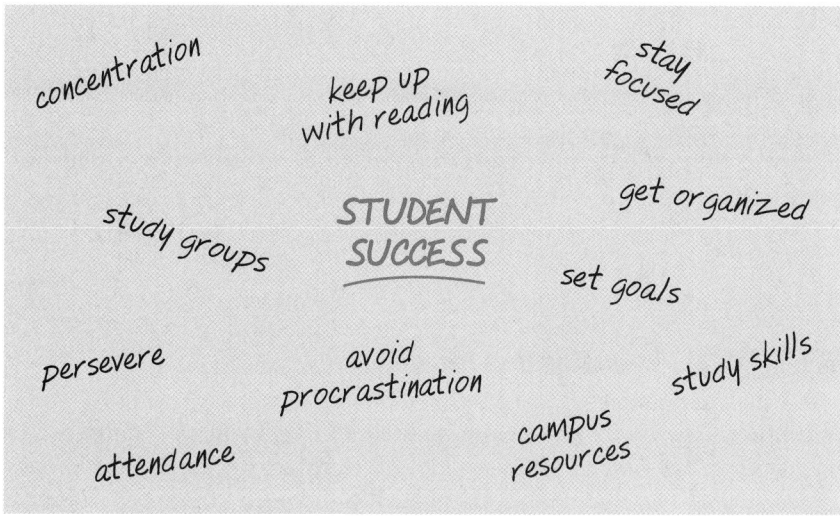

Figure 2.2 Brainstorming the Topic "Student Success"

Maya looked over her brainstorming and decided that she was most interested in writing about getting organized. She herself had good organizational skills that helped her keep up with her academic responsibilities, so she thought she might be able to share some tips that other students might find valuable. She decided to prewrite again, this time using freewriting to generate more ideas:

> I think that getting and staying organized is essential to being a good student. If your not organized then things can get away from you and

you'll miss deadlines and you won't be prepared for class or tests.
That's why I use a monthly calendar to record all due dates and test
dates. Some of my friends really need to get better organized. Emily
and Frank never know where anything is. . I keep separate notebooks
for each class so things don't get mixed up. Studying in several sessions is important too. I write down tasks I need to complete on certain days to stay current. Like study for math test. And I write it on
my To Do list for that day. I check off each thing as I finish it. I can
just glance at the calendar and get a picture of my responsibilities for
the whole month. On the same calendar, I write my work schedule too
and my softball practice times. And I carry my calendar everywhere so
I can update it right away.

Based on this freewriting, Maya realized that she uses several essential tools to
keep herself organized. She wrote down this main idea:

Student success depends upon getting organized.

Then she realized that she could write a more specific main idea statement:

Student success depends upon using tools that will help you organize your
responsibilities and your materials.

In Chapter 3, you will see how Maya organized and outlined her ideas for her
paragraph.

 **EXERCISE 2.8**   **Prewriting for a Paragraph**

In this chapter, you will begin to write a paragraph, and you will continue to work
on this paragraph in stages as you study the chapters on the writing process. In
this chapter, you will complete prewriting about your topic and formulate a
main idea. As part of your work for Chapters 3–6, you will organize your ideas,
write the paragraph, revise it, and then edit and prepare it for submission to your
instructor.

To get started, choose a topic that seems interesting to you from the following
list:

My favorite sport
My goals
An embarrassing moment
Artistic expression

Now use at least two different prewriting methods to generate ideas about this topic. If you use the talking method of prewriting, write down what you learned or what became clearer to you during your conversation.

Finally, write a main idea statement that would be suitable for a paragraph.

CHAPTER 2 REVIEW

Fill in the blanks in the following statements.

1. The five main steps of the writing process are _____, _____ _____, _____, _____, and _____.

2. Eliminating or trying to combine steps in the writing process makes this process more _____ and time-consuming.

3. Techniques that help you discover ideas for writing are known as _____.

4. Prewriting helps writers find a _____ to write about, find a _____ or interesting aspect of a topic, identify _____ they already know or determine what they need to research, and decide what they want to say about a topic.

5. _____ about a topic with another person will help your ideas about that topic become clearer in your mind.

6. _____ involves recording, in sentence form, the flow of thoughts going through your mind.

7. _____ involves writing down words and phrases that spring to mind when you think about a subject.

8. _____ involves writing down words or phrases that are grouped together as trains of thought.

9. Asking _____ such as *Who? What? When? Where? Why?* and *How?* is another good way to generate ideas for writing.

10. A _____ statement includes two components: a topic and the _____ the writer wants to make about that topic.

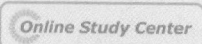

WebWork

Using an Internet browser such as Yahoo.com or Google.com, conduct a search for the topic "prewriting techniques" and read the information at several of the Web sites you find. Then, using your own paper, complete the following tasks.

1. Find a prewriting technique that is not covered in this chapter. Write a brief description of it. Do you think this additional technique might work for you? Why or why not?

2. Share your description of the technique with a classmate, and read your classmate's description of a new technique.

3. Try one of these new techniques to generate ideas for the topic you selected in Exercise 2.8.

Online Study Center   For additional information and practice with prewriting, go to the Houghton Mifflin Online Study Center for this book, at **http://www.college.hmco.com/pic/dolphinwritertwo**.

Organizing and Outlining

GOALS FOR CHAPTER 3

▶ Explain why organizing ideas before writing is an important step.

▶ Follow a three-step process to group and order relevant ideas.

▶ Explain the difference between natural and logical organization.

▶ Complete formal and informal outlines.

▶ Create a formal or informal outline.

In Chapter 2, you learned how to use prewriting to generate ideas. The next step of the writing process is to organize those ideas and prepare an outline to follow as you write.

Organizing

When you are generating ideas, those ideas will rarely occur to you in an organized manner. Nor should they. When you prewrite, you want to free your creative mind to let the ideas flow without worrying about their order. However, before you write, you must bring some organization to these thoughts. When you read something, you expect the author to have grouped ideas together, divided them into paragraphs, and linked thoughts together so that you can follow them. Likewise, the readers of your writing will expect you to have done the same. If you offer your readers a collection of disorderly, random thoughts, they are likely to become confused about what you are trying to say. They are also likely to miss important connections that you want them to make.

Determining the right order for ideas can be a challenging task because there are often several different ways to arrange your thoughts. To find the most effective pattern, you might have to think of several different possibilities before you can decide which one is best. It is important to devote some time and

35

attention to examining all of the pieces and figuring out how to fit them together, for your organization (or lack of it) can make or break your paper. This chapter shows you some techniques you can use to organize your ideas.

Determining a Framework

In Chapter 2, you learned that prewriting helps you discover your topic and what you want to say about that topic. Prewriting should include the creation of a main idea statement that will keep your writing focused on just one point. Next, you will need to determine the best framework for arranging your thoughts about your main idea. You begin to create this framework when you examine your main idea statement and your prewriting (brainstorming, freewriting, cluster, or whatever you used) and go through a three-step process to decide on what to include and how to order that information:

Step 1: Circle ideas and information that match your main idea statement, and ignore or cross out ideas that seem irrelevant.

Step 2: Group like ideas and information together.

Step 3: Decide on the best way to put these groups of ideas in order.

In Step 1, you look at the ideas you collected during prewriting with your main idea statement in mind. You evaluate each thought or piece of information, asking yourself if it relates to or supports the point in your main idea statement. Then you circle, highlight, or otherwise mark these relevant ideas. At the same time, you either ignore or cross out the ideas and information that do not relate to the point in your main idea. Do not erase these ideas; you might decide later that one or two really are useful, so you should not eliminate them completely. But develop a system for marking the ideas that will be useful. For example, one student was asked to write a paragraph on the topic of a famous person who is admirable. The student decided to freewrite about television talk-show host Oprah Winfrey, and she came up with the following main idea statement:

Oprah Winfrey is an admirable celebrity.

When she looked over her freewriting for ideas that matched this point, she circled some key words and phrases:

I just love Oprah. Her show is great. Always very informative yet it touches your heart too. She has interesting guests and topics. Things that real people want to know about. She's been going strong for many years and she's recognized all over the country. And she is so far above those other trashy talk shows that encourage people to fight and scream at each other about their personal problems. Oprah wants her show to do good not be sleazy entertainment. And her magazine gives people good advice. Oprah is a very spiritual person she encourages people to remember their higher purpose and I admire her for that. She wants to help people and she supports many charities. She especially helps girls and women realize their full potential. She's a very real person. You can tell that she genuinely cares about her fellow human beings and that she wants to use her life to make the world a better place. Personally, she's a great role model for young women— strong and independent and goal-oriented and smart. She travels all over sharing with people what she's learned.

What this student looked for were reasons that she admires Oprah Winfrey or characteristics that Oprah possesses that are admirable. She circled these reasons and characteristics, and she ignored the sentences that did not focus on why she admires Oprah as an individual.

Another student, given the same assignment, chose to brainstorm about golfer Tiger Woods. He generated this main idea statement:

Tiger Woods is admirable because he is a great role model for young athletes.

This student's main idea statement focuses on why Tiger Woods is an admirable athlete, so he looked for ideas that relate to Tiger Woods's athletic qualities. In addition, he crossed out those ideas that seemed unrelated. Notice that some of the ideas are neither circled nor crossed out, for this student was not yet sure whether they would be useful.

As you complete this first step of the organizing process, you will need to honestly evaluate the quantity of your ideas. Did you generate enough ideas in your prewriting, or did you come up with only a few? If the number of ideas you have generated seems skimpy, go back to the prewriting stage, perhaps selecting another technique, and try to think of more.

EXERCISE 3.1   **Evaluating the Relevancy of Ideas**

Examine the main idea statement and the cluster provided here. In the prewriting, circle words or phrases that match the main idea statement. Either ignore or cross out words and phrases that do not relate to the main idea statement.

Main idea statement: Television does not deserve its bad reputation because it offers many benefits.

After you have identified relevant ideas in Step 1, you are ready to go on to Step 2, which involves grouping like things together. Before you see how to do this with prewriting, consider how you would go about doing it with common household items. Say you are going to organize your kitchen cabinets by putting like things together in the same place. You have the following items on your kitchen table:

three cans of soup	forks	plastic containers
dish detergent	salt and pepper	glass bowls
plates	drinking glasses	boxes of macaroni and cheese
knives	scouring powder	a ladle
a box of cereal	sponges	tea bags

If you mix all of these items up, it might be more difficult to locate something when you need to find it. Therefore, you want to group them together logically. How would you go about doing it? You could group the soup, cereal, macaroni and cheese, and tea bags together because they are all food items. The salt and pepper could go in this group, too. You might put the silverware and utensils (forks, knives, ladle) together in another group and the dishware (plates, bowls, glasses) in yet another. The cleaning items (dish detergent, scouring powder, and sponges) probably belong in a different group, and so on. This is not the only method for grouping these items, but it is probably the most common one because it makes the most sense to the most people.

However, how would you group this next set of items?

paper clips	a watch	a napkin	the sun
a football field	leaves	a pencil	a ring
a dollar bill	a mailbox	a radio	green beans
a basket	a dime	cake	

Different groupings are possible for this set of items. For example, you could group them according to shape (some of these things are round, and some are square or rectangular), function (some of these things relate to food or eating, for example), color (several of these things are green), material (some of these things are made of metal), or some other criterion. As you can see, these things can be grouped in a number of different ways. Such will be the case when you look at the ideas you generate for writing. Sometimes, the right grouping will be immediately apparent to you. At other times, you may have to experiment with different ways to group thoughts together.

Now you can apply this same procedure to ideas generated in a prewriting exercise. When you were circling key words and phrases in Step 1, you probably circled some things that actually go together or say the same thing in different words. For example, look back at the student's freewriting about Oprah Winfrey on pages 36–37. Which of the circled phrases seem to belong together? Several of the phrases relate to Oprah's interest in helping people:

wants her show to do good	gives people good advice
wants to help people	supports many charities
genuinely cares	make the world a better place

If you examine this list further, though, you might realize that some of the things in this list are desires and goals and that some of them are actions:

Desires/goals	*Actions*
wants her show to do good	gives people good advice
wants to help people	supports many charities
genuinely cares	
make the world a better place	

Other circled words and phrases in the freewriting relate to Oprah's personal qualities:

Personal qualities

spiritual	great role model	strong
independent	goal-oriented	smart

When you sort the items into groups, you can see three different aspects of Oprah that are admirable: her desires and goals, her actions, and her personal qualities.

Of course, this is not the only way to group these thoughts. You could, for instance, group things according to *how* Oprah helps people. The freewriting mentions her show, her magazine, and her travels, during which she shares what she has learned with people. It is also possible to group these ideas according to *whom* she has helped: television show audiences, charities, and girls and women. There may be other possibilities as well.

Now look back at the brainstorming on Tiger Woods on page 37. How would you group those ideas together? Here is one possibility:

Physical	*Mental*
hard work	determined
long practices	stays focused
always strives to improve	does not give up
challenges himself	

Alternatively, you could group these items according to three important qualities for athletic success: perseverance, dedication to improvement, and concentration/focus.

EXERCISE 3.2   **Sorting Items into Groups**

Group each set of the following sets of items according to how they are alike. On the blank provided, write any item that does not belong with the others.

1. cookies   soda   milk   rice   water   sweater   juice   potato

   Group 1: _____

   Group 2: _____

   Item that does not belong: _____

2. diamond   bricks   emerald   rose   lumber   ruby   concrete

   Group 1: _____

   Group 2: _____

   Item that does not belong: _____

3. museum   paintings   clay   colored pencils   drawings   sculptures   paint

   Group 1: _____

   Group 2: _____

   Item that does not belong: _____

4. heights   anger   friendship   snakes   sorrow   grief   the dark   flying

   Group 1: _____

   Group 2: _____

   Item that does not belong: _____

5. honesty   generosity   greed   fame   kindness   gold   faithfulness   fear

   Group 1: _____

   Group 2: _____

   Item that does not belong: _____

> **EXERCISE 3.3**   **Grouping Ideas from a Prewriting**
>
> Go back to Exercise 3.1 and examine the items you circled. How would you group the relevant items in this cluster? List your groups in the space provided here:

_____

_____

_____

_____

_____

_____

_____

_____

_____

_____

_____

_____

_____

_____

_____

_____

After you have determined possible groupings for relevant items, Step 3 involves deciding on the order in which you should present these groups to your reader. Sometimes, the groups will naturally organize themselves, as you will see in the next section. For those topics that do not naturally order themselves, you will have to use logic, letting the relationships between the groups suggest the best arrangement.

Natural Versus Logical Organization

When you are deciding on the best order for your ideas, you will have to decide whether to use natural organization or logical organization. Some topics organize themselves, so they are arranged with **natural organization**. When you tell a story, for instance, or write a set of directions to explain how to do something, you will give your readers the events or the steps chronologically, in the order in which they occur.

However, many more topics do *not* naturally organize themselves. For these topics, you will have to use **logical organization**. In other words, you will have to evaluate the groups you created and apply logic to decide whether they are related to each other in some way. These relationships may indicate a certain order for presenting the groups. For example, the items in one of the groups may actually be the cause of the items in another of the groups. Recall, for example, the three groups of admirable things about Oprah Winfrey: her desires and goals, her actions, and her personal qualities. Does one of these things cause another? You could say that her personal qualities and her desires and goals lead her to act in certain ways. As a result, you might want to present her actions last, after you have explained the other two admirable aspects. Should you present her desires and goals first, or should you discuss her personal qualities first? You could argue that it is her personal qualities that give rise to her particular goals, so you might cover her personal qualities first. Once again, this is not the only way to arrange these groups, but it seems logical when we consider how one thing leads to another.

When you examine your groups, you might decide that some are more important than others. Order of importance may affect how you arrange your ideas. Sometimes it is best to present the most important information first, and sometimes it is best to save it for last. In either case, though, consider whether you should order groups by their relative importance. You might do this, for instance, with the ideas about Tiger Woods. Is it more important for an athlete to concentrate on the physical or the mental? Is concentration more important than dedication to improvement? If you believe that it is, then order your groups accordingly.

One common mistake that you should avoid as you work on organizing ideas is trying to use natural organization when you should use logical organization. It is not advisable, for example, to present your ideas to the reader in the order in which you thought of them. If you do that, you will have altogether skipped Steps 1 and 2 of the organization process. Nor do you want to try to use a story form to present information about a topic that is not really a story. For example, telling a story about the time you were in the audience of Oprah Winfrey's show and mentioning here and there the things about her you admire is probably not the best way to address why she is an admirable person.

 **EXERCISE 3.4**   **Determining the Right Order for Ideas**

In what order would you place the groups you created in Exercise 3.3? In the space provided here, write each of your groups in order, numbered 1, 2, 3, and so forth.

 **EXERCISE 3.5**   **Natural or Logical Organization?**

Read each of the following main idea statements, and label each one **N** if it would lend itself to natural organization or **L** if it would require logical organization.

_____ **1.** You should not expose your skin to the radiation in tanning beds.

_____ **2.** My last camping trip quickly turned into a nightmare.

_____ **3.** My neighbor Don is a good father.

_____ **4.** Anyone can boil water by following three simple steps.

_____ **5.** The martial arts, such as karate and judo, are great for children.

_____ **6.** If you do not learn how to relax, you will wind up with health problems.

_____ **7.** Americans could do more to cut down on pollution.

_____ **8.** The library is the best place on campus to study.

_____ **9.** My childhood was a very happy one.

_____ **10.** You must see Paris sometime during your life.

Outlining

During or after your completion of the three steps of the organization process, you should create an outline of your ideas. **Outlines** come in different forms, but they all list the ideas or information you will present in the order in which you will present them. The best outlines also indicate how ideas are related to one another. Regardless of their form, they all provide the writer with a guide to follow as he or she writes.

Myths About Outlining

When people object to creating an outline prior to writing, they usually argue that they can save time by skipping the outline and just working out their organization as they write. Or they may argue that it is pointless to create an outline that may not match the finished product. Both of these arguments, however, rest on myths about outlining.

Myth #1: Skipping the outlining step saves time. On the contrary, failing to outline actually *adds* time to composition. When you do not spend time determining and writing down a plan of organization before you begin writing, you force your brain to juggle two challenging mental tasks (organizing and composing) at the same time. Because doing this is more complicated, the writing usually takes longer. Separating the outlining stage and the organization stage before you begin to write might actually save you valuable time in the long run by making the writing step easier and, therefore, faster.

Myth #2: An outline is useless because the final paper rarely matches it. The outline is your best determination of your composition's overall structure. However, it is not carved in stone, and you may very well find better ways to organize your thoughts as you write. Altering your original plan does not mean that it was not useful for getting you started.

WRITING FOR SUCCESS

Outlining and PowerPoint Presentations

In your academic life or later in your career, you may have to create slide presentations using Microsoft PowerPoint or some other slide-show program. A series of slides that summarizes your main points is a very effective audiovisual tool that will help your audience follow your presentation and remember more of it when it is over.

To illustrate, say that you are going to teach a group of other students how to follow the three-step process for grouping and ordering ideas that was covered in this chapter. The following illustrations demonstrate how you might represent this information on PowerPoint slides:

STEP 2: Group like things together

- Sort ideas into groups according to their similarities.
- Experiment with different groupings.

STEP 3: Decide on the best order for your groups

- Natural organization: chronological topics like stories and directions.
- Logical organization
  — Causes
  — Order of Importance

STEP 1: Identify info that matches the main idea

- Circle, highlight, or mark relevant ideas.
- Ignore or cross out info that does not relate to main idea.
- Do not erase anything.
- Prewrite again if you need more info.

Learning how to organize and outline your ideas is critical to a successful PowerPoint presentation. Many of your slides will include main points and indicate how those points are related to one another, just as an outline does. As a matter of fact, an outline of a speech often becomes the slide show. The PowerPoint program even allows you to transform an outline into an entire slide presentation in just a few steps.

Creating an outline of your ideas before you write will help you keep the overall big picture in mind as you concentrate on the smaller details. It will also prevent you from

- straying from your main point and including information or ideas that are irrelevant

- rambling or jumping from thought to thought in a manner that confuses the reader

- mixing different kinds of information together

- discussing an idea in the wrong place

Formal Outlines

When you think of an outline, you may picture one that includes Roman numerals. A **formal outline** uses some combination of Roman numerals, letters, and/or Arabic numbers. One common type of formal outline, for example, uses all three:

I. Main idea
    A. Supporting detail
       1. Statistic
       2. Example
    B. Supporting detail
       1. Expert opinion
       2. Data

In this type of outline, the Roman numerals correspond to the main ideas, whereas the letters and Arabic numbers indicate supporting information. This is the type of outline that is usually a required part of longer assignments such as research papers, for it serves as a kind of table of contents for a lengthy paper.

However, creating a formal outline is worthwhile even if it is not a required part of an assignment. This format not only is useful for showing the order of your ideas but also serves another valuable purpose: it clearly indicates the relationship of your ideas to one another. Thus, as you write, one glance at this outline can help you keep in mind your overall structure for the entire paper, allowing you to stay organized *and* make important connections for your reader. Obviously, it takes some time to create a detailed outline like this, but the time and effort are worth it, for the composition process is often faster and yields a more successful finished product.

Using an Outline to Identify Needed Information

Your outline for your paragraph or essay will help you know what kind of information you will need to gather about your topic. When you create your outline, you can add notes about needed pieces of information. One student, for example, created this informal outline for his paragraph about the benefits of learning a foreign language:

1. Helps improve overall academic performance
   - Find studies of children who are learning foreign languages
   - Get SAT statistics

2. Good skill for job market
   - What is the percentage of jobs in which foreign language is an asset?
3. Helps kids understand other cultures—leads to tolerance and world peace
   - Find examples of real kids learning languages

Under each group in this outline, the student listed the pieces of information he will need. Next, he can begin to locate those facts and examples.

EXERCISE 3.6   **Completing a Formal Outline**

Fill in the blanks in the following formal outline with the words and phrases in the list.

Main idea: Regular, brisk walking offers many benefits.

Cardiovascular health	Lower risk of heart attack	Benefits of brisk walking
Lower blood pressure	Physical benefits	Stress relief
Disease prevention	Mood improvement	
Increased brain power	Weight loss	

I. _____

   A. _____

      1. _____

         a. _____

         b. _____

      2. _____

      3. Improved muscle tone

      4. _____

   B. Mental benefits

      1. _____

      2. _____

      3. _____

Informal Outlines

If an outline is not required for your assignment and if you are creating one just as a tool for yourself, then you are free to use a less formal method. Informal types of outlines can take the form of brief lists of ideas in the order in which you want to discuss them. For example, the following sketch is an informal outline:

> Main idea: Planning a large wedding can be very stressful.
>
> 1. Many decisions, preparations
>   – dress, wedding party, reception, invitations
> 2. Worrying about observing proper etiquette
>   – invitations, procession, seating at reception
> 3. Anxiety about things going wrong
>   – weather, saying or doing something embarrassing during ceremony, flowers wrong, cake ruined

An informal outline can also take the form of **branching.** This form looks a lot like the clustering prewriting technique. It starts with a topic and then draws "branches" of subtopics and details radiating from that central topic. Here is an example of branching:

Main idea: A fish aquarium is worth the effort it takes to clean and maintain it.

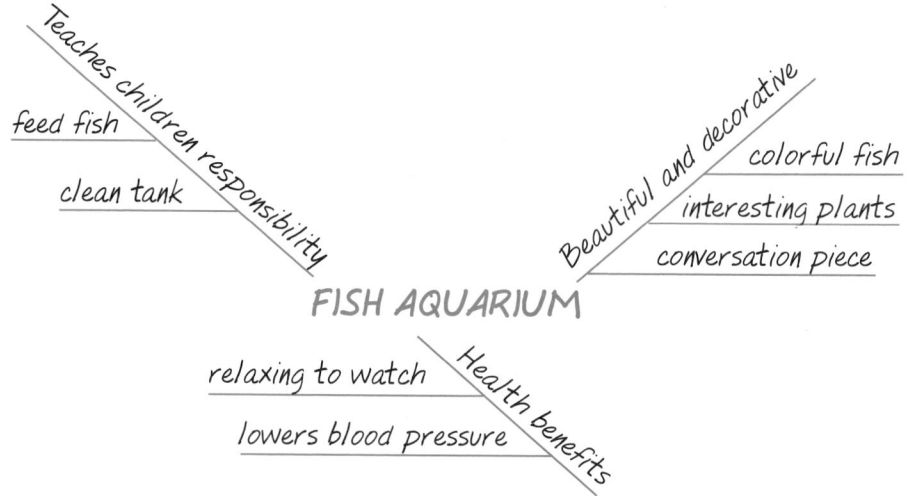

Figure 3.1 An Example of Branching

EXERCISE 3.7 **Completing an Informal Outline**

Complete the following informal outline by filling in the blanks.

Main idea: For distances of 300 miles or less, driving is a better form of transportation than flying.

1. _____
   – Gas costs less than plane ticket

   – _____

2. Convenience of having your own car

3. _____

4. Sometimes faster, especially during holidays and bad weather

   – _____

   – _____

Organizing and Outlining: A Student Demonstration

In Chapter 2, you saw the prewriting generated by Maya, a student who was assigned to write about student success. Maya's main idea statement was

Student success depends upon using tools that will help you organize your responsibilities and your materials.

Next, Maya needs to complete the three-step organizing process. First, she circled relevant ideas in her freewriting.

I think that getting and staying organized is essential to being a good student. If your not organized then things can get away from you and you will miss deadlines and you will not be prepared for class or tests. That's why I use a monthly calendar to record all due dates and test dates. Some of my friends really need to get better organized. Emily and Frank never know where anything is. I keep separate notebooks for each class so things don't get mixed up. Studying in several sessions is important too. I write down tasks I need to complete on certain days to stay current. Like study for math test. And I write it on my To Do list for that day. I check off each thing as I finish it. I can just glance at the calendar and get a picture of my responsibilities for the whole month. On the same calendar, I write my work schedule too and my softball practice times. And I carry my calendar everywhere so I can update it right away.

Then she moved on to Step 2 of the organizing process and discovered that she had already thought of three tools for organization: a monthly calendar, separate notebooks for each class, and a daily To Do list. She created groups of ideas:

Monthly calendar
record all due dates and test dates
write my work schedule too and my softball practice times

Separate notebooks for each class

To Do list
check off each thing as I finish it

Although she discovered three good ideas for her paragraph, she noticed that she had not generated very many ideas about the To Do list and the notebooks, so she decided to do some more prewriting on those two topics.

In Step 3, she realized that natural organization would not apply to her topic, so she would have to logically order the groups. She decided that two of the tools—the calendar and the To Do list—are tools for organizing responsibilities and that the third tool is for organizing materials. Because her calendar determines what she writes on her daily To Do list, she decided to discuss the calendar first and then the list. She decided to save her discussion of using separate notebooks for class materials for last.

Finally, she created a brief, informal outline to guide her as she wrote her paragraph:

Main Idea: Student success depends upon using tools that will help you organize your responsibilities and your materials.

1. Monthly calendar
2. Daily To Do list
3. Separate notebook for each class

In Chapter 4, you will see how Maya completed the next step, composing her paragraph.

EXERCISE 3.8   **Preparing an Outline for Your Paragraph**

In Chapter 2, you generated some ideas about one of the following topics: your favorite sport, your goals, an embarrassing moment, or artistic expression. Then you wrote a main idea statement. Reread this main idea statement and examine the prewriting you generated. Follow the three-step organization procedure. First, circle all of the words and phrases that seem relevant to your main idea. Second, group like ideas and information together. Third, decide on the best order for those groups.

Finally, create either a formal or an informal outline of your ideas. You will use this outline again in Chapter 4 when you actually write your paragraph.

CHAPTER 3 REVIEW

Fill in the blanks in the following statements.

1. You begin to create a framework for your ideas when you examine your _____ and your _____ and go through a three-step process to organize your ideas.

2. Step 1 of the organization process involves circling ideas and information that are _____ to your main idea statement and ignoring or crossing out ideas that seem _____.

3. Step 2 of the organization process involves _____ like ideas and information together.

4. Step 3 of the organization process involves deciding on the best way to put your groups of ideas in _____.

5. Some topics, such as stories and sets of directions, arrange themselves with _____ organization.

6. For other topics, the writer must evaluate relationships of idea groups to one another and determine a plan of _____ organization.

7. Two common types of logical order are _____ and _____ _____.

8. An _____ lists the ideas and information you will present in the order in which you will present them; it should also indicate how ideas are _____ to one another.

9. One myth about outlining says that skipping the outlining step saves _____.

10. A second myth about outlining is that an outline is useless because it rarely _____ the final paper.

11. Creating an outline will prevent you from digressing from your main point and including information or ideas that are _____.

12. Creating an outline will also prevent you from _____ from thought to thought in a confusing manner, from mixing different kinds of information together, and from discussing an idea in the wrong place.

13. A _____ outline is one that uses some combination of Roman numerals, letters, and/or Arabic numbers; this format shows not only the order of your ideas but also the _____ of ideas to one another.

14. An _____ outline can take the form of a brief list or branching.

WebWork

For more practice with organizing and outlining, work with a partner to complete the outlines at the following Web sites:

http://mrcoward.com/slcusd/org3.html
http://mrcoward.com/slcusd/org4.html
http://mrcoward.com/slcusd/org5.html

 *Online Study Center*   For additional organizing and outlining information and activities, go to the Houghton Mifflin Online Study Center for this book, at **http://www.college.hmco.com/pic/dolphinwritertwo**.

4

Writing a Paragraph

GOALS FOR CHAPTER 4

▶ Revise ineffective topic sentences.

▶ Write effective topic sentences.

▶ Write a paragraph that includes layers of development and transitions.

In Chapter 2, you learned some prewriting techniques for generating ideas, including a main idea, and in Chapter 3, you practiced organizing and outlining ideas. This chapter focuses on the third step of the writing process, composing a draft of a paragraph.

The Paragraph and Its Purpose

A **paragraph** can be defined as a group of sentences that all support or develop one particular idea about a topic. Paragraphs vary in length from just a few sentences to many sentences. A paragraph can stand alone, or it can be combined with other paragraphs to form a longer piece of writing, such as an essay.

The purpose of a paragraph, particularly in a longer piece of writing, is to group related sentences together so that readers can clearly understand the writer's ideas. Imagine that books or articles you have read contained no paragraphs and presented thoughts and information in no particular order, leaving you to try to make sense of them all. Reading such a book or article would be a confusing and unpleasant task. Just as you expect writers to have grouped their sentences into related units of thought, the readers of your writing will expect you to have done the same with your own ideas.

The following diagram shows the form of a paragraph. The first sentence of a paragraph is indented five spaces from the left margin. The remaining sentences follow each other with only two spaces between them, and blank space follows the last word of the last sentence.

*First sentence
indented 5
spaces*

_____

_____   *Sentences two
spaces apart*

_____

_____

*Left side lines
up along
margin line*

_____   *Line blank
after last word
of last sentence*

_____.

A paragraph has two main parts: a topic sentence and a body. The topic sentence states the paragraph's main idea, and the remaining sentences—the body—develop that idea with more information and explanation.

The Topic Sentence

In Chapter 2, you practiced generating main idea statements as part of your prewriting practice. This main idea statement becomes the **topic sentence,** the sentence in the paragraph that states the main idea. Therefore, just like the main idea statement that you generate in prewriting, the topic sentence has two parts: it states the topic of the paragraph, and it also states the writer's point about that topic. Notice how each of the following topic sentences contains both a topic and an idea about that topic:

Topic	*Point*
My hobby	offers me several different benefits.

Topic	*Point*
Friends	should not try to resolve a conflict via e-mail.

Topic	*Point*
My mother	is the person I admire most.

Remember that the term *topic sentence* might seem a little misleading, for the topic sentence does more than state the topic of the paragraph. It also states an idea about that topic.

EXERCISE 4.1   **Identifying the Parts of Topic Sentences**

In each of the following topic sentences, circle the topic and underline the point the writer makes about that topic.

1. My two best friends are as different as night and day.

2. Your exercise program will be most successful if it matches your personality.

3. Dusting is the household chore I hate the most.

4. Going to preschool offers children several advantages.

5. Volunteering to help others builds character and values.

In a well-written paragraph, the topic sentence will be apparent. It will be the most general statement in the paragraph, and all of the other sentences will clearly develop the point that it makes. A topic sentence is often the first sentence of the paragraph, but it does not have to be. It can appear anywhere in the paragraph: at the beginning, in the middle, or at the end. Read the following paragraph, and see if you can underline the sentence that expresses the main idea.

> Chickens make perfect pets. They're great with children; they are never noisy. (It's the roosters that are noisy, and for egg-laying purposes, hens need roosters like fish need bicycles.) "They like to be with people, and they like to be in the community," testifies recent chicken convert Chris Williams, a Gloucester sculptor whose pet hen, Mrs. Miller, hops up on his lap during break time. (Alex Beam, "Why Did the Chicken Get in This Column?" *Boston Globe*, June 10, 2003, p. D1.)

Did you underline the first sentence? That is the sentence in the paragraph that states the paragraph's main idea. Then the rest of the paragraph goes on to offer three reasons why the main idea is true.

 **EXERCISE 4.2**   **Recognizing Topic Sentences in Paragraphs**

Underline the topic sentence in each of the following paragraphs.

1. At one time management could simply assume that most workers came to the job believing that hard work and sacrifice paid off. This was a correct assumption. However, a decreasing percentage of younger workers believe in the value of hard work. While they are willing to work hard under the right conditions, they're too smart to believe that sweat and elbow grease[1] automatically guarantee success. Younger workers are much more likely to be dedicated to self-fulfillment and leisure pursuits than company loyalty and hard work for its own sake. And if they don't like the job or the way they're being treated, you can count on them to leave—or worse yet, retire psychologically and continue to draw a paycheck. (Michael LeBoeuf, "Turning On Turned-Off Workers," in *A Basic Reader for College Writers,* ed. D. I. Daniels et al., [Marlton, NJ, Townsend Press, 1995], p. 231.)

2. On the train the other day, on another crowded morning, I watched a young man in an expensive suit slip into an open seat without so much as losing his place in *The New York Times*, smoothly beating out a silver-haired gentleman and a gaggle[2] of young women in spike heels. My first thought was that his mother would be ashamed of him. And then I thought, with some amusement, that I am hopelessly behind the times. For all I know, the older man would've been insulted to be offered a seat by someone two or three decades his junior. And the women, I suppose, might consider chivalry[3] a sexist[4] custom. Besides, our young executive or investment banker probably had to compete with women for the job that's keeping him in Italian loafers; why would he want to offer a potential competitor a seat? Of course, this sort of confusion about expectations is about much more than etiquette[5] on public transportation; it's about what we should do for each other, and expect of each other, now that our roles are no longer closely dictated by whether we are male or female, young or old. (Adapted from Caroline Miller, "Civil Rites," in *The Simon and Schuster Short Prose Reader*, ed. R. Funk et al., 2nd ed. [Upper Saddle River, NJ: Prentice-Hall, 2000], p. 90.)

3. Maybe it was typical male naiveté[6], but it took me a long time to realize that for girls the [prom] dress is infinitely more important than the date. Some have had their dresses for months; a few made the five-hour trip to exclusive

---

1. **elbow grease:** hard work; effort
2. **gaggle:** group or cluster
3. **chivalry:** qualities—such as courtesy, honor, and bravery—exhibited by knights
4. **sexist:** showing discrimination against the opposite sex
5. **etiquette:** good manners
6. **naiveté:** lack of experience or sophistication

New York shops to guard against what they saw as a potential disaster: another girl arriving in the same dress. Senior Emily Ewell says, "For the girls, it's glamour night; the excitement of the dress, of getting the shoes, nails and makeup that matches. It's seeing all your friends dressed up." Indeed, Emily and her date, Colin O'Neil, were among the night's more elegant couples—Emily in a tangerine evening gown and Colin in a black tux with an orange rose boutonniere[1] that matched the gown. Barbara Harslem . . . took Amy, her youngest child, shopping for a prom dress. "It took a whole day and visits to five stores," Harslem says. "At one store, there were over 30 girls trying on prom dresses with their mothers standing around. The mother's job was to take the dresses the girls didn't like back and bring new ones." (Patrick Welsh, "Proms Equalize High School Lives," *USA Today*, June 4, 2003, p. 11A. Reprinted by permission of the author.)

When you write topic sentences for paragraphs of your own, remember that an effective topic sentence has three essential characteristics: it is a complete sentence that includes both a topic and a point, it is not too broad or too narrow, and it takes into account not just the topic but also the audience and purpose of the paragraph.

First of all, a topic sentence must contain both of its required parts: a topic and some point about that topic. A topic in the form of a sentence fragment is not a topic sentence:

Incomplete:	The importance of exercise
Complete topic sentence:	Exercise is important to good health.
Incomplete:	The damage caused by Hurricane Katrina
Complete topic sentence:	Hurricane Katrina was one of the most destructive storms in American history.
Incomplete:	Moths and butterflies
Complete topic sentence:	Moths and butterflies differ from one another in several ways.

If you try to begin writing with only a topic in mind, then you will probably not produce a coherent and well-developed paragraph. When you are unsure about exactly what you mean to say, then your paragraph will probably ramble aimlessly. Make sure that before you begin to write, you have a complete topic sentence that includes both your topic and your point.

---

1. **boutonniere:** a flower worn in a buttonhole

In addition to being complete, a topic sentence must also be appropriately specific. If an idea is too broad or too vague, it will not keep you properly focused as you write. For example, look at the following examples:

Too broad: Summer activities are a lot of fun.
Too vague: Something should be done about the traffic in this city.

Neither of these statements expresses one clear idea, so each would probably lead to rambling when it came time to write. To improve these two statements, rewrite them to narrow the topic and/or the idea:

Swimming at the lake is my family's favorite summertime activity.

Expanding and improving bus service would help reduce city traffic.

On the other hand, though, you do not want to make your topic sentence so specific or limited that you cannot develop it at all:

Too specific: The temperature rose to 98 degrees last week.

Because this sentence states a fact, there is not much more you can say about it. To improve it, broaden the topic and the idea:

Last week's 98-degree heat caused a number of serious problems.

Be aware that your topic sentence may not be perfect on your first try. You may have to work on it, experimenting with the wording and rewriting it even after you have begun writing, until it says exactly what you want to express.

EXERCISE 4.3   **Revising Ineffective Topic Sentences**

On the blanks provided here, rewrite each of the following topic sentences that is either incomplete, too broad, too vague, or too specific. If the main idea seems complete and appropriately specific, write **OK** on the blank.

1. My worst job.

_____

2. Education is important.

_____

3. I know how to speak Spanish.

_____

_____

4. Something should be done about the state of public school education in this country.

_____

_____

5. Fast-food restaurants are contributing to soaring obesity rates among Americans.

_____

So far, you have learned that effective topic sentences are complete and appropriately specific. A good topic sentence also takes into account the audience and purpose of the paragraph. When you are composing your topic sentence, you will not only want to consider _what_ you want to say but also _why_ and _to whom_ you want to say it. Therefore, in addition to the topic, there are two other factors—audience and purpose—that will affect how you express your topic sentence.

The first of these factors is your audience, or readers. _Who_ is going to read your writing? _What_ does this person need to know or want to know about the topic? Your topic sentence should take into account this audience's needs and desires.

The second factor is your purpose. Do you want to entertain your readers? Do you want to inform them about your topic so they can learn something new? Or do you want to persuade them to believe what you believe about the topic? Your topic sentence should clearly reflect this purpose.

For example, take the topic sentence "Massage has several important health benefits." The writer intends to explain to someone who is interested in health how massage affects the body in positive ways. But notice how the purpose of this next statement differs:

You should get a cardiovascular workout at least three times a week.

Although the audience is probably the same, the words "you should" indicate that the writer's purpose is persuasive. If the first topic sentence were changed to have a persuasive purpose, it might read: "If you want to feel great and improve your health, you must get regular massages."

 **EXERCISE 4.4**   **Topic, Audience, and Purpose in Topic Sentences**

A. Answer the question that follows each topic sentence by circling the letter of the correct response.

1. In many retail stores, the quality of customer service is declining.

The writer's purpose is to

    a. entertain customer service representatives with a story about a shopper.
    b. inform readers about how and why customer service is declining.
    c. persuade retail store managers to improve their customer service.

2. *Raiders of the Lost Ark* was the best movie ever made.

The writer's purpose is to

    a. entertain readers by telling the story of *Raiders of the Lost Ark.*
    b. inform readers about *Raiders of the Lost Ark.*
    c. persuade readers that *Raiders of the Lost Ark* was the best movie ever made.

3. Our ride on the roller coaster at Busch Gardens was a lot of fun.

The writer's purpose is to

    a. entertain readers with a description of the roller coaster ride at Busch Gardens.
    b. inform readers about the roller coaster at Busch Gardens.
    c. persuade readers that the roller coaster at Busch Gardens is the best one around.

4. *Time* magazine is a weekly publication that includes current events, international news, entertainment news, and sports news.

The writer's purpose is to

    a. entertain readers with an amusing story about *Time* magazine.
    b. inform readers about what kind of magazine *Time* is.
    c. persuade readers that they should subscribe to *Time.*

5. You should think about joining Premiere Athletic Club because of its excellent facilities.

The writer's purpose is to

    a. entertain readers with a story about Premiere Athletic Club.
    b. inform readers about the facilities at Premiere Athletic Club.
    c. persuade readers to join Premiere Athletic Club.

B. Use prewriting techniques to generate ideas, and then write a topic sentence for each topic/audience/purpose set provided here.

Topic: A good film you have seen
Audience: People who enjoy films
Purpose: To inform

1. Topic sentence: _____

Topic: A good film you have seen
Audience: People who are deciding whether or not they should see the film
Purpose: To persuade

2. Topic sentence: _____

Topic: A trip you took
Audience: Your friends
Purpose: To entertain

3. Topic sentence: _____

Topic: A trip you took
Audience: People who are interested in taking the same trip
Purpose: To inform

4. Topic sentence: _____

Topic: Gun control
Audience: People who want to learn more about the issue
Purpose: To inform

5. Topic sentence: _____

Topic: Gun control
Audience: People who are opposed to new gun-control laws
Purpose: To persuade

6. Topic sentence: _____

The Body

The **body** of the paragraph includes all of the sentences that support, explain, or prove the idea expressed in the topic sentence. These sentences provide all of the evidence the reader will need in order to accept the main idea as true, and this evidence can take a variety of different forms, including

> facts
> statistics and other data
> examples
> stories
> reasons
> comparisons
> descriptive details

In the following paragraph, the topic sentence is highlighted. Read the paragraph and try to decide which of the different kinds of evidence in the preceding list is given to support the topic sentence.

> The biggest lesson I've learned from being on welfare is that most people assume I don't want to work. When I list my job skills for the caseworkers, they can't seem to understand why I don't have a job. To them, and the rest of society, I am just one of the 7 million people on welfare who survive off less than 1 percent of the federal budget. **But I'm more than just a statistic.** I graduated in the top 10 percent of my high-school class. I'm studying nursing at my community college. I've played the flute since I was 5. My parents have been married 30 years. I can type more than 80 words a minute. I'm bilingual. I know half a dozen computer programs inside and out. I'm 24 years old. (Elyzabeth Joy Stagg, "From the Welfare Rolls, a Mother's View," in *Viewpoints*, ed. W. R. Adams, 4th ed. [Boston: Houghton Mifflin, 2001], p. 240.)

This paragraph supports the topic sentence with an example of someone (the writer herself) who does not fit the stereotype of a welfare recipient and includes statistics and facts to help develop the main idea.

The next sections of this chapter will cover some techniques for writing the body of a paragraph.

A Step-by-Step Guide to Composing a Paragraph

After you have generated ideas through prewriting and then organized them and created an outline, you are ready to write your paragraph.

Step One: Transform Your Main Idea into a Topic Sentence

As mentioned earlier, a topic sentence does not have to be the first sentence of a paragraph. However, as you work on strengthening your writing skills, it is usually best to begin your paragraph with this statement because it will help you stay focused as you write the rest of the paragraph. Therefore, look first at the main idea statement you generated during the prewriting stage of your process. Evaluate it to make sure it is complete (containing a topic and an idea about that topic), appropriately specific, and suited to your purpose and audience, and rewrite it if necessary. Once it contains all of these characteristics, write it down as the first sentence of your paragraph.

Look, for example, at one student's main idea statement. John generated prewriting on the topic "A Memorable Trip" and came up with the following: *My trip to Hong Kong to meet my grandmother for the first time.* But then he realized that this statement was not a complete sentence, so he revised it to read: *My trip to Hong Kong to meet my grandmother for the first time helped me learn more about my cultural heritage.*

Another student, Luisa, generated prewriting on the same topic and decided on this main idea: *My scuba diving trip to the Florida Keys was interesting.* When she evaluated whether or not it would be a good topic sentence, she decided that it was too vague. She revised it to read: *My scuba diving trip contributed to my personal development.*

As you can see, main idea statements and topic sentences may not be perfect the first time. If yours seems to be lacking something, do not proceed with writing the rest of the paragraph until you have figured out what is missing and have corrected the problem. If you are not sure of exactly what you are trying to communicate to your readers, then you will be in greater danger of rambling or failing to adequately develop what you want to say.

 **EXERCISE 4.5**   **Writing Topic Sentences**

Prewrite on the topic *friendship*. Generate three main idea statements for different aspects of that topic, and write those three statements on the blanks provided. Next, evaluate whether each statement is complete, appropriately specific, and suited to your audience and purpose. If you decide that the statement does not possess all three characteristics, rewrite it on the blank provided so that it does.

Main idea statement #1: _____

Is it complete?	Yes _____	No _____
Is it appropriately specific?	Yes _____	No _____
Is it suited to audience and purpose?	Yes _____	No _____

Revised statement (Topic Sentence): _____

Main idea statement #2: _____

      Is it complete?   Yes _____   No _____

      Is it appropriately specific?   Yes _____   No _____

      Is it suited to audience and purpose? Yes _____   No _____

      Revised statement (Topic Sentence): _____

Main idea statement #3: _____

      Is it complete?   Yes _____   No _____

      Is it appropriately specific?   Yes _____   No _____

      Is it suited to audience and purpose? Yes _____   No _____

      Revised statement (Topic Sentence): _____

Step Two: Reevaluate Your Outline and Consider Common Strategies for Organizing Ideas

Once you have written down your topic sentence, the next step involves reevaluating your outline to make sure that it still matches the idea you have expressed in the topic sentence. Make sure this outline still includes the right kinds of supporting ideas, and decide whether they are still listed in the right order. Make any necessary adjustments to your outline before you begin.

    Look, for example, at Luisa's revised topic sentence and existing outline:

My scuba diving trip contributed to my personal development.

       – saw fascinating fish and underwater plant life
       – improved my scuba skills
       – brought back interesting souvenirs
       – met people and made some new friends

The topic sentence and outline no longer seem to match because the revised topic sentence focuses more specifically on the writer's personal development. So Luisa made a few changes to her outline:

My scuba diving trip contributed to my personal development.

       – improved my scuba skills
       – challenged myself by diving deeper than I thought I could
       – learned to cope with several of my fears

After Luisa revised her outline, it seemed more appropriate for the topic sentence she planned to develop.

As part of this step, you will want to consider the common strategies for organizing ideas. Chapters 9–18 of this book provide in-depth explanations of these common patterns. The list that follows provides a brief description of each one:

- **Narration.** Tell a story from your own or someone else's experience. (See Chapter 9.)

- **Description.** Provide details about people, places, and things so that readers can picture them in their minds. (See Chapter 10.)

- **Process.** Explain the steps of a procedure. (See Chapter 11.)

- **Illustration.** Provide specific examples that illustrate the main idea. (See Chapter 12.)

- **Classification.** Group items in categories. (See Chapter 13.)

- **Division.** Examine the parts of something. (See Chapter 14.)

- **Comparison/Contrast.** Examine how two things are alike and/or different. (See Chapter 15.)

- **Cause/Effect.** Explain why something occurred or examine the results or outcomes. (See Chapter 16.)

- **Definition.** Explain the meaning of a term. (See Chapter 17.)

- **Argument.** Present a series of reasons to convince readers to change their minds or behaviors. (See Chapter 18.)

Often, your topic sentence will either dictate or suggest how to organize your paragraph according to one or more of these patterns. For example, the topic sentence *Moving to a new town when I was sixteen years old resulted in a number of good and bad effects* indicates that the essay will discuss effects. Therefore, the paragraph's supporting details should be the various effects of moving. The thesis statement *My new home is much different from the town where I spent my childhood* indicates comparison/contrast, and the supporting details should be in the form of points of comparison.

When you write topic sentences, be aware of clue words that indicate an appropriate pattern for the supporting details. The following list provides some examples of words in topic sentences that often suggest a certain pattern:

Narration: *several events, a number of developments, over time*
Description: *features, characteristics*
Process: *three steps, several stages, process, procedure*
Illustration: *examples*
Classification: *types, categories, groups, classes, kinds*
Division: *parts, pieces, sections*
Comparison/contrast: *similarities, differences, likenesses, comparisons, contrasts*
Cause/effect: *causes, effects, consequences, reasons*
Definition: *defined, definition, is*
Argument: *reasons*

 **EXERCISE 4.6**   **Evaluating Outlines**

In each of the following outlines, circle the point that does not match the topic sentence.

1. Topic Sentence: Americans should not drive sport-utility vehicles.

   A. They use too much gas.

   B. They are very popular vehicles.

   C. They roll over too easily.

2. Topic Sentence: My trip to Hong Kong to meet my grandmother for the first time helped me learn more about my cultural heritage.

   1. I got more information about my family members and ancestors.

   2. I learned more about the history of the Chinese people.

   3. I made several new friends on the airplane during my journey.

3. Topic Sentence: Teaching preschool is physically demanding work.

   – reading stories

   – chasing after toddlers to keep them safe

   – lifting kids to change diapers, comfort crying

   – helping kids on playground equipment (pushing them on swings, helping them climb, and so on)

   – cleaning constantly (sweeping, mopping, scrubbing, wiping)

Step Three: Using Your Outline as a Guide, Compose with Layers of Development and Transitional Expressions

After you have made the final adjustments to your outline, you are ready to begin writing the body sentences of your paragraph. Using your outline as a guide, write about the first group of ideas you have listed. Then write about the second group, and so on.

As you write, think of using layers of development to explain each of your ideas. **A layer of development** provides more specific information about a general idea in the sentence that came before it. So a layer of development anticipates and answers questions that pop into readers' heads as they read. For example, suppose you write the sentence "Joe is a very neat person." The word *neat* is a relatively general one that could mean a lot of different things. As your readers read this sentence, they will probably immediately think, *What do you mean by "neat"?* or *How is Joe a neat person?* Instead of going on to another new idea, you need to add some information—a layer of development—to answer these questions. In other words, you need to explain what you mean. So you might add this sentence:

For example, all of Joe's CDs and books are tidy and organized.

This sentence helps the reader better understand what *neat* means. However, you should ask yourself, *Will readers have any questions about this sentence?* They might be asking, for instance, *What do you mean by "tidy and organized"?* or *What do his CDs and books look like?* You might add another layer of development to answer these questions:

They are all lined up in alphabetical order on dust-free shelves.

By adding these two sentences, you have made it very clear to readers how neat Joe is.

Every time you write a sentence, ask yourself this question: *Is there some idea here that I should explain more by giving another fact, detail, or example?* There is no rule about how many layers of development should be included in a paragraph. The number of layers you include will always depend on the idea or information in each different sentence you write. But if you get in the habit of wondering whether you just wrote something that might need further development, then you will be less likely to leave readers guessing about what you really mean, and your ideas will be clear.

EXERCISE 4.7   **Adding Layers of Development**

For each of the following pairs of sentences, circle the letter beside the one that needs to be explained with a more specific fact, detail, or example.

1. a. It is very hot out today.
   b. It was 95 degrees in the shade today.

2. a. Rick works a total of 60 hours per week in his job at the convenience store.
   b. Rick is a very hard worker.

3. a. Rose was wearing a red beret, yellow dress, and purple sneakers.
   b. Rose looks like a clown today.

4. a. It is fun to go on a cruise.
   b. Activities that are fun on a cruise include swimming, dancing, playing games, and even rock climbing.

5. a. Swimming in the ocean can be dangerous.
   b. Rip tides in shallow water cause hundreds of people to drown every year.

To create *transitions* to help your readers see how the sentences are related to each other, add transitional words. **Transitional words** and **phrases** are those whose function is to show the relationships between thoughts and ideas. The word *transition* comes from the Latin prefix *trans*, which means "across." Transitions bridge the gaps across sentences and paragraphs and reveal how they are related. The following box gives some common types of transitional words with a few examples of each type.

Transitional words that signal addition

also	in addition
too	first
second	third
furthermore	finally
and	another

Transitional words that show time order

now	then
today	next
soon	later
finally	previously
eventually	meanwhile

Transitional words that indicate causes or consequences

so	therefore
as a result	consequently
hence	because
thus	for this reason

Transitional words that signal examples

for example	for instance
in one case	as an illustration
to illustrate	

Transitional words that signal comparisons

also	too
likewise	similarly
however	but
yet	in contrast
on the other hand	

EXERCISE 4.8   **Adding Transitional Words and Phrases**

Add transitional words in the blanks in the following passage.

Be Proactive About Studying

Stephen R. Covey, author of *The Seven Habits of Highly Effective People*, says that people are either reactive or proactive in their responses to life's circumstances. *Reactive* people lack initiative[1]. Instead of taking responsibility for what happens, they blame other people or outside events. *Proactive* people, _____, take initiative and accept responsibility for what

comparison

happens to them. Being proactive means accepting responsibility for your own success or failure. _____, being proactive means choosing your actions,

addition

accepting the consequences, and modifying your behavior as needed to achieve success.

When it comes to studying, are you reactive or proactive? The language you use will tell you. The language of reactive people, according to Covey, relieves them of responsibility. _____, if you say, "I can't make a good grade in

example

1. **initiative:** power or ability to begin or follow through with a task

that class," you are saying that you are not responsible. Someone or something is preventing you from making good grades in the class. _____, if you say, *comparison* "I don't have time to study," instead of managing your time, you are allowing the factor of limited time to control you. If you say, "I have to study," you mean that you are not free to choose this action; instead, someone or something is forcing you to do it.

You can become proactive about studying. _____, take control of your *time order* language, which can either limit or expand your horizons. _____, *example* when you say, "I can't make a good grade in that class," you convince yourself that there is no reason to try. _____, you give up. You stop *cause or consequence* studying. The belief that you can't make a good grade becomes a self-fulfilling prophecy. _____, if you become proactive and instead say, *comparison* "I choose to make good grades in that class," you realize that grades are the result of your own decisions and your own effort. _____, you can accurately *time order* assess what your strengths and weaknesses are. _____, you can choose *time order* appropriate study systems or strategies that will get you the results that you want. (Carol C. Kanar, *The Confident Student*, 5th ed., Boston: Houghton Mifflin, 2004, p. 214.)

Some Helpful Tips for Composition

1. As you write your paragraph, keep rereading your topic sentence to stay focused on the one point you want to develop. Doing this will prevent you from including unnecessary or irrelevant information.
2. If you get stuck, go back and reread what you have written so far. Often, revisiting where you have been will act as a springboard to propel you forward again.
3. As you write a first draft, stay focused on the overall big picture. Do not stop to agonize over one particular word or to track down a piece of information you need. Instead, draw a blank, or make a note in the margin about the missing detail and then keep writing. You can find the missing word or information later when you are concentrating on the details.
4. Be willing to go back to the prewriting and organizing stages if your ideas and information seem skimpy or if your ideas do not seem to be flowing logically from one to another.

WRITING FOR SUCCESS

Advantages and Disadvantages of Composing on a Computer

Some people prefer to compose a paragraph by writing it down on paper. Others like to sit down in front of a computer and compose the paragraph by typing it directly into a word processing program. Which method works best? Both have advantages and disadvantages, so writers have to decide for themselves.

Composing a draft using a word processing program may speed up the writing process a little. Because you eliminate a step by not recording all of your thoughts on paper, you may save some time. Many people who are proficient typists also find composing on the computer to be less laborious than writing their papers by hand because they can type on a keyboard more easily than they can write. Slow typists, however, are usually better off writing at least the first draft by hand so that they do not unnecessarily slow down their creative process as they hunt for the right keys. Many writers believe, too, that writing by hand is an essential part of the creative process. The physical act of forming letters and words with a pen or pencil, they say, connects the writer's mind and body more intimately to his or her creation.

Some people prefer to type a first draft because a written one is just too messy. When you scribble your thoughts quickly onto a page, crossing out sentences and writing over them again as you search for the right words, the resulting draft can indeed be difficult to read. But one benefit of a handwritten draft is that all of your experiments with different ways to word your thoughts remain there on the page. Even if you scratch out a sentence (never erase anything in a first draft!), you can still read and retrieve it later if you need it elsewhere in the paper. Conversely, a deleted portion of a computer-generated first draft is gone forever. Of course, one way to overcome this drawback is to stop "erasing" your experiments on the screen. Get in the habit of striking (drawing a line) through anything you do not want just as you would on paper. Then those words will still be available if you need them later.

One final disadvantage of a computer-generated draft, especially one produced by a high-quality laser printer, is its finished appearance. It is neatly typed and attractive, so you might be tempted to send it off "as is" to your reader. In reality, though, it probably needs further revision and polishing. A messy handwritten draft, on the other hand, still looks like it needs more work.

Writing a Paragraph: A Student Demonstration

In Chapter 3, you saw how Maya organized her ideas from her prewriting about student success. Here are her main idea and informal outline again:

Main Idea: Student success depends upon using tools that will help you organize your responsibilities and your materials.

1. Monthly calendar
2. Daily To Do list
3. Separate notebook for each class

Next, she began composing her paragraph. She started by examining her main idea statement and decided that she could revise it to be clearer about her topic and her point about that topic. Her revised main idea became this topic sentence:

Three tools will help students organize their responsibilities and their materials so they will be more successful.

Next, Maya evaluated her outline. She decided that it still included the ideas she wanted to discuss in the order in which she wanted to discuss them. So she began composing her paragraph, consciously adding layers of development and transitions to help readers follow her ideas from one sentence to the next. Here is her first draft:

Three tools will help students organize their responsibilitys and their materials so they will be more successful. A calender is the first tool, I carry my calender wherever I go. In it, I write down duedates for all of my assignments in all my classes. Like math tests and papers due. Papers are always the hardest assignments. I also write down my work schedule and practices for softball. So I can just glance at the whole month and know what I need to do when. Next I write a To Do list every day. I look at the day on my calendar and see what I need to do. Then I make a list of things to get done. I will write items like "study for math test" and "read chapter 6 of english book." Crossing them off as I do them. I keep a seperate notebook for my materials for each class. I have a notebook for english, one for math, and one for my computer class. I put handouts, class notes, and other class information in each one and take it to class always. To be a good student, it is important to be prepared for class.

Notice that Maya did a good job of adding layers of development and transitions as she wrote. Her paragraph is just a first draft, so it is not perfect. However, it is a good start. In Chapter 5, you will see how she revised and improved it.

 **EXERCISE 4.9**   **Writing Your Paragraph**

In Chapter 3, you created an outline for your main idea about one of the following topics: your favorite sport, your goals, an embarrassing moment, or artistic expression. Now write a paragraph that develops this main idea. First, compose your topic sentence. Then reevaluate your outline. Finally, follow your outline to write the paragraph, adding layers of development and transitions.

Fill in the blanks in the following statements.

1. A _____ is a group of sentences that all support or develop one particular idea about a topic.

2. The purpose of a paragraph is to group related _____ together so that readers can clearly understand the writer's ideas.

3. The _____ is the sentence in the paragraph that states the paragraph's main idea.

4. A topic sentence has two parts: it states the paragraph's _____, and it also states the writer's _____ about that topic.

5. An effective topic sentence has three essential characteristics: it is a _____ sentence, it is not too _____ or too _____, and it takes into account not just the topic but also the paragraph's _____ and _____.

6. The _____ of the paragraph includes all of the sentences that support, explain, or prove the idea expressed in the topic sentence.

7. The body of a paragraph provides _____, such as facts, statistics, examples, and reasons, which helps the reader accept the main idea as true.

8. A _____ provides more specific information about a general idea in the sentence that came before it.

9. _____ words and phrases are those whose function is to show the relationship between thoughts and ideas.

WebWork

Go to the Paragraph Punch Web site at **www.paragraphpunch.com**. This Web site provides questions that you answer as you are guided step-by-step through the actual process of composing a paragraph. Follow the directions to create your own paragraph, and print that paragraph.

Online Study Center For additional information and activities related to writing paragraphs, go to the Houghton Mifflin Online Study Center for this book, at **http://www.college.hmco.com/pic/dolphinwritertwo**.

Revising

GOALS FOR CHAPTER 5

▶ Explain the difference between revising and editing.

▶ Name the three characteristics that should be evaluated as part of the revision process.

▶ Identify areas for revision in paragraphs.

▶ Use a peer review sheet to identify needed revisions for a paragraph.

In Chapter 4, you practiced the third step in the writing process, composing a draft. However, even after a paragraph is written, you are still not quite finished. The fourth step of the process is revising.

Revising Versus Editing

Take a moment and think about the word *revision*. Notice that it includes the prefix *re-*, meaning "back or again," and the root word *vision*. So *revision* literally means "to look at again." Once you have written your paragraph, you need to look at it again to make sure you have successfully explained your main idea for your readers.

Revising and editing, which is the fifth step of the writing process, are not the same thing. When you revise a paragraph, you are looking for and then correcting paragraph-level problems. In other words, you are evaluating and improving, if necessary, the way your whole paragraph is organized or developed. Editing, which is discussed in Chapter 6, involves examining the paragraph at the sentence and word levels and correcting errors in sentence construction, grammar, word choice, and spelling. It is best to accomplish revision and editing as two separate, distinct steps, for each process involves looking at different aspects of the paragraph.

To revise a paragraph, you will need to evaluate it for the three C's: completeness, cohesiveness, and coherence.

Revising for Completeness

In Chapter 4, you learned about including layers of development as you wrote your first draft. A layer of development provides more specific information about a general idea in the sentence that came before it. It anticipates and answers readers' questions about more general statements, so it increases their understanding.

When you are examining a paragraph to make sure it is *complete*, or adequately developed, you evaluate the layers of development in the paragraph. Does it provide enough information and explanation of general ideas? Should you add more facts or examples to develop your ideas? To determine whether or not you have provided enough development, consider using the following techniques.

Use different colors of highlighter markers to identify the layers in your paragraph. Use one color, such as yellow, to highlight the topic sentence, which is the most general sentence in the paragraph. Use another color, such as pink, to highlight the second sentence, which should develop the first sentence. If the third sentence develops the second sentence, use yet another color to highlight it. If the third sentence develops the first sentence, highlight it with the same color you used for the second sentence. Follow this same procedure for all of the other sentences in the paragraph. Then, after you have highlighted every sentence, see how colorful your paragraph is. In general, paragraphs that contain more colors are probably developing the main idea with sufficient details. A paragraph that is highlighted with only two colors, however, may need the addition of more specific information and examples.

Use the highlighting technique to determine the sentence in the following paragraph that needs more development:

> There are three main kinds of annoying drivers on the roads. The first kind is the people who are paying attention to everything but driving. This category includes women who are putting on makeup as they speed down the road, people who are chatting away on cell phones, and people who are sightseeing instead of looking at the road in front of them. Another group of annoying drivers are those who drive too slowly. And then there is the opposite: the aggressive drivers. These are the people who speed, weave in and out of traffic, and tailgate other drivers who are obstacles to their progress. Many of them honk their horns and even shout out their windows at other motorists who are in their way.

Did you identify the fourth sentence as the one that needs more development? Following this sentence should be at least one layer of development that further describes or gives examples of people who drive too slowly.

Count the sentences in your paragraphs. There is no magic minimum or maximum number of sentences for a paragraph. The number of sentences a paragraph contains will depend on the main idea and supporting information. However, if a paragraph contains only three or four sentences, it may be incomplete because it is not adequately developed. Get in the habit of scrutinizing short paragraphs, in particular, to make sure that they include enough layers of development.

Scan your drafts for the phrase *for example.* This phrase often begins sentences that really help readers grasp your ideas. If you never begin sentences this way, you may not be including the specific information your reader needs in order to understand your thoughts on a topic.

EXERCISE 5.1   **Identifying Sentences That Need Development**

Underline the one sentence in each of the following paragraphs that is *not* adequately developed with more specific information or examples.

1. According to lifeguards, there are four main dangers that threaten swimmers at the beach. The first one is rip currents. A rip current is a strong, river-like flow of water that can pull swimmers out into deep water if they try to swim against it by heading directly for shore. The second danger is sandbars. Swimmer overconfidence is a problem, too. People believe they can swim out far away from shore, and then they get tired before they make it all the way back. A final danger is swimming alone. When people swim by themselves, they cannot send someone for help if they get into trouble. (*USA Weekend*, "Lifeguard Lessons," July 5–7, 2002, 7.)

2. Yoga offers quite a few benefits. For one thing, it's great for improving one's physical health. For example, yoga helps lower blood pressure, boost the immune system, and even alleviate[1] headaches. It helps the body become more flexible and mobile[2], and it can reduce back pain. Yoga also helps lower stress. It reduces tension throughout the body, and it can be used to achieve a meditative state that helps one feel calm and centered. And yoga has spiritual benefits as well. ("Benefits of Yoga," www.triadyoga.com/Benefits%20of%20Yoga.htm)

3. I prefer camping to staying in hotels. For one thing, camping is a lot less expensive than staying in a hotel. Staying at a campground is also a much more sociable experience than staying at a hotel. Camping gets you away from the television and encourages you to interact with your companions.

1. **alleviate:** make more bearable   2. **mobile:** able to move

When you camp, you usually pass the time by talking and playing games. Plus, you sit outside nearby others' campsites, so it also gives you more opportunities to meet new friends. At hotels, everyone stays in his or her individual room and does not interact much.

EXERCISE 5.2   **Adding Layers of Development**

Each of the following paragraphs lacks adequate layers of development. On the blanks provided, add sentences that further explain or illustrate the idea in the preceding sentence.

1. Your appearance tells people a lot about you. Your hairstyle is one thing that reveals aspects of your personality. _____

   _____

   _____.

   Your clothes express many of your preferences and values. _____

   _____

   _____.

   And the jewelry you wear (or do not wear) speaks volumes about you, too.

   _____

   _____

   _____.

2. People complain about the poor quality of television shows today, but there are actually some very interesting programs to choose from. For one thing, some of the dramatic series are really quite fascinating. _____. In addition, several of the comedy series will make you laugh out loud. _____. Several other programs offer valuable information. _____. And if you like reality TV, you have a lot of interesting shows to choose from. _____.

3. Cell phones may have a few drawbacks, but they have many more benefits. Cell phones are, first of all, valuable for safety. _____. Cell phones have also helped families. _____. Cell phones also allow Americans to take advantage of time that used to be wasted. _____.

Revising for Cohesiveness

If a paragraph is *cohesive*, all of its sentences "stick together" to support one main idea. In other words, a cohesive paragraph has unity because it focuses on just one point.

After you decide whether your paragraph includes enough layers of development, the next step is to make sure that every sentence in your paragraph relates to the idea in your topic sentence. When you are writing, it is easy to get sidetracked and to go off on tangents when new thoughts come to mind. Evaluating a paragraph for cohesiveness is a process of looking for any sentence that does not directly relate to the main idea.

Can you find the sentence in the following paragraph that does not relate to the main idea? Read the paragraph, and underline the sentence that prevents cohesiveness.

> Being a single parent is very difficult. The hardest part, of course, is making ends meet. Even when one's former spouse pays child support, it can be a challenge to pay all of the bills with just one income. Money problems then cause a lot of stress in the one-parent family. The second most difficult thing about single parenting is the amount of work that the custodial[1] parent faces. A single parent usually works an eight-hour day outside the home and then must take care of at least another eight hours' worth of household chores and parenting responsibilities, such as helping the children with their homework. Homework is beneficial because it helps teach children responsibility. However, single parents often do not get much time to themselves.

Did you underline the second-to-last sentence in this paragraph? Because it is about a benefit of homework rather than about single parenting, it disrupts the unity in this paragraph.

To determine whether or not you have included any sentence that prevents cohesiveness, try two techniques:

Count the sentences in your paragraph. When you evaluate a paragraph for completeness, you learn to become aware of especially brief paragraphs. When you evaluate for cohesiveness, pay particular attention to especially long paragraphs. A relatively long paragraph might be trying to develop too many different ideas, so it may not be cohesive. It may need to be divided up into smaller, more unified units.

Read the sentences of your paragraph backward, beginning with the last sentence. After you read each sentence, reread the topic sentence. Decide whether each individual sentence truly relates to the main idea.

---

1. **custodial:** having the responsibility for the care of a child

 **EXERCISE 5.3**   **Recognizing Sentences That Prevent Cohesiveness**

In each of the following paragraphs, underline the sentence that does not directly relate to the main idea.

1. The playground was not just run-down; it was also dangerous. The bolts holding down the slide had come loose, and the slide wobbled whenever a child climbed the ladder. The wooden teeter-totter, weather-beaten and rotten, looked as though it would break if anyone tried to sit on it. An old tire swing hung precariously[1] from a frayed rope. The swing set was rusty, and its plastic seats were cracked with age. Swinging helps children learn to coordinate several different body movements at once.

2. Child rearing is easier and more safety-conscious than it was when my parents were raising kids. Today, we have convenient products such as canned baby formula, disposable diapers, and baby wipes in handy dispensers. My mother had to make her own baby formula, and she had only cloth diapers, which she herself had to wash and reuse. She had to create her own baby wipes, too. Safety equipment for children was also nearly nonexistent. Not only was there no such thing as a car seat, but my parents' car did not even have any seat belts. Now, of course, most states require motorists to wear seat belts. My parents did not have safe cribs, fireproof pajamas, or baby monitors, either, which most parents believe to be essential today.

3. When I go to the grocery store, I ask for old-fashioned paper bags instead of plastic ones. Groceries in flimsy plastic bags get crushed too easily. When bread is placed in a plastic bag, it is almost always squashed by the time it gets home. Paper bags are sturdier and stand up, so purchases can be packed so that they do not get damaged during transport. Plus, if they are recycled, paper bags are better for the environment. They are not only biodegradable[2], but they can also be put to many good uses. For example, they can be used as book covers or kindling for fireplaces. Unlike plastic bags, paper bags do not necessarily end up in our overflowing landfills. I like the fact that I am helping conquer America's problem with trash when I use paper bags. I try to conserve water, too.

1. **precariously:** dangerously lacking in stability

2. **biodegradable:** capable of decomposing or decaying

Revising for Coherence

In addition to being complete and cohesive, a paragraph needs to be coherent. If a paragraph is *coherent*, it makes sense because it offers a clear progression of thought. In other words, readers can easily follow the writer's ideas from sentence to sentence.

Evaluating a paragraph's coherence involves examining its overall organization and its transitions as well as repetition of key words and ideas.

Organization and Transitions

The ideas in paragraphs are often presented in certain types of order that are familiar to readers. For example, paragraphs that relate a series of events or explain the steps in a process are organized with **time order**. In other words, the events or steps are presented in chronological order, or the order in which they happened. In addition, transitional words and phrases—words such as *first, next, then, finally, later, afterward,* and *eventually*—help readers more easily see how the ideas and information are related.

To recognize how readers use both time order and transitions to make sense of information, number the following four sentences in the order in which they should appear:

_____ State legislatures responded to the crime problem by building more new prisons and making penalties tougher in the 1990s.

_____ In the 1980s, crime rates were high.

_____ Now crime rates have dropped and state budgets are tight, so many prisoners will probably be released.

_____ By the year 2000, the population of America's prisons and jails had risen from 1.2 million in 1990 to more than 2 million in 2000. (David Crary, "Many States Rethinking Lock-Up Policies for Criminals, *Salt Lake Tribune*, March 7, 2003.)

You should have numbered these four sentences 2, 1, 4, 3. If you did, you used the time order of these statements, along with transitional phrases such as *In the 1980s, Now,* and *By the year 2000,* to figure out the order in which they should be arranged.

A second common type of order in paragraphs is **order of importance**. Using this order, a series of ideas or reasons may be presented with the most important item either given first or saved until last. Transitional words and phrases—such as *first, second, third, last, in addition, plus, most important,* and *for one thing*—help readers understand when a new item is being presented. See if you can use order and transitions to help you put these next four sentences in the order in which they should appear:

_____ Fifteen percent of the meal should be composed of protein, like meat or eggs.

_____ The next most important element of a nutritious breakfast is actually fat; 25 percent of the meal should be fat, such as that in butter or cream.

_____ The most important ingredient of a good breakfast is carbohydrates, which should account for 60 percent of what you eat.

_____ Finally, a good breakfast should contain plenty of vitamins, such as those found in grains, cereals, and breads. (From "Breakfast, the Most Important Meal," Milo Web site.)

Did you number these sentences 3, 2, 1, 4? Order of importance, as well as transitions, helps you determine how these four sentences should be arranged.

Another kind of order is **spatial order**, which is used in descriptions of people, places, or things. This order can take the form of front to back, left to right, top to bottom, inside to outside, or whatever other pattern best suits the topic. It usually includes transitional words and phrases—such as *in front of, beside, above, below, next to,* and *on the left*—that help the reader mentally picture how the descriptive details are related to one another. Use spatial order and transitions to order this next group of sentences:

_____ The Christmas decoration store entices[1] strolling shoppers with its window displays in front, which are filled with sparkling, ornament-laden trees.

_____ At the back of the store, bins filled with discounted merchandise offer shoppers excellent bargains on holiday decorations.

_____ As shoppers move farther into the store, they are surrounded by twinkling lights and glittering decorations on trees of green, white, and even blue.

1. **entices:** attracts by arousing desire for something

_____ Just inside the front door, shoppers are greeted with the sights, sounds, and smells of the holiday season, including the scent of pine and the familiar tunes of Christmas carols.

These four sentences should appear in this order: 1, 4, 3, 2. These sentences should appear in front-to-back order, which is indicated by the transitions.

In Chapter 3, you practiced determining the best order for ideas during the organizing and outlining step of the writing process. After the paragraph is written, however, you should evaluate again whether or not your choice of order is effective. Do your ideas lead logically from one to another? Is the progression of thought easy to follow from sentence to sentence? Have you included transitions that help the reader understand how ideas are related to one another? These are the elements of a coherent paragraph.

 **EXERCISE 5.4** **Evaluating the Coherence of Paragraphs**

In each of the following paragraphs, underline the sentence that is out of order and preventing the paragraph from being coherent.

1. Although the year was 2003, the fourteen-year-old girl looked just like a 1970s hippie. Over her long, straight, center-parted hair, she wore a floppy leather hat. Around her neck were beads and a chain with a peace-sign charm. She wore her loose peasant-style blouse off her shoulders, and a wide, beaded leather belt encircled her waist. On her feet were a pair of platform shoes. And she also wore a pair of hip-hugging jeans that flared into bell bottoms at the knee.

2. Scientists have figured out how mosquitoes locate and feed upon humans. First, they find their prey by detecting the carbon dioxide we breathe out. Then, they zero in on their targets by detecting our body heat. Next, the mosquito lands, reveals a sharp cutting instrument called a "stylet," and pierces its victim's skin. Injecting a substance that keeps blood from clotting, the insect drinks. It can draw blood for up to five minutes before it gets its fill. It also finds its victims by detecting lactic acid secreted by human skin. (Jeffrey Kluger, "Bzzzz . . . Slap!" _Time,_ July 7, 2003.)

3. People rank the features of vehicles differently as they are deciding on which one to buy. To me, a car's style and color are its least important features. The safety features of a vehicle are at the top of my list, so I will not consider owning one that lacks air bags or antilock brakes. I want to drive a car that

has performed well in crash tests. The second most important feature to me is the vehicle's fuel economy. I do not want to spend too much on gasoline, and I am definitely not interested in gas-guzzlers.

Repetition of Key Words and Ideas

Another feature of coherent paragraphs is the repetition of key words and ideas, which link the sentences of the paragraph together. Repeating the words that name the topic, along with synonyms and pronouns that either re-name or refer to the topic, causes the whole paragraph to "stick together." In the following paragraph, for example, note the highlighted words and phrases:

> Assigning children household **chores** is one of the best ways to build self-esteem and a feeling of competence. Regular **chores** establish helpful habits and good attitudes about **work. They** also teach valuable lessons about life and create an understanding that there are **jobs** that must be done to run a household. Children who grow up perceiving **chores** as a normal part of life will find the flow into adulthood much easier than those without responsibility will. (Adapted from Elizabeth Pantley, "Kids and Chores," *ParentsTalk*, http://www.parents-talk.com/expertsadvice/ea_pa_0006.html)

These repetitions and substitutions help to give the paragraph coherence.

EXERCISE 5.5   **Recognizing the Repetition of Key Words and Ideas**

In the following paragraph, circle all repetitions of the highlighted topic, along with all of the synonyms and pronouns that either rename or refer to the topic.

Dating is a relatively new form of courtship[1] ritual that shifted the balance of power from women to men. Until the beginning of the 20th century, dating as we know it did not exist. If a man wanted to get to know a young lady, he came "calling" at her parents' home. He would sit in the parlor, drink lemonade, and chat with his love interest, all beneath the watchful eyes of her

---

1. **courtship:** attempts to gain the love and affection of another person

parents. During this era, power in courtship belonged to women, for mothers and their daughters were the ones who decided which young men would be invited to call. Men had to be properly introduced and then impress the ladies enough to secure an opportunity to romance them. Our great-grandparents, however, changed courtship by supplanting[1] calling with dating. Young women wanted to be free to spend time alone with their suitors[2] out in public places. They wanted men to take them out dancing and enjoy commercial amusements. So dating was relocated from family parlors to restaurants, theaters, and dance halls. These new rituals shifted control and power in courtship from women to men. In the old days, men had to wait for women to invite them to their homes, but now women had to wait for men to invite them on dates. (Anne Morse, "The Dating Game: The Dangers of Cash-Based Courtship," *Boundless*, from www.boundless.org/2000/departments/beyond_buddies/a0000234.html. Reprinted by permission of the author.)

Two Important Revision Tips

1. Allow time for your draft to sit for a few days between the writing and revising steps. If you give yourself a few days to develop some distance between yourself and the draft you wrote, you may be better able to see the aspects of it that could use improvement.

2. Often, it is difficult to evaluate your own writing. You are so intimately connected with your creation that it can be challenging to see its flaws and figure out how to make it better. Therefore, it is often beneficial to ask others, such as classmates, family members, coworkers, or friends, to read your draft and provide you with feedback about the strengths and weaknesses of your paragraph. Get in the habit of allowing enough time to ask one or more people you know to read your paragraph and offer their comments and suggestions. Even those who are not teachers can read your draft simply as readers and tell you what they like and what confuses them. Consider using some type of peer review sheet to guide your readers' feedback. These sheets ask reviewers to examine specific aspects of a paragraph and comment on each one. Sample Peer Review Sheet #1 focuses on the specific qualities of an effective paragraph covered in this chapter.

1. **supplanting:** substituting for   2. **suitors:** men who are courting women

Sample Peer Review Sheet #1

Writer: _____

Reviewer: _____

Topic of paragraph: _____

	Yes	No

1. Does the paragraph contain a topic sentence that clearly states one main idea? _____ _____

   Suggestions for improvement:

2. Does every sentence in the paragraph support the main idea? _____ _____

   Suggestions for improvement:

3. Does the paragraph seem complete, or adequately developed? _____ _____

   Suggestions for improvement:

4. Is the paragraph organized effectively? _____ _____

   Suggestions for improvement:

5. Has the author included transitions to help readers follow the progression of thought from one sentence to the next? _____ _____

   Suggestions for improvement:

6. Does the paragraph repeat key words and ideas? _____ _____

   Suggestions for improvement:

   Additional suggestions for improvement:

This sheet guides reviewers to evaluate the paragraph's topic sentence as well as its completeness, cohesiveness, and coherence.

Another version, Sample Peer Review Sheet #2, is more general. It allows reviewers to comment on any strength or weakness they see.

Sample Peer Review Sheet #2

Writer: _____

Reviewer: _____

Topic of paragraph: _____

1. **State the paragraph's focus.** In your own words, write down what you believe the writer was trying to say.

2. **Offer a commendation.** What did you like best about this paragraph? Why? What did the writer do well?

3. **Ask a question.** What would you like to know more about? What was confusing or unclear?

4. **Make a recommendation.** Give the writer at least one specific suggestion for improving the paragraph.

If you use this type of review sheet, pay particular attention to your reviewer's response to the first item. The reader's understanding of the main idea should match your intention. If these two things do not match, you need to reevaluate the wording of your topic sentence as well as the support you have included.

You may have noticed that these peer review sheets do not ask for information about errors in grammar and spelling. Those sentence- and word-level issues are addressed in the next chapter.

WRITING FOR SUCCESS

Qualities of a Good Peer Reviewer

As you and your classmates practice your writing skills, you may be asked by your instructor or by other students to serve as a peer reviewer who can offer other writers suggestions for improving their paragraphs. Your goal as peer reviewer is to help the writer improve his or her writing. Here are some tips for accomplishing that goal:

1. When you are asked to evaluate someone else's writing, read the paragraph carefully, all the way through, at least twice. You need to gain a good understanding of the whole composition before you begin commenting on the details.
2. Begin by offering the writer praise. We all like to know what we did right. So identify the strengths of the paragraph and tell the writer what you liked best.
3. Concentrate on paragraph-level issues such as the clarity of the main idea, the development of that idea, and the organization of the developing details. The revising stage of the writing process is the time to discover and correct any weaknesses in these major areas. Later on, during the editing stage of the process, you can help the writer identify sentence-level mistakes such as grammar and spelling errors.
4. Phrase your comments with tact and sensitivity by offering your opinions as suggestions. For example, instead of saying, "I have no idea what your main idea really is," say, "Maybe you could reword your topic sentence to make your main idea more clear."
5. Make notes for the writer of the paragraph to use while he or she is working on the paragraph later. Either fill out a Peer Review Sheet or jot down your suggestions so that the writer will not forget any of your advice.

Revising a Paragraph: A Student Demonstration

In Chapter 4, you saw the first draft of Maya's paragraph about three tools for student success. Here is her draft again:

> Three tools will help students organize their responsibilitys and their materials so they will be more successful. A calender is the first tool, I carry my calender wherever I go. In it, I write down duedates for all of my assignments in all my classes. Like math tests and papers due. Papers are always the hardest assignments. I also write down my work schedule and practices for softball. So I can just glance at the whole month and know what I need to do when. Next I write a To Do list every day. I look at the day on my calendar and see what I need to do. Then I make a list of things to get done. I will write items like "study for math test" and "read chapter 6 of english book." Crossing them off as I do them. I keep a seperate notebook for my materials for each class.

I have a notebook for english, one for math, and one for my computer class. I put handouts, class notes, and other class information in each one and take it to class always. To be a good student, it is important to be prepared for class.

After Maya wrote this paragraph, she set it aside for two days. She was then ready to look at it again and evaluate it for the three C's. In addition, she asked one of her classmates to read her paragraph and complete a peer review sheet. Her classmate's feedback is shown on the Sample Peer Review Sheet.

Sample Peer Review Sheet #1

Writer: *Maya*

Reviewer: *Randy*

Topic of paragraph: *Three tools to help students*

	Yes	No
1. Does the paragraph contain a topic sentence that clearly states one main idea?	✓	

Suggestions for improvement:

2. Does every sentence in the paragraph support the main idea?		✓

Suggestions for improvement:
I think that the 5th sentence and the last sentence may not go with your topic sentence.

3. Does the paragraph seem complete, or adequately developed?	✓	

Suggestions for improvement:

4. Is the paragraph organized effectively?	✓	

Suggestions for improvement:

5. Has the author included transitions to help readers follow the progression of thought from one sentence to the next?	✓	

Suggestions for improvement:
You might consider using "first," "second," "third" to make it clearer what the three tools are. The third tool is not signaled by a transition at all.

6. Does the paragraph repeat key words and ideas?	✓	

Suggestions for improvement:
You could think of synonyms for the word "tool."

Additional comments and suggestions for improvement:
I think these are three very good tips for students!

Maya considered Randy's suggestions and revised her draft to eliminate the sentences that prevented cohesiveness and then altered the transitions. Her revision follows:

> Three tools will help students organize their responsibilitys and their materials so they will be more successful. A calender is the first tool, I carry my calender wherever I go. In it, I write down duedates for all of my assignments in all my classes. Like math tests and papers due. I also write down my work schedule and practices for softball. So I can just glance at the whole month and know what I need to do when. The second organization technique I use is a To Do list, which I write every day. I look at the day on my calendar and see what I need to do. Then I make a list of things to get done. I will write items like "study for math test" and "read chapter 6 of english book." Crossing them off as I do them. The third tool for student success consists of seperate notebooks for my materials for each class. I have a notebook for english, one for math, and one for my computer class. I put handouts, class notes, and other class information in each one and take it to class always.

In the next chapter, you will see how Maya got help with editing her paragraph and producing a final draft.

 **EXERCISE 5.6**   **Revising Your Paragraph**

Ask one of your classmates to read the paragraph you wrote about your favorite sport, your goals, an embarrassing moment, or artistic expression. Then ask that classmate to complete the Peer Review Sheet.

Use the feedback on this sheet to decide what revisions to make to your paragraph. Also, evaluate your paragraph yourself for the three C's: completeness, coherence, and cohesiveness. Finally, rewrite your paragraph, making any necessary changes.

Sample Peer Review Sheet #1

Writer: _____

Reviewer: _____

Topic of paragraph: _____

	Yes	No

1. Does the paragraph contain a topic sentence that clearly states one main idea?   _____ _____

   Suggestions for improvement:

2. Does every sentence in the paragraph support the main idea?   _____ _____

   Suggestions for improvement:

3. Does the paragraph seem complete, or adequately developed?   _____ _____

   Suggestions for improvement:

4. Is the paragraph organized effectively?   _____ _____

   Suggestions for improvement:

5. Has the author included transitions to help readers follow the progression of thought from one sentence to the next?   _____ _____

   Suggestions for improvement:

6. Does the paragraph repeat key words and ideas?   _____ _____

   Suggestions for improvement:

   Additional suggestions for improvement:

CHAPTER 5 REVIEW

Fill in the blanks in the following statements.

1. The word _____ literally means "to look at again."

2. When you _____ a paragraph, you are looking for and then correcting paragraph-level problems; in other words, you are evaluating and improving, if necessary, the way your whole paragraph is organized or developed.

3. To revise a paragraph, you will need to evaluate it for the three C's: _____, _____, and _____.

4. When you are examining a paragraph to make sure it is _____, or adequately developed, you evaluate layers of development in the paragraph.

5. If a paragraph is _____, all of its sentences "stick together" to support one main idea.

6. Evaluating a paragraph for cohesiveness is a process of looking for any sentence that does not directly relate to the _____.

7. If a paragraph is _____, it makes sense because it offers a clear progression of thought; in other words, readers can easily follow the writer's ideas from sentence to sentence.

8. Paragraphs that relate a series of events or explain the steps in a process are organized with _____ order.

9. Using order of _____, a series of ideas or reasons may be presented with the most important item either given first or saved until last.

10. _____ order, which is used in descriptions of people, places, or things, can take the form of front to back, left to right, top to bottom, or another pattern that suits the topic.

11. Coherent paragraphs include the repetition of _____, which link the sentences of the paragraph together.

12. If you allow time for a draft to sit for a few days between the _____ and _____ steps, you will be better able to see the aspects of it that could use improvement.

13. Because it can be challenging to see the flaws in your own writing, it is often beneficial to ask others to read your draft and provide you with _____ about the strengths and weaknesses of your paragraph.

14. _____ ask reviewers to examine specific aspects of a paragraph and comment on each one.

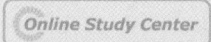

WebWork

Most colleges and universities have writing labs or centers where students can go to get help with their writing. These writing centers, which are typically staffed by either teachers or students with excellent writing skills, usually offer one-on-one tutorials and/or assistance with the revision of a paper.

Many colleges have also created online versions of their writing centers. An online writing lab (OWL), which is also known as an online writing center, is a Web site on the Internet that often offers students online resources to help them with their writing. These resources usually include tutorials and exercises. Some of them even allow students to send their writing to staff members for feedback and advice.

Find out about the kind of help your own college offers. Go to your college's Web site on the Internet, and locate information on that Web site about your college's writing lab or center. Then answer the following questions:

1. Does your school have a writing lab or center? If so, what resources and services does it offer?

2. If your school has an online writing lab or center, who staffs this lab? What is the procedure a student follows to get help with a paper?

3. If your school does not have an online writing lab or center, search for a school that does. Use a search engine such as Google to locate schools with online writing facilities. Then answer questions 1 and 2.

Online Study Center For additional revision information and activities, go to the Houghton Mifflin Online Study Center for this book, at **http://www.college.hmco.com/pic/dolphinwritertwo.**

6

Proofreading, Editing, and Preparing a Final Draft

GOALS FOR CHAPTER 6

▶ Proofread and edit sentences for style, sentence errors, grammatical and mechanical errors, and spelling errors.

▶ Use a peer review sheet to identify errors that need editing.

▶ Prepare a final draft of a paragraph according to certain guidelines.

The fifth and final step of the writing process involves editing and preparing a final draft. When you reviewed your writing during the revision step, you were searching for large-scale errors, such as problems with the overall organization or development of your idea. To edit your writing, you **proofread**, or search for errors at the sentence and word levels. In other words, you comb through the paper carefully, searching for grammatical and spelling errors and making adjustments to sentences to improve your overall style. **Editing** means making the necessary corrections. After locating and fixing errors, you prepare your final draft for submission.

This chapter briefly covers the kinds of errors you will need to find and correct as part of the editing stage of the writing process. For more information about how to recognize and eliminate errors of this type, see the Handbook at the end of this text.

Editing to Improve Style

The **style** of writing refers to the words the writer has chosen and the way sentences are constructed. There are many different kinds of writing styles, and you will surely develop your own style as you continue to improve your overall writing skills. Right now, however, you should concentrate on choosing words and constructing sentences so that your writing will be interesting, clear, and easy to read. You can do that by paying attention, especially during proofreading, to the length and type of your sentences as well as to the words you have selected.

Sentence Length

Writing that is composed mostly of very short sentences usually sounds dull and monotonous to readers. If readers are bored by your sentence structure, they will have a more difficult time concentrating on your meaning. Also, short sentences may not be making important connections, so readers may not fully understand your ideas. The following paragraph contains too many short sentences.

> I really love vacationing at the beach. I enjoy strolling along the shore. I like the cool ocean breezes. I like to pick up shells for my collection. Swimming is always fun. Body-surfing in the waves is one of my favorite things. I like to build sandcastles with my kids. I enjoy just relaxing, too. It is restful to sit under an umbrella. I can read a book. Or I can take a nap.

As this example shows, too many short sentences make the whole paragraph sound unsophisticated. But notice how the paragraph becomes clearer, easier to read, and less childish when the length of sentences is varied:

> I really love vacationing at the beach. I enjoy strolling along the shore in the cool ocean breezes and picking up shells for my collection. Swimming is always fun, and body-surfing in the waves is one of my favorite things. I like to build sandcastles with my kids, but I enjoy just relaxing, too. While I sit under an umbrella, I can read a book or take a nap.

Now the paragraph includes a mix of shorter and longer sentences, which not only are more pleasurable to read but also sound much more sophisticated.

Techniques for Combining Sentences

If you have a tendency to write too many short sentences, try to combine some of them using the following techniques:

1. Join two sentences with a coordinating conjunction—*and, or, but, nor, for, yet,* or *so*—preceded by a comma.

   Two short sentences: He sings in the choir.
   He plays on the football team.

Combined sentence: He sings in the choir, and he plays on the
                         football team.

2. Turn one sentence into a dependent clause and attach it to an independent clause. (See the Handbook at the back of this text for more discussion of clauses.)

Two short sentences: I want to finish my degree.
                         Then I hope to find a good job.
Combined sentence: After I finish my degree, I hope to find
                         a good job.

3. Embed the information of one sentence into another sentence.

Two short sentences: Jane is the new manager.
                         She starts work next week.
Combined sentence: Jane, the new manager, starts work
                         next week.

EXERCISE 6.1   **Combining Sentences**

On the blank provided, combine each group of sentences to write one new sentence. Try to use each of the three techniques for combining sentences at least once.

1. Bob is turning twenty-one years old.

We are throwing a party for him.

_____

2. Our basketball team has not lost a game.

The team will play in the state championship.

_____

_____

3. Cabbage is a healthy food.

We eat cabbage every day.

_____

4. Jessica got a sunburn.

She was not wearing sunscreen.

She stayed out in the sun too long.

_____

_____

5. The children built the snowman.

The snowman was built yesterday.

The snowman was melting in the warm sunshine.

Sentence Types

Another way to achieve a style of writing that is interesting is to vary not only the length but also the type of sentence you write. There are four types of sentences—simple, compound, complex, and compound-complex—that are illustrated here. See the Handbook at the back of this text for how to use independent and dependent clauses to create these sentence types.

A **simple sentence** contains just one independent clause:

subject   verb

She   earned an A on her research paper.

A **compound sentence** contains two or more independent clauses. Each contains at least one subject and one verb and could stand alone as a complete sentence.

subject   verb   *subject verb*

Mary decided to learn French, and **Juan chose** German.

A **complex sentence** contains a dependent clause and an independent clause:

dependent clause   *independent clause*

If you do not brush your teeth every day, you will get cavities.

A **compound-complex sentence** includes at least one dependent clause and two or more independent clauses:

          independent clause #1
  dependent clause   *subject   verb*

Because the dog was wearing an ID tag, **they** located its owner, and

  independent clause #2
  subject   verb

the **children got** their pet back.

When you check over your sentences during the editing stage, determine the type of each sentence in your paragraph. Then, if you see that you are relying too heavily on simple sentences, combine some of them to add more variety.

EXERCISE 6.2   **Identifying Sentence Types**

On the blank next to each sentence, identify it as either simple (S), compound (C), complex (CX), or compound-complex (CC).

___ **1.** Americans need lessons in cell phone manners.

___ **2.** Half of all Americans use cell phones, and some of them can behave inconsiderately.

___ **3.** During one out of every five funerals, a cell phone rings during the service.

___ **4.** Cell phones also interrupt weddings, courtroom proceedings, church services, romantic dinners, and movies.

___ **5.** Some people speak more loudly than normal on their cell phones, so their conversations have been described as "cell yell."

___ **6.** If you are in a meeting, courtroom, or restaurant, you should let your caller leave a message.

___ **7.** If you are with others when your phone rings, you should first find a secluded spot for your conversation, and then you can answer the call.

___ **8.** Before you enter a movie theater or a church, you should turn your phone off.

___ **9.** When you expect a call you cannot postpone, alert your companions beforehand, and then excuse yourself when your phone rings.

___ **10.** Your companions should always take precedence[1] over your phone calls. (Adapted from Karen H. Long, "PLEASE! Turn Off Cell Phone During Funeral," *The News Herald*, August 1, 2003, p. 7A. Reprinted with permission of the *Tampa Tribune*.)

Diction

Diction refers to the individual words you choose. These words affect your style, so you should make sure that they are appropriate in a number of respects. In particular, you should evaluate the formality, specificity, emotion, and originality of your words. To determine whether a word is appropriate or not, you must consider your readers and decide whether the word is suitable for those readers.

First of all, evaluate your choices of words for their **level of formality**. Although each pair of words in the following chart is made up of synonyms, notice that the words in the two columns vary in their level of formality.

1. precedence: priority

Formal	*Informal*
apartment	pad
companion	buddy
brave	has guts
pilfer	rip off
gentleman	guy
suspicious	fishy
supervisor	head honcho
relax	take it easy
chicanery	monkey business
trepidation	cold feet

Many writing situations, including academic papers and work-related documents, call for a relatively high level of formality. It is unlikely that the words labeled *Informal* in the preceding chart would be appropriate in such documents, for readers expect a more elevated style. In contrast, more personal kinds of writing, such as e-mail messages and letters to family members and friends, can be much more informal. They are likely to include slang terms and conversational words such as those in the chart labeled *Informal*.

EXERCISE 6.3   **Identifying Inappropriately Informal Words**

The following passage was submitted to an English professor for an academic assignment that asked students to paraphrase a poem. Circle all of the words and phrases that are inappropriately informal.

Robert Frost's poem "Stopping By Woods on a Snowy Evening" is about a dude who is traveling in a horse-drawn sleigh through the woods. He stops just to chill out and admire the beauty and tranquility of the winter scene. It is cold and dark, though, so he realizes that his horse must think that he has totally flipped out. He wishes he could hang out and enjoy the lovely and peaceful setting, but he realizes that he still has stuff to do. He is still a long way from home, so he decides that he had better motor.

You will also need to evaluate whether your words are **specific** enough. Specific words help readers form clear images in their minds so that they can grasp your meaning more easily. Using general or vague terms makes it harder for readers to understand your ideas. Notice how the following sentence becomes clearer with the substitution of more specific terms.

Too general: She was going very fast in her large vehicle.
More specific: She hurtled down the road in her nine-passenger Ford
                  Expedition at speeds exceeding 80 miles per hour.

Words and phrases such as *going very fast, large*, and *vehicle* do not provide the reader with much information. The revised sentence, however, substitutes more specific terms that provide readers with much more detail and help them form a clear mental image.

Which words in the following sentence are too vague and general? Circle them as you read the sentence.

Jennifer is a very nice person who helps others.

Did you circle the words *nice, helps*, and *others*? These are the words that provide little information. If this sentence were rewritten to read "Jennifer volunteers a lot of her free time to help children learn how to read," it would be much clearer for the reader.

EXERCISE 6.4   Identifying Vague Words

Rewrite each of the following sentences on the blanks provided to replace vague, general words and phrases with more specific words and phrases.

1. He is very good at what he does.

   _____

2. Her bad behavior often gets her into trouble.

   _____

3. She looked great at the big event.

   _____

   _____

4. It is really nice outside.

   _____

5. His poor performance cost him dearly.

_____

The next aspect of diction to examine is the **emotion** in the words you have chosen. Some words, such as *cat*, are relatively neutral. That is, they carry no particular emotional suggestion. But compare the word *kitty*, which indicates affection for that animal. Notice in the following chart how some synonyms reveal more about the feelings of the person who chose to use the word:

Neutral	*Emotional*
waste products	trash
shelter	home
investigate	snoop
spouse	soul mate
discipline	spank
penitentiary	slammer
attorney	shyster

When you are evaluating your word choices, think about the emotions they reveal. Although it is fine to feel strongly—either positively or negatively—about the subject you are writing about, you must also think about your reader, especially when your topic is a controversial one. You do not want to offend, insult, or annoy readers. If you do, they will reject your ideas. So make sure that your words are not inappropriately emotional.

For example, the following sentence contains emotional word choices:

Fat people should not blame fast-food restaurants for their own failure to maintain a normal weight.

The words *fat* and *failure* may offend or insult some readers because of the negative, judgmental emotions attached to the words. Revising the sentence to contain fewer emotional words might be a good idea.

EXERCISE 6.5   **Identifying Inappropriately Emotional Words**

On the blanks provided, rewrite each of the following sentences so that they express the same idea with more neutral language.

1. Kids who are failures need extra attention.

_____

2. The pushy salesperson refused to take no for an answer.

_____

3. That politician is a liar.

_____

4. She did not realize that the cashier had cheated her until later.

_____

5. She is just a housewife who takes care of the kids.

_____

Finally, you will need to determine whether or not your word choices are **original**. In other words, locate and eliminate from your writing all **clichés**, overused expressions that everyone has heard before. Here are just a few examples of the thousands of clichés we hear often:

> the blind leading the blind
> a bull in a china shop
> dead as a doornail
> fish out of water
> out of the woods
> playing with fire
> running around like a chicken with its head cut off
> bottom line
> it is six of one, half a dozen of the other
> let us get this show on the road
> a dime a dozen
> strong as an ox
> better than sliced bread
> two peas in a pod
> the grass is always greener on the other side
> no-brainer
> light at the end of the tunnel
> up the creek without a paddle
> took him to the cleaners

These expressions often creep into our writing because we have heard them over and over, and they naturally pop into our minds as we compose. But they make writing dull and unoriginal, so replace them with other words that say the same thing.

Notice how the revised sentences below are more interesting than the versions containing clichés:

Sentence with cliché:	We will have to cross that bridge when we come to it.
Revised:	We will deal with that problem when it is on our doorstep ringing the bell.
Sentence with cliché:	Do not count your chickens before they hatch.
Revised:	Do not deliver your victory speech before the votes are counted.

 **EXERCISE 6.6**   **Eliminating Clichés**

Rewrite each of the following sentences to eliminate the clichés.

1. She decided to throw caution to the wind.

_____

2. When it comes to dancing, I cannot hold a candle to you.

_____

3. All was quiet, but it was only the calm before the storm.

_____

4. You need to wake up and smell the coffee.

_____

5. He is head over heels for her.

_____

Eliminating Wordiness

When you are examining the diction of your writing, one last problem to look for is **wordiness,** or unnecessary words. Clear writing always expresses an idea in as few words as possible. Wordy writing just makes it more difficult for readers to understand your thoughts, for the extra words slow them down and get in the way. Notice how the following wordy sentences express ideas that become clearer when the unnecessary words are eliminated:

Wordy: Subsequent to completing his studies at his current institution of higher learning, he is planning to secure a position as a sales associate for a retail company that provides its customers with wireless communication devices.

Revised: After finishing college, he plans to sell cell phones.

Wordy: To develop your ability to put words on paper effectively and with success, read the words that have been written in other documents by individuals who have a facility and talent for creating good sentences, paragraphs, and essays.

Revised: To learn to write well, read the works of good writers.

Always ask yourself, *Can I find a way to say this in fewer words?* Notice how in the first example, the word *after* substitutes for *subsequent to*, the word *college* substitutes for *institution of higher learning*, and the phrase *cell phones* substitutes for *wireless communication devices*. In the second example, *learn* replaces *develop your ability*, *write* replaces *put words on paper*, and *good writers* replaces *individuals who have a facility and talent for creating good sentences, paragraphs, and essays.*

It is quite natural to be wordy when you are writing your first draft and trying to find the right words for expressing your ideas. However, you should get in the habit of examining your drafts in the editing stage and eliminating the words that are not contributing anything. When you are examining your writing for wordiness, look for the following common expressions, which add unnecessary words:

Instead of . . .	*Use . . .*
due to the fact that	because
in order to	to
for the purpose of	to
in the near future	soon
in the event that	if
at this point in time	now
at the present time	now
at that point in time	then
in today's world	today
this day and age	today
has the ability	can
during the same time that	while

Instead of . . .	Use . . .
until such time as	until
in spite of the fact that	although
are of the opinion that	think
green in color	green
small in size	small
short in length	short
the reason why is that	because
given the fact that	because
put forth an effort	try
a number of	some

Also, look for redundant expressions, which contain words that simply repeat each other. Here are a few common redundant expressions:

Instead of . . .	Use . . .
close proximity	proximity
each and every	each
he is a man who	he
my personal feeling	my feeling
first and foremost	first
is located in	is in
past history	past (or history)

Finally, get in the habit of examining the especially long sentences that you write. Ask yourself if you can pare these sentences down so that they say the same thing in fewer words.

EXERCISE 6.7   Eliminating Wordiness

On the blanks provided, rewrite each of the following sentences to eliminate unnecessary words.

1. We had to postpone to a later date our picnic due to the fact that precipitation had begun to fall from the sky.

   _____

2. During the time that Jill was moving in an upward motion on the hillside, Jack was engaging in the exact same activity.

   _____

3. Each and every one of my close personal friends knows that at this point in time, I now have the ability to operate a vehicle.

_____

4. She is a woman who has put forth a lot of effort to keep herself slim and to avoid getting overweight.

_____

5. Many Americans are of the opinion that we should increase the amount of funding provided to the institutions that teach our children on a daily basis.

_____

Editing to Correct Major Sentence Errors

In addition to proofreading your drafts for sentence variety, appropriate language, and wordiness, you will need to find and eliminate major errors in sentence structure. These errors include sentence fragments, run-on sentences, dangling or misplaced modifiers, and faulty parallelism.

Sentence Fragments

A **sentence** contains at least one independent clause with at least one subject and one verb. It expresses a complete thought and ends with a period, an exclamation point, or a question mark. A **sentence fragment** is a group of words punctuated like a sentence but unable to stand alone. It may lack a subject, a verb, or both; it may also be a dependent clause or a phrase that does not express a complete idea. The missing element(s) must be added for the sentence to be grammatically correct.

> _No subject:_   Hopes to earn her college degree.
> _Corrected:_   She hopes to earn her college degree.
>
> _No verb:_   A talented pianist.
> _Corrected:_   Joe, a talented pianist, entertained the audience.
>
> or
>
> A talented pianist will be performing here next week.

No subject or verb:	Studying for hours.
Corrected:	Studying for hours, they went over the material in every chapter.

or

They had been studying for hours.

Often, correcting a sentence fragment is a matter of attaching a dependent clause or a phrase to a sentence that comes before or after it:

Dependent clause fragment:	Because she has a beautiful voice. They asked her to sing the national anthem.
Correct:	Because she has a beautiful voice, they asked her to sing the national anthem.
Dependent clause fragment:	Where we like to vacation.
Corrected:	Disney World, where we like to vacation, is crowded at this time of year.
Phrase fragment:	He sent her flowers. To apologize for his behavior.
Correct:	He sent her flowers to apologize for his behavior.
Phrase fragment:	During the severe storm.
Corrected:	During the severe storm, the power went out.

For more information about sentence fragments, including more practice in correcting them, see the Basic Sentence section of the Handbook at the end of this text.

EXERCISE 6.8   **Correcting Sentence Fragments**

On the blanks provided, rewrite each of the following sentence fragments to correct them. You may need to add information to create complete sentences.

1. In the spring.

_____

2. When I am earning more money.

_____

3. A generous person.

_____

4. To find her lost dog.

_____

5. Feeling sad and lonely.

_____

Comma Splices and Run-on Sentences

A **comma splice** consists of two independent clauses that are connected with only a comma, which is inadequate punctuation:

> It should not rain today, weather forecasters predicted a sunny day.

> Ray writes the music, Charlene writes the lyrics.

In both of these examples there are two complete thoughts expressed in two different independent clauses. However, they are separated with only a comma.

A **run-on sentence** consists of two independent clauses that are not separated by any punctuation:

> The break was over it was time to get back to work.

> She is majoring in business her real love is cooking.

Comma splices and run-on sentences can be corrected in one of three ways. First of all, we could simply use a semicolon to connect the two independent clauses:

> It should not rain today; weather forecasters predicted a sunny day.

> Ray writes the music; Charlene writes the lyrics.

> The break was over; it was time to get back to work.

> She is majoring in business; her real love is cooking.

Note that each independent clause could also be written as a separate sentence. Or we could connect the clauses with a comma and an appropriate coordinating conjunction:

> It should not rain today, for weather forecasters predicted a sunny day.

> Ray writes the music, and Charlene writes the lyrics.

The break was over, so it was time to get back to work.

She is majoring in business, but her real love is cooking.

A third way to correct a comma splice or a run-on sentence is to add a semicolon and an appropriate conjunctive adverb followed by a comma:

It should not rain today; indeed, weather forecasters predicted a sunny day.

Ray writes the music; afterward, Charlene writes the lyrics.

The break was over; therefore, it was time to get back to work.

She is majoring in business; however, her real love is cooking.

For more information about comma splices and run-on sentences, including more practice in correcting them, see the Coordination section of the Handbook at the end of this text.

EXERCISE 6.9 **Correcting Comma Splices and Run-on Sentences**

On the blanks provided, rewrite each of the following comma splices and run-on sentences to correct them. Try to use each of the different methods for correcting these errors at least once.

1. She will drink coffee, she prefers hot tea.

_____

2. The governor wants to serve another term, he hopes to be reelected.

_____

3. He was ill yesterday today he feels better.

_____

4. Only three people registered for the class it will probably be cancelled.

_____

_____

5. Eat more fruits they are good for you.

_____

WRITING FOR SUCCESS

Careful Use of Computer Checks

Most word processing programs can help you identify potential grammatical and spelling errors in your writing. In Microsoft Word, for example, you can activate a feature of the program that identifies faulty sentence structure by marking possible errors with a green wavy underline. This feature also identifies possible spelling errors with a red wavy underline and even suggests corrections.

Before you print your final, finished draft, pay special attention to words and sentences the computer has labeled as possible errors. Although the computer program is not foolproof, it can be a valuable tool for editing.

The following example is a draft of the previous two paragraphs, with errors identified by Microsoft Word:

> Most word processing programs can help you identify potential grammatical and spelling errors in you're writing. In Microsoft Word; for example you can activate a feature of the program that identifies faulty sentence structure by marking possible errors with a green wavey underline. Possible spelling errors are identified with a red wavy underline the program will even suggest corections.
>
> Before you print your final, finished draft. Pay special attention to words the sentences the computer has label as possible errors. The computer program are not foolproof. it can be valuable tool for editing.

Note, however, that this passage contains errors that Word did not identify. Can you spot them?

Misplaced or Dangling Modifiers

A modifier, especially an adjective, must be placed next to the word it describes. If a modifier is not next to the word it describes, it is called a **misplaced modifier**:

> **Running for her life**, the pantyhose Diana was wearing snagged on the chain link fence.

In this sentence, the phrase *running for her life* modifies *pantyhose* because that is the closest word to the phrase. Therefore, this sentence is saying that the pantyhose was running for its life. Actually, though, it is Diana who was doing the running. To correct this sentence, rewrite it so that the modifier is next to the word it is supposed to describe:

Running for her life, Diana snagged her pantyhose on the chain link fence.

Misplaced modifiers can be phrases or single words. The word *only,* for example, is commonly misplaced:

She only won six dollars.

In this sentence, the word *only* is modifying the verb, but it should be modifying the word *dollar.* So it needs to be moved:

She won *only* six dollars.

If the word the modifier is supposed to be describing is not in the sentence at all, the error is called a **dangling modifier.**

As a child, my family flew to Hong Kong to see my grandmother.

In this sentence, the modifier *as a child* is incorrectly describing *family.* It is not the family that was a child but the speaker of the sentence. To correct the error, rewrite the sentence to add the missing information:

As a child, **I** flew with my family to Hong Kong to see my grandmother.

For more information about dangling and misplaced modifiers, including more practice in correcting them, see The Basic Sentence section of the Handbook at the end of this text.

✦ **EXERCISE 6.10** **Correcting Misplaced and Dangling Modifiers**

On the blanks provided, rewrite each of the following sentences to correct misplaced and dangling modifiers. You may need to add information to correct dangling modifiers.

1. I watched the monster trucks eating a corn dog.

_____

2. I like to listen to music cleaning my room.

_____

3. While strolling in the rain, thunder could be heard in the distance.

_____

4. Rolling in the mud, the children laughed at the pigs.

_____

5. Typing like mad, the paper was almost finished.

_____

Faulty Parallelism

When pairs or series of words, phrases, or clauses express parallel ideas, they must be parallel in structure:

He loves garden**ing**, sew**ing**, and cook**ing**.

Either **we mow** the grass today, or **we mow** it tomorrow.

I told her **that** I loved her and **that** she should marry me.

Notice how changing the structure of one of the items in the pair or series makes the relationships in the sentence a little harder to understand:

He loves gardening, sewing, and to cook.

Either we mow the grass today, or tomorrow would be a good day for doing it.

I told her that I loved her and marrying me is what she should do.

These sentences are not only more difficult to understand, but their lack of balance also causes them to sound cumbersome and awkward.

Now read two more sentences that lack parallelism, and try to determine how the structure changes:

French diners enjoy snails as a gourmet delicacy, and frog legs are considered to be tasty, too.

She is hoping that their team will win and to bring home the big trophy.

In the first sentence, the verb in the first independent clause is active, and the verb in the second independent clause is passive. To correct the error, rewrite the second independent clause to make the verb active. Now the subjects of both independent clauses are performing the action: _French diners enjoy snails as a gourmet delicacy, and they find frog legs tasty, too._

In the second sentence, one of the direct objects is a noun dependent clause that begins with _that_ and the other is an infinitive phrase. To correct this sentence, change the infinitive phrase to a noun dependent clause beginning with *that* to match the form of the first direct object: *She hopes that their team will win and that it will bring home the big trophy.*

For more information about faulty parallelism, including more practice in correcting it, see the Parallelism section of the Handbook at the end of this text.

EXERCISE 6.11   **Correcting Faulty Parallelism**

On the blanks provided, rewrite each of the following sentences to correct faulty parallelism.

1. Successful students attend class, take notes, and studying every night.

_____

2. He not only speaks Italian, but Greek is one of the languages he knows.

_____

3. He knows the date of their wedding anniversary and what day it was when they met for the first time.

_____

4. She is an excellent writer and who is also a genius in math.

_____

5. Because she smokes and her avoidance of exercise, Mary finds climbing stairs difficult.

_____

_____

Editing Errors in Grammar and Mechanics

In addition to locating and correcting major sentence errors—such as fragments, comma splices, dangling modifiers, and faulty parallelism—you will need to check your writing for many other kinds of grammatical and mechanical errors, including subject-verb agreement errors, errors in verb tense, and capitalization and punctuation errors.

The best way to find errors is to learn to recognize them yourself. Increase your knowledge of grammar and mechanics so that you will stop making the same mistakes over and over again. Use the Handbook at the end of this text to review, and complete the exercises provided to make sure you understand how to correct the various kinds of errors. Also, pay special attention to your instructors' comments. If an instructor identifies subject-verb agreement errors in a paper you have written, go to the Handbook and review the material on subject-verb agreement errors and how to correct them.

Another way to locate errors is to have others read your drafts and point them out. Consider adding questions about possible word- and sentence-level errors to the Peer Review Sheet you give your reviewers to fill out. Doing so will encourage your reviewers to look for very specific kinds of errors that may be reducing the effectiveness of your writing. You could add a page like the one that follows, for example, to your Peer Review Sheet:

Peer Review Sheet (page 2)

	Yes	**No**
1. Does the writer include a mixture of sentence lengths and types?	_____	_____
Suggestions for improvement:		
2. Is the diction appropriately formal, specific, original, and emotional?	_____	_____
Suggestions for improvement:		
3. Is the writing free of wordiness?	_____	_____
Suggestions for improvement:		
4. Is the writing free of major sentence errors, such as sentence fragments, comma splices, run-on sentences, dangling or misplaced modifiers, and faulty parallelism?	_____	_____
Suggestions for improvement:		

(continued)

Peer Review Sheet (page 2) (*continued*)

	Yes	No
5. Is the writing free of other grammatical and mechanical errors?	___	___

Suggestions for improvement:

If you use a Peer Review Sheet, ask your reviewers to identify the specific locations of possible errors in your draft. Then make sure you correct all of those errors before or during your preparation of your final draft.

Correcting errors in your writing is very important because submitting a final draft that is marred with errors will undermine your credibility as a writer. When a paper contains errors, readers often question the writer's intelligence and overall writing ability, or they assume that the writer did not care enough about the document to ensure that it was error-free.

Editing Spelling Errors

Your final draft should always be free of spelling errors. There are three ways to identify and correct errors in spelling:

1. **Whenever you have the slightest doubt that a word is spelled correctly, look it up in a dictionary.** Always check the spellings of words you question in a book or online version of a dictionary. You can find several different online dictionaries at www.onelook.com. Looking up the correct spelling will help you remember how to spell the word the next time you use it.

2. **Use a computer spell-checker.** If you have an electronic version of your draft, use the spell-check feature of your word processing program to locate errors. Most of these spell-checkers will suggest possible alternative spellings for each error identified. Note, however, that these spell-checkers are not foolproof. They may actually ignore words that are incorrectly spelled.

3. **Ask someone to proofread your draft for spelling errors.** Ask someone you know who is a good speller to circle possible errors in spelling in your draft.

 **EXERCISE 6.12**   Proofreading a Passage for Grammar and Spelling Errors

Edit the following passage to correct grammar and spelling errors. Cross out the errors and add corrections directly to the text of the passage.

Do You Want to Be a Millionaire?

Today, it seems like everyone wants to be a millionaire, each week over 32 million people tune in to get-rich-quick game shows such as ABCs *Who Wants to Be a millionaire* and Fox's *Greed*. The increasing popularity of this type of programing illustrates the public's fascination with getting money fast. The contestant's that sit in the hot seat can walk away with thousands of dollars in as little as thirty minutes. Ben stein, whom has his own game show, *Win Ben Stein's Money*, explained that america doesn't want to wait years to get rich anymore. What many viewers don't realize is that becoming a participant in these game shows are not a quick and easy process, it may take months of phone calls, e-mails, and preliminery quizzs just to get a chance to become a televised player. And if your one of the lucky contestant's to get on television the odds are that you won't become the world's next millionaire. In fact, there is only one sure-fire method to acquire that kind of money, you have to create a long-term investment plan.

Financial planners often tell client's that there is no substitute for a long-term investment plan. If you start an investment program when your young, make quality investments in individual stocks or mutual funds, and let your investment earnings acummulate, you wont have to worry about money when you reach retirement age. For example if you begin an investment program when you are 25 and invest $150 a month, or $1,800 a year, and choose investments that earn 11 percent a year. Your investments will be worth $1,047,294 when you reach age 65. However if you wait until you are 35 to start your investment program and invest in the same investments over a 30-year period, the value of your investments when you reach age 65 will be just $358,236. By waiting 10 years to invest. You would lose almost $700,000. Regardless of your age, its time to start investing. (Adapted from William M. Pride et al., *Business*, 7th ed. [Boston: Houghton Mifflin, 2002], p. 617.)

Preparing the Final Draft

After you have edited your paragraph for style and errors, you are ready to prepare your final draft for submission. You will, of course, need to follow your instructor's guidelines for final drafts. Regardless of the final format of your paragraph, however, it should always be neat, clean, and professional looking. It should be typed or handwritten, as your instructor requires, and its appearance should reflect the fact that you have invested time and effort in your paragraph.

In general, both typed and handwritten final drafts usually have one-inch margins at the top, bottom, left, and right sides of the paper. This means that the first sentence begins an inch from the top edge of the paper and that the last line on the page stops an inch away from the bottom edge of the paper. Each line begins one inch from the left edge of the paper and reaches all the way to one inch from the right edge of the paper. Every new paragraph is indented five spaces. Many instructors require assignments to be double-spaced, which means that a handwritten paragraph should skip every other line on the page. At the top of the first page, include your name and any other information the instructor wants you to list (such as course name or number and date).

After you prepare your final draft, you should go over it one more time to look for **typographical errors**, which are accidental mistakes that occur during the typing or printing of a document. If you find such an error, you should always neatly correct it by either carefully striking through the error and writing in the correction with a black pen or covering the error with correction fluid and then writing the correction.

 ## Editing a Paragraph: A Student Demonstration

In Chapter 5, you saw how Maya revised her paragraph about three tools for student success. Here is her revised draft again:

> Three tools will help students organize their responsibilitys and their materials so they will be more successful. A calender is the first tool, I carry my calender wherever I go. In it, I write down duedates for all of my assignments in all my classes. Like math tests and papers due. I also write down my work schedule and practices for softball. So I can just glance at the whole month and know what I need to do when. The second organization technique I use is a To Do list, which I write every day. I look at the day on my calendar and see what I need to do. Then I make a list of things to get done. I will write items like "study for math test" and "read chapter 6 of english book." Crossing them off as I do them. The third tool for student success consists of seperate notebooks for my materials for each class. I have a notebook for english, one for math, and one for my computer class. I put handouts, class notes, and other class information in each one and take it to class always.

Next, she needed to look over her draft for word- and sentence-level errors. So she asked her peer reviewer, Randy, to help her find grammatical and mechanical errors and to help her polish her style. Randy completed an addition to the first Peer Review Sheet.

Peer Review Sheet (page 2)

	Yes	No
1. Does the writer include a mixture of sentence lengths and types?		✓

Suggestions for improvement:
Your sentences are mostly short and simple. Combine a few of them to add variety?

2. Is the diction appropriately formal, specific, original, and emotional?	✓	

Suggestions for improvement:

3. Is the writing free of wordiness?	✓	

Suggestions for improvement:

4. Is the writing free of major sentence errors, such as sentence fragments, comma splices, run-on sentences, dangling or misplaced modifiers, and faulty parallelism?		✓

Suggestions for improvement:
The second sentence is a comma splice. Combine what are now the third and fourth sentences and the tenth and eleventh sentences to eliminate two sentence fragments.

5. Is the writing free of other grammatical and mechanical errors?		✓

Suggestions for improvement:
I see a few capitalization errors (Chapter 6, English). I think you have misspelled "responsibilities," "calendar," and "separate."

After receiving Randy's feedback, Maya found the errors he mentioned and edited her paragraph to eliminate these mistakes. Then she typed her final draft according to her teacher's guidelines. Here, finally, is the draft she submitted:

Three Tools for Student Success

By Maya Johnson

Three tools will help students organize their responsibilities and their materials so they will be more successful. A calendar is the first tool. I carry my calendar wherever I go. In it, I write down due dates for all of my assignments in all my classes, like math tests and papers due. I also write down my work schedule and practices for softball, so I can just glance at the whole month and know what I need to do when. The second organization technique I use is a To Do list, which I write every day. I look at the day on my calendar and see what I need to do, and then I make a list of things to get done. I will write items like "study for math test" and "read Chapter 6 of English book," crossing them off as I do them. The third tool for student success consists of separate notebooks for my materials for each class. I have a notebook for English, one for math, and one for my computer class. I put handouts, class notes, and other class information in each one and take it to class always.

Because Maya completed all five steps in the writing process to create this paragraph, it is clearly developed, well organized, and easy to read and understand.

EXERCISE 6.13 **Editing Your Paragraph**

For your paragraph on either your favorite sport, your goals, an embarrassing moment, or artistic expression, ask a classmate to complete the following peer review sheet to help you identify errors that need correction.

Peer Review Sheet (page 2)

	Yes	No
1. Does the writer include a mixture of sentence lengths and types?	_____	_____

Suggestions for improvement:

| 2. Is the diction appropriately formal, specific, original, and emotional? | _____ | _____ |

Suggestions for improvement:

| 3. Is the writing free of wordiness? | _____ | _____ |

Suggestions for improvement:

| 4. Is the writing free of major sentence errors, such as sentence fragments, comma splices, run-on sentences, dangling or misplaced modifiers, and faulty parallelism? | _____ | _____ |

Suggestions for improvement:

| 5. Is the writing free of other grammatical and mechanical errors? | _____ | _____ |

Suggestions for improvement:

Use the feedback on this sheet to edit your paragraph, and then prepare your final draft according to the following guidelines:

1. Type the paragraph with double spacing, or write it neatly by hand, skipping every other line on your paper.

2. All margins should be one inch.

3. Include a title for your paragraph and your name somewhere at the top of the page.

CHAPTER 6 REVIEW

Fill in the blanks in the following statements.

1. To edit your writing, you _____, or search for errors at the sentence and word levels.

2. *Editing* means making the necessary _____.

3. The _____ of writing refers to the words the writer has chosen and the way sentences are constructed.

4. Writing that is composed mostly of very short sentences usually sounds _____ to readers; short sentences also may not be making important _____, so readers may not fully understand the ideas.

5. To combine sentences, join them with a _____ (*and, or, but, nor, for, yet,* or *so*), turn one sentence into a _____ and attach it to an independent clause, or embed the information of one sentence into another sentence.

6. A _____ sentence contains just one independent clause.

7. A _____ sentence contains two independent clauses.

8. A _____ sentence contains a dependent clause and an independent clause.

9. A _____ sentence includes at least one dependent clause and two or more independent clauses.

10. _____ refers to the individual words you choose; these words must be appropriately formal, specific, emotional, and original.

11. _____ are overused expressions that everyone has heard before.

12. Writing that suffers from _____ includes unnecessary words.

13. In addition to proofreading your drafts for sentence variety, appropriate language, and wordiness, you need to find and eliminate major errors in sentence _____.

14. A _____ may lack a subject, a verb, or both, or it may be a dependent clause or a phrase that cannot stand on its own as a complete idea.

15. A _____ consists of two independent clauses that are separated with only a comma, which is inadequate punctuation.

16. A _____ consists of two independent clauses that are not separated by any punctuation mark.

17. If a modifier is not next to the word it describes, it is called a _____.

18. If the word the modifier is supposed to be describing is not in the sentence at all, the error is called a _____.

19. When pairs or series of words, phrases, or clauses express parallel ideas, they must be parallel in _____.

20. Two ways to locate errors in your drafts involve learning to recognize errors yourself and asking peer reviewers to fill out a _____.

21. Correcting errors in your writing is very important because submitting a final draft marred with errors will undermine your _____ as a writer.

22. Three ways to identify and correct spelling errors are (1) look up possible misspellings in a _____, (2) use a _____, and (3) ask someone to proofread your draft for spelling errors.

23. Regardless of a paper's final format, it should always be _____, _____, and _____.

24. _____ are accidental mistakes that occur during the typing or printing of a document.

WebWork

After your instructors help you identify grammatical errors in your writing, you should review the ways to correct these errors so that you will not make the same mistakes over and over again. One useful tool for reviewing grammar is the Guide to Grammar and Writing Web site at http://grammar.ccc.commnet.edu/grammar/index.htm. This Internet site not only explains grammatical concepts but also includes computer-graded quizzes that give you instant feedback, so you know immediately whether or not you have understood the information.

Find one of your graded papers and choose an error (such as a sentence fragment or faulty parallelism) that you made. Go to the Guide to Grammar and Writing Web site and find the tutorial about that particular error. Then complete at least one of the quizzes provided at the end of the lesson.

Online Study Center   For more practice with spotting and correcting errors during proofreading, go to the Houghton Mifflin Online Study Center for this book, at **http://www.college.hmco.com/pic/dolphinwritertwo.**

Writing the Essay

▶ Identify the parts of an essay, and explain the purpose of each part.

▶ Write introductions that use techniques for interesting readers and that include necessary background information.

▶ Rewrite ineffective thesis statements.

▶ Write thesis statements that reflect a certain audience and purpose.

▶ Identify thesis statements, topic sentences, and supporting details in essays.

▶ Evaluate an essay using a peer review sheet.

▶ Proofread and edit an essay.

▶ Follow all five steps of the writing process to write an essay.

The previous five chapters of this text have focused on following the steps in the writing process to compose a paragraph. This chapter focuses on how you can use that same process to write a longer composition, the essay. First, though, we examine the essay and its parts.

The Essay and Its Parts

An **essay** is a multiparagraph composition that develops one idea or opinion, which is called the **thesis**. Like a paragraph, an essay focuses on one point and includes details that support that point. As a matter of fact, the parts of the paragraph often correlate with those of an essay, as the following diagram shows:

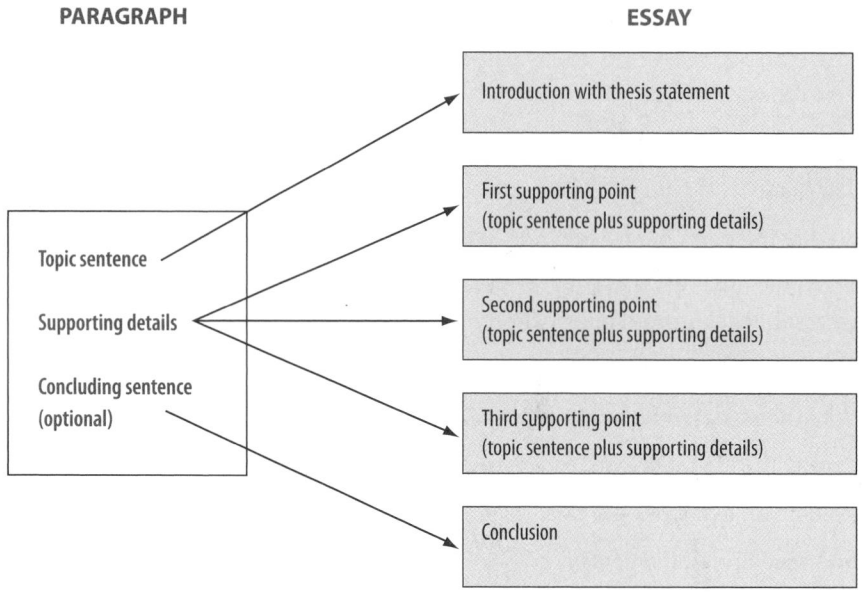

However, an essay is not just an expanded paragraph. For one thing, the thesis usually expresses an idea that requires more development than the idea expressed in the topic sentence of a paragraph. Therefore, an essay is broader in scope and thus needs to be longer.

An essay has three main parts: an introduction, a body, and a conclusion. The **introduction** gives readers background information, gets them interested, and provides the thesis statement. The **body** is composed of several paragraphs that include all of the evidence to explain or prove the thesis. The **conclusion** provides a satisfying ending to the essay. Each of these parts is labeled in the essay that follows:

The Best Job I Have Ever Had

1 We all hope to earn our college degrees and go on to find jobs that we love. But one of my favorite jobs was one I had *while* I was in college. I worked in a flower shop, and my responsibilities included taking orders, helping customers, INTRODUCTION helping keep records of orders organized, keeping the shop tidy, and occasionally delivering an order. I usually worked on the weekends and in the afternoons

Thesis Statement after my classes were over. I did not earn very much, of course. **But looking back, I realize that my flower shop job was one of the best ones I have ever had.**

2   I love flowers, so it was wonderful to be around thousands of them for hours at a time. Their fragrance was always so pleasant; as a matter of fact,

smelling the flowers' perfume never failed to soothe me or lift my spirits, even when I was feeling glum[1]. I liked them so much that I did not even mind sweeping out the large walk-in cooler where we kept the buckets of fresh flowers. Even though my job was to cull[2] the dead or dying blooms and keep the buckets filled with water, I never minded cleaning up because it gave me a chance to look at their beautiful colors and inhale their scents.

3   The people I worked with were another aspect of the job that I loved. The owner of the flower shop, Harry, and another man named Rick were the designers who created all of the arrangements. They were fun-loving and had a good sense of humor. Several of the delivery people became my friends, too. There was a lot of laughter and joking in the shop, so it made the workday pleasant. Even during busy, stressful holidays like Valentine's Day and Mother's Day, when everyone in the world needs flowers delivered on the same day, we all got along and worked well as a team.

BODY

4   I also loved working in a business that makes people happy. Everyone loves to get a delivery of flowers, and the flower arrangements that Harry and Rick created were especially beautiful. On the occasions when I got to make a delivery, I loved seeing the look of delight and surprise on the recipient's face. Even the flowers that went to funerals would often lift people's spirits and let them know that people cared about them. It was nice to know that I was helping to make many people's days a little brighter by doing my small part to get the orders taken, made, and delivered.

5   I ended up leaving my job at the flower shop to take a job that paid me more money. I know I could not have worked there forever, but I do miss it. Working there helped me understand that there are other aspects of a job that are just as important as the wages.

CONCLUSION

 **EXERCISE 7.1**   **Identifying the Parts of an Essay**

Read the following essay and underline the thesis statement. Then label the introduction, the body, and the conclusion.

Satellite or Cable?

1   Do you enjoy watching television? Do you have cable TV, or are you thinking about getting it? If you answered yes to either one of these questions, you might want to consider getting a satellite TV system instead. This system, which includes a small satellite that a technician installs atop the roof of your home, allows you to receive hundreds of TV channels. Indeed, satellite TV is better than cable TV for two reasons.

---

1. **glum:** depressed   2. **cull:** pick out; select

2   For one thing, satellite TV is more cost-effective than cable TV. My cable TV bill used to go up every year. By the time I switched to satellite, I was paying about $30 per month for about 60 channels, most of which I never even watched. For the $40 a month I now pay for satellite TV, I get 130 channels, which is more than twice the number of cable channels I had for only $10 more a month. Plus, the satellite TV channels are better, and I always have the option of adding even more when I can afford an additional charge. With cable, you do not have these kinds of options.

3   The second reason I like satellite better than cable is satellite's reliability. When I had cable, my service was interrupted often. Every time there was a thunderstorm or a heavy snow, the cable would go out and stay out for hours, just when I had to stay indoors and wanted to watch TV. My satellite TV service is rarely interrupted in any kind of weather. And when it is, it is out only briefly, never for hours at a time.

4   So I would recommend that you look into satellite TV and consider installing it in your home. Then you can enjoy hours of relaxation in front of the TV, enjoying the channels you like at a good price.

The Introduction

The **introduction** is also known as the opening, for it is composed of one or more paragraphs at the very beginning of the essay. The introductions of the essays you write should fulfill three purposes. First of all, the introduction should grab readers' attention and get them interested in the essay's topic and the author's point about that topic. To make readers want to read on, you can use one of several methods:

Begin with an anecdote. Everyone likes to hear stories, so you can tell a brief story that is related to your topic and leads to your main point. An anecdote is a tried-and-true technique for hooking readers' interest and making them want to continue reading.

> A few weeks ago, as I was driving one morning on Interstate 40, I witnessed a terrible accident. Up ahead of me, on a long, straight stretch of road, a police cruiser was stopped on the shoulder. A sport-utility vehicle pulling a trailer was in the right lane, headed toward the parked cruiser. The driver of the SUV must have gotten distracted by something because all of a sudden, he veered toward the cruiser and hit it. As I watched in horror, the SUV jerked back to the left and began tumbling. By the time I slowed and stopped my own car, the SUV had rolled several times and then come to rest upside down, on its roof, in the middle

of the highway. Amazingly, no one was killed in the accident, but the driver and two passengers in the SUV, as well as the officer in the cruiser, had to be taken by ambulance to the hospital. The people in the SUV were lucky, for rollovers are the number one cause of death in SUV wrecks. Drivers may think that they are safer in these huge, heavy vehicles, but that is just an illusion. SUVs are actually very dangerous both for their owners and for the other drivers on the road.

Begin with an example. You can make the topic immediately interesting by showing how it relates to a specific individual.

Richie was really looking forward to seeing the Shocking Flamingoes perform live in concert. The band had always been one of his favorites, so when it scheduled a performance in the city where Richie lived, he spent $40 on what he thought would be a great seat. But his seat was not anywhere near the stage, and the crowd around him ended up ruining the whole experience for him. Richie was one of many concertgoers who are finding out that concerts can sometimes be a waste of money.

Provide an interesting fact or statistic. You can also arouse readers' curiosity by providing some information that is surprising, startling, or even shocking.

While you read this essay, another person will probably die because he or she needed an organ transplant and there were no donors. According to the U.S. Department of Health and Human Services' National Organ and Tissue Donation Initiative, about 10 people die every day while waiting for a donated kidney, liver, heart, lung or other organ. And there are more than 55,000 people presently on the national organ transplant waiting list. Statistics show that there is only a 38 percent chance that an individual on this waiting list will get an organ. You can help raise their odds, though, by becoming an organ donor. (The 11th Annual *Discover* Awards, July 2000, http://www .discover.com/jul_00/explain.html)

Provide a direct quotation. Beginning with a clever or humorous statement made by someone else can be a good way to get readers interested in the topic.

Ralph Waldo Emerson said that you are a successful person "if even one life has breathed easier because you have lived." My grandparents were not rich or famous. On the contrary, my grandfather worked as a janitor, and my grandmother worked on an assembly line in a factory. When they finally retired, each lived only a few more years before dying, so they had little time to devote to other accomplishments. But according to Emerson's definition, they were both very successful individuals.

Ask readers a question. You can often draw readers into your essay by asking them questions to get them thinking about their own ideas or opinions about the topic.

> Do you feel stressed out and overwhelmed? Do you wish you could find a good technique for relaxing and soothing your frazzled nerves? You may want to try yoga, a series of stretches and poses designed to calm the mind while they strengthen and tone the body. Yoga is not people looking for a mystical, New Age[1] experience. As a matter of fact, yoga's popularity among many different age groups has been steadily increasing because of its physical and mental benefits.

Explain the topic's relevance or significance to the reader. Immediately connect the topic to your readers' interests, goals, or desires.

> If you are like most people, you are probably tired of answering your phone and having to listen to a telemarketer try to sell you something. Telemarketing companies think nothing of bothering people by calling them during dinner or while they are trying to relax in the evening. Many people get multiple phone calls every night from different telemarketers. But now, if you want to put a stop to these interruptions, you can. There are now several different ways to prevent unwanted sales calls.

Begin with a contradiction. Present to the reader some commonly held idea or opinion, and then go on to contradict or refute it.

> When the Internet began to grow rapidly, offering computer users books, magazines, and huge amounts of other information in electronic form, some people predicted that traditional libraries would become a thing of the past. Of course, that did not happen. As a matter of fact, libraries are still thriving all over the nation. Although it is true that conducting online research is very convenient, the Internet will never completely replace libraries, which will always have an important place in our communities.

 **EXERCISE 7.2**   **Writing Interesting Introductions**

Choose two of the following thesis statements, and complete the statements by filling in the blanks. For each thesis statement you choose, write on your own paper

1. **New Age:** related to spiritual or natural methods

two different introductions, each of which uses a different technique for interesting the reader.

1. The most peaceful place on Earth is _____.

2. _____ should be a required course for every college student.

3. I have the biggest personality conflict with _____.

4. _____ is a great author.

5. I love to collect _____.

The second purpose of the introduction is to provide readers with necessary background information about the topic. After you have gotten readers interested, you may need to provide some facts or explanation about your topic so that they will understand the point you make in your thesis. Notice how, in the following example, the author gets readers interested by asking a question. But then he goes on to explain some things to readers. He tells them who the coaches are, what kinds of games he is talking about, and how he is involved with youth sports.

> Which kind of youth sports coach is better: the kind that puts the kids through their paces and focuses on improving their skills, or the kind that emphasizes having fun and enjoying the game? The answer usually depends upon whom you ask, for different parents and children prefer different coaching styles. But over the last three years, as I worked for our town's recreation center and assisted at a lot of kids' baseball, basketball, and soccer games, I have found that all of the really good coaches have some similarities, regardless of their overall style. They are all moms and dads who have volunteered to lead and supervise teams of children. **But I speak from experience when I say that the best coaches are the ones who have three qualities: patience, firmness, and good teaching ability.**

Do not assume that readers will know all about your topic. Provide them with a brief orientation so that you are sure they have the information they need to understand your ideas. For example, look at this thesis statement:

> The Bible's Ten Commandments should not be posted in schools, courthouses, or any other government building.

What do you think readers will need to know before they can understand this point? The writer will need to answer the following questions: *What are the Ten Commandments? Who are the people who want to post them in schools, courthouses, and other government buildings? Why do these people want to post the Ten Commandments? What situation prompted the controversy?* If readers do not get the answers to these questions, they may not understand the thesis statement.

EXERCISE 7.3   **Including Background Information in Introductions**

Choose two of the following thesis statements. For each one, write on your own paper an introduction that provides necessary background information about the topic.

1. The International Space Station is a worthwhile project that should continue to receive funding.

2. Reality television shows have been criticized for being mean-spirited, but most of them have many redeeming qualities.

3. Attendance in college classes should (or should not) be mandatory.

4. The penalties for drunk driving need to be even more severe.

5. Every young American should have to serve at least two years in the military.

The third and final purpose of an introduction is to clearly state the thesis, the overall main point the writer wants to make about the topic. Like the topic sentence of a paragraph, the thesis statement includes both a topic and a point:

Topic	*Point*
The Tampa Bay Buccaneers	should go all the way to the Super Bowl this year.

Topic	*Point*
Rock climbing	offers physical and psychological benefits.

Topic	*Point*
My best friend Tom	is the most generous person I know.

 **EXERCISE 7.4** Identifying the Parts of Thesis Statements

In each of the following thesis statements, circle the topic and underline the point the writer makes about that topic.

1. Credit cards should not be available to people under twenty-one years of age.

2. Many of today's musical artists try to camouflage their lack of talent with their good looks and flashy performances.

3. Teenagers in our community need a place where they can hang out together safely.

4. My brother Joe is my hero.

5. For thousands of years, tattoos have been used for a number of diverse purposes.

Like topic sentences, thesis statements must be complete, appropriately specific, and suited to your audience and purpose. To review these three characteristics, refer back to pages 57–61 of Chapter 4.

 **EXERCISE 7.5** Revising Ineffective Thesis Statements

On the blanks provided, rewrite any of the following thesis statements that are either incomplete, too broad, too vague, or too specific. If the thesis statement seems complete and appropriately specific, write **OK** on the blank.

1. There is a lot wrong with today's fashions for young people.

   _____

2. The problem with income taxes.

   _____

   _____

3. Computers are helping family members who live far apart from one another stay connected.

   _____

4. I graduated from high school in 1999.

   _____

5. How to kick a bad habit.

   _____

 **EXERCISE 7.6** **Topic, Audience, and Purpose in Thesis Statements**

Use prewriting techniques to generate ideas, and then write a thesis statement for each topic/audience/purpose set provided here.

> Topic: College education
> Audience: High school students
> Purpose: To persuade

1. Thesis statement: _____

> Topic: A cultural tradition in your family
> Audience: People of other cultures
> Purpose: To inform

2. Thesis statement: _____

> Topic: A funny thing that happened to you
> Audience: Your peers
> Purpose: To entertain

3. Thesis statement: _____

> Topic: A raise in your wages or salary
> Audience: Your supervisor at work
> Purpose: To persuade

4. Thesis statement: _____

> Topic: One of your sports or hobbies
> Audience: People who are interested in trying this sport or hobby
> Purpose: To inform

5. Thesis statement: _____

In review, an introduction must fulfill three purposes: to interest the reader, to provide necessary background information, and to state the thesis. An introduction may not necessarily fulfill these three purposes in the order in which they are presented here. In most cases, it will probably be best to get readers' attention and orient them *before* stating the thesis, but there may be times when it seems most appropriate to begin the essay with the background information or even with your thesis statement. Just make sure that each introduction you write accomplishes all three goals.

The Body

The **body** of an essay supplies all of the ideas and information that explain or prove the point made in the thesis statement. The body consists of several paragraphs, one for each separate idea or reason that supports the thesis. Each idea or reason is usually stated in a clear **topic sentence.** Then the rest of the paragraph develops this topic sentence with details such as facts, examples, observations, or other kinds of support. Therefore, the paragraphs that you have been examining in the preceding five chapters of this text have all been the kinds of paragraphs that you would find in the body of an essay.

In the following essay, the thesis statement, body, topic sentences, and supporting details have all been labeled.

The Best Job I Have Ever Had

1 We all hope to earn our college degrees and go on to find jobs that we love. But one of my favorite jobs was one I had *while* I was in college. I worked in a flower shop, and my responsibilities included taking orders, helping customers, helping keep records of orders organized, keeping the shop tidy, and occasionally delivering an order. I usually worked on the weekends and in the afternoons after my classes were over. I did not earn very much, of course. **But looking back, I realize that this job was one of the best ones I have ever had.**

INTRODUCTION

Thesis Statement

2 I love flowers, so it was wonderful to be around thousands of them for hours at a time. Their fragrance was always so pleasant; as a matter of fact, smelling the flowers' perfume never failed to soothe me or lift my spirits, even when I was feeling glum. I liked them so much that I did not even mind sweeping out the large walk-in cooler where we kept the buckets of fresh flowers. Even though my job was to cull the dead or dying blooms and keep the buckets filled with water, I never minded cleaning up because it gave me a chance to look at their beautiful colors and inhale their scents.

Topic Sentence

Supporting Details

3 The people I worked with were another aspect of the job that I loved. The owner of the flower shop, Harry, and another man named Rick were the designers who created all of the arrangements. They were fun-loving and had a good sense of humor. Several of the delivery people became my friends, too. There was a lot of laughter and joking in the shop, so it made the workday pleasant. Even during busy, stressful holidays like Valentine's Day and Mother's Day, when everyone in the world needs flowers delivered on the same day, we all got along and worked well as a team.

Topic Sentence

BODY

Supporting Details

4 I also loved working in a business that makes people happy. Everyone loves to get a delivery of flowers, and the flower arrangements that Harry and Rick created were especially beautiful. On the occasions when I got to make a delivery, I loved seeing the look of delight and surprise on the recipient's face.

Topic Sentence

Supporting
Details

Even the flowers that went to funerals would often lift people's spirits and let them know that people cared about them. It was nice to know that I was helping to make many people's days a little brighter by doing my small part to get the orders taken, made, and delivered.

5   I ended up leaving my job at the flower shop to take a job that paid me more money. I know I could not have worked there forever, but I do miss it.

CONCLUSION   Working there helped me understand that there are other aspects of a job that are just as important as the wages.

EXERCISE 7.7   **Recognizing the Essay's Body and Its Parts**

In the essay that follows, draw a bracket, as in the preceding example, to label the body. Then underline and label the thesis statement and the topic sentence of each body paragraph.

Satellite or Cable?

1   Do you enjoy watching television? Do you have cable TV, or are you thinking about getting it? If you answered yes to either one of these questions, you might want to consider getting a satellite TV system instead. This system, which includes a small satellite that a technician installs atop the roof of your home, allows you to receive hundreds of TV channels. Indeed, satellite TV is better than cable TV for two reasons.

2   For one thing, satellite TV is more cost-effective than cable TV. My cable TV bill used to go up every year. By the time I switched to satellite, I was paying about $30 per month for about 60 channels, most of which I never even watched. For the $40 a month I now pay for satellite TV, I get 130 channels, which is more than twice the number of cable channels I had for only $10 more a month. Plus, the satellite TV channels are better, and I always have the option of adding even more when I can afford an additional charge. With cable, you do not have these kinds of options.

3   The second reason I like satellite better than cable is satellite's reliability. When I had cable, my service was interrupted often. Every time there was a thunderstorm or a heavy snow, the cable would go out and stay out for hours, just when I had to stay indoors and wanted to watch TV. My satellite TV service is rarely interrupted in any kind of weather. And when it is, it is out only briefly, never for hours at a time.

4   So I would recommend that you look into satellite TV and consider installing it in your home. Then you can enjoy hours of relaxation in front of the TV, enjoying the channels you like at a good price.

Later in this chapter, you will see how to follow the steps in the writing process to compose the body of an essay.

The Conclusion

In a brief essay, the **conclusion** is the very last paragraph. It is usually unnecessary to repeat or summarize all of the ideas you have just presented. Instead, think of the purpose of the conclusion as providing closure, or a satisfying ending, for the reader. View the conclusions you write as opportunities to wrap up your essay and to suggest how your readers might respond. Write your conclusion under the assumption that you have convinced your readers that the idea or opinion in your thesis is true. Now that they agree with you, what should happen next? To achieve closure, you might use one of the following methods:

Describe the consequences of the idea or opinion in your thesis statement. Briefly explain the effects of what you have just shown to be true.

> Once you have selected one or more of these options for preventing telemarketing calls, you will see a significant reduction in the number of calls you receive. As a result, you will finally be able to enjoy a family dinner or your favorite TV show without being interrupted by someone who is trying to sell you something.

Make a prediction that arises from the idea or opinion in your thesis statement. Tell what you think will happen in the future.

> Because libraries offer all of these valuable services, computers will never make them obsolete[1]. Of course, traditional libraries will probably have to continue to make alterations in what they do and how they do it to keep pace with improved technologies. For example, they may have to incorporate more computers and train staff to help library patrons find what they need in cyberspace[2]. But these alterations might cause libraries to *expand* rather than shrink or die out altogether.

End with a suggestion that readers act in some way. Call readers to action, and ask them to do something such as join an organization, donate time or money, or make some kind of change.

> Now that you have learned how important it is to become an organ donor, take the next step to make your wishes known. Tell your family members that you want to donate your organs to help others. Complete a donor card, and when

---

1. **obsolete:** no longer in use

2. **cyberspace:** the electronic medium of computer networks

you renew your driver's license, say yes when you are asked if you want to be an organ donor.

End with a question that keeps readers thinking. Just as you can begin an essay by asking questions that draw readers in, you can end with a question or two that encourage readers to continue reflecting upon the topic or issue.

As you can see, SUVs are definitely making our roads and highways more dangerous. People who choose to drive an SUV may think that they need all that extra room, and they might believe they look hip and trendy in these gigantic vehicles. But is it not time for us to stop listening to car manufacturers and advertisers who want to sell us expensive SUVs and start making more safety-conscious choices?

EXERCISE 7.8   **Recognizing Methods of Concluding an Essay**

Write the answer to each question on the blank provided.

1. In the essay on pages 126–127, which of the four techniques does the writer use to conclude the essay? _____

2. In the essay on pages 127–128, which of the four techniques does the writer use to conclude the essay? _____

3. The technique used in the following conclusion is _____

When you consider becoming an organ donor, put yourself in the shoes of those who are on the waiting list for an organ. They live every day hoping to get the call that says a new organ has become available. They also live in fear that this call will never come. If you needed a new heart, liver, or kidney, would you not hope that someone out there cared enough to leave his or her organs to those in need?

Steps in Writing an Essay: A Student Demonstration

Now that you know the elements of the essay, you can see how to use the steps in the writing process to compose one. You learned about and practiced each of these steps as you completed Chapters 2–6 of this text. The steps are the same for writing essays as they are for writing paragraphs:

Step 1: Prewriting
Step 2: Organizing and outlining
Step 3: Writing a draft
Step 4: Revising
Step 5: Proofreading, editing, and preparing the final draft

For an illustration of these five steps, you will be following the process that a student named Joel went through in order to complete an essay.

Prewriting

Joel's assignment was to write an essay about a memorable experience. As you learned in Chapter 2, the first step of the writing process is prewriting. Techniques such as talking, freewriting, brainstorming, clustering, and asking questions are all effective prewriting methods. Joel began by brainstorming a list of his most memorable experiences:

high school graduation
trip to the Bahamas
summer camp
volunteering at the animal shelter
my first date
my car wreck

He decided that he wanted to write his essay about his trip to the Bahamas. So he did some prewriting again, this time using freewriting to explore his specific memories of the trip:

My trip to the Bahamas was definitely a memorable experience but not a good one! It was truly awful, the worst trip I ever took. Steve got sick and had to stay in the room. The weather was terrible—a hurricane wrecked the whole trip. It was the worst vacation of my life. The food was what must have made Steve sick but the hotel was not that great. The air conditioner in our room was not working correctly so it was warm and humid. The TV got only about 4 stations. It rained every day we were there. I was glad to finally get home.

After Joel generated some ideas, he needed to begin thinking about his main idea, the overall point he wanted to make. He wrote this main idea statement:

I did not enjoy my trip to the Bahamas.

Then he decided that he could improve this statement by beginning the sentence with his topic. He revised his statement to read:

> My trip to the Bahamas turned out to be the worst vacation I have ever had.

 **EXERCISE 7.9**   **Prewriting for an Essay**

Choose one of the following topics and generate some ideas by brainstorming, freewriting, clustering, or asking questions.

The benefits of one of my hobbies
The reasons I chose to attend a particular college
The worst (or best) date I have ever had
A decision that had a major impact on my life
My favorite kind of exercise
The best kind of instructor

Organizing and Outlining

The second step of the writing process is organizing and outlining. Just as you learned to organize ideas for a paragraph in Chapter 3, you need to group all of the relevant ideas together and then determine the best order for the paragraphs in the essays you write.

Joel reviewed his freewriting and saw that there were three main things that ruined the trip: the weather, his friend's illness, and problems with the hotel room. He decided to write a paragraph about each one. But he knew that before he could create his outline, he would have to figure out the best order for his paragraphs. He decided that he should discuss the bad weather first because it made the other two problems even worse. He created this outline, adding a few more details that he wanted to include in each paragraph:

> Main idea: My trip to the Bahamas turned out to be the worst vacation I have ever had.
>
> 1. Bad weather
>   – hurricane passing close by
>   – heavy rains every day
>   – no sunshine
>   – nothing to do but stay inside

2. Problems with hotel
   – broken air conditioner
   – few TV channels
3. Steve getting sick
   – he probably ate something bad
   – stayed in bed 3 of the 4 days we were there

After completing this outline, Joel was ready to write the body of his essay.

EXERCISE 7.10 **Organizing and Outlining an Essay**

Complete each of the following main idea statements, and then fill in the outline that follows each one. Use prewriting techniques to generate ideas.

1. _____ is the perfect career for me.
   A. _____
   B. _____
   C. _____
2. _____ are the healthiest people I know.
   A. _____
   B. _____
   C. _____
3. One of the best movies I have ever seen is _____.
   A. _____
   B. _____
   C. _____

Writing a Draft

The third step of the writing process is writing a draft. When you practiced writing a paragraph, you turned the main idea statement you wrote during the prewriting stage into a topic sentence that was complete, appropriately specific, and appropriate to your purpose and audience. When you write an essay, you turn your main idea statement into a thesis statement that has these same three characteristics.

For example, Joel's main idea statement was

My trip to the Bahamas turned out to be the worst vacation I have ever had.

Is this thesis statement complete? In other words, does it include both a topic and some point about that topic? Joel's thesis statement included his topic, *my trip to the Bahamas*. It also included his point: *It turned out to be the worst vacation I have ever had*. So it was indeed complete.

Is Joel's thesis statement appropriately specific? It seems to be. If Joel's topic was all of the trips he has ever taken or all of the times when things went wrong, then his thesis might be too broad or vague. If he focused on only one thing that went wrong on his trip, then his thesis might be too narrow for an entire essay. Remember that an essay is longer than a paragraph, though, so the thesis statement can be broader than a topic sentence.

Finally, is Joel's thesis statement appropriate for his purpose and audience? He decided to write this essay for a general audience of his peers, and he wanted to inform them about what happened to him on this particular trip. His thesis matched that intention. Compare his thesis statement with the thesis statement "You should never try to go to the Bahamas during hurricane season," which clearly has a more persuasive purpose.

After you have settled on a particular thesis statement, make sure that this statement still matches the outline you created in the second step of the process. If it does not, make the necessary adjustments to your thesis, your outline, or both. Also, consider your outline in light of the modes of development. These familiar patterns, which are explained and illustrated in Chapters 9–18 of this text, will often provide an effective organizational framework for your ideas.

As you begin to write your draft, consider skipping the introduction and writing the body of the essay first. Afterward, when you know exactly what you need to introduce, you can go back and write an opening that fits.

As you compose each body paragraph, consciously write a clear topic sentence for each one, and use layers of development (see pages 54–69 in Chapter 4) to make sure you fully explain each idea. As you begin each new paragraph, think about how you can link your paragraphs together to develop a clear progression of ideas and to make relationships clear. For example, you can refer back to a word or idea in a previous paragraph, or you can use transitional words that indicate how a paragraph is related to the one before it.

With all of this information in mind, Joel wrote a draft of the body of his essay:

When you go to the Bahamas, you expect sun, sand, and surf. You picture in your mind laying on the beach getting a tan and going for a dip when it gets hot. But the only sun I saw was on the day we got there. Because a hurricane was passing nearby. Thick clouds quickly blotted out the sun completely so you could not see it. We maybe

could of lived with that. But then it started to rain. It rained the entire rest of our four day trip. So we could not swim or do anything but
basically sit in the hotel room.

   Our hotel was not that great. It was free, so I guess we could not
gripe too much. Although, I was pretty bummed. The air conditioner
was not working right, so the room was too warm and humid. The dude
at the front desk said there was no other room available for us to
move to because the hotel was full. So we had to tough it out. Besides
that, the TV in our room got like only four channels, so we were stuck
inside with nothing much to watch.

   I guess Steve and me could of found someplace to play video
games or just hang out. Then Steve got sick. It must have been something he ate. Because all of a sudden he is feeling terrible and throwing up. This happened to me once when I went with my parents on a
cruise. I do not know if I was seasick or the shrimp was spoiled; but I
was sicker than a dog.

EXERCISE 7.11   **Examining the Draft of an Essay**

**Answer the following questions about Joel's essay by writing your answers on the
blanks provided.**

   1. Did Joel seem to follow his outline as he wrote the draft of his essay? Why
      or why not?

      _____

      _____

   2. Do all three of Joel's paragraphs include clear topic sentences with sufficient
      layers of development? Explain your answer.

      _____

      _____

      _____

   3. Joel needs to write an introduction next. Which technique can he use to get
      his reader interested?

      _____

   4. Based on these body paragraphs, what background information will Joel
      need to provide in his introduction?

      _____

      _____

5. What type of conclusion would be effective for this essay?

_____

_____

After Joel wrote the body of his essay, he turned his attention to his introduction. He remembered that he needed to write a paragraph that got his readers interested, provided background information, and stated his thesis. Here is his first attempt at an introduction:

> I was real excited when I won a trip to the Bahamas in a radio contest. I called up and answered some trivia questions, and I won! Everything was free; the plane tickets, the hotel, and food. I got to take one friend with me, so I picked my buddy Steve. But the trip was good only during a certain time, that time turned out to be September. We were psyched because we knew it would still be warm and sunny. Unfortunately though that is hurricane season. My trip to the Bahamas turned out to be the worst vacation I have ever had.

Next, Joel wrote his conclusion. He looked at the different techniques he could use to conclude his essay (see pages 137–138 of this chapter), and he decided to describe the consequences or effects of his thesis statement:

> It was definitely an awful trip. Fortunately, though, Steve and I can just laugh about it now. It was not funny at the time but now its a good story about one of our many adventures that we tell our friends. We also tell them not to go to the Bahamas during hurricane season!

EXERCISE 7.12   **Writing Introductions and Conclusions**

Write an introduction and a conclusion for the body of the essay that follows. The thesis of this essay is _You can do several things to improve your performance on tests._

Introduction:_____

_____

_____

_____

_____

_____

You can do several things to improve your performance on tests.

The first thing you will have to do if you want to make better test grades is adequately prepare yourself before you take tests. Obviously, you have to study. But you should not wait until the night before the test because cramming is just not effective. Instead, plan to study the material a little at a time over a longer period of time, a method that will help you learn and retain the material better. It will also allow you to ask your instructor questions about anything you do not fully understand. In addition, consider forming a study group that meets regularly to review the information. As part of your preparation, familiarize yourself with the format of the test as well as likely test questions. Ask your instructor to give you some idea of what to expect, and pay careful attention to material the instructor emphasizes in class or during review sessions.

If you are sufficiently prepared but still struggle during tests, you may suffer from test anxiety. So the next step is to use techniques to help yourself stay calm. Get to a test early, and spend a few minutes getting your materials ready and then just breathing deeply to relax. Use positive affirmations; in other words, remind yourself that you studied and that you are ready. When the test is distributed, look it over, and do all of the easy questions first to build your confidence. Then go back and complete the more challenging questions.

So let us say that you got through the test. You studied, you were able to conquer your test anxiety, and you made a grade you can be proud of. But you are still not finished. If you want to improve your test-taking skills, make sure you do not just stuff your graded test into a notebook where you will never see it again. Instead, study your incorrect answers until you understand what you did wrong. If necessary, make an appointment to discuss with your instructor how you can improve your performance on the next test. If you try to learn from your mistakes, you should see your skills continue to improve.

Conclusion: _____

_____

_____

_____

_____

_____ .

WRITING FOR SUCCESS

Beyond College Essays

You can count on writing quite a few essays in the college courses you take, for the essay is a common academic assignment. But what about after college? You may be wondering if you will ever have to write essays in your personal and professional life.

It is true that you will probably not be generating the academic form of essays after you complete your college education. However, you will in all likelihood be generating other types of documents—such as memos, business letters, proposals, and reports—that have many similarities to the essay form. All of these documents, for example, begin with an introduction and offer details in support of main ideas. So you will be able to apply what you learned about the essay to compose other kinds of writing.

Even when a document—such as a lab report or a passage of text for a Web site—seems to bear very little resemblance to an academic essay, you will still be able to use many of the skills you learned from writing essays to compose it. For example, as you learn to write effective essays, you sharpen your organizational skills, and you develop your ability to anticipate and answer the reader's questions. These and many other skills that are necessary for writing essays are directly applicable to any other kind of writing.

Revising

In Chapter 5 of this text, you learned how to revise a paragraph by evaluating whether it is complete (adequately developed), cohesive (focused on one main idea only), and coherent (well organized). When you evaluate the draft of an essay, you examine these same three aspects. In addition, you evaluate the effectiveness of the introduction and the conclusion.

A peer review sheet is an effective tool to use when you are looking for areas of improvement in your own or someone else's draft. The following peer review sheet, which has been expanded to include questions about essays, was completed by a student who read the draft of Joel's essay:

> I was real excited when I won a trip to the Bahamas in a radio contest.
> I called up and answered some trivia questions, and I won! Everything
> was free; the plane tickets, the hotel, and food. I got to take one

friend with me, so I picked my buddy Steve. But the trip was good only during a certain time, that time turned out to be September. We were psyched because we knew it would still be warm and sunny. Unfortunately though that is hurricane season. My trip to the Bahamas turned out to be the worst vacation I have ever had.

When you go to the Bahamas, you expect sun, sand, and surf. You picture in your mind laying on the beach getting a tan and going for a dip when it gets hot. But the only sun I saw was on the day we got there. Because a hurricane was passing nearby. Thick clouds quickly blotted out the sun completely so you could not see it. We maybe could of lived with that. But then it started to rain. It rained the entire rest of our four day trip. So we could not swim or do anything but basically sit in the hotel room.

Our hotel was not that great. It was free, so I guess we could not gripe too much. Although, I was pretty bummed. The air conditioner was not working right, so the room was too warm and humid. The dude at the front desk said there was no other room available for us to move to because the hotel was full. So we had to tough it out. Besides that, the TV in our room got like only four channels, so we were stuck inside with nothing much to watch.

I guess Steve and me could of found someplace to play video games or just hang out. Then Steve got sick. It must have been something he ate. Because all of a sudden he is feeling terrible and throwing up. This happened to me once when I went with my parents on a cruise. I do not know if I was seasick or the shrimp was spoiled; but I was sicker than a dog.

It was definitely an awful trip. Fortunately, though, Steve and I can just laugh about it now. It was not funny at the time but now its a good story about one of our many adventures that we tell our friends. We also tell them not to go to the Bahamas during hurricane season!

Peer Review Sheet

Writer: *Joel*

Reviewer: *Nicholas*

Topic of essay: *A trip to the Bahamas*

	Yes	No
1. Does the essay's introduction get you interested in the topic and thesis of the essay?		✓

Suggestions for improvement:
I thought it was pretty interesting that you won the contest, but using one of the techniques for introductions might make it even better.

2. Does the introduction provide all of the necessary background information?   ✓ _____

Suggestions for improvement:

3. Does the introduction include a clear thesis statement?   ✓ _____

Suggestions for improvement:

4. Do all of the main ideas in the body of the essay support the thesis statement?   ✓ _____

Suggestions for improvement:

5. Does each body paragraph contain a topic sentence that clearly states one main idea?   _____ ✓

Suggestions for improvement:
I think the topic sentences are a little hard to recognize. Maybe make them clearer?

	Yes	No
6. Is each body paragraph complete, cohesive, and coherent?		✓

Suggestions for improvement:
The third body paragraph is not cohesive because you start talking about getting sick on a cruise. After you delete that part, the paragraph will need more development.

	Yes	No
7. Is the organization of the essay's body effective?	✓	

Suggestions for improvement:

	Yes	No
8. Has the writer included transitions and repetition of words to help the reader follow the progression of thought from one paragraph to the next?		✓

Suggestions for improvement:
You have made a few connections between the paragraphs, but you could add some transitions, too.

	Yes	No
9. Does the conclusion provide a satisfactory ending for the essay?	✓	

Suggestions for improvement:
The conclusion is good. It gives the effects, which was an effective way to wrap up.

Additional suggestions for improvement:
I think you made it clear why this was such a terrible trip. During editing, you should think about changing some of the informal language and fixing some verb tense shifts.

On the basic of this feedback, Joel revised his essay. You can see his revised draft in Exercise 7.14.

EXERCISE 7.13 **Evaluating an Essay Using a Peer Review Sheet**

Read the next essay, which was written by a student named Beth. Then complete the peer review sheet on pages 151–152 that follows to give Beth your advice for improvement.

The Joys of Cooking

I come from a long line of good cooks. My grandmother and my mother are both great cooks, and I even have an aunt who is a professional chef. So I guess it is only natural that I like to cook, too. Cooking is fun.

Cooking gives me a chance to be creative. I like to follow recipes, but I also like to experiment while I am in the kitchen. I like to alter recipes and substitute different ingredients, and I also enjoy trying to come up with my own unique dishes. For example, I am working right now on trying to perfect a spaghetti sauce recipe that I created. It gives me a sense of satisfaction to begin working with ingredients and coming up with new and tasty combinations.

I can go into the kitchen stressed out. An hour later, I feel much calmer and less tense. Cooking helps me forget about things that are bothering me for a while so I can relax. I also jog every morning as a way to reduce stress.

I like to cook for my friends and family. When I cook for them, I feel like I am letting them know that I care for them. They always appreciate it, too.

Cooking is a great way to relieve stress and be creative, so that is why many people enjoy it.

Peer Review Sheet

Writer: _____

Reviewer: _____

Topic of essay: _____

	Yes	No

1. Does the essay's introduction get you interested in the topic and thesis of the essay?   _____ _____

   Suggestions for improvement:

2. Does the introduction provide all of the necessary background information?   _____ _____

   Suggestions for improvement:

3. Does the introduction include a clear thesis statement?   _____ _____

   Suggestions for improvement:

4. Do all of the main ideas in the body of the essay support the thesis statement?   _____ _____

   Suggestions for improvement:

5. Does each body paragraph contain a topic sentence that clearly states one main idea?   _____ _____

   Suggestions for improvement:

	Yes	No

6. Is each body paragraph complete, cohesive, and coherent?   _____ _____

Suggestions for improvement:

7. Is the organization of the essay's body effective?   _____ _____

Suggestions for improvement:

8. Has the writer included transitions and repetition of words to   _____ _____
help the reader follow the progression of thought from one
paragraph to the next?

Suggestions for improvement:

9. Does the conclusion provide a satisfactory ending for the   _____ _____
essay?

Suggestions for improvement:

Additional suggestions for improvement:

Proofreading, Editing, and Preparing the Final Draft

In Chapter 6 of this text, you learned to proofread a paragraph for style, sentence errors, grammatical errors, and spelling errors. These are the very same things you are looking for when you proofread an essay. A peer review sheet such as the one on page 86 in Chapter 5 can provide a handy list of the errors you should look for.

EXERCISE 7.14 Proofreading and Editing an Essay

After Joel received Nicholas's suggestions, he revised his essay. The following is Joel's revised draft. Proofread this essay for style, sentence errors, grammatical errors, and spelling errors, and correct them in the text. (HINT: Here are some of the errors present in Joel's draft: missing commas, inappropriately informal word choices, verb tense shifts, sentence fragments, and wordiness.)

My mom has always said, if it seems too good to be true, it probably is. It turns out that she was right about a trip I took to the Bahamas in September of last year. I was excited when I won the trip in a radio contest by calling and answering some trivia questions. It sounded great, the plane tickets, the hotel, and food were all free for myself and one other person, so my buddy Steve went with me. The trip was only good during the month of September but we were psyched because we knew it would still be warm and sunny. Unfortunately though that is hurricane season. So my trip to the Bahamas turned out to be the worst vacation I have ever had.

The first thing that ruined our trip was the weather. When you go to the Bahamas, you expect sun, sand, and surf. You picture in your mind laying on the beach getting a tan and going for a dip when it gets hot. But the only sun I saw was on the day we got there. Because a hurricane was passing nearby. Thick clouds quickly blotted out the sun completely so you couldn't see it. We maybe could of lived with that. But then it started to rain. It rained the entire rest of our four day trip. So we could not swim or do anything but basically sit in the hotel room.

If the hotel had been really nice, then the trip might still have been pretty decent. But problems with our hotel room contributed to our bad experience. I guess we should not have expected too much since it was free. Although, I was pretty bummed. The air conditioner was not working right, so the room was too warm and humid. The dude at the front desk said there was no other room available for us to move to because the hotel was full. So we had to tough it out. Besides that, the TV in our room got like only four channels, so we were stuck inside with nothing much to watch.

But then the third problem came up when Steve got sick. It must have been something he ate. Because all of a sudden he is feeling terrible and throwing up. He spends the last three days of our four day trip in bed in a hot hotel room. He can't eat anything or get up until the day it was time to get back on the plane to go home. So he ended up being miserable for the whole trip.

It was definitely an awful trip. Fortunately, though, Steve and I can just laugh about it now. It was not funny at the time but now its a good story about one of our many adventures that we tell our friends. We also tell them not to go to the Bahamas during hurricane season!

After getting some help with proofreading and editing his essay, Joel prepared his final draft according to his instructor's directions. He typed it with double spacing and added a title page. He decided to title his essay "Bad Days in the Bahamas."

EXERCISE 7.15   Writing an Essay

In Exercise 7.9, you did some prewriting for one of the following topics. Follow the five steps in the writing process to generate an essay of your own about one of them.

The benefits of one of my hobbies
The reasons I chose to attend a particular college
The worst (or best) date I have ever had
A decision that had a major impact on my life
My favorite kind of exercise
The best kind of instructor

CHAPTER 7 REVIEW

Fill in the blanks in the following statements.

1. An _____ is a multiparagraph composition that develops one idea or opinion, which is called the _____.

2. A thesis usually expresses an idea that requires more _____ than the idea expressed in the topic sentence of a paragraph.

3. An essay has three main parts: an _____, a ____, and a _____.

4. The _____ gives readers background information, gets them interested, and provides the thesis statement.

5. The ____ is composed of several paragraphs that include all of the evidence to explain or prove the thesis.

6. The _____ provides a satisfying ending to the essay.

7. To get readers interested and make them want to read on, writers can begin with an _____ or an _____, provide an interesting _____, provide a _____, ask readers a _____, explain the topic's _____, or begin with a _____.

8. A thesis statement includes two parts: a ____ and the ____ the writer makes about that topic.

9. Like topic sentences, thesis statements must be _____, appropriately _____, and suited to the _____ and _____.

10. In body paragraphs, each idea or reason that supports the thesis is usually stated in a clear _____.

11. The purpose of the conclusion is to provide closure, or a _____ ending, for the reader.

12. To achieve closure in the conclusion, writers can describe the _____ of the idea in the thesis statement, make a _____, end with a suggestion that readers ____ in some way, or end with a _____ that keeps readers thinking.

13. The five steps in writing an essay are _____ _____.

WebWork

Go to the Essay Punch Web site at **www.essaypunch.com.** This Web site provides questions that you answer as you are guided step by step through the actual process of composing an essay. Follow the directions to create your own essay, and print that essay.

Online Study Center   For additional information and activities for writing essays, go to the Houghton Mifflin Online Study Center for this book, at **http://www.college.hmco.com/pic/dolphinwritertwo.**

8

The Reading/Writing Connection

▶ Explain how reading and writing are connected.

▶ Actively read a passage.

▶ Read a passage critically.

▶ Write reading journal entries.

Reading and writing are linked, and each strengthens the other. When you read, you get ideas about *what* to write and *how* to write it. When you write, practice in crafting sentences and paragraphs often ends up improving your reading skills, too. In this chapter, you will focus on how to get more from your reading and how to use what you read to improve your writing skills.

Reading for Ideas

Where will your ideas for compositions come from? Sometimes they will arise from your own experiences in life, from television or films, or from talking to other people. Often, though, they will come to you as you read the writing of others. Reading can provide a springboard of ideas for your own compositions.

For example, read the following essay, titled "What Makes a True Sports Hero?" As you read, try to think of possible essay topics, and write your ideas in the margin or on a separate sheet of paper.

What Makes a True Sports Hero?

By Robert Lipsyte

1 The hill is just too steep for my bursting lungs and burning thighs. My body wants to stop pedaling and walk the bike, but my mind has another idea. I shout (actually, croak), "Lance Armstrong! Lance Armstrong![1]" As usual, the four magic words push me to the top.

2 This is not an inspirational essay. The hill is no metaphor for life. This is just about riding a bike a bit harder or faster than I think I can, and about a role model who helps me do it.

3 Lance Armstrong is the only sports hero I have ever had. I wouldn't dream of letting him advise me in the purchase of cereal, sneakers or a car. But he gets me out and moving, which is more than good enough.

4 Maybe because I've been a sportswriter for so long, I tend to see celebrity athletes as ordinary people with extraordinary skills. While not jaded or cynical, I'm rarely transported when, for example, the San Antonio Spurs' veteran center, David Robinson, turns out to be a good guy; nor am I outraged when the Cubs' home-run hitter, Sammy Sosa, gets caught cheating on his bat. Cork happens.

5 But when Armstrong won his first Tour de France[2] in 1999, I bought a $300 bicycle, my first since childhood. Now, as he tries to win what is probably the world's most demanding sporting event for an amazing fifth consecutive[3] time— on Sunday, he seized the lead in this year's race—I'm still on my bike and riding farther and faster than ever. While I'm not a hard-core bike-racing fan, I think of Armstrong every time I snap shut my helmet strap and kick into speed.

6 We have a connection. In 1996, five years after my third operation for testicular cancer, Armstrong received his own diagnosis, a far more advanced stage than mine. His cancer had reached his brain. He was 25, a world-class racer who had yet to realize his potential.

7 As cancers go, testicular has become "carcinoma lite," thanks to effective chemotherapy drugs. But the chemo can be brutal; two years of it shook up this writer. One can only imagine what far more toxic doses did to that rider.

8 One positive side effect we shared was an intensification of focus and an appreciation of our own capacity for endurance. Intimations[4] of mortality[5] can do that. I wrote harder and faster, concentrating on what felt important to me, confident that I could finish the course.

1. **Lance Armstrong:** a champion bicycle racer
2. **Tour de France:** a bicycle race
3. **consecutive:** following one after the other without interruption
4. **intimations:** suggestions or hints
5. **mortality:** being subject to death

9   Armstrong rode harder and faster, concentrating on training for the long races, especially the three-week, 2,142-mile Tour. His old team had dropped him, but he never lost faith in himself. He was a survivor, and there is something magnetic about such toughness. Doctors, nurses, friends and coaches rallied around him, sharing energy with him.

10   He came back to the races in 1997, the same year he established a foundation for cancer education and research and instituted the fund-raising Ride for the Roses in his hometown, Austin. He was married in 1998, and in 1999, riding for the U.S. Postal Service team, he won the Tour. And my fandom[1]. Among other things, I appreciated how he was reaching out to other cancer survivors. Two years ago, he reached out to me.

11   I was surprised at how reluctant I was about meeting Armstrong. Was I afraid the real person would not live up to the imagined object? That he would turn out to be another pampered jock brat? Some tough sportswriter. He wanted me to moderate[2] a panel his foundation was sponsoring at Stanford University. Was he just using the event to promote himself?

12   Had I been disappointed, I probably would not be writing this. Armstrong turned out to be tough, smart, decent and unsentimental about cancer. When someone in the audience asked him how his belief in God had helped him as a patient, he replied with a bracing[3] directness: "Everyone should believe in something, and I believed in surgery, chemotherapy and my doctors." No politician, he obviously wasn't playing to the crowd.

13   In his absorbing autobiography, *It's Not About the Bike: My Journey Back to Life*, written with Sally Jenkins, it is clear how much of Armstrong's athletic success comes out of his psychic pain. His mother was 17 when he was born. His biological father left two years later. A stepfather abused him. In bike racing, he found a way to inflict physical pain on himself that smothered the emotional pain.

14   "Cycling is so hard," he said, "the suffering is so intense, that it's absolutely cleansing." Just like chemotherapy.

15   I worry about Armstrong. He has three kids now, but his marriage seems shaky at times. He and his wife, Kristin, publicly announced their separation in February. They have since announced their reconciliation[4]. Does that drive to win isolate him from the normal give-and-take of a relationship? He is bothered by the European press's continual accusation that he takes drugs. How else, it asks, could he come back from a cancer that reached into his brain?

16   He answered that question for me obliquely[5], but in a way he knew I would understand. "I approached cancer the way I would prepare for the Tour," he

1. **fandom:** state of being a fan or admirer
2. **moderate:** lead a meeting, forum, or debate
3. **bracing:** invigorating or refreshing
4. **reconciliation:** reestablishment of a close relationship
5. **obliquely:** indirectly

said. "Get in shape, find out as much as you can, be motivated by small results. The lesion[1] shrinking a little gave me the same kind of encouragement to keep going that I would get when my uphill times got slightly faster."

17   No wonder I call on Armstrong when the hill looks too steep.*

Here is a list of topic ideas generated by one student:

> My own sports hero
> A difficult obstacle I conquered
> My own definition of the word hero
> Celebrities as heroes or role models
> Someone who has inspired me
> Meeting a celebrity
> America's fascination with celebrities
> Mental benefits of physical fitness

You probably have additional ideas on your own list. As you can see, this one brief essay was the springboard for many topic ideas.

 **EXERCISE 8.1**   **Generating Essay Topic Ideas from Reading**

Read the following essay. Then, on the blanks provided, write down possible essay topics that occurred to you as you read.

Pain Gains

By Abraham Verghese

1   In the early mornings, when I head out to work, I often see the same middle-aged jogger go by, fussing with his stopwatch. Though his pace is rapid, it is also shuddering like a cart with a wobbly wheel. I picture bone grinding on bone with no cartilage[2] left to intervene. And yet it is not pain that shows on his face but pleasure. I speculate[3] about this man even as I envy him. Exercise for him is its own reward. It is life affirming and it is his addiction.

---

1. **lesion:** infected or diseased part of the body
2. **cartilage:** tough connective tissue in the body

3. **speculate:** reflect upon

---

*Source: "What Makes a True Sports Hero?" by Robert Lipsyte, *USA Today*, July 14, 2003, p. 11A. Reprinted by permission of the author. Robert Lipsyte is a former sports and city columnist of the *New York Times* and the author of sixteen books, including *In the Country of Illness: Comfort and Advice for the Journey*. His young adult novels include *The Contender* and *Raiders Night*.

2   My addiction is tennis. In summer I may hobble around home and office, but on the court, once I hear the opening pop of a new can of balls, pain is forgotten, and I lunge and sprint with abandon. My game peaked 10 years ago and then came down to a steady club level. Since then, the biggest change is in the time it takes to recover from my on-court exertions[1]. There was a week not long ago, for example, when I dreaded shaking hands because my elbow hurt, I limped from Achilles tendonitis, lying flat was preferable to sitting because my back ached and the Advil was taking its toll on my stomach. And yet, when my partner called to see if I would play, I couldn't get out the door fast enough. I felt comforted that even President Bush, a committed exerciser, had complained just that month of aching knees. Last month, it was revealed he had torn his calf muscle in April.

3   He is no exception. On the courts, I see players his age, or mine (upper 40s), wearing strange patellar[2] bands or air-filled forearm straps or thigh wraps or wrist braces, not to mention magnets parked over various body sites. No doubt at home they have gel packs cooling in the freezer and supersize bottles of Motrin[3]. All for good health!

4   As a nation, our waistlines are expanding. Missives[4] regarding the salutary[5] effects of exercise on lipids[6], on blood pressure, on risk for heart disease and diabetes bombard us from all sides. But when we exercise, moderation does not come easily to our society. If you are inclined to cycle, a pedal pusher won't do; a feather-light bike and every last accessory is *de rigueur*[7]. The billions we Americans spend on just the right shoes for our particular sport is a measure of serious intent. What is tricky is finding the sport or exercise we can sustain. So many yard sales feature newish exercise bikes, treadmills, weight benches and ski machines all destined to go from one dusty garage to another. If good intention were the measure of health, we would be a very healthy nation. It is only when exercise becomes its own reward, a compulsion[8], that it sticks. Regular exercise seems to have taken the highest place in the pantheon[9] of modern American virtues.

5   Mass media and Madison Avenue[10] have driven us to identify closely with professional athletes, particularly athletes who defy the age limits of their sport, like Andre Agassi or Martina Navratilova[11], or who overcome major medical obstacles. Arnold Schwarzenegger, a former Mr. Universe, had a heart valve

1. **exertions:** efforts	8. **compulsion:** irresistible impulse to act
2. **patellar:** related to a bone in the knee	9. **pantheon:** group of gods or things highly regarded
3. **Motrin:** a pain reliever	
4. **missives:** written messages	10. **Madison Avenue:** the U.S. advertising industry
5. **salutary:** promoting good health	
6. **lipids:** fats, oils, and waxes	11. **Andre Agassi and Martina Navratilova:** two tennis champions
7. *de rigueur:* required by custom	

replaced. And in his 50s the Terminator[1] remains a formidable[2] figure, a living invitation for us all to pump it up.

6   It is an invitation many have accepted. I see more people who were never jocks in school and who are no longer in the prime of youth but who have recently transformed themselves into muscle-bound hulks. We live in an age when machines, robots and microchips have retooled work, not only making our manual skills redundant but also shaming us at many cognitive[3] tasks. If we buff and shape our bodies and if we sport six-pack abs and arms the size of thighs, perhaps it is in reaction to this fear of obsolescence[4], to feel as if we can assert control when we want. Though our pumped-up muscles are the result of tremendous work performed with weights in air-conditioned gyms, they do no *useful* work. We get chiseled and ripped, we chow down and beef up, all so that the body can serve as it own billboard and so that we reassure ourselves in the mirror that the human machine is still supreme.

7   One thing machines cannot do, but humans can, is take personal risks. More people seem to be pursuing extreme sports, pushing themselves to new and dangerous levels. Triathlons, endurance races, mountain climbs, sky dives, Antarctic treks—the risk list goes on. Success is now defined by our personal best. Joshua Cooper Ramo, author of *No Visible Horizon*, is an extreme flyer— a sport that by his estimate kills 1 in 30 of its participants. Ramo describes extreme flying as "a conversation with myself about what I am capable of."

8   And what about those of us whose pastimes are more earthbound and ordinary? We play hard, long and unwisely at times, often to the point of injury. Like bodybuilders, we care about how we look, but even more we care about how playing makes us feel. Time vanishes in an activity that takes us beyond cognition, takes us into the zone, a transcendent[5] place no machine will ever enter. The universe is condensed[6] in our play.

9   How are we to view the pain that follows later? I admit there is something self-indulgent and almost narcissistic[7] in the way I apply the ice packs or in the way I massage my inflamed tendons or sink into a hot tub. Pain makes me aware of my body in a way that pain's absence never does—in that sense pain is a gift Arnold's Terminator will never know. Pain reminds me to treat the instrument better, to tape it, stretch it and cushion it. This pain from sport is delicious, even

1. **the Terminator:** a character Arnold Schwarzenegger played in films
2. **formidable:** inspiring awe, admiration, or wonder
3. **cognitive:** related to thinking or mental activity
4. **obsolescence:** state of being out of use or useless
5. **transcendent:** beyond ordinary perception
6. **condensed:** reduced; made more compact
7. **narcissistic:** loving oneself

as it is terrible. Pain allows entry into its own culture where you compare notes on a message board and where you receive advice about heel lifts, magnets, even the faith healer and the witch doctor who made tennis champion Yannick Noah's pain vanish. We wish for the pain to be gone and work hard to get rid of it. When it has disappeared, however, we are almost nostalgic for its companionship. This is the paradoxical[1] pain of exercise: pain that becomes the emblem[2] of the new virtue.*

Topic ideas: _____

_____

_____

_____

_____

_____

_____

EXERCISE 8.2   **Generating Ideas from a Photograph**

Study the photograph below. Then, on the blanks provided, write down possible essay topics that occurred to you as you looked at the image.

Source: © Jim Arbogast/Getty Images

1. paradoxical: seemingly contradictory   **2. emblem:** symbol or sign

*Source: Abraham Verghese, "Pain Gains," *New York Times Magazine,* July 27, 2003. Copyright © 2003, Abraham Verghese. Reprinted by permission.

Topic ideas:

_____

_____

_____

_____

Reading for Learning and Critical Thinking

In addition to giving us topic ideas, reading also provides us with information we can include in our own compositions. From our reading, we glean facts, examples, direct quotations, and other kinds of information that helps us develop and support our own thoughts about a subject.

Furthermore, reading exposes us to others' thoughts about important topics and leads us to reflect more on those topics. As a result, reading helps us form or confirm our own thoughts and beliefs. In other words, reading encourages us to think critically by holding what we know up to scrutiny and then deciding whether our opinions are still valid.

You do not have to agree with everything you read. Critical thinking involves considering what a writer has to say and then applying your own powers of logic and observation to decide whether those ideas are valid.

EXERCISE 8.3   **Reading for Learning and Critical Thinking**

Read the following essay and then answer the questions that follow by writing your answers on the blanks provided.

A Tale of Two Nations

By Michael Barone

1   Who has not been impressed by the American military personnel we have been seeing over these past two months? Calm, terse[1], determined, brave, confident—above all, competent, able to vanquish the enemy and spare the innocent with

1. **terse:** brief and to the point

astonishingly low casualties. And yet a few years ago most of these young men and women were typical American 18-year-olds, most of whom don't seem competent at much of anything.

2   One of the peculiar features of our country is that we produce incompetent 18-year-olds and remarkably competent 30-year-olds. Americans at 18 typically score lower on standardized tests than 18-year-olds from other advanced countries. Watch them on their first few days working at McDonald's or behind the counter in chain drugstores, and it's obvious that they don't really know how to make change or keep the line moving. But by the time Americans are 30, they are the most competent people in the world. They produce a stronger and more vibrant private-sector economy; they produce scientific and technical advances that lead the world; they provide the world's best medical care; they create the strongest and most agile military the world has ever seen. And it's not just a few meritocrats[1] at the top: American talent runs wide and deep.

3   Why? Because from the age of 6 to 18, our kids live mostly in what I call Soft America—the part of our society where there is little competition and accountability. In contrast, most Americans in the 12 years between ages 18 and 30 live mostly in Hard America—the part of American life subject to competition and accountability; the military trains under live fire. Soft America seeks to instill self-esteem. Hard America plays for keeps.

4   Soft America for a long time has been running most of our schools. Since early in the 20th century, as Diane Ravitch has shown in *Left Back*, educators have had a mistrust of testing and competition and a yearning to protect children from their rigors. Educators ban tag and dodge ball, because some kids lose. Teacher unions seek tenure[2], higher pay, and lower accountability. Parents' expectations are often low: Mom and Dad, busy working in Hard America, don't want to notice that their kids are not learning much. There are exceptions of course: many schools do a good job despite all this. But for most kids who are not on the track to the relatively few select colleges, junior high and high school are something like the Soviet system: they pretend to teach, and we pretend to learn.

5   Then at 18, kids encounter Hard America—competitive colleges and universities and community colleges, competitive private-sector employers, training institutions from McDonald's to the military. Some fall behind and don't get much of anywhere. Others seek out enclaves of Soft America—soft corners in the civil service or corporate bureaucracies. But most figure out pretty quickly that how they do depends on what they produce. They develop skills that astonish those who knew them at 18. That is what we have been seeing in the American military forces in Iraq.

1. **meritocrats:** people who have advanced because of their abilities or achievements

2. **tenure:** status of holding one's position on a permanent basis and not subject to periodic renewal of a contract

6   Soft America took over much of society because in the early and middle 20th century, America seemed to many people to be too Hard. Not many kids made it up the educational and job ladders. Much work was hard labor, and in the 1930s, jobs were scarce and charity inadequate. Educators wanted to make schools Soft, and New Dealers wanted to shield people from the marketplace with strong unions and Social Security. By the 1970s Soft America was trying to Soften Hard America with guaranteed incomes, job tenure, and comparable worth (bureaucrats, not markets, setting salaries).

7   In the 1980s and 1990s Hard America fought back. Surging private-sector growth brushed aside attempts to Soften the Hard economy. The military, hobbled[1] by public contempt after Vietnam[2], built a voluntary force in which people could gain benefits and honor by performing. Politicians started passing laws to make the people who run the schools accountable for results. A sensible society wants to keep some part of itself Soft: We don't want to subject kindergartners to the rigors of the Marine Corps or to leave old people helpless and uncared for. But a sensible society also understands—and the military has been driving home the lesson—that Soft America lives off the productivity, creativity, and competence of Hard America. And that we have the luxury of keeping part of our society Soft only if we keep most of it Hard.*

1. List two pieces of information that you learned from reading this essay.

a. _____

b. _____

2. Do you agree or disagree with the author's opinion that typical American 18-year-olds "don't seem competent at much of anything"? Why or why not?

_____

_____

_____

3. Do you agree with the author that "Soft America . . . has been running most of our schools"? Why or why not?

_____

_____

_____

1. **hobbled:** hampered in movement   2. **Vietnam:** the Vietnam War, 1954–1975

*Source: Michael Barone, "A Tale of Two Nations," *U.S. News and World Report,* May 12, 2003.
Copyright © 2003, *U.S. News & World Report,* L.P. Reprinted with permission.

4. According to the author's descriptions, are you now living in Soft America or Hard America? Explain your answer.

_____

_____

_____

Reading to Improve Writing Skills

Another benefit of reading is the opportunity to study the writing of others and find models of successful essays that can help you when you create your own documents. Thus, the more you read—especially if you read the writings of capable and talented authors—the more exposure you will get to the different ways to organize and develop a topic.

 **EXERCISE 8.4**   **Reading to Improve Writing Skills**

Read the following essay and answer the questions by writing your answers on the blanks provided.

Not All in the Family

By Steve Salerno

1 We are in my home office one night, my son and I. He's living with us again, trying to regroup after the loss and humiliation of California. There is a computer for each of us, and until moments ago, we were both intent on our respective monitors. Graig, headset on, was stringing together the digital rock music he writes in the hope of being discovered. It's the latest in a long series of attempts at validation[1] on his part; the others were undone by the bad luck that clings to him like some malevolent[2] shadow. My son, 26, has an uncanny[3] knack for getting in his own way.

1. **validation:** proof of one's worth
2. **malevolent:** evil

3. **uncanny:** eerie or unsettling

2   Right now he's taking a breather, hunched up behind me on the carpet, knees to his chest, his back braced against the futon[1]. "Look at Sophia in that picture," he says, "the one where she's just standing by herself in the pink dress."

3   They are the first words spoken in a room where for hours the only sound has been the overlapping clatter of computer keyboards. We have never been able to find much common ground. As far back as I can remember, our interactions have followed the same pattern: what few words we do speak lead quickly to arguments, then there are no words again for a long while. We even argued our way through Disneyland once when Graig was 5 or 6. My wife and I joked about it for a while. As the years passed, it seemed less funny.

4   I stop working and glance up at the picture of his daughter on the wall. I know exactly which one he means without having to search for it among the framed photos of family and extended family. I hear myself simply say, "Uh-huh." I have no idea where he's going with this. He hasn't mentioned Sophia in months.

5   Of the half-dozen pictures of Sophia I could not bring myself to box up, Graig unknowingly has singled out the one I like best. At 18 months, she stands with her chubby arms at her sides, in the shade of a large oak, amid ankle-high green grass; in her flowered dress she looks as if she sprouted there. My wife, Kathy, snapped the photo during a weeklong visit with our children, both of whom then lived in California.

6   We didn't know it that day, but it would be the last time we would see Sophia—the last time before her mother scooped the baby up one afternoon and ran out on Graig. Then, when he reported her for abducting his daughter, she played her trump card[2], admitting for the first time that my son might not be Sophia's biological father. Within a month, mismatched DNA settled the matter. At that point, Graig's ex decided that since Sophia had been the only thing binding her to Graig, she now wanted nothing more to do with any of us. Her relationship with my son, not unlike my own, had been an endless succession of quarrels. And though Kathy and I always got along well with her, she now blamed us for showing partiality[3] during the legal wrangling[4]. Just like that it was over. Legally, none of us had any further right to see Sophia if her mother didn't want us to. And she didn't want us to.

7   My fingers still poised above the keyboard, I wait for Graig to say something more. I know that Sophia is in his thoughts more than he lets on. He talks

---

1. **futon:** a thin mattress that folds to create a couch
2. **trump card:** key to winning
3. **partiality:** bias or favoritism
4. **wrangling:** quarreling; fighting

about her to his mother every once in a while. Last fall, as she and Graig drove past a store that was putting up its holiday display, he reminisced[1] about his final Christmas with his daughter—the obligatory[2] visits to Santa and how he got to show Sophia off to out-of-town friends. Kathy said his voice was tinged with a softness you hear only when he speaks of his daughter. Graig went quiet for a moment; his smile faded. "And then she went away," he said, before receding somewhere deep within himself.

8   I believe Graig had his doubts about being the baby's father all along but put them aside. (He admitted as much once in a moment of beer-induced introspection.) After barely surviving high school, seeing his sports career derailed by an injury and mourning his best friend's suspected suicide, my son must have felt Sophia was something for people to talk about besides his failures. For that, he was willing to leave the hard questions unasked.

9   Sitting there, I realize that even if I did have something to say, I probably wouldn't be able to get the words out. After a moment, Graig pulls himself to his feet and without a word leaves the room. Closing the French doors behind him, he plops on the couch, digs the remote out from between the cushions and clicks on the TV. *Monday Night Football* is on, so he settles in to watch the game. I go back to typing.

10   I had hoped that Sophia might somehow give me and Graig what had always eluded us: a chance to grow as she grew and grow to understand each other. In the meantime, maybe I could see her do something for my son I'd never been able to do in all my years of trying: make him happy. And then she went away.*

1. What was your favorite part of this essay? Why? What did the author do that made this part especially powerful or interesting to you?

_____

_____

_____

2. How does the author build suspense about what happened and why?

_____

_____

_____

1. **reminisced**: remembered   2. **obligatory**: required

*Source: Steve Salerno, "Not All in the Family," *New York Times Magazine*, Aug. 17, 2003, p. 60. Copyright © 2003. Reprinted with permission.

3. Which paragraph is especially descriptive to you? What details does the author include that help you picture in your mind what he is describing?

_____

_____

_____

4. With which individual in this story—the author, his son Graig, Graig's mother Kathy, Sophia, or Sophia's mother—do you most identify? Why? What details about that individual cause you to feel sympathetic or similar to him or her?

_____

_____

_____

5. Why does the author include himself in this story instead of just telling about what happened to Graig and Sophia? Why does he tell you about what he is doing and about his and his son's relationship?

_____

_____

_____

6. Why do you think the author titled this essay "Not All in the Family"?

_____

_____

_____

Active Reading

Obviously, reading will benefit your writing in a number of ways. But how can you get the most out of your reading to make sure you will reap all of these benefits? You must learn to become an active reader. What do active readers do that makes them more successful at comprehending and retaining information?

- Active readers do more than just run their eyes over the text in front of them.

- Active readers interact with the text and think as they read.

- Active readers read with a pen or pencil in hand, marking key words or ideas or jotting notes in the margins.

- Active readers reread the text if necessary and consciously try to connect the information in the text to their own experiences and beliefs.

The techniques that active readers use are essential to understanding and remembering ideas and information, especially those in more challenging reading selections. In the next four sections of this chapter, you will learn about some tried-and-true techniques of the active reader.

Preview the Text

The first step in reading any selection involves previewing, or surveying, the text. To *preview* means to obtain a preliminary sample of something. When you preview a reading selection, you skim, or glance over, it to try to get a sense of the piece's content and organization. You are not looking for specific details or information; instead, you skim a reading selection to get an idea of the author's subject, main point, overall focus, or purpose.

Here are some tips for previewing a text:

- To get this sense of the "big picture," you should read the title of the selection, which will usually state the subject and sometimes even indicate the main point.

- Then try to find the thesis statement, or main point, of the selection. The thesis, which is the idea the author wants you to know or to believe by the time you finish reading, usually appears somewhere near the beginning of the selection, often in the first paragraph.

- Also, glance over the headings in the selection, which function as "minititles" for the different sections. If there are no headings to guide you, read the first sentences of the paragraphs to get some idea of the topics they address.

- Read the titles of any visual aids, such as graphs or charts, that are included with the text.

- Read over any introductory material—such as a brief summary paragraph—that may offer clues about the main point of the selection.

Your goal in previewing the text is to get an overview of its topics, main idea, and overall organization. This overview will allow you to assemble a rough mental framework of the whole selection. Then, as you read more thoroughly later on, you will be able to fit the specific ideas and information into this framework as you go. You will have a better understanding of how the specific details relate to one another. As a result, your comprehension while reading will increase.

Formulate Questions and Read for Answers

A second proven active reading technique involves formulating questions and then reading for the answers to these questions. Completing this step helps to keep readers focused on finding certain kinds of information in a text, so it often improves concentration and, therefore, comprehension.

To formulate questions, simply turn the title, headings, or topic sentences of a selection into questions before you read the text. For example, if the title of a selection is "The Benefits of Exercise," you could turn it into "*What are* the benefits of exercise?" Then, as you read, you can search for the answers to that question. If the heading is "Walking Versus Jogging," you could turn it into "How are jogging and walking alike and different?" or "Which is better: walking or jogging?" If you own the text you are reading, actually write your questions in the margins. If you have borrowed the text and cannot write in it, consider making a photocopy of it and then writing your questions in the margins of that photocopy. Or you can take notes on a separate sheet of paper by writing your questions and leaving a blank space for each of the answers, which you will fill in later as you read.

Underline and Highlight Key Words and Phrases

A third tried-and-true technique for active reading is underlining and/or highlighting key words and phrases in a text with your pen or highlighter marker. This method is valuable for two reasons. First, it encourages you to look for important information while you are reading, which helps to keep you focused on the main points or information. Second, it makes a review of the information more efficient because you can scan the important words you have already identified rather than reread the entire text.

What do you highlight or underline in a text? The following is a list of information that is usually worth marking:

- Any words or phrases in distinctive typeface. If an author has put key terms in bold print or color, highlight them to make them stand out even more.

- The answers to the questions you formulated from headings or topic sentences. Read with the question in mind, and every time you discover an answer (or part of the answer), highlight it.

■ Words or phrases referring to major details that develop the idea stated in each paragraph's topic sentence. Look for and underline or highlight the main reasons, examples, or other kinds of the details provided to explain the point of the topic sentence.

The key to effective highlighting is to avoid overdoing it. Highlighting whole sentences or paragraphs is pointless, for the major ideas will not stand out when you go back to the text again later. Instead, you will end up unnecessarily re-reading long sections of the text. Also, highlighting whole passages will not help you focus on finding the most essential information. So concentrate on marking only those words that will help you quickly piece together the general gist or essence of the text when you are reviewing it later.

Take Notes on the Text

One final effective active reading technique involves taking notes. Taking notes means recording in writing the major information and ideas in a text. You might choose to take these notes in the margins of the text itself (which is called *annotating*), or in a notebook, or on separate sheets of paper.

Regardless of where you write them, notes offer two important benefits. First of all, good notes often increase comprehension of the text. Taking notes requires you to think more about what you are reading, so you wind up understanding it better. Second, writing down information and ideas helps you remember them better. For many people, taking the extra time to hand-write the main points helps implant them in the memory more securely.

Good notes always begin with highlighting or underlining main ideas or key terms. When you write notes, they might take one or more of the following forms:

■ **A list of the main ideas in all of the paragraphs.** Put these ideas in your own words and condense them whenever possible. Do not try to include all of the details, just the most important points.

■ **A summary of the chapter or article.** In your own words, write a paragraph or two to tell about the main ideas of the selection.

■ **An outline.** Outlines not only list the major and minor details of a reading selection, but they also reveal the relationships among those details. You can use a Roman numeral outline, but the notes are usually for your eyes only, so you could also adopt or create a more informal system. No matter what kind of outline you use, though, make sure it clearly demonstrates the general and specific relationships among the ideas.

The passage that follows is the first part of an article entitled "Can E-mail Be Saved from 'Spam'?" Notice how it has been annotated by a reader using many of the active reading techniques.

Can E-mail Be Saved from "Spam"?

By John Merline

1 Just about anyone who uses a computer these days knows that spam doesn't just refer to a brand of canned meat anymore. Once marketers realized they could cheaply and easily promote their products through e-mail messages, unsolicited junk e-mail—dubbed spam—started to explode. For those with e-mail accounts today, that means wading through and deleting piles of junk e-mail pitches for everything from low-interest mortgages to herbal supplements. Also spam soon may be coming in the form of text messages to a cell phone or pager near you. Both cell phones and pagers are being targeted by spammers, with unwanted junk mail accounting for almost 10% of the 1 billion text messages sent last December, according to a recent *USA Today* article. In Japan, junk mail on mobile phones is already a scourge[1], with some getting up to 30 spam messages a day, and paying for it, since cell phone companies typically charge for each text message received.

spam = unsolicited junk e-mail sent via computers, cell phones, pagers

2 The avalanche of spam may be good for marketers who find it a cheap way to reach millions of potential customers. The only real cost to the marketer is the nominal[2] one of gathering up e-mail addresses. Marketers can buy lists of about a million e-mail addresses for as little as $500.

cheap marketing tool

3 Unlike regular mail, e-mail doesn't cost anything to send, beyond the monthly service fee for Internet access. And companies like Microsoft and Yahoo offer free e-mail accounts to anyone with access to the Web. So moderate e-mail users pay the same monthly rate as aggressive e-mail users. But spam is becoming a decidedly costly annoyance to most e-mail users who receive it. And if recent trends continue, it will become an unbearable problem within a few years, if not months. Just since 2001, spam e-mail messages have grown from 7% of all e-mail sent to an estimated 51%, according to Brightmail, which tracks this trend. To get an idea of how massive the spamming industry has become, consider that America Online, the most popular online service provider, blocked an astonishing 2.4 billion pieces of spam in a single day.

spam already half of all e-mail and still growing

---

1. **scourge:** a cause of suffering   2. **nominal:** insignificantly small

Spam's Cost ?

4   Not surprisingly, <u>consumers are getting increasingly agitated[1] about spam</u>. A *USA Today*/CNN/Gallup poll taken in April found that two-thirds said they get "a lot" of spam. That compares with 37% who said so three years ago. Consumers pay <u>more in terms of time and frustration</u> spent deleting unwanted e-mail. But they <u>also pay in dollar terms</u>. Spam now costs American businesses $10 billion a year— costs that eventually get translated into higher product prices. Consumers also pay about $2 a month in higher bills for Internet service. Because <u>spam is eating up so much of the Internet traffic capacity</u>, ISPs[2] are forced to increase their capacity to transmit and receive data so they can handle the flood of junk e-mail without ad- versely[3] affecting their customers' Internet needs.

5   There are <u>other costs to consumers</u>. Much of the spam consumers receive is deceptive. According to the Federal Trade Commission, two-thirds of the spam messages it examined in a recent sampling contained <u>false information</u>. The false information ranged from phony return addresses to misleading subject lines to false claims in the text of the message. Spam may contain <u>computer viruses</u>, which can render all or parts of a computer unworkable when unleashed. And <u>spam can be used to gather information surreptitiously[4] about the recipient</u>.

6   Spam is also making it harder for legitimate businesses to reach their own customers, who in slogging through their daily spam pile are <u>more likely to delete any commercial e-mail messages</u>, even those from firms with which they have a business relationship. Worse, <u>e-mail itself as a communication tool is being harmed</u>. Imagine if every time you picked up the phone to make a call you first had to listen and delete dozens of commercial messages. Consumers would likely grow increasingly reluctant to use their phones at all.*

 **EXERCISE 8.5**   **Reading Actively**

Actively read the remainder of the article about e-mail and spam.

Finding Solutions

1   While the size and scope of the spam problem is obvious, workable solutions are much harder to come by.

2   On the one hand, private efforts should be the primary means of dealing with spam. To the extent that consumers dislike junk e-mail, ISPs will have an incentive[5] in guaranteeing their services "spam free." Those that do a better

1. **agitated:** upset
2. **ISPs:** Internet service providers
3. **adversely:** with negative consequences

4. **surreptitiously:** secretly and stealthily
5. **incentive:** something that motivates effort

Source: John Merline, "Can E-mail Be Saved from 'Spam'?" *Consumers' Research*, July 2003, pp. 10–12, 21. Reprinted by permission.

job will attract more customers. And ISPs have been trying to do this, with various spam-blocking offerings. New versions of ISP software typically boast of "new, improved" anti-spam filters. In addition, the three biggest online services—America Online, Microsoft, and Yahoo—recently announced plans to combine their anti-spam efforts. Consumers, too, have options—with varying prospects of success—in getting rid of spam on their own.

3   But spam is different from other consumer services in one important way: The spammer does not bear the full cost of his marketing campaigns. With traditional junk mail, marketers must pay the cost of printing up every copy of their solicitations[1], and pay to have them delivered by hand into mailboxes. That puts limits on the amount of junk mail delivered. Imagine, however, if traditional mail was paid for by service fees rather than postage stamps. Everybody would send more mail—especially marketers. Most likely every mailbox would be stuffed to overflowing with junk mail. In economics, these sorts of costs are "externalities." In many cases, forcing these externality costs back onto the producer requires some form of government intervention. Such actions have taken many forms. The FTC[2] has stepped up law enforcement against fraudulent spammers. Congress, meanwhile, is considering several pieces of legislation that would regulate the spam industry more strictly. But there is no guarantee that any legislative solution will be effective in eliminating the spam problem.

4   One way of addressing the "externality" issue would be simply to charge users a fee per e-mail sent, akin to the postage stamp. That would sharply raise the cost of sending millions of e-mails indiscriminately[3] to e-mailboxes, and dramatically lower the amount of spam. But there's a "first mover" problem. Since nobody charges for e-mail use today, the first to do so isn't likely to attract much business. There potentially is a way around this, by awarding bonuses to infrequent e-mail users, or by putting a toll on total use of the Internet, including e-mail, downloading music files and the like. Improvements in metering technology could make this economically feasible[4] down the road.

5   Here is the range of other options and their potential limitations:

6   **Better Technology.**   The most straightforward solution is for consumers and ISPs to deal with the problem of spam either through filtering technology or by simply deleting the unwanted e-mail. In an opinion piece written for the *Wall Street Journal*, Microsoft chairman Bill Gates explained the many steps his company, along with America Online, Yahoo and Earthlink, is taking to battle spam. Among them: coordinating efforts to find spammers who set up multiple e-mail accounts from which to launch their spam efforts; identifying messages that try to conceal the sender's identity through "spoofing" techniques; creating systems to verify senders' addresses.

---

1. **solicitations:** efforts to persuade people to buy something
2. **FTC:** Federal Trade Commission
3. **indiscriminately:** not selectively
4. **feasible:** capable of being accomplished

7   But these solutions have serious limitations. First, ISPs have so far been in a losing arms race with spammers. ISPs develop improved spam-blocking technologies only to find clever spammers quickly getting around them. The result: consumers are getting more spam than ever. On the other hand, spam filters can filter out too much. According to one study, an average 15% of wanted e-mail was blocked by spam filters at the major ISPs in the last three months of 2002. That means users must still wade into the spam pile, if only to make sure they aren't missing important e-mails.

8   Consumers can program their e-mail service to accept e-mail only from designated friends, family or businesses. But that can also mean missing important e-mail messages if they haven't programmed their e-mail software to accept them. Consumers can also set up multiple e-mail accounts, using some only for personal e-mail exchanges, and others more widely for commercial activities, chat-room exchanges, and the like. The problem with this approach comes in the complexity that juggling all these accounts can create. In any case, why should consumers, who don't want the junk mail, bear the burden of getting rid of it?

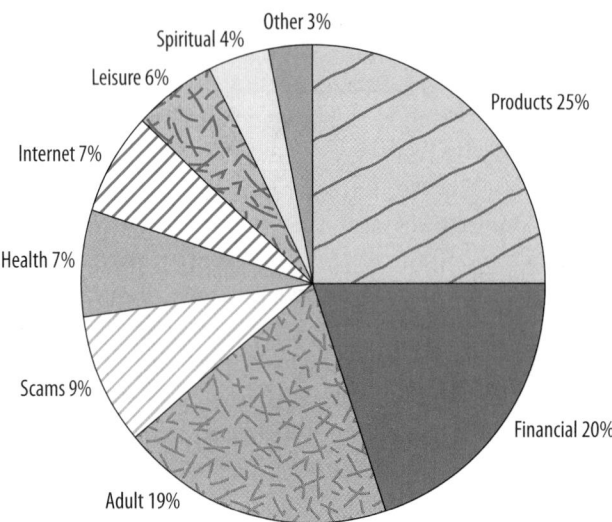

Types of Spam

- Other 3%
- Spiritual 4%
- Leisure 6%
- Internet 7%
- Health 7%
- Scams 9%
- Adult 19%
- Products 25%
- Financial 20%

9   **Tighter Regulations.** Sen. Conrad Burns (R-Mont.) and Sen. Ron Wyden (D-Ore.) earlier this year introduced legislation, called "CAN-SPAM," which would, among other things, require all junk e-mail to have a valid return e-mail

address so recipients can be asked to be removed from future mailings. A mailer who continued to send messages to those e-mail accounts could be fined $10 for each message.

10   Other reform ideas lawmakers have proposed:

- Set up a national "do not e-mail" list. Under such a plan, consumers who didn't want to receive any junk e-mail would put their accounts on the list, and direct marketers would then be forbidden from e-mailing to them. Violators would be fined. The FTC recently started up a similar "do not call" list for those who don't want to be bothered at home by phone solicitations. So far, the service has been hugely popular, with consumers putting more than 10 million phone numbers on the list. The Senate Commerce Committee approved a "Do Not Spam" bill in June.

- Require mass e-mailers to put the letters "ADV"—which stands for "advertisement"—in the subject line of their messages. That would make it easier for consumers and ISPs to block the messages.

- Create a regulatory "safe harbor" for those who follow industry best practices. Any commercial e-mailer who complies with a check-list on sending spam would be exempt from fines and other regulations.

As with technology solutions, these approaches have their limits, not least of which is compliance[1]. Many spammers already are breaking the law. The FTC survey found that just 2% of spam included the "ADV" notification, which means most of it was operating outside the laws of the states that have already passed that requirement. Another concern is that putting regulations on what constitutes legal spam could backfire, resulting in far more spam than exists today. The reason is that if companies know the legal boundaries for sending junk e-mail, more of them might do it. And it wouldn't take much to overwhelm e-mailboxes completely.

11   **Legal Action.** In April, the Federal Trade Commission went to court to shut down a deceptive e-mail scheme that was luring people to pornographic web sites. It was, the FTC said, the first case of targeting junk e-mail for putting deceptive information in the subject line of the e-mail message. Also in April, America Online filed five lawsuits targeting spammers that, the company said, were responsible for 1 billion junk e-mail messages to its members. In May, Virginia toughened its anti-spam laws to include criminal penalties for violations.

12   A problem with litigation[2] is that courts move slowly, and law enforcement generally has other priorities than spam. That means enforcement might not be

---

1. **compliance:** acting in accordance with someone's rules, requests, or wishes

2. **litigation:** legal proceedings

there to back up any new stiff anti-spam penalties. And if spammers don't have to worry about getting caught, the penalties likely won't act as much of a deterrent[1].

13 **Ban It.**   The most straightforward solution is an outright ban on junk e-mail. Under such a plan, sending unsolicited e-mail would be illegal, punishable by fines. Consumers who receive unwanted mail also could file in small claims court. Congress has already been down this road. In the late 1980s, when fax machines were the new communications technology, marketers had similarly realized how cheap and easy it was to advertise by blast-faxing large numbers of fax machines. The problem was, as with spam, that senders had to bear little of the cost of their advertising campaign. The sender just had to print up one copy of his ad. Fax owners, meanwhile, found that their fax machines were continually clogged with unwanted junk faxes, which ate up paper and toner supplies as well.

14   In the early 1990s, Congress passed a law that banned the practice of sending commercial faxes to anyone who hadn't specifically requested them. The result was that the problem pretty much disappeared. This spring, the U.S. Court of Appeals for the Eighth Circuit ruled that the law was constitutional, saying it didn't violate advertisers' First Amendment rights. The court made an interesting observation, which is relevant to the current spam debate: "It was not unreasonable for Congress to choose a system that protects those who would otherwise be forced to bear unwanted burdens over those who wish to send and receive unsolicited fax advertising."

15   The problem with an outright ban, like the weaknesses of other solutions, is that while it would effectively eliminate most legitimate forms of spam, it would likely have little impact on those spammers already breaking the law by using phony return addresses or other fraudulent means to get recipients to open up the messages.

16   In the end, some combination of all these approaches may be needed. With the growth of spam, e-mail itself, which has been an incredibly valuable communications tool, is becoming more of a headache than a help. Left unchecked, spam could make cell phones and pagers equally aggravating.*

Critical Reading

Critical reading does not mean reading to criticize or find fault with a text. Instead, *critical reading* is the process of determining whether or not a text is valid and then deciding whether or not you agree with the ideas presented.

1. **deterrent:** something that discourages action

Source: John Merline, "Can E-mail Be Saved from 'Spam'?" *Consumers' Research,* July 2003, pp. 10–12, 21. Reprinted by permission.

The ultimate goal of critical reading is critical thinking, an important skill in all areas of life, not just in your academic courses. Critical thinkers do not just believe everything they hear or read. Instead, they approach new ideas and information with a healthy skepticism. They have learned how to analyze texts and ideas not only to understand them better but also to decide whether they should accept those ideas, reject them, or think about them further. College students, in particular, are expected to read critically. Professors assign textbook chapters, journal articles, and other readings not just to have you memorize facts but also to encourage you to think about the texts so you can expand and refine your ideas.

Critical reading, of course, begins with active reading. In order to evaluate an author's ideas or information, you need to completely understand them, and practicing the active reading techniques will increase your comprehension of the material. After actively reading a text, a critical reader thinks in depth about what he or she has read. Thinking critically about a reading selection involves all of the following:

- Evaluating the evidence given in support of the thesis and main idea. Does it seem to be adequate? Does it seem to be accurate?

- Scrutinizing the author's conclusions. Do they arise logically from the evidence presented? Does the author exhibit any bias—in other words, does he or she obviously have certain opinions or prejudices?

- Comparing the ideas and information to your own experiences and observations.

- Agreeing or disagreeing with the author after doing all of the preceding.

To assist critical reading and thinking, you can engage in several activities:

- As you read, you can **annotate,** or write brief comments in the margin of the text. These comments can include your reactions to specific points or details and your questions about those points and details. They can take the form of words or phrases (such as *True, Seems exaggerated*, and so on) or even symbols (such as writing an exclamation point next to a sentence that surprises you or writing a question mark in the margin when you are confused). Annotation is a valuable skill for critical thinking because it can become a kind of dialogue between you and the author as the author tries to convince you to accept his or her ideas.

- You can also **answer the questions** that may follow a text. In textbooks, in particular, authors provide a list of questions that help you focus on the most important information or even begin to apply the information to your own life. Even if your instructor does not assign these questions, think about how you would answer them.

■ Finally, you can **discuss the text with others.** Participate in class discussions about reading selections, and suggest to your classmates that you discuss texts more informally as well. By talking about what you read with others, you will confirm your understanding of the text. Also, you will get the opportunity to compare your reactions to the thoughts of other critical readers. These conversations will help all of you decide whether the text is valid.

The following passage has been annotated to show how one writer responded to a text.

Encourage Organ Donors with a Little Quid Pro Quo[1]

By Lawrence W. Reed

1   Before you read tomorrow's newspaper, 16 Americans probably will die waiting for a heart, kidney, lung or another body organ—a daily death toll that adds up to about 6,000 a year. The time is long overdue to supplement the charitable impulse to donate organs with some financial incentives[2]—and, in fact, there are signs that Congress and expert opinion may be warming to the idea.

interesting idea

2   The organ problem does not stem from a shortage of people dying with harvestable organs. It's that too few of them—less than 30%—ever consented to donating and that the families of half of all potential donors refuse donor consent, even in many cases when that means they are vetoing[3] the wishes of the deceased.

I wonder why most people do not donate

3   At an Orlando conference in 2003, donor experts agreed to promote "donor authorization," which would allow organs to be harvested if the deceased had signed donor cards, even if their families disapprove. If widely adopted, that would modestly alleviate[4] the crisis—but still leave us with needless deaths among potential organ recipients.

I agree— donor's wishes should be followed

4   More than simple goodwill is required to increase organ donations. Incentives—financial and otherwise—do matter; the lack of them is a major reason for the current widespread shortages. Today's system relies on little more than altruism.[5] Leave your organs for others because it's a good thing to do. Admirable—but far more in life gets done because of a little self-interest.

I disagree— people choose not to donate for other reasons (fear, religion)

1. **quid pro quo:** an equal exchange
2. **incentives:** rewards or punishments that motivate behaviors
3. **vetoing:** rejecting
4. **alleviate:** lessen the severity of something
5. **altruism:** unselfish concern for the welfare of others

Some people are repulsed[1] by the thought of a true, unrestricted "market" in organs, but there are more modest ways to employ the incentives and self-interest that make free markets so remarkably productive.

A new death benefit

5 Some think the government should be involved, but there's no need to use tax dollars. Instead, we need to think creatively. Richard DeVos, co-founder of Amway Corp. (now Alticor) and a heart-transplant recipient, champions an insurance-like incentive plan: An individual would sign a legal document promising to donate his or her organs if an accident or illness rendered the individual brain-dead (that avoids the risk of healthy people trying to donate organs for profit). If the individual's organs are donated, $10,000 would be paid to a person of the donor's choice. As DeVos testified to Congress in May, insurers probably would gladly pay the $10,000, because each patient taken off the organ-transplant list saves them hundreds of thousands of dollars. Congress, however, would have to amend or repeal[2] a 1984 law that makes such arrangements illegal.

interesting idea, but $10,000 is not very much

donor still does not get the money

why are they illegal?

Unethical payments?

6 Other hurdles exist. The National Kidney Foundation is among the national organizations that strongly oppose any efforts in this direction as unethical. "There is no way to do this and maintain our values as a society," said its chairman, Andrew Baur. But to many others, voluntary measures that allow for modest compensation under careful guidelines could save many lives without doing violence to ethical concerns.

I agree — it seems unethical to sell body parts

7 The American Medical Association and the American Society of Transplant Surgeons have called for Congress to authorize tests of financial incentives to see whether they increase organ donations. So has the United Network for Organ Sharing, which operates the national organ distribution system. A bipartisan[3] group of senators, including [former] Majority Leader William Frist, R-Tenn., have proposed allowing such trials.

8 A new non-profit network of organ donors, LifeSharers, is working to increase the organ supply by putting incentives to work now. LifeSharers' members direct that their organs first be offered to other members. Non-members can have a member's organs if no member can use them when they become available. As LifeSharers grows (people can join at no charge at www.lifesharers.com), so does the incentive to become a registered donor: equal access to an ever-larger

this idea is better — agree to donate your organs in case you yourself need one some day

1. **repulsed:** disgusted
2. **repeal:** withdraw; eliminate
3. **bipartisan:** consisting of both major political parties

pool of donated organs. That will also make the system fairer, because your chances of receiving an organ will be greater if you've agreed to be a donor.

9   The 16 Americans who likely died in the past day as they waited in vain for a donor's gift are all the reason this country needs to explore new, incentive-based approaches to organ donations.*

 **EXERCISE 8.6**   **Reading Critically**

Actively read the following passage and then answer the questions that follow by writing your answers on the blanks provided.

Student Problems Begin at Home: Public Schools Struggle to Fulfill Rearing Roles Abandoned by Parents

By Nick Jans

1   It's the start of another school year with those first magical weeks of classes, when each student is eager and everything seems possible.

2   But for me this year is different. Though I've been a teacher since 1977, this September school is going on without me. These first months of retirement should be, I suppose, a time to reflect proudly on what I've accomplished and perhaps even to wax a bit nostalgic. Instead, I find myself tired and troubled, overcome by the notion that I've escaped rather than retired.

3   Over the years that I taught both junior and senior high, there's been a notable decline in the quality of our schools. Standardized test scores have diminished; college professors complain that high school graduates—some of them straight-A valedictorians[1]—are incapable of writing a decent paragraph.

4   Of course, the issue is well publicized. Countless studies and dollars have been focused on poor public school performance and how to address it. The two-year-old No Child Left Behind Act is merely the latest and most elaborate fix offered in a quarter century of handwringing, finger-pointing and pontificating[2].

5   Unfortunately, most of that time, the effort and money have been wasted, bypassing the issue's true heart. There is something terribly wrong with our

1. **valedictorians:** students who graduated at the top of their classes

2. **pontificating:** expressing opinions or judgments

Source: "Encourage Organ Donors with a Little Quid Pro Quo," by Lawrence W. Reed, *USA Today,* July 24, 2003, p. 13A. Reprinted by permission of the author. Lawrence W. Reed is the president of the Mackinac Center for Public Policy in Midland, Michigan.

schools, but it has nothing to do with the quality of teachers, the curricula or textbooks—or even how much money we spend. The problem is far simpler and more ominous[1]: the students themselves.

6   This opinion is common among teachers who've served double-digit years in the trenches. Kids these days ain't what they used to be. I know that rant has been popular since the time of the Romans. But these children are different from those of just two decades ago—not in raw ability, but in their essential attitudes and readiness to learn. If I had a hundred bucks for every time a student cheated on a test, or had the nerve to tell me, in the middle of an impassioned lecture, that my presentation was "boring," I could be driving a new car.

7   I'd suspect I was at fault, except that teacher friends of mine from Michigan to California to Alaska (where I taught) have similar stories.

8   Of course there are many wonderful students. But today's kids, as a group, just don't buy into the entire adult-run institution that is modern public education. Caught up in the narcissistic[2] values of hip-hop, immersed in ultra-violent video and computer games, casually and brazenly[3] sexual, these kids consider themselves grown and independent by age 14, in no need of further guidance.

9   Consider, for example, an April study by Jupiter Research indicating that 95% of teenage boys and 67% of teen girls regularly play video games—including the best-selling *Grand Theft Auto*, where players gain points by murdering cops and beating prostitutes to death with bats.

10   At the same time, a national survey in *Education Week* found that 74% of students admitted to engaging in "serious" cheating during the past year. Is it any wonder that a 2000 Gallup poll cited education and a decline in ethics as the two most serious problems facing our country?

11   If we consider that the main function of schooling is to socialize tomorrow's citizens and acclimate[4] them to our values, America is in big trouble. Schools, after all, mirror society; the shortcomings of the former are inextricably[5] tied to the latter's failings. Blaming teachers because your kid can't read makes as much sense as blaming the dentist for a mouthful of cavities.

12   So if not the schools' fault, whose?

13   The music, movies and computer games are just symptoms. The fault lies squarely in the failures of the home, and in the disintegration of the traditional family. For many reasons—dual incomes, divorce, separation and more— quality face time between parent and child has shriveled. Schools struggle to take its place.

1. **ominous:** threatening
2. **narcissistic:** showing love of oneself
3. **brazenly:** boldly
4. **acclimate:** get used to something
5. **inextricably:** incapable of being separated

14   Today, our public schools are expected to provide (in addition to academic instruction) up to two meals a day, homework help, daycare, entertainment, a sense of well-being and a basic respect for society and its laws.

15   Not so long ago—certainly in the supposedly turbulent[1] 1960s and early '70s, when I was in school—everyone assumed these were the home's provinces. Yet while today's parents have abdicated[2] these basic responsibilities, they become incensed if a school disciplines their child for an issue as basic as academic dishonesty or cussing out a teacher. And, according to the National Center for Education Statistics, parent satisfaction with secondary schools continues to decline.

16   Am I just another buck-passer? I sincerely hope not. I agree that our public school system bears responsibility for instructing our children. I believe it faces that task head on. U.S. schools are, in most respects, the best they've ever been. Ho-hum books and hands-off approaches disappeared decades ago. Educational theory has become a well-honed science, and new strides are being made and applied daily.

17   Compare the schools of today with the first public schools in Puritan New England, when students of all levels sat on rock-hard benches in a single classroom, copying on slates and memorizing passages from dog-eared copies of the classics. The teacher received little respect in the community, and was paid accordingly. Yet no one complained about the failings of the system, and literacy rates were arguably the highest in the world. The difference then was that the home was doing its job.

18   Today we indeed face a crisis in education. The stakes are just as enormous, the outcome just as uncertain, as those in the war on terrorism. Our society's very fiber is being tested.

19   While it's up to our schools to continue to improve, it's also time for parents to take back the responsibility of raising and educating their own children. It's simple, actually: Read to them. Play catch with them. Discipline them. Discuss and model ethical behavior. According to the National Center for Education Statistics, "research supports the belief that high-quality education cannot be successfully accomplished without the active involvement of parents."

20   Help does indeed start in the home.*

1. What is the thesis of this selection? Express this idea in your own words.

_____

_____

1. turbulent: violently disturbed   **2. abdicated:** gave up power or responsibility

*Source: "Student Problems Begin at Home: Public Schools Struggle to Fulfill Rearing Roles Abandoned by Parents," by Nick Jans, USA Today, September 2, 2003, p. 11A. Reprinted by permission of the author.

2. Does the author provide adequate and accurate support for this thesis? List the evidence that the author includes and decide whether it is adequate and accurate.

_____

_____

_____

_____

3. Does the author exhibit any bias? If so, where?

_____

_____

_____

_____

4. Do you agree or disagree with the author's assertions about today's students? Why?

_____

_____

_____

_____

5. Compare the author's ideas and information about today's students, schools, and education, in general, with your own experiences.

_____

_____

_____

_____

Keeping a Reading Journal

A reading journal is a notebook in which you record your responses to what you read. This can be a very valuable tool for improving reading comprehension, for stimulating critical thinking, and for generating ideas for your own papers. Responding in writing also helps to clarify what you have learned about the topic and to identify what you still need to find out. Often, you do not really know exactly what you think about a topic until you sit down and try to put your ideas into words. The act of finding language for your thoughts helps you understand what you know and what you believe about the topic, especially those topics with which you are unfamiliar.

A reading journal can contain a number of different kinds of reactions, but the following are all particularly effective:

- A summary of what you learned

- Your feelings about the ideas or information

- The reasons why you agree or disagree with the author

- An explanation of how your own experiences either support or disprove the information

- Questions you have about the information

- A comparison of the information with other authors' writings on the topic

As an example, read the following passage, and then read one student's reading journal entry about this passage.

Parenting for the Long Haul: Success in High School May Not Carry into Adulthood

By Anne Becker

1 Parents aren't necessarily in the clear when their children walk across the stage to claim their high school diplomas, according to a study by the University of Michigan's Institute for Social Research.

2 About 20 percent of students who were doing well as high school seniors were not meeting their stated—or expected—goals at age 26, according to a study called Monitoring the Future.

3 "What's scary is that it's unpredictable," says John Schulenberg, Ph.D., professor of developmental psychology at the University of Michigan in Ann Arbor, and the study's lead researcher. "We used to think that if things were going well in high school, they'd continue to go well."

4 The ongoing study analyzed data from more than 2,900 young people initially surveyed as 18-year-old high school seniors, and again at ages 21 to 22, and 25 to 26, to assess whether respondents were thriving in key developmental areas.

5   By age 26, the study showed 29 percent were not financially independent, which they defined as supporting themselves alone or with the help of a spouse. Another 21 percent had strayed from previously stated educational goals, which included graduating from two-year or four-year colleges.

6   Transitioning to adulthood may be more difficult in the U.S., says Schulenberg. American youths lack institutional structures such as apprenticeship programs, which guide young Europeans in their careers. But there is a flip side to the U.S. story: many young adults who feel stifled and unhappy in high school thrive on their new freedom and responsibility after graduation, according to Schulenberg.

7   The study did not track how parental influence affected post–high school success.*

How 26-Year-Olds Are Doing

Area of Life	Thriving	Surviving	Floundering[1]
Education	43%	36%	21%
Employment	28%	58%	14%
Financial independence	41%	29%	29%

Source: University of Michigan Institute for Social Research

Here is one student's response to this article:

> Anne Becker's article "Parenting for the Long Haul" states that even though students might do well in high school, they may not continue to do well in school or life. The author supports her thesis with statistics from a study. By age twenty-six, 29 percent of students in a given study were not financially independent, and 21 percent had not met their educational goals. One expert says that making the transition

1. **floundering:** struggling

Source: Anne Becker, "Parenting for the Long Haul: Success in High School May Not Carry into Adulthood," *Psychology Today,* May-June 2003. Reprinted with permission from *Psychology Today* magazine, copyright © 2003, Sussex Publishers, Inc.

to adulthood may be more difficult in the U.S. because our country does not have apprenticeship programs, which Europe has. But many American students think that they have more freedom when they graduate from high school. I disagree with some of the material presented because all of my friends and I are very committed to getting our degrees and moving out of our houses as soon as possible. Financial independence will not be a problem because many of us have thought about getting good jobs, setting up apartments with roommates and making plans for the future. It is hard for me to believe that almost one-third of the students surveyed have trouble achieving financial independence, based on what I know about me and my friends.

When you write, you continue to think, which leads to new insights. As a result, compositions are a common college assignment, for professors know that writing helps students learn more. Use the power of writing, then, to get more out of what you read.

 **EXERCISE 8.7**   **Writing Reading Journal Entries**

On your own paper, write a reading journal entry for each of the following reading selections in this chapter:

"Pain Gains" (pages 161–164)
"A Tale of Two Nations" (pages 165–167)
"Not All in the Family" (pages 168–170)
"Can E-mail Be Saved from 'Spam'?" (pages 175–180)

In the next eleven chapters, you will be examining the different modes for arranging ideas in paragraphs and essays. Each of these chapters will include readings that will give you ideas for compositions of your own and that will stimulate your critical thinking. Part III of this text, too, includes a variety of longer reading selections that will provide you with more topic ideas.

An Introduction to Research

As you write paragraphs and essays of your own, you will often need to find information from other sources to develop or to prove your ideas and opinions on a subject. This information may take the form of facts, statistics, examples, expert testimony, or the observations of others. To find what you need, you will have to conduct research, usually in a library or via the Internet. To help you improve your skills in researching, managing information, and incorporating source materials into your own writing, the remaining chapters in this book contain *Focus on Research* boxes like this one. Each of these boxes will explain and illustrate procedures and techniques for locating source information and integrating it smoothly into your compositions.

When you are deciding whether or not you need information from other sources to support your ideas, you can use the first three steps of the writing process as both guides and stepping-stones. In Step 1, the prewriting stage, for example, as you generate ideas for your composition, you will probably get a sense of not only what you *do* know about a topic but also what you *do not* know and need to find out. At this stage of the process, after you have decided upon a tentative main idea statement, you can probably jot down a list of information that you are going to need to acquire through research. Turn this into a "shopping list" that you can take to the library or to a computer, and check off each item once you have found it.

In Step 2 of the writing process, when you are organizing your ideas, do not forget to account for source material in your outline. Under the appropriate outline heading, list the facts or other kinds of information you plan to use in that particular paragraph or section. And think again about each point you want to make so that you can decide whether any additional source material might help you make that point clearer for your readers.

Finally, in Step 3, take a careful look at the paragraphs you have written. Are there ideas that could be made clearer or supported more strongly with facts, statistics, examples, observations, or expert opinions? Evaluate your layers of development, especially in shorter paragraphs, and decide whether you should find more information to bolster your point.

CHAPTER 8 REVIEW

Fill in the blanks in the following statements.

1. Along with your own experiences in life, television or films, or your discussions with other people, _____ can provide a springboard of ideas for your own compositions.

2. _____ involves considering what a writer has to say and then applying your own powers of logic and observation to decide whether those ideas are valid.

3. _____ participate in their reading by interacting with the text and by thinking as they read.

4. To _____ means to obtain a preliminary sample of something. When you do this, you skim, or glance over, a reading selection to get a sense of the piece's content and organization.

5. To formulate _____ about a reading selection, turn the title, headings, or topic sentences into questions before you read the text.

6. When you _____ key words and phrases in a text, it encourages you to look for important information while you are reading, which helps you stay focused on the main points or information.

7. _____ means recording in writing the major information and ideas in a text.

8. _____ is the process of determining whether or not a text is valid and then deciding whether or not you agree with the ideas presented.

9. A _____ is a notebook in which you record your responses to what you read.

WebWork

Go to the site **www.criticalreading.com** and review "Critical Reading: The Steps," "Principles of Critical Reading," and any other links that the author provides. Using your critical reading and thinking skills, evaluate this site. Do you detect any bias in the author's presentation of this material? Is the material adequately and accurately supported? Why or why not? How do you think this site could be improved, if at all?

Online Study Center   For more on the reading/writing connection, go to the Houghton Mifflin Online Study Center for this book, at **http://www.college.hmco.com/pic/dolphinwritertwo**.

Narration

GOALS FOR CHAPTER 9

▶ Define the term *narration*.

▶ Describe the steps in writing a narrative paragraph.

▶ Write a narrative paragraph.

▶ Recognize the features of longer narratives.

In Chapter 4 of this book, you practiced developing the main idea of a paragraph or essay with various kinds of information and examples. In the next eleven chapters (Chapters 9–19), you will look more closely at different patterns, or modes, that will help you organize your development of your topic sentence or thesis. You will begin in this chapter with the narrative mode of development.

Writing a Narrative Paragraph

You probably use **narration,** or storytelling, fairly often. You tell stories to your friends and your family members about the things that happen to you, and you also tell stories you have heard about other people's experiences. As a writer, you will need to be able to tell a good story in order to develop some point or idea. Sometimes the story will be something that happened to you. At other times, you will tell a story that happened to someone else. In either case, though, you will need to incorporate some features that are common to all effective narratives. These essential features are discussed in the following sections of this chapter.

Determining a Main Idea and Writing a Topic Sentence

The first step in writing an effective narrative paragraph involves deciding on the point you want to make about the events you will relate. As you look at the

193

details you generated during the prewriting stage, ask yourself *why* you want to tell the story. Is there some moral or lesson to be gained from hearing the story? Does the story illustrate some truth about your life or the lives of everyone? Do you want to help readers learn something, or do you want to entertain them? These questions will help you decide on the one main idea you would like your readers to know or to accept. Then write a topic sentence that states this main idea.

For an example, look at a brainstorming sample generated by a student who was assigned to write about a time she stood up for herself.

> – skinny 4th grader
> – picked on, bullied by a 5th grader named George
> – he would make me give him things from my lunch
> – he would laugh at me and tell me I was "ugly" and "scrawny"
> – I would cry and run
> – One day I just got really mad
> – I screamed at him to leave me alone
> – I was crying and red-faced—I just exploded
> – I must have scared him
> – He left me alone from then on, ignoring me as though I was invisible
>   from then on

After completing this brainstorming, the student decided that she wanted to entertain readers with her story about the time she stood up to the schoolyard bully. She wrote this topic sentence:

> I stood up for myself when I insisted that a bully stop tormenting me.

As you complete this step in the process, remember what you learned in Chapter 4 about topic sentences. A topic sentence does not always have to be the first sentence of a paragraph. It may be more appropriate to save it for last or to put it in the middle of the paragraph.

✦ EXERCISE 9.1   Writing Topic Sentences for Narratives

For each of the following topics, use some prewriting techniques to generate ideas for your own paper, and then write a topic sentence you could use for a narrative paragraph.

1. A time I learned something about myself

Topic Sentence: _____

2. An occasion when I felt like an outcast

Topic Sentence: _____

3. An important first day (of work, school, camp, and so on)

Topic Sentence: _____

4. An amazing or extraordinary event I witnessed or experienced

Topic Sentence: _____

5. An important event experienced by someone I know

Topic Sentence: _____

Selecting the Right Details for a Narrative

The next step toward writing an interesting narrative paragraph is selecting the right details to include. You cannot include everything that happened or every little detail because the finished product would be too tedious to read and your point could get lost in irrelevant information. Therefore, you will have to examine your prewriting and decide which pieces of information are essential to your narrative. You will, of course, need to include all of the major, important events, so make sure you circle those events in your prewriting. Then you will need to think about the minor events in the story, evaluating each one in terms of the main idea you want to express. If a minor event does not directly relate to your main idea, you will probably want to leave it out because providing unnecessary information slows down your story and makes it less interesting. Finally, you will need to consider the details of the events you will include and omit information that is not essential to the story.

For some practice in selecting details, look back at the student's brainstorming about standing up to a bully (page 194). Put check marks next to details in the following list that seem important to understanding what happened.

_____ The clothes the writer was wearing the day she screamed at the bully
_____ The names the bully called the writer
_____ The writer's statements to the bully
_____ The weather on the day the writer screamed at the bully
_____ The bully's behavior after the writer screamed at him
_____ A physical description of the bully
_____ The names of the bully's friends

You should have checked the second, third, fifth, and sixth items in this list. Knowing about the writer's clothing, the weather, and the names of the bully's friends is not essential to understanding the story. The other pieces of information, however, are important in helping readers see what happened and why.

 **EXERCISE 9.2**   **Selecting Details for Narratives**

Choose one of the topic sentences you wrote for Exercise 9.1, and list the major, important events that you would definitely need to include if you developed that statement in a narrative paragraph.

Organizing Details and Using Transitions

Of all the modes for writing, narratives tend to be among the easiest to organize. As a matter of fact, narratives are naturally organizing because the events are almost always presented in chronological, or time, order. Of course, writers can move around in time as they tell their stories. In a flashback, for instance, a writer can take readers back to the past for a while before returning to the present to move the story forward again. However, the events in most narrative paragraphs are simply told in the order in which they occurred. Preparing the outline, then, is usually just a matter of listing the important events in order, from beginning to end.

To help the reader understand the time frame of the events, writers include transitional words and phrases. The following list includes some common time-related transitional expressions:

first, second, third	next	as
before	soon	when
now	in the beginning	until
then	once	later
after	today	eventually
while	previously	last
finally	often	meanwhile
over time	during	
in the end	in, on, or by (followed by a date)	

In addition, writers include information about the passage of time, usually in short phrases or statements such as *in a few hours* or *two weeks went by* or with specific dates. Notice how the writer of the following paragraph uses both time-related transitional words and information about how much time has passed to help you follow the events in the story.

> **Not long ago** I was in a popular local coffeehouse and noticed a spill near the entrance. **When** I brought it to the attention of the idle clerk, she shouted in the direction of the kitchen for assistance. **Minutes passed,** the clerk continued to dawdle[1], and the spill went untended. **Finally,** I decided to dab it up with some napkins. But **before** I could start, the clerk called me off with, "Oh, don't worry about that. We'll take care of it." **Then** she barked toward the kitchen again for "a hand out here." **Eventually** a sweaty and bedraggled[2] figure emerged with a mop large enough to tar a roof. With one deft[3] swab, he made the pool vanish. But he couldn't conceal his annoyance with the impassive[4] clerk. **As** he returned to the kitchen he hurled some uncharitable[5] remark her way. "Well, that's not *my* job!" she fired back. I couldn't help wondering whether she thought general neatness and safety were her job, not to mention protecting the business against lawsuits. (Vincent Barry, "It's Not in My Job Description," in Michelle Christopherson, *Growing Ideas* [Boston: Houghton Mifflin, 2001], p. 137.)

EXERCISE 9.3 **Organizing Events in Narratives**

On your own paper, prewrite to generate ideas, and then complete each of the following topic sentences by filling in the blank. Then, on the other blanks provided, prepare an informal outline by listing the major events of the story in the order in which they occurred.

1. I had never been so afraid as when I _____ .

_____

_____

_____

_____

_____

1. **dawdle:** waste time
2. **bedraggled:** dirty and rumpled
3. **deft:** quick and skillful
4. **impassive:** revealing no emotion
5. **uncharitable:** intolerant; judgmental

2. _____ was a very frustrating experience for me.

_____

_____

_____

_____

_____

3. I was extremely angry when _____.

_____

_____

_____

_____

EXERCISE 9.4   **Recognizing Narrative Transitions**

Circle all of the transitional words and time-related information in the following paragraph.

> When I was three years old, I learned how to swim in a lake called Snow Pond, in Maine, where my mother's father had taught her to swim. I swam there in the summer, and the rest of the year I took lessons in an indoor heated pool. I started entering swim meets a couple of years later, but it wasn't until my family moved to California, in 1969, and I participated in a race in the Pacific that I realized how much I loved swimming in open water. In August, 1971, when I was fourteen years old, I swam twenty-seven miles, from Catalina Island, in Southern California, across the Catalina Channel to the mainland. The swim took twelve hours and thirty-six minutes, and, as I touched the shore, I knew that I wanted to swim the English Channel, the Mount Everest[1] of distance swimming. (Excerpted from Lynne Cox, "Swimming to Antarctica," *The New Yorker*, February 3, 2003, pp. 66–67.)

EXERCISE 9.5   **Writing a Narrative Paragraph That Includes Transitions**

Choose one of the topic sentences and outlines you prepared in Exercise 9.3. Write the paragraph, including transitions that indicate the time frame of the events.

1. **Mount Everest:** tallest mountain on Earth

Using Vivid Language

Using vivid and interesting language is important in all types of writing. However, it is especially important in narrative writing, in which your goal is to enable readers to picture people and events in their minds. There are three kinds of vivid language that will help you re-create experiences in words.

Specific Words

You will create more vivid mental images for your readers if you choose specific words over more general ones. For example, the word *dance* is a relatively general term that includes many different kinds of dancing. So to help your readers picture the scene more clearly, substitute a more specific word, such as *waltz* or *moonwalk*. Instead of writing *magazine*, write *Reader's Digest*; instead of writing *martial art*, write *karate*; and so on. The more precise your word choice, the sharper the picture becomes in the mind's eye of your readers.

Factual and Sensory Details

Like specific words, factual and sensory details will create more vivid mental images for your reader. **Factual details** offer information such as names, quantities, dates, and dimensions (height, length, width, weight). So in describing your own or someone else's actions, you might want to specify when and where these actions took place as well as how long they lasted. **Sensory details** provide information about what something looks, smells, tastes, sounds, or feels like. When you write narratives, include information about the sights, sounds, and other sensations one could experience in the scenes you are re-creating in words.

One special type of factual detail in narratives is dialogue. **Dialogue** is the exact statements of the participants, enclosed in quotation marks. Consider including the exact words of the people in your story because dialogue assists readers in picturing exactly what happened.

Action-Oriented Verbs

In narratives, especially, you will want to use action-packed verbs to describe the events and the participants' behaviors. So instead of writing *Bob entered the room*, write *Bob strolled into the room*, wording which provides more of a mental picture of *how* he entered. Also, choose verbs that offer the most precise explanation of what happened. For example, instead of writing that Joe *spoke*, you might want to say that Joe *shouted* or *whispered*. The more specific the verb, the easier it is for readers to picture what happened.

EXERCISE 9.6   Writing with Vivid Language

Rewrite each of the following sentences to substitute more specific words, to add factual and sensory details, and to use more action-oriented verbs.

1. The person moved across the area.

_____

2. That individual was helpful to me.

_____

3. The animal did an amazing trick.

_____

4. The task was difficult.

_____

5. The people left the scene as rapidly as they could.

_____

Writing Longer Narratives and Narrative Essays

So far, this chapter has focused only on narrative paragraphs. However, a narrative may need several paragraphs for development. For example, read the following story:

> [A gang known as] the "Dukes," unknown to us, had terrorized all the shopkeepers in the area. In order to be able to stay in business without being harassed[1] by vandalism[2], shoplifting, out and out robberies, and, in certain cases, beatings, [shopkeepers paid] the Dukes . . . whatever [the gang] felt the traffic could bear. In their opinion, we were to be no exception.
>
> One day three of the young men swaggered[3] into the store. At the time, my husband was in the cellar arranging a shipment of merchandise that had just arrived, and I, expecting him momentarily, was preparing a sandwich which was

1. **harassed:** irritated or tormented
2. **vandalism:** destruction of property

3. **swaggered:** walked arrogantly; strutted

to be my lunch. As I glanced up, I saw one of them quickly grab some Hostess Cupcakes and put them in his pocket; another leaned against the fruit bin which was immediately minus an apple. Such was my naiveté[1] that I firmly believed the only reason anyone stole food was hunger. My heart broke and at the same time opened and embraced them in the mother syndrome. They asked to speak to my husband. "He's not here at the moment, but if you don't mind waiting, he should be back in a jiffy." They nodded.

As they started to turn to walk around the customer area, I proceeded to introduce myself and, at the same time, commenced[2] making three more sandwiches. While I made small talk (actually, it was a monologue[3]), they stood silent, looking fiercely, albeit hungrily at the masterpieces I was concocting[4]: Italian rolls, piled high with juicy roast pork and, on top, my husband's wonderful homemade cole slaw. I placed them on paper plates along with pickles and plenty of potato chips, then I said, "Come on, you'll have to eat in the kitchen, because we're not licensed to serve in the store. Do you want milk or soda?" "Don't you know who we are?" "I've seen you around, but I don't know your names," I replied. They looked at me in disbelief, then shrugging their shoulders, marched as one into the kitchen, which was the first room behind the store. They ate to their hearts' content and, before they left, emptied their pockets, depositing each purloined[5] article in its appointed[6] place. No apologies were given, none were expected. **But from that day on, we were protected, and the only payment we ever made was that which we also received: friendship, trust, and acceptance.** (Excerpted from Carmen Machin, "The Deli," in Mary Lou Conlin, *Patterns Plus*, 7th ed. [Boston: Houghton Mifflin, 2002], pp. 44–45.)

Although this story covers three paragraphs, it, too, is a narrative that develops a topic sentence, which is highlighted. It includes factual details; for example, readers learn that one of the Dukes steals Hostess cupcakes, and the writer tells exactly what she gives the gang members to eat. The writer also incorporates dialogue by providing the word-for-word conversation she had with the gang members. The story includes sensory details, too. The writer tells us, for instance, that the roast pork is *juicy*. And movement is conveyed through action-oriented verbs: the gang members *terrorized* and *swaggered* and *marched*. Yet all of these details are necessary to the story. And the writer helps readers follow the events with the use of transitional words such as *then*, *while*, and *as*.

1. **naiveté:** lack of experience or sophistication
2. **commenced:** began
3. **monologue:** a speech made by one person
4. **concocting:** making
5. **purloined:** stolen
6. **appointed:** designated

Narratives can also take the form of complete essays. To write a narrative essay, follow the same steps for writing a narrative paragraph. First, prewrite to generate ideas and to decide on your main idea. For an essay, the main idea is expressed in a thesis statement, which will appear somewhere within the essay. Next, select relevant details, including only events and information that are essential to understanding the idea in the thesis statement. Arrange these events in a chronological outline. The paragraphs of your essay will usually correspond to the major events or scenes of the story. As you write, include transitions that indicate the time order of the events and consciously include specific words, factual and sensory details, and action-oriented verbs.

FOCUS ON RESEARCH

Conducting Library Research

When you are searching for information about a topic, the library is the obvious place to go. The two main types of library sources are books and periodicals.

Books

There are usually two main types of books in libraries. The general collection, which contains works of fiction as well as nonfiction books such as biographies, includes all of the books that can be checked out by those with a library card. In most college libraries, these books will be organized according to the Library of Congress Subject Headings system, which assigns a letter and number (the **call number**) to each book so that you can locate it on the shelves. The library's online catalog or card catalog allows you to look up books by subject, author, or title and then write down the call numbers of the books you want to examine.

The other type of book is the reference work, which provides factual information about a wide variety of topics. Reference works include general and specialized encyclopedias, statistical sources, dictionaries, and many other works that usually cannot be checked out. They, too, are arranged by call number, and they are usually shelved in a particular section of the library.

Periodicals

The periodicals include magazines, journals, and newspapers that are published periodically, such as every day, once a month, or twice a year. They contain articles on a variety of different subjects. To find articles about your topic, you locate that topic in a printed index, such as *The Reader's Guide to Periodical Literature*. Or you can use one of many different computerized indexes, which allow you to search by subject, author, or title.

Spend some time familiarizing yourself with the locations and the methods of retrieval for the different types of sources in your library. Then, when you need information, you will know where and how to get it.

> **EXERCISE 9.7** **The Narrative Essay**

Read the following narrative essay. Then answer the questions by writing your responses on the blanks provided.

A Thanksgiving Feast in Aburi

1 The music of the Fanti[1] language was becoming singable to me, and its vocabulary was moving orderly into my brain.

2 Efua took me to a durbar, a thanksgiving feast in Aburi, about thirty miles from Accra.[2] Thousands of gaily dressed celebrants had gathered, waving, singing and dancing. I stood on the edge of the crowd to watch the exotic parade. Hunters, rifles across their shoulders, marched in rhythm to their own drummers. Soldiers, with faces set in grim determination, paced down the widened roads behind their drummers while young girls screamed approval. Farmers bearing scythes[3] and fishermen carrying nets were welcomed loudly by the throng.

3 The annual harvest ritual gave each segment in the society its opportunity to thank God and to praise its workers and their yield.

4 I was swaying to the rhythm when the drums stopped, and the crowd quieted. The restless air steadied. A sound, unlike the other sounds of the day, commenced in the distance. It was the harsh tone of hundreds of giant cicadas[4] grinding their legs together. Their rasping floated to us and the crowd remained quiet but edgy with anticipation. When men appeared out of the dust scraping sticks against corrugated[5] dry gourds, the crowd recovered its tongue.

5 "Yee! Yee! Awae! Awae!"

6 The scrapers, like the paraders who preceded them, gave no notice to the crowd or to the small children who ran unceremoniously close to their serried[6] ranks.

7 Rasp, Rasp. Scrape! Scrape, Scour, Scrunch, Scrump. Rasp, Rasp! Scree! The raspers faded into a dim distance.

8 The deep throb of royal drums was suddenly heard in the distance and again the din[7] of celebration stopped. The people, although quiet again, continued to

1. **Fanti:** an African ethnic group
2. **Accra:** the capital of Ghana, in Africa
3. **scythes:** a tool with a long, curved blade used for mowing or reaping
4. **cicadas:** insects that make a high-pitched sound
5. **corrugated:** with ridges
6. **serried:** pressed or crowded together
7. **din:** loud noise

move, sidle, exchange places and wipe their brows. Women adjusted the clothes which held babies securely to their backs. Rambunctious children played tag, men and women waved at each other, smiled, but kept looking toward the sound of the drums.

9   Efua touched my shoulder and offered me a large white handkerchief.

10   I said, "Thank you, but I'm all right." She kept her hand extended. I took the handkerchief.

11   Men emerged out of the dim dust. One set had giant drums hefted onto their shoulders, and others followed in splendid cloth, beating the drums with crooked sticks. The powerful rhythms rattled my bones, and I could feel the vibrations along the edges of my teeth.

12   People began clapping, moving their feet, their hands, hips and heads. They shouted clamorously, "Yee! Yee! Aboma!" And there was still a sense of anticipation in the turbulence. They were waiting for a climax.

13   When the first palanquin[1] hove[2] into view, I thought of a Chinese junk[3] on the Yangtze (which I had never seen), and a ten-ton truck on a California freeway (which I knew well). Long poled hammocks, sturdy as Conestogas[4], were carried by four men. In the center of each conveyance[5] sat a chief, gloriously robed in rich hand-woven Kente cloth. At his side (only a few chiefs were female) sat a young boy, called the Kra, who, during an earlier solemn ceremony, had received the implanted soul of the chief. If the chief should die during the ritual, there would be no panic, for his people would know that his soul was safe in the young boy's body and, with the proper ritual, could be placed into the body of the chief's successor.

14   The drums beckoned, the kings appeared, and the air nearly collapsed under the weight of dust and thudding drums and shouting jubilation.

15   Each chief was prouder than the one preceding him. Each dressed in more gold and richer colors. Each black beyond ebony and shining with oil and sweat. They arrived in single file to be met by the adoring shouts of their subjects. "Na-na. Na-na." "Yo, Yo, Nana." The shouting united with the thumping of the drums and the explosion of color. Women and men bounced up and down like children's toys, and children not tall enough to see over the crowd were lifted by the nearest adults to see their passing royalty.

16   A flutter of white billowed over that excited scene. Thousands of handkerchiefs waving from thousands of black hands tore away my last reserve. I started

---

1. **palanquin:** a couch mounted on poles, which is carried on the shoulders of four or more people
2. **hove:** was hauled

3. **junk:** a type of ship
4. **Conestogas:** covered, horse-drawn wagons
5. **conveyance:** a vehicle for transportation

bouncing with the entranced Ghanaians, my handkerchief high above my head, I waved and jumped and screamed, "Na-na, na-na, na-na." *

1. Write, in your own words, the main idea of this essay.

   _____

   _____

2. What are the main events of this story?

   _____

   _____

   _____

   _____

3. Which part of this story is especially easy for you to picture in your mind? Give examples of the vivid language (specific words, factual and sensory details, and action-oriented verbs) that the writer used to narrate that part of the story.

   _____

   _____

In Summary: Steps in Writing Narratives

1. Prewrite to generate ideas and determine a main idea.
2. Select relevant details, including only events and information that are essential to understanding the main idea, and create an outline of the major events in chronological order.
3. As you write, include time-related transitions and information. Also, use vivid language, including specific words, factual and sensory details, and action-oriented verbs.

*Source: From Maya Angelou, *All God's Children Need Traveling Shoes*, (New York: Random House, 1986). Copyright © 1986. Used by permission of Random House, Inc.

CHAPTER 9 REVIEW

Fill in the blanks in the following statements.

1. A narrative is a _____ about your own or others' experiences.

2. The first step in writing an effective narrative paragraph involves deciding on the _____ you want to make about the events.

3. The next step in writing an interesting narrative is selecting the right _____ to include.

4. Narratives are naturally organizing because the events are almost always presented in _____ order.

5. In a _____, a writer can take readers back to the past for a while before returning to the present to move the story forward again.

6. Preparing an outline for a narrative is usually just a matter of listing the important _____ in the order in which they occurred.

7. To help the reader understand the time frame of the events, writers include _____ words and phrases, such as *in the beginning, after, next,* and *meanwhile.*

8. _____ language helps readers picture people and events in their minds.

9. Three kinds of vivid language are _____ words, _____ and _____ details, and _____.

10. _____ offer information such as names, quantities, dates, and dimensions.

11. _____ provide information about what something looks, smells, tastes, sounds, or feels like.

12. _____ is the participants' exact statements, enclosed in quotation marks.

13. A narrative may need several _____ for development.

14. Narratives can also take the form of complete essays in which a _____ _____ expresses the main idea.

Topic Ideas for Narratives

Exercise 9.1 includes topic ideas you may want to develop into narrative paragraphs or essays. Here are some additional ideas:

- An incident that caused you to change your mind about something
- An event that made you who you are today
- A memorable moment you shared with a friend
- A historical event that fascinates you
- A day you regret
- The story told by the following photograph

© Joshua Blake/Istockphoto

WebWork

Visit Web sites that focus on storytelling. Explore the Web site of the International Storytelling Center at **http://www.storytellingcenter.com/.** Also, conduct a search for other sites about storytelling by using an Internet browser such as Google.com or Yahoo.com. Then answer the following questions:

1. Why is it important to tell stories? What are the benefits to individuals? Cultural groups? Entire societies?

2. What stories do you have to tell that might benefit others?

3. What is a family story that is meaningful to you? Why is this story meaningful?

Online Study Center   For additional information and practice with writing narrative paragraphs and essays, go to the Houghton Mifflin Online Study Center for this book, at **http://www.college.hmco.com/pic/dolphinwritertwo**.

Description

GOALS FOR CHAPTER 10

▶ Define the term *description*.

▶ Describe the steps in writing a descriptive paragraph.

▶ Write a descriptive paragraph.

▶ Recognize the dominant impression, details, organizational pattern, and figurative language in a longer description.

In Chapter 9, you examined the narrative as a method of developing an idea. In this chapter, you will focus on **description**, which provides details about what something or someone looks like, sounds like, smells like, and so forth. Description is often used along with narration, for telling a story usually requires that you give some information about a scene or the people in it. However, description can also be a mode of development of its own.

Writing a Descriptive Paragraph

Sometimes you will need to develop a topic sentence by describing someone or something. When you describe, you provide factual and sensory details that help readers form a mental image of your subject. To write an effective description, you will need to include the essential features that are illustrated in the next sections.

Prewriting

Although you can use any of the prewriting methods described in Chapter 2 of this text to generate ideas for description, clustering is especially useful. Re-creating a person, place, or thing in words for your readers will require you

Figure 10.1 A Sample Prewriting Cluster

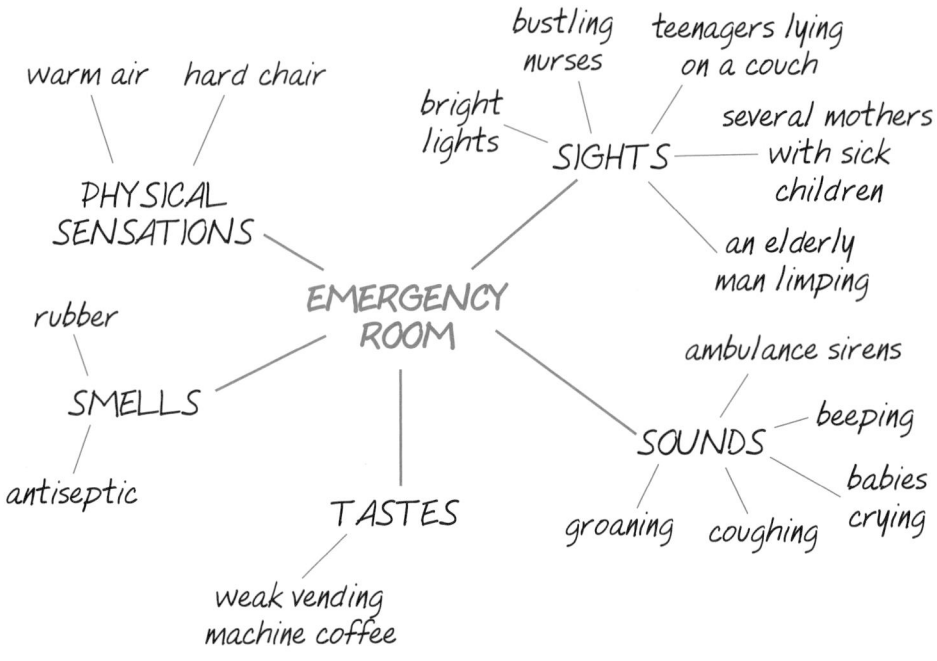

to provide details related to all five senses, so you might want to add a group of details for each sense to your cluster. For example, if you were going to describe a busy hospital emergency room, your cluster might look like Figure 10.1.

Determining a Main Idea and Writing a Topic Sentence

The first step in writing an effective descriptive paragraph involves deciding on the point you want to make about the subject you are describing. This point offers a **dominant impression**, an essential quality that you want to convey about your subject. Sometimes you will know before you begin writing what your dominant impression will be. For example, if you are assigned to write about a place that is peaceful to you, then "peaceful" is your dominant impression, and you would select a subject that fits this impression. However, if you are assigned to write about the room you are sitting in right now, then you may not know what your dominant impression is until you generate some details.

For example, here is one student's list of details:

bright fluorescent lights
no windows
polished tile floor
cinder block walls painted beige
no pictures on walls

rows of metal and plastic desks
rustling of papers
sound of other students' pens and pencils on paper
blank blackboard
smell of someone's perfume

When you consider this list of details, what one impression do most of them convey to you? Would you say this room seems to be sterile? Dull? Stark? Plain? Most of the details indicate that this classroom would fit any of these characterizations. If the student were to write a topic sentence for a paragraph about this classroom, she might write something like

Our classroom is as stark as the inside of a prison.

Almost all of the details in this particular example would convey that impression. However, be aware that other lists of details might suggest more than just one dominant impression. Think for a moment about what you would see, hear, smell, taste, and feel as you were sitting at a public beach. Your list of details would be long, and it would probably include everything from the sound of children playing in the waves to the smell of suntan oil to the heat of the sun beating down on you. Different writers might choose to convey different dominant impressions about this scene. One writer might find the subject to be a relaxing place, whereas another writer would describe it as lively, and a third could pronounce it to be annoying. The topic sentence should clearly indicate the dominant impression that you will convey.

As you complete this step in the process, remember what you learned in Chapter 4 about topic sentences. A topic sentence does not always have to be the first sentence of a paragraph. It may be more appropriate to save it for last or to put it in the middle of the paragraph.

EXERCISE 10.1   **Writing Topic Sentences for Descriptive Paragraphs**

For each of the following topics, use some prewriting techniques to generate ideas, and then write a topic sentence you could use for a descriptive paragraph.

1. Someone I know very well

   Topic Sentence: _____

2. A room I am in frequently

   Topic Sentence: _____

3. A good vacation spot

   Topic Sentence: _____

4. A gift I received

Topic Sentence: _____

5. An animal that is (or was) special to me

Topic Sentence: _____

Selecting the Right Details for a Description

The next step in writing an interesting descriptive paragraph is selecting the right details to include. You cannot include every detail about your subject because your paragraph would be too long and too tedious to read, and your point would get lost in irrelevant information. Therefore, you will have to examine your prewriting and decide which pieces of information will convey your dominant impression. Circle every detail that supports the idea in your topic sentence, and ignore the other details.

For some practice in selecting details, think back to the previous example about describing a beach scene. On the blank next to each of the following details, write an *R* if you think that detail suggests "relaxing," an *L* if the detail suggests "lively," and an *A* if the detail suggests "annoying." Some details might warrant more than one label.

_____ cool ocean breeze on my skin
_____ three teenagers throwing a football
_____ people riding jet skis
_____ sand on my sandwich
_____ radio blaring rock music
_____ sound of waves lapping the shore
_____ hot sun beating down

Did you label the details in this list *R, L, L, A, L/A, R,* and *R/A*? This is how you would go about deciding which details match your dominant impression.

EXERCISE 10.2   **Selecting Details for Descriptive Paragraphs**

Choose one of the topic sentences you wrote for Exercise 10.1, and list the details that you would definitely need to include if you were to develop that statement in a descriptive paragraph.

Organizing Details and Using Transitions

Once you have circled all of the appropriate details in your prewriting, you next need to decide how to organize these details. Descriptions require some type of spatial organization. In other words, they orient the specific details for the reader by explaining how those details relate to one another in space. Some common spatial patterns for arranging details are

> front to back (or vice versa)
> left to right (or vice versa)
> top to bottom (or vice versa)
> inside to outside (or vice versa)
> near to far (or vice versa)

Descriptive details can also be arranged using a narrative pattern. For example, if you are describing a parade that passed before you, you could describe each element of the parade in chronological order.

The best pattern is often dictated by the subject itself. For example, if you are describing a house, you might use an outside-to-inside pattern. If you are describing a landscape, however, it would be more appropriate to use a near-to-far or left-to-right pattern. Once you select a pattern, list in your outline your details in that order. Follow your outline as you write to avoid jumping around. Particularly in descriptions, readers must understand the arrangement of the details in order to create a mental picture.

As you write descriptions, use transitional words that help your reader understand how the details are related. The following list includes common spatial transitional words:

above	to the left, to the right	overhead
below	nearby	underneath
under	in the distance	between
inside	on top	among
outside	at the bottom	across
toward	in the center	next to
away	close by	far away
in front	in back	up
down		

Notice in the following paragraph how the spatial transitional words and information, which are highlighted, help you organize the details in your mind and form a mental picture of the subject:

> I remember walking out on the black asphalt of the parking lot of the nursing home. It was heat-cracked and eroded already, and grass had veined itself **into**

the interstices[1]. There were coconut trees **around**, a cane field I could see **across the street**, and the ocean I knew was pitching a surf **just beyond** it. The green Ko'olaus[2] came up **behind us. Somewhere nearby, alongside the beach,** there was an abandoned airfield **in the middle** of the canes. (Garrett Hongo, "Kubota," in *The Best American Essays*, ed. Robert Atwan, 3rd college ed. [Boston: Houghton Mifflin, 2001], p. 97.)

EXERCISE 10.3 **Organizing Details in Descriptive Paragraphs**

Prewrite to generate ideas, and then complete each of the following topic sentences by filling in the blank. Then, on the other blanks provided, prepare an informal outline by listing the major details with an appropriate type of spatial order.

1. My most prized possession is my _____.

_____

_____

_____

_____

_____

2. _____ is one of the most attractive people I know.

_____

_____

_____

_____

3. My kitchen is a very _____ place.

_____

_____

_____

_____

_____

1. **interstices:** narrow spaces   2. **Ko'olaus:** mountain range in Hawaii

EXERCISE 10.4 **Recognizing Spatial Transitions**

Circle all of the transitional words and space-related information in the following paragraph.

There is a home movie of the two of us, sitting on the edge of the swimming pool at my grandma and grandpa's old apartment building in Culver City. The movie, taken some time in early 1960, is in color, though the color has faded, leaving my brother Brad and me milk-white and harmless children, me a year and a half old, Brad almost four. Our mother, impossibly young, is in the movie, too. She sits next to me, on the right of the screen. Her hair, for all the fading of the film, is coal black shoulder length and parted in the middle, curled up on the sides. She has on a bathing suit covered in purple and blue flowers, the color in them nearly gone. Next to me, on the left of the screen, is Brad in his white swimming trunks, our brown hair faded to only the thought of brown hair. I am in the center, my fat arms up, bent at the elbows, fingers curled into fists, my legs kicking away at the water, splashing and splashing. I am smiling, the baby of the family, the center of the world at that very instant, though my mother is pregnant, my little brother Tim some six or seven months off, my little sister Leslie, the last child, still three years distant. The pool water before us is only a thin sky blue, the bushes behind us a dull and lifeless light green. There is no sound. (Excerpted from "Brothers" by Bret Lott, the *Antioch Review,* vol. 51, no. 1. Copyright © 1993 by the Antioch Review, Inc. Reprinted by permission of the editors.)

EXERCISE 10.5 **Writing a Descriptive Paragraph That Includes Transitions**

Choose one of the topic sentences and outlines you prepared in Exercise 10.3. Write the paragraph, including transitional words that indicate how the details are arranged in space.

Using Vivid Language

In Chapter 9, you learned how to include specific words, factual and sensory details, and action-oriented verbs in your writing. The first two types of vivid language are particularly important in descriptive paragraphs such as the following:

Erie County had "condemned"[1] the Weidel property. The downstairs windows were carelessly boarded over, and both the front and rear doors were unlocked,

---

1. **condemned:** declared unfit for further use

collapsing on their hinges. Broken glass underfoot and a sickish stench of burn, mildew, decay. Yet there were "touches"—on what remained of a kitchen wall, a Holstein[1] calendar from a local feed store, a child's crayon drawing. Upstairs, children's clothes, socks and old shoes heaped on the floor. I recognized with a thrill of repugnance[2] an old red sweater of Ruth's, angora[3]-fuzzy. There were broken Christmas tree ornaments, a naked pink plastic doll. Toppled bedsprings, filthy mattresses streaked with yellow and rust-colored stains. The mattresses looked as if they'd been gutted, their stuffing strewn about. The most terrible punishment, I thought, would be to be forced to lie down on such a mattress. (Adapted from Joyce Carol Oates, "They All Just Went Away," in *The Best American Essays*, ed. Robert Atwan, 3rd college ed. [Boston: Houghton Mifflin, 2001], p. 232.)

Notice how the author paints the scene by including specific words. Instead of saying that there were toys on the floor, for example, she says there was a "naked pink plastic doll." She also provides facts, such as specific names, and sensory information about colors and smells and physical sensations.

In addition to specific words and factual and sensory details, try to add some figurative language to your descriptions. **Figurative language**, or *figures of speech*, make interesting, often clever comparisons between two unlike things in order to help the reader form a clear mental image of or better understand the thing being described. **Metaphors** are direct comparisons in which one thing is called another:

The moon was *a bright lamp* in the night sky.

Similes are indirect comparisons that use the words *like* or *as*:

A wealthy but unhappy woman, she was *like a bird imprisoned in a gilded cage.*

Personification compares an inanimate or nonhuman object to humans by giving the object human characteristics:

The wind *whistled* through the trees.

The tea kettle *shrieked* on the stove.

Try to come up with a few original comparisons to add to your own writing. They will add clarity and a spark of creativity to your descriptions. However,

1. **Holstein:** a type of dairy cow
2. **repugnance:** great dislike
3. **angora:** a type of soft yarn

as you learned in Chapter 6 of this text, you should avoid clichés, overused and tired expressions such as "hungry as a bear," "sweet as sugar," and "happy as a clam."

Can you spot the figurative language in the following excerpt from a description of an ice storm in the Deep South?

> When my wife and I awoke, civilization as we knew it had mainly shut down. Luckily we had gas heaters. All electricity and water were gone; no telephone, all local radio stations kaput[1]. Outside, the trees were draped sculptures in white, but in their quietness, a whole new storm of ghouls.
>
> At noon when limbs and then whole trees began falling around me, nothing was nice. The picturesque[2] had turned into terror. Whatever we were, whatever good and rotten had transpired in this, our little jewel of a city, these trees had witnessed it. Now they were splitting apart and falling wholesale with mournful cracks and awful thuds. They were coming in the window glass like dead uncles. Next door, an 80-foot tree fell on a neighbor woman's Mercedes, the fetish[3] of her life. She came out into the driveway wailing. . . . But you see a whole tree go over like that, and your grip on the universe goes. A small mob of slackers[4] came down the block and stood around the big tree over the Mercedes. They grinned, sort of worshiping the event. But the woods running down a hill to the east went into an exploding mutual collapse too much like the end of the world, and everyone fled back inside.
>
> All of these old trees were like family in the act of dying, their agony was more terrible than the storm itself. We had been confident, even arrogant, with them around us, I realized. They'd been comforting brothers and sisters. Now the town was suddenly half as tall. ("The Ice Storm" by Barry Hannah, *Outside Magazine,* March 1995. Reprinted by permission of the author.)

Notice how the author includes all three kinds of figurative language. For example, he uses metaphors such as "the trees were draped sculptures in white," and he writes that the trees had been "comforting brothers and sisters." He includes similes such as "They [the trees] were coming in the window glass like dead uncles" and "All of these old trees were like family in the act of dying." And he personifies the trees when he gives them the ability to "witness" the acts of the townspeople and to be in "agony" when they collapse under the weight of the ice.

1. **kaput:** not working
2. **picturesque:** something attractive or interesting enough to be suitable for a picture
3. **fetish:** an object of excessive attention or obsession
4. **slackers:** people who avoid work or responsibility

EXERCISE 10.6   **Writing with Vivid Language**

Rewrite each of the following sentences to substitute more specific words and add factual and sensory details and figurative language.

1. She is a beautiful woman.

_____

2. The view is quite amazing.

_____

3. The meal was delicious.

_____

4. The thing was not perfect.

_____

5. The sunset was the prettiest one I have ever seen.

_____

EXERCISE 10.7   **Describing a Photograph Using Vivid Language**

Use vivid language to describe the scene in the accompanying photograph.

© Yann Layma/Getty Images

Writing Longer Descriptions and Descriptive Essays

So far, this chapter has focused mostly on descriptive paragraphs. However, a description may need several paragraphs for development. For example, read the following passage, a description of the Vietnam Veterans Memorial (which is also known as "The Wall") in Washington, DC. This passage was written by Maya Ying Lin, the architect who designed the monument.

Maya Ying Lin's Design Submission
to the Vietnam Veterans Memorial Competition

1 The memorial appears as a rift[1] in the earth—a long, polished black stone wall, emerging from and receding into the earth. Near the memorial, the ground slopes gently downward, and the low walls emerging on either side, growing out of the earth, extend and converge[2] at a point below and ahead. Walking into the grassy site contained by the walls of the memorial, we can barely make out the carved names upon the memorial's walls. These names, seemingly infinite in number, convey the sense of overwhelming numbers, while unifying those individuals into a whole. For this memorial is meant not as a monument to the individual but, rather, as a memorial to the men and women who died during this war, as a whole.

2 **The memorial is composed not as an unchanging monument, but as a moving composition, to be understood as we move into and out of it; the passage itself is gradual, the descent to the origin slow, but it is at the origin that the meaning of the memorial is to be fully understood.** At the intersection of these walls, on the right side, at the wall's top, is carved the date of the first death. It is followed by the names of those who have died in the war, in chronological order. These names continue on this wall, appearing to recede into the earth at the wall's end. The names resume on the left wall, as the wall emerges from the earth, continuing back to the origin, where the date of the last death is carved, at the bottom of this wall. Thus the war's beginning and end meet; the war is "complete," coming full circle, yet broken by the earth that bounds the angle's open side, and contained within the earth itself. As we turn to leave, we see these walls stretching into the distance, directing us to the Washington Monument, to the left, and the Lincoln Memorial, to the right, thus bringing the Vietnam Memorial into an historical context. We the living are brought to a concrete realization of these deaths.

3 It is up to each individual to resolve or come to terms with this loss. For death is in the end a personal and private matter, and the area contained with

---

1. **rift:** a long crack or opening   2. **converge:** come together

this memorial is a quiet place, meant for personal reflection and private reckoning. The black granite walls, each two hundred feet long, and ten feet below ground at their lowest point (gradually ascending toward ground level) effectively act as a sound barrier, yet are of such a height and length so as not to appear threatening or enclosing. The actual area is wide and shallow, allowing for a sense of privacy, and the sunlight from the memorial's southern exposure along with the grassy park surrounding and within its walls contribute to the serenity of the area. Thus this memorial is for those who have died, and for us to remember them.

4   The memorial's origin is located approximately at the center of the site; its legs each extending two hundred feet towards the Washington Monument and the Lincoln Memorial. The walls, contained on one side by the earth, are ten feet below ground at their point of origin, gradually lessening in height, until they finally recede totally into the earth, at their ends. The walls are to be made of hard, polished black granite, with the names to be carved in simple Trajan[1] letters. The memorial's construction involves recontouring[2] the area within the wall's boundaries so as to provide for an easily accessible descent, but as much of the site as possible should be left untouched. The area should remain as a park, for all to enjoy. (Source: The National Park Service, http://www.nps.gov/vive/memorial/description.htm)

Although this description covers four paragraphs, it, too, develops one dominant impression, which is highlighted. It includes factual details such as lengths, distances, and materials of construction. It also includes sensory information, such as "hard, polished black granite." The writer helps us make sense of all the details by arranging details using a far-to-near pattern and by including spatial transitional words such as "near the memorial" and "at the intersection of these walls."

Descriptions can also take the form of complete essays. To write a descriptive essay, follow the same steps for writing a descriptive paragraph. First, prewrite to generate ideas and to decide on your main idea. Express your dominant impression in your thesis statement, which will appear somewhere within the essay. Next, select relevant details, including only information that is essential to understanding the idea in the thesis statement. Arrange these details in an outline according to some type of spatial organizational pattern. As you write, include transitions that indicate how the details are arranged, and consciously include specific words, factual and sensory details, and figurative language.

---

1. **Trajan:** a style for writing letters of the alphabet   2. **recontouring:** reshaping

Internet Sources

The Internet offers a wealth of information about nearly any topic you can name. By using a search engine, such as Google or Yahoo, you can type in a search term, and you will see lists of Web sites that may offer information.

You can also use a search engine to access the specific Web sites of organizations, government agencies, and businesses.

In addition, you will find many publications online. For example, newspapers such as the *New York Times* and *USA Today* post their content online every day. Magazines such as *Time, Newsweek,* and *U.S. News and World Report,* too, post some or all of their articles online.

You can also subscribe to electronic libraries or databases that allow you to search for information from a wide variety of electronic texts. Some of these, such as Highbeam Research, require you to pay an annual fee for access to the content. Other databases, especially those available through your local library or campus library, may provide the same kind of information at no charge.

EXERCISE 10.8 **The Descriptive Essay**

Read the following essay, which describes the aftermath of terrorists' destruction of New York's World Trade Center. Then answer the questions by writing your responses on the blanks provided.

As Eyes Pan Ground Zero, Words Fail

1 My own words fail, because I was a gawking[1] idiot of a tourist, walking around the worst thing that words have tried to describe in America.

2 So I desperately grab for the words of a man who helped invent the atomic bomb. After seeing the first one tested, Robert Oppenheimer turned to ancient Indian scripture: "I am become death, the destroyer of worlds."

3 I think I can start there because the most famous address in New York is no more. The forwarding address comes from an age of atomic bombs.

4 "Where you headed to, sir?" is the question at a police checkpoint.

5 "Down to Ground Zero," says a state police investigator named Paul DeSalvador. Ground Zero is the patch of earth right above where an A-bomb goes off underground.

6 Since two planes were turned into bombs on September 11, there are so many people missing they would fill an entire Orange County village. There are enough grieving survivors to fill an entire country.

1. **gawking:** staring

7 So many of those men and women have tried to describe what they saw and felt. Mostly, they end up saying the same thing: It has to be seen with one's own eyes. Then, only then, can a description be attempted.

8 Photographer Jeff Goulding and I tried.

9 It could be described as a war zone because only an act of war could rip a piece of New York's skyline right out of the sky.

10 Only in a war zone could you find the pieces of that skyline lying on the ground. They were crumpled, burnt, smashed like a kid's Tinker Toy set after a tantrum.

11 But then you look around, and you see hard hats everywhere, and a skyline of cranes, their booms extended like the arms of gigantic spiders. The air gets loaded down with gluey, burnt chemical smells, so loaded you want to push it out of the way like a smelly old curtain.

12 There are men with barbed-wire stubble and far-away looks in their eyes, wearing police and fire uniforms. There are contractors with their jaws set, getting out of pickups from Virginia, Cleveland, Missouri.

13 So maybe it's not a war zone, maybe it's the biggest demolition site you've ever seen, the aftermath of a hurricane or a tornado.

14 And then three National Guardsmen blurt out, "Whoa, whoa, whoa!" as you cross a checkpoint and they ask for IDs. One of them asks to borrow your binoculars so he can see if someone's got a camera mounted in a building nearby, trying to take pictures of body parts being recovered from nearby 5 World Trade Center.

15 There are red Xs marked on the mountain of metal and pulverized[1] concrete where the south tower used to be. They mark the places where K9 dogs[2] have hit upon the odor of human beings.

16 So, maybe it's not a demolition scene, maybe it's a crime scene, and you can't imagine how there could ever be enough detectives and investigators in this world, or any other, to gather the evidence and solve the crime.

17 There is the steady hum of generators, and the howl of backhoes[3] making a precarious[4] climb up what used to be the Twin Towers.

18 It takes about 45 minutes to make a circle around the place that is a war zone and a demolition site and a crime scene with a name taken from the language of atomic bombs.

---

1. **pulverized:** demolished; pounded or crushed to dust
2. **K9 dogs:** police dogs
3. **backhoes:** large machines used for digging
4. **precarious:** dangerously lacking in stability or security

19   Near the blackened skeleton of a building that used to be 7 World Trade Center, there is smoke rising from the piles. The temperature is 400 degrees in some spots.

20   It is heat from hell. And if the devil himself saw this place, he would take a detour.

21   But there are people working here and all through the city, binding the city's wounds and their own. They work through 400-degree heat and emotion and pain that burns even hotter than that.

22   Unlike words, these people will not fail. They will not be stopped.

23   Not even by death, destroyer of worlds.*

1. What is the dominant impression conveyed by this description?

_____

_____

2. How does the author organize the details of his description?

_____

_____

_____

3. What part of the author's description was particularly vivid to you? How did the author use factual and sensory details to paint the scene?

_____

4. Find one of the author's metaphors and write it on the blank.

_____

_____

_____

5. Find one of the author's similes and write it on the blank.

_____

_____

_____

6. What is personified in this essay?

_____

*_Source:_ Oliver Mackson, "As Eyes Pan Ground Zero, Words Fail," _Times Herald-Record,_ Nov. 11, 2001, www.recordonline.com/adis/62/stories/mackson.htm. Reprinted by permission of the author.

In Summary: Steps in Writing Descriptions

1. Prewrite to generate ideas and determine a main idea.
2. Select relevant details, including only information that is essential to understanding the main idea, and create an outline using an appropriate type of spatial order.
3. As you write, include space-related transitional words and information. Also, use vivid language, including specific words, factual and sensory details, and figurative language.

CHAPTER 10 REVIEW

Fill in the blanks in the following statements.

1. _____ provides details about what something or someone looks like, sounds like, smells like, and so forth.

2. When you generate ideas for description, the _____ method of prewriting is especially useful.

3. The _____ is the essential quality that you want to convey about the subject you are describing.

4. The _____ you include in your paragraph must match or contribute to the dominant impression you want to convey.

5. _____ organizational patterns such as front to back, left to right, and inside to outside help orient the specific details for the reader by explaining how those details relate to one another in space.

6. _____, including specific words and factual and sensory details, is important in descriptions.

7. _____ language makes interesting, often clever comparisons between two unlike things in order to help the reader form a clear mental image of the thing being described.

8. Three types of figurative language are _____, _____, and _____.

9. _____ are direct comparisons in which one thing is called another.

10. _____ are indirect comparisons that use the word *like* or *as*.

11. _____ describes an inanimate or nonhuman object by giving the object human characteristics.

12. A description may need several _____ for development.

13. Descriptions can also take the form of complete essays in which the dominant impression is expressed in a _____.

Topic Ideas for Descriptions

Exercise 10.1 includes topic ideas you may want to develop into descriptive paragraphs or essays. Here are some additional ideas:

- My favorite place to relax

- My place of employment

- My favorite store

- An unusual food or meal I like to prepare

- My favorite celebrity

(*See the following page for more ideas*)

- An object that is special or meaningful to me
- The scene in the following photograph

© David Trood/Getty Images

 WebWork

To practice your descriptive skills, go to the National Geographic photography Web site at **http://www.nationalgeographic.com/photography/.** Click on "Photo Galleries," select a category, and then choose one photograph. Write a description of the scene in that photograph, including as many sensory details as possible.

Online Study Center   For additional information and practice with writing descriptive paragraphs and essays, go to the Houghton Mifflin Online Study Center for this book, at **http://www.college.hmco.com/pic/dolphinwritertwo.**

11

Process

GOALS FOR CHAPTER 11

▶ Define the terms *directive process* and *informative process*.

▶ Describe the steps in writing a process paragraph.

▶ Write a process paragraph.

▶ Recognize the purpose, steps, organizational pattern, and transitions in a longer process passage.

Process is an explanation of how something is done or should be done. There are two types of processes: *directive process* and *informative process*. A **directive process** provides directions for accomplishing some task. The goal of this type of process is to give readers the information they need in order to re-create the process themselves. Recipes, instructions for assembling a toy, and "how-to" articles are all examples of directive process analysis. The following passage illustrates directive process:

> The secret to skipping[1] is spin and speed, the world-record holder says, and careful attention to form. Pick a smooth stone that fits in your palm, has a uniform[2] thickness, and is neither too heavy nor too light. Champion stone skipper Jerdone Coleman McGhee likes ones that are about as heavy as tennis balls. Rectangular stones will veer off[3] at an angle; triangular stones are the most stable on choppy water. Irregular stones are McGhee's favorites. Stand at an angle to the water, your feet apart at shoulder width. Take a few warm-up throws with increasingly heavy stones. When you're ready, gather some stones and hold them in your non-throwing hand as a counterbalance[4]. Then place one in the crook of your index finger and cock your wrist. Breathe in slowly through your

1. **skipping:** making a rock bounce off the surface of water
2. **uniform:** regular; even
3. **veer off:** turn aside from a particular course or direction
4. **counterbalance:** a weight that acts to balance another

nose, extending your arm high above your head. When your lungs are full, whip your non-throwing arm across your body, then bring your throwing arm down and forward, rotating your shoulders 180 degrees. Exhale forcefully as you throw, shifting your weight onto your lead foot. Snap your wrist at the end of its arc[1], releasing the stone parallel to the water with as much spin and speed as possible. If you are standing at the water's edge, your stone should first splash down no more than 15 feet away. Follow through with your throwing arm's motion after the stone is released. (Adapted from Cameron Walker, "Stone Skipping 101." This article originally appeared in *Discover Magazine*, August 2003, p. 23. Reprinted by permission of the author.)

This paragraph teaches readers how to skip stones on water by explaining the process as a series of steps.

An **informative process** provides information about how some process works. The goal of this type of process is to explain a procedure so that readers can understand it, not so that they can re-create it. Thus, a paragraph or article that explains how bees make honey or how e-mail works is designed to inform the reader about the process. This next passage illustrates informative process:

Earthquakes can be caused by explosive volcanic eruptions or even explosions detonated[2] by humans, but the great majority are associated with the movement of lithospheric[3] plates. These movements form large crustal features called faults. In a fault, the rock on one side of the fracture has moved relative to the rock on the other side of the fracture. Movement of neighboring plates exerts stress on the rock formations along the plate margins. Because rocks possess elastic[4] properties, energy is stored until the stresses acting on the rocks are great enough to overcome the force of friction[5]. Then the fault walls move suddenly, and the energy stored in the rocks is released, causing an earthquake. After a major earthquake, the rocks may continue to adjust to their new positions, causing additional vibrations called *aftershocks*. (Adapted from James T. Shipman et al., *An Introduction to Physical Science*, 10th ed. [Boston: Houghton Mifflin, 2003], p. 590)

This paragraph explains what happens during an earthquake so that readers can *understand* the process rather than *perform* the process.

To write effective process paragraphs of both types, follow the principles presented in the next section.

1. **arc:** something shaped like a curve
2. **detonated:** caused to explode
3. **lithospheric:** related to the outer part of the earth
4. **elastic:** flexible or springy
5. **friction:** rubbing of one object against another

Writing a Process Paragraph

Some topic sentences need to be developed with an explanation of how something is done or should be done. When you develop an idea in the process mode, you explain the steps in a procedure using chronological order.

Determining a Main Idea and Writing a Topic Sentence

The topic sentence of a process paragraph will identify the process you are explaining and state the goal or end result of this process:

> Anyone can learn how to whistle.

The topic sentence may also identify the number of steps in the process. So, for example, a paragraph giving an explanation of how new vaccines are tested might begin with this topic sentence:

> New vaccines are usually tested in three stages.

EXERCISE 11.1   **Writing Topic Sentences for Process Paragraphs**

For each of the following topics, use some prewriting techniques to generate ideas, and then write a topic sentence that you could use for a process paragraph.

1. Getting rid of a bad habit

   Topic Sentence: _____

2. Saving money

   Topic Sentence: _____

3. How a certain process in nature takes place

   Topic Sentence: _____

4. Losing weight

   Topic Sentence: _____

5. How to register for a class

   Topic Sentence: _____

Organizing Details and Using Transitions

Most process paragraphs, like narrative paragraphs, are naturally organizing. The writer breaks the process down into a series of clear steps and then presents those steps chronologically, in the order in which they occur. Other process paragraphs may take the form of a series of tips or advice. In that case, the writer must determine the best order for presenting those tips if they are not chronologically related. Order of importance is a common pattern to use for those types of tips. Your outline for your paragraph should list the steps or tips in the order in which you will discuss them.

As you write, show how the steps in the process are separated from or related to one another by using transitions formed with either transitional words or organizational markers. In a process that presents the steps chronologically, transitions will help the reader follow the steps' order in time. The following list includes common process transitional words:

first, second, third	next	as
before	soon	when
now	in the beginning	until
then	once	later
after	often	meanwhile
while	finally	last
in the end	afterward	

Organizational markers—such as numbers, bullet points, or headings—are also useful in helping the reader follow your ideas. You may want to identify the steps in the process as Step 1, Step 2, and so forth. In the following, for example, the author chooses to present the steps in a numbered list:

Shark attacks, while well publicized, are fairly rare; in fact, bees, wasps and snakes cause far more fatalities[1] each year. Sharks do attack humans, however, even when unprovoked[2]—but the attacks aren't necessarily deadly. "Most shark attacks result in wounds that are readily survivable," says Rick Martin, a marine biologist who studies sharks. If you see a shark, follow these steps:

1. **Do not panic.** Clear thinking offers your best chance of survival.
2. **Maintain eye contact.** As the shark approaches, face it head-on, to communicate that you won't be caught off guard and thus are not easy pickings.

---

1. **fatalities:** deaths

2. **unprovoked:** not brought about deliberately

3. **Observe.** Watch the shark carefully. Often, initial bites or bumps are simply exploratory, because sharks sometimes use their gums and teeth to obtain tactile[1] cues about an object.

4. **Don't overreact.** Waving arms and legs suddenly or charging a shark aggressively may startle the animal and elicit[2] a defensive attack.

5. **Fend off[3] the shark if it continues to attack,** using only enough force to deflect[4] the animal.

6. **Attack or injure the shark only as a last resort.** Attempting to injure a shark may provoke a defensive or retaliatory[5] attack. Still, if you feel the shark is intent on multiple bites, attack the eyes or gills[6], which are the most sensitive areas. (Excerpted from "The Summer of All Fears" by Joshua Piven and David Borgenicht, *USA Weekend*, July 5–7, 2002, p. 6. Originally appeared in the July 5–7, 2002 issue of *USA Weekend*. Reprinted with permission.)

If you are presenting a series of tips that are not chronologically related, however, you could separate them into sections labeled with headings or marked with bullet points.

EXERCISE 11.2 **Organizing Details in Process Paragraphs**

Prewrite to generate ideas, and then complete each of the following topic sentences by filling in the blank. Then, on the other blanks provided, prepare an informal outline by listing the major steps in chronological order or the major tips in order of importance.

1. If you want to _____, follow these steps.

_____

_____

_____

_____

_____

1. **tactile:** related to the sense of touch
2. **elicit:** bring forth
3. **fend off:** try to prevent
4. **deflect:** turn away
5. **retaliatory:** paying back; getting revenge
6. **gills:** breathing organs of animals that live in water

2. _____ is a process that occurs in
three distinct stages.

_____

_____

_____

_____

3. To be a better _____, here are some tips.

_____

_____

_____

_____

EXERCISE 11.3   **Recognizing Process Transitions**

Circle all of the transitional words and time order information in the following
paragraph.

> There are a series of steps that your body goes through in fighting off a vaccine-
> preventable disease. First, a vaccine is given by a shot or liquid by mouth. An
> alternative needle-free route is the use of inhalation[1] by aerosol and powder.
> Most vaccines contain a weakened or dead disease germ or part of a disease
> germ. Other vaccines use inactivated[2] toxins[3]. Some of the bacteria that cause
> disease do so by producing toxins that invade the bloodstream. Next, the body
> makes antibodies[4] against the weakened or dead germs in the vaccine. Then,
> these antibodies can fight the real disease germs—which can be lurking[5] all
> around—if they invade the child's body. The antibodies will know how to
> destroy them and the child will not become ill. Most vaccines don't cause the
> diseases that are usually caused by viruses and bacteria. Finally, protective

1. **inhalation:** breathing in
2. **inactivated:** made unable to function
3. **toxins:** poisons
4. **antibodies:** substances in the body that fight disease
5. **lurking:** lying in wait, waiting to cause harm

antibodies stay on guard in the child's body to safeguard it from the real disease germs. (Centers for Disease Control and Prevention, "How Do Vaccines Work?" http://www.cdc.gov/nip/publications/fs/gen/howvacswork.htm)

EXERCISE 11.4 **Writing a Process Paragraph That Includes Transitions**

Choose one of the topic sentences and outlines you prepared in Exercise 11.2. Write the paragraph, including transitions that indicate the order of the details.

Developing a Process Paragraph

Although the topic sentence and organizational pattern for a process essay tend to be relatively easy to generate, writers must take care to include all of the essential information about the procedure. Have you ever tried to put something together by following unclear or incomplete instructions? The process was probably time-consuming and frustrating. So to help the reader easily re-create or comprehend the procedure you are explaining, do not make any assumptions about the reader's knowledge, and do not leave out even the smallest critical detail. You must anticipate all of your readers' questions and make sure you provide answers.

Avoid Making Assumptions. Considering your intended audience is very important if you are going to explain the process clearly enough for readers to understand it or follow it. How much basic knowledge will your readers have about your subject? How much will readers know about the materials involved in the process? If you refer to a *hex nut* or a *zipper footer*, will your readers know what that is? Will you need to provide definitions of terms, or can you be reasonably sure that the reader will know what they mean? Will the reader know how to accomplish minor steps—such as "thread the needle," "whisk together the ingredients," or "contract your abdominal muscles"—or should you explain those, too?

Include Relevant Details and Information. As you write your process paragraph, make sure that you do not overlook any essential steps or materials, especially for minor actions or events. So if you tell readers to breathe in, do not forget to tell them to breathe out. Also, be very specific. If you tell readers to sit, specify whether they should sit in a chair or on the floor. If you tell readers to attach two things, specify whether that attachment should be made with glue, nails, screws, or something else.

Writing Longer Process Passages and Process Essays

So far, this chapter has focused only on process paragraphs. However, a process may need several paragraphs for development. For example, read the following passage:

> Every day we all make hundreds of decisions with hardly a thought. We decide what to have for breakfast, what to wear, which bits of the newspaper to read and which to ignore. Yet most of us feel guiltily indecisive at work, much of the time. In our hearts, we alone know what terrible procrastinators[1] we are.
>
> **Can you improve yourself? You bet.** First and foremost, in any situation, you must determine your objectives[2]. The ends will almost always justify the means—but you must be absolutely clear about the ends you're aiming for. Are you willing to let your personal life suffer, or do you want to keep work and home life in balance? Are you keen to be popular or don't you give a stuff?[3] Are you willing to be ruthless[4] in pursuit of your ambitions, or do you find ruthless behavior unethical? The more guidelines you can lay down for yourself, the faster you will decide which activities will help you achieve your goals and which won't. If you constantly hem and haw[5] about where you are going, you'll never decide how to get there.
>
> On any project, one of the immediate analyses you need to make is: does it need to be perfect or does it need to be fast? As in cooking, excellence often takes time—time that may not be available. . . . There is never any excuse for shoddiness[6], but there is often a trade-off between speed and perfection. Find out what's needed before you start or you'll end up falling out of the frying pan and into the fire. . . .
>
> Next, evaluate the downside. What is the worst that can happen if things go pear-shaped? When you're making a decision, carefully analyze the conse-

1. **procrastinators:** people who put things off instead of doing them
2. **objectives:** goals
3. **give a stuff:** care
4. **ruthless:** merciless; having no compassion or pity

5. **hem and haw:** hesitate; avoid decision making
6. **shoddiness:** poor quality

quences of everything coming utterly unstuck. The downside will rarely be quite as disastrous as it first appears.

Then, don't delay—but don't rush. If you have a little time in hand, take it: you'll find the decision keeps resurfacing in your mind, helping you to reexamine all the angles. Many of the most senior and successful business managers I have met view themselves as rather cautious decision-makers. They're not, of course. Their skill is to act as quickly as the circumstances dictate, while taking as much time as the circumstances allow. "More haste less speed" is as true in business as in life generally.

A couple more tips. If you are hesitating, ask yourself how somebody you admire would tackle the problem: the head of the company, perhaps, or a previous boss you really rated.[1] Put them in your shoes and see what they would do. It will force you to look at the problem from a different standpoint. Similarly, don't be too proud to ask for advice. Phrase your enquiry properly and it won't make you look stupid; it will make you look smart. Whereas you will indubitably[2] look a right idiot if you make the wrong decision when your colleagues knew the right one all along. The propensity[3] of managers to re-invent wheels is prodigious[4]. Don't do it. (Excerpted from Winston Fletcher, "It's Time to Make Up Your Mind," *Management Today,* Sept. 1998, p. 31. Reprinted by permission of *Management Today.*)

Although the explanation of this process covers six paragraphs, it develops just one topic sentence, which is highlighted. The details are arranged as several major steps presented in chronological order. Note the author's use of process transitional words, such as *first and foremost, next,* and *then.* The passage ends with a paragraph of tips.

Processes can also take the form of complete essays. To write a process essay, follow the steps for writing a process paragraph. First, prewrite to generate ideas and to decide on your main idea. Identify in your thesis statement the process you are explaining and state the goal or end result of this process. Next, select relevant details, including only information that is essential to understanding the idea in the thesis statement. Arrange these details in an outline according to some type of appropriate organizational pattern, using either chronological order or order of importance. As you write, include transitions that indicate how the steps or tips are related, and avoid making assumptions about the reader's knowledge of the procedure you are explaining.

1. **rated:** respected
2. **indubitably:** unquestionably; without a doubt
3. **propensity:** tendency
4. **prodigious:** enormous

F CUS ON RESEARCH

Nonprint Sources

In Chapters 9 and 10, you learned about using the library and the Internet for research. Although these two resources are the obvious places to go when you need information, do not overlook a third valuable resource: nonprint sources.

Other people who are experts on the subject you are researching are an especially useful source of information. You can set up interviews with these individuals and then prepare a list of questions to ask them. With your interviewee's permission, tape-record your interview so that you will be able to extract direct quotations to use to support your ideas.

Television shows, radio programs, and films are other good nonprint resources. Often, you can obtain a transcript of a television or radio program by contacting the station or network that aired the program.

Do not overlook works of art, either. You may find it useful to use a painting, sculpture, photograph, or musical composition as a source.

 **EXERCISE 11.5**   **The Process Essay**

Read the following essay. Then answer the questions by writing your responses on the blanks provided.

How to Write a Personal Letter

1   We shy persons need to write a letter now and then, or else we'll dry up and blow away. It's true. And I speak as one who loves to reach for the phone and talk. The telephone is to shyness what Hawaii is to February, it's a way out of the woods. *And yet:* a letter is better.

2   Such a sweet gift—a piece of handmade writing, in an envelope that is not a bill, sitting in our friend's path when she trudges home from a long day spent among wahoos and savages, a day our words will help repair. They don't need to be immortal, just sincere. She can read them twice and again tomorrow: *You're someone I care about, Corinne, and think of often, and every time I do, you make me smile.*

3   We need to write, otherwise nobody will know who we are. They will have only a vague impression of us as A Nice Person, because, frankly, we don't shine at conversation, we lack the confidence to thrust our faces forward and say, "Hi, I'm Heather Hooten, let me tell you about my week." Mostly we say "Uh-huh" and "Oh, really." People smile and look over our shoulder, looking for someone else to talk to.

4   So a shy person sits down and writes a letter. To be known by another person—to meet and talk freely on the page—to be close despite distance. To escape from anonymity[1] and be our own sweet selves and express the music of our souls.

5   We want our dear Aunt Eleanor to know that we have fallen in love, that we quit our job, that we're moving to New York, and we want to say a few things that might not get said in casual conversation. *Thank you for what you've meant to me. I am very happy right now.*

6   The first step in writing letters is to get over the guilt of *not* writing. You don't "owe" anybody a letter. Letters are a gift. The burning shame you feel when you see unanswered mail makes it harder to pick up a pen and makes for a cheerless letter when you finally do. *I feel bad about not writing, but I've been so busy,* etc. Skip this. Few letters are obligatory,[2] and they are *Thanks for the wonderful gift* and *I am terribly sorry to hear about George's death.* Write these promptly if you want to keep your friends. Don't worry about the others, except love letters, of course. When your true love writes *Dear Light of My Life, Joy of My Heart,* some response is called for.

7   Some of the best letters are tossed off in a burst of inspiration, so keep your writing stuff in one place where you can sit down for a few minutes and—*Dear Roy, I am in the middle of an essay but thought I'd drop you a line. Hi to your sweetie too*—dash off a note to a pal. Envelopes, stamps, address book, everything in a drawer so you can write fast when the pen is hot.

8   A blank white 8" × 11" sheet can look as big as Montana if the pen's not so hot—try a smaller page and write boldly. Get a pen that makes a sensuous[3] line, get a comfortable typewriter, a friendly word processor—whichever feels easy to the hand.

9   Sit for a few minutes with the blank sheet of paper in front of you, and let your friend come to mind. Remember the last time you saw each other and how your friend looked and what you said and what perhaps was unsaid between you; when your friend becomes real to you, start to write.

10   Write the salutation—*Dear You*—and take a deep breath and plunge in. A simple declarative[4] sentence will do, followed by another and another. As if you were talking to us. Don't think about grammar, don't think about style, just give us your news. Where did you go, who did you see, what did they say, what do you think?

11   If you don't know where to begin, start with the present: *I'm sitting at the kitchen table on a rainy Saturday morning. Everyone is gone and the house is quiet.* Let the letter drift along. The toughest letter to crank out is one that is

---

1. **anonymity:** the state of being unknown or unacknowledged
2. **obligatory:** required
3. **sensuous:** appealing to or satisfying the senses
4. **declarative:** making a statement

meant to impress, as we all know from writing job applications; if it's hard work to slip off a letter to a friend, maybe you're trying too hard to be terrific. A letter is only a report to someone who already likes you for reasons other than your brilliance. Take it easy.

12   Don't worry about form. It's not a term paper. When you come to the end of one episode, just start a new paragraph. You can go from a few lines about the sad state of rock 'n' roll to the fight with your mother to your fond memories of Mexico to the kitchen sink and what's in it. The more you write, the easier it gets, and when you have a True True Friend to write to, a soul sibling, then it's like driving a car; you just press on the gas.

13   Don't tear up the page and start over when you write a bad line—try to write your way out of it. Make mistakes and plunge on. Let the letter cook along and let yourself be bold. Outrage, confusion, love—whatever is in your mind, let it find a way to the page. Writing is a means of discovery, always, and when you come to the end and write *Yours ever* or *Hugs and Kisses,* you'll know something you didn't when you wrote *Dear Pal.*

14   Probably your friend will put your letter away, and it'll be read again a few years from now—and it will improve with age.

15   And forty years from now, your friend's grandkids will dig it out of the attic and read it, a sweet and precious relic[1] of the ancient Eighties that gives them a sudden clear glimpse of the world we old-timers knew. You will have then created an object of art. Your simple lines about where you went, who you saw, what they said, will speak to those children and they will feel in their ears the humanity of our times.

16   You can't pick up a phone and call the future and tell them about our times. You have to pick up a piece of paper.*

1. What is the thesis of this essay? Write it on the blank below in your own words.

_____

2. What kind of order arranges the major steps explained in this essay?

_____

3. What is a process transition that the author uses? Do you think he should have used more process transitions throughout the rest of his essay?

_____

_____

1. **relic:** something treasured for its age or historic interest

*Source: Excerpted from "How to Write a Personal Letter" by Garrison Keillor, copyright © 1987 by International Paper Company. Reprinted by permission of Garrison Keillor/ Prairie Home Productions and the November 1987 issue of *Reader's Digest.*

4. Does the writer make any assumptions about his readers' knowledge, or does he leave out any crucial details? Explain your answer.

_____

5. After reading this process essay, do you feel as though you yourself could write an effective personal letter? Why or why not? If you answered no, what else would you like to know before attempting to follow the author's advice?

_____

In Summary: Steps in Writing About a Process

1. **Write a topic sentence or thesis that mentions the process and the end result.**
2. **Organize the steps in the process.** Create an outline that lists these steps in chronological order or in another kind of order as appropriate.
3. **Develop each step with all of the essential information.** Make sure you define terms, explain the use of materials, and describe each step as appropriate for your intended readers. Use transitions that help readers understand how the steps are related.

CHAPTER 11 REVIEW

Fill in the blanks in the following statements.

1. A _____ is an explanation of how something is done or should be done.

2. There are two types of processes: _____ and _____.

3. A _____ process provides directions for accomplishing some task. The goal of this type of process is to give readers the information they need in order to re-create the process themselves.

4. An _____ process provides information about how some process works. The goal of this type of process is to explain a procedure so that readers can understand it, not so that they can re-create it.

5. The topic sentence of a process paragraph will identify the process you are explaining and state _____ of this process.

6. Most process paragraphs break the process down into a series of steps and then present those steps _____, in the order in which they occur.

7. Other process paragraphs may take the form of a series of tips or advice; _____ is a common pattern to use for those types of tips.

8. As you write, show how the steps in the process are separated from and related to one another by including either _____ or _____.

9. Common process _____ include *first, second, third, then, next, finally,* and *meanwhile.*

10. Numbers, bullet points, and headings are examples of _____ _____.

11. To help the reader easily re-create or comprehend the procedure you are explaining, do not make any _____ about the reader's knowledge, and do not leave out even the smallest critical _____. You must anticipate all of your readers' _____ and make sure you provide answers.

12. A process may need several _____ for development.

13. Processes can also take the form of complete essays in which the goal or end result of the process is stated in a _____.

Topic Ideas for Process Writing Assignments

Exercise 11.1 includes topic ideas you may want to develop into process paragraphs or essays. Here are some additional ideas:

- How to make something related to one of your hobbies
- How to prepare for a job interview
- How to do a particular exercise correctly
- How to be a happier person
- How to find the information you need on the Internet
- How to choose a career that is right for you
- How a certain product is manufactured

- How e-mail works

- How to create your own Web site

- How to tie a necktie (see the accompanying diagram)

WebWork

Go to the Guide to Grammar and Writing Web site's information about writing process essays at **http://grammar.ccc.commnet.edu/grammar/composition/process.htm.** Read the information on this page, including the sample essay. Then, on your own paper, write your answers to the questions in the "Points to Ponder" box.

    For more examples of process essays, click on the links under the "Additional Readings" heading.

Online Study Center   For additional information and practice with writing process paragraphs and essays, go to the Houghton Mifflin Online Study Center for this book, at **http://www.college.hmco.com/pic/dolphinwritertwo.**

12 Illustration

GOALS FOR CHAPTER 12

▶ Define the term *illustration*.

▶ Describe the steps in writing an illustration paragraph.

▶ Write an illustration paragraph.

▶ Recognize the features of an illustration essay.

Illustrating ideas by providing specific examples is a valuable way to help readers understand ideas. We often make general or vague statements or use abstract terms that readers will not be able to understand or correctly interpret if we do not provide one or more examples. Look, for instance, at the following statement:

> Japanese culture has developed indirectness to a fine art.

Do you know what the writer means by this statement? What does *indirectness* mean? You probably need additional clarification and explanation. When the writer provides an example, the meaning of this statement becomes much clearer:

> Japanese culture has developed indirectness to a fine art. For example, a Japanese anthropologist[1], Harumi Befu, explains the delicate exchange of indirectness required by a simple invitation to lunch. When his friend extended the invitation, Befu first had to determine whether it was meant literally or just *pro forma*[2], much as an American might say, "We'll have to have you over for dinner some time" but would not expect you to turn up at the door. Having decided the invitation was meant literally and having accepted, Befu was then asked what he would like to eat. Following custom, he said anything would do, but his friend, also following custom, pressed him to specify. Host and guest repeated this exchange an appropriate number of times, until Befu deemed[3] it polite to answer

---

1. **anthropologist:** scientist who studies the behavior of humans
2. *pro forma:* done as a formality
3. **deemed:** thought

the question—politely—by saying that tea over rice would be fine. When he arrived for lunch, he was indeed served tea over rice—as the last course of a sumptuous[1] meal. Befu was not surprised by the feast, because he knew that protocol[2] required it. Had he been given what he had asked for, he would have been insulted. But protocol also required that he make a great show of being surprised. (Deborah Tannen, "His Politeness Is Her Powerlessness," in *Identities*, ed. Ann Raimes [Boston: Houghton Mifflin, 1996], p. 158)

This paragraph provides one long, extended example of a lunch invitation to illustrate the main idea. After you had read this example, the idea stated in the topic sentence probably made a lot more sense.

Other paragraphs might offer several examples instead of just one longer example:

The Puritans[3] were a daring lot, but they had a mean streak. They hated the theater and banned Christmas. They punished people in a cruel and inhuman manner. They killed children who disobeyed their parents. When they came in contact with those whom they considered heathens[4] or aliens, they behaved in such a bizarre and irrational manner that this chapter in American history comes down to us as a late-movie horror film. They exterminated the Indians, who taught them how to survive in a world unknown to them, and their encounter with the calypso[5] culture of Barbados resulted in what the tourist guide in Salem's Witches' House refers to as Witchcraft Hysteria. (Excerpted from Ishmael Reed, "America: The Multinational Society," in *Identities*, ed. Ann Raimes [Boston: Houghton Mifflin, 1996], pp. 483–484.)

In this paragraph, the author provides multiple examples to illustrate his point that Puritans were mean.

Writing an Illustration Paragraph

Some topic sentences will need to be illustrated with specific examples. When you develop a paragraph using illustration, you give specific instances that back up the claim you make in your topic sentence.

1. **sumptuous:** of a size or splendor suggesting great expense; lavish
2. **protocol:** code of correct conduct
3. **Puritans:** a group of religious sixteenth- and seventeenth-century settlers in America
4. **heathens:** people who are not religious or do not acknowledge the God worshiped by the followers of Christianity, Judaism, or Islam
5. **calypso:** a type of music originating in the Caribbean

Determining a Main Idea and Writing a Topic Sentence

A topic sentence that will need to be developed with one or more examples usually states a general observation or opinion (its main idea):

> Too many children today are spoiled and undisciplined.
>
> Many modern companies are trying to make the workplace more fun.
>
> Television offers several good shows that help prepare kids for school.

To prove that the observation in each topic sentence is valid, each paragraph would need to be developed with one longer example or several shorter examples.

EXERCISE 12.1   **Writing Topic Sentences for Illustration Paragraphs**

For each of the following topics, use some prewriting techniques to generate ideas, and then write a topic sentence you could use for an illustration paragraph.

1. Funny television shows

Topic Sentence: _____

2. Dangerous jobs

Topic Sentence: _____

3. Cheating among students

Topic Sentence: _____

4. Turning setbacks into opportunities

Topic Sentence: _____

5. Overrated (or underrated) actors or musicians

Topic Sentence: _____

Selecting Relevant Examples

In Chapter 10, you learned to convey a dominant impression in a description by carefully choosing the right details. Similarly, illustration must incorporate only those examples that develop the main idea. Whether you choose to include one example or several, all examples must directly relate to the point you are trying to make. Therefore, if you were trying to illustrate that modern Americans are far too busy and overscheduled, you would choose several examples of people you know who are busy and overscheduled. You would not bring up people who do not demonstrate these qualities.

To discover the best examples, begin by prewriting. Then weed out any example that does not exactly match your main point.

EXERCISE 12.2 **Selecting Relevant Examples**

For each of the following topic sentences, circle the letter of the example in the list that would not develop the topic sentence.

1. Topic sentence: Exercising can be a lot of fun.

   a. Get together with friends to play childhood games like kickball and dodgeball.
   b. Go out to dance clubs and work up a sweat by dancing to your favorite music.
   c. Do 100 sit-ups on your living room floor.

2. Topic sentence: The police officers in our town harass young people.

   a. They will not let teenagers loiter outside the movie theater, even when the young people are just hanging out.
   b. They frequently set up road blocks to check to make sure motorists are wearing their seatbelts.
   c. They will not let kids ride their skateboards at a vacant and abandoned old strip mall.

3. Topic sentence: My aunt is a very frugal person.

   a. She makes a high salary in her position as a loan officer at a bank.
   b. She clips coupons and uses them to save a lot of money in stores.
   c. She shops only in discount stores and never buys anything that is not on sale.

4. Topic Sentence: Computers can help you manage the details of your personal life.

   a. You can store information in computer calendars and address books.
   b. You can play games on your computer.
   c. You can manage your finances with computer software that allows you to create budgets and track expenses.

5. Topic Sentence: Elements of Mexican culture are entering the American mainstream.

   a. More Americans celebrate Cinco de Mayo, a Mexican holiday.
   b. Tortillas are a Mexican food that has become a popular ingredient of "wrap" sandwiches in many American restaurants.
   c. More and more Americans are choosing to vacation in Mexico.

Including Adequate Examples

After prewriting to generate the examples you want to include, consider whether or not you are providing an adequate number of examples. Readers will not be able to understand or agree with your main point if they do not feel as though they have been given enough information. In the case of a controversial idea, or one that is difficult to believe, you will have to provide sufficient examples to get the reader to accept that idea. For example, if you are trying to convince readers that several recent sightings of the Loch Ness Monster prove that it is indeed a real, living dinosaur, you will need to provide several examples of these sightings to persuade skeptical readers that this opinion is valid. If you give only one example of a particular encounter, you will probably not have offered enough evidence in support of your point.

If you decide that one extended example will provide adequate support, then make sure you fully develop that example with plenty of detail. (See "Developing an Illustration Paragraph" later in this chapter.)

 **Adding Examples**

Read the following paragraph. Then, on the blanks provided, list two or three additional examples the writer could add to better support the paragraph's main idea.

Reality TV shows are really quite fascinating. Take *Survivor*, for instance. It includes exciting challenges that have viewers rooting for their favorite contestants. It also offers an interesting look at teamwork and at how people develop personal relationships in adverse circumstances.

Additional examples:

_____

_____

_____

Organizing Details and Using Transitions

If you include several examples in support of your main idea, you will need to decide on the best order in which to present them. Sometimes the order will not matter. If all of your examples are equal in importance, you can arrange them in any order. At other times, though, some examples will be more significant than others. In that case, you will need to decide whether you should present the most important examples first or save them for last. In the paragraph about the Loch Ness Monster, for instance, you might want to present your strongest example first so that readers will not dismiss your point out of hand and stop reading. Then save the weaker evidence for later in the paragraph, after you have convinced readers that your claim is possible.

After you have decided on the best order for your examples, list them in that order in an outline. Then, as you write, make sure that you include transitions to help readers follow your organizational pattern and progression of thought. Some common illustration transitional expressions are

for example	an illustration of this is
for instance	one example
to illustrate	another example (or instance)
in one case	a case in point is

EXERCISE 12.4   **Organizing Details in Illustration Paragraphs**

Prewrite to generate ideas, and then complete each of the following topic sentences by filling in the blank. Then, on the other blanks provided, prepare an informal outline by listing the examples you would include in an appropriate order.

1. Many inventors have helped to make the world _____.

_____

_____

_____

_____

_____

2. People who _____ are usually happier and less stressed.

_____

_____

_____

_____

_____

3. Being successful is a matter of _____.

_____

_____

_____

_____

_____

EXERCISE 12.5   **Recognizing Illustration Transitions**

Circle all of the illustration transitional words in the following paragraph.

There has never been another generation of Americans whose intellect and achievements have equaled those of this country's Founding Fathers[1]. Take Benjamin Franklin, for example. He was not only a successful businessman but also an inventor, author, philosopher, and statesman. It was Franklin who persuaded the French to help the American patriots win the Revolutionary War, and it was Franklin whose wisdom guided the creation of the new American republic by helping to settle disagreements about how it should be formed. He was the only person to sign all four documents—the Declaration of Independence, the Alliance with France, the Peace Treaty with England, and the Constitution—that established the United States as an independent nation. Another example was Franklin's colleague[2] Thomas Jefferson. He, too, was a philosopher, inventor, and writer. He wrote the Declaration of Independence, served as third president of the United States, and founded the University of Virginia. A third case in point is Jefferson's friend and colleague James Madison, the fourth president of our country as well as the father of the U.S. Constitution. And do not forget about many of the other great Founding Fathers, such as George Washington, John Adams, and Alexander Hamilton.

EXERCISE 12.6   **Writing an Illustration Paragraph That Includes Transitions**

Choose one of the topic sentences and outlines you prepared in Exercise 12.4. Write the paragraph, including transitions that indicate how the details are related.

---

1. **Founding Fathers:** members of the convention that drafted the U.S. Constitution in 1787

2. **colleague:** a fellow member of a profession or group

Developing an Illustration Paragraph

If you have decided to develop your illustration paragraph with several shorter examples, you will probably only briefly mention each one. Thus, you will probably write just one to three sentences to explain each example.

If you have decided to include just one extended example, however, you will need to develop this example with even more specific detail. These specific details will often take the form of narratives or descriptions, which are discussed in Chapters 9 and 10 of this book. As you are developing each example with one or both of these modes, remember what you have learned about structuring a narrative, creating a dominant impression in a description, using descriptive language such as specific words and factual and sensory details, and all of the other principles of effective narration and description.

Look back at the paragraph about indirectness in Japanese culture (pages 242–243); it is developed with a narrative. The story includes many details about what happened, what both people said, and how they behaved.

FOCUS ON RESEARCH

Evaluating the Credibility of Sources

In Chapters 9, 10, and 11, you learned about the different library, Internet, and nonprint sources that can provide material to help you develop your ideas. But finding information about your topic is not enough. You must also evaluate it to make sure it is *credible*, or believable and trustworthy. If you do not use credible sources, then you will weaken your support for your own ideas. Information on Internet Web sites, in particular, should be carefully examined for its worthiness and accuracy. Here are questions to ask yourself when you are considering a source's credibility:

1. **Is the information current and up-to-date?** When was the book or article published? When was the Web site posted or updated? You will want to include only the latest information, so avoid facts and statistics that seem too old.

2. **Who wrote or posted the information?** Is an author identified? What are the author's credentials? Does he or she seem qualified to be considered an "authority" on the topic? If not, the information may not be credible. Be careful when using Internet Web sites, in particular, for anyone can create a Web site and post information or opinions on it.

3. **Do the ideas and information agree with those in other reputable sources you have found?** Beware of outlandish claims that are contrary to everything else you have read about a topic.

4. **How objective does the information seem?** Does the author provide information about his or her sources, and are those sources reputable? If the author seeks to persuade you, could he or she have manipulated the facts or data to support his or her position? Could the information actually be a form of advertising?

Writing Longer Illustration Passages and Illustration Essays

So far, this chapter has focused only on illustration paragraphs. However, an illustration may need several paragraphs for development. For example, read the following passage:

> **If you learn that failing even a little penalizes[1] you (e.g., being wrong only 15%** **of the time garners[2] you only a "B" performance), you learn not to make mistakes.** And more important, you learn not to put yourself in situations where you might fail. This leads to conservative[3] thought patterns designed to avoid the stigma[4] our society puts on "failure."
>
> I have a friend who recently graduated from college with a Master's degree in journalism. For the last six months, she has been trying to find a job, but to no avail[5]. I talked with her about her situation, and realized that her problem is that she doesn't know how to fail. She went through eighteen years of schooling without ever failing an examination, a paper, a midterm, a pop quiz, or a final. Now, she is reluctant to try any approaches where she might fail. She has been conditioned to believe that failure is bad in and of itself, rather than a potential stepping stone to new ideas.
>
> Look around. How many middle managers, housewives, administrators, teachers, and other people do you see who are afraid to try anything new because of this fear of failure? Most of us have learned not to make mistakes in public. As a result, we remove ourselves from many learning experiences except for those occurring in the most private of circumstances. (Roger von Oech, "To Err Is Wrong," in *Viewpoints,* ed. W. Royce Adams, 4th ed. [Boston: Houghton Mifflin, 2001], pp. 84–85.)

Although this illustration covers three paragraphs, it develops just one topic sentence, which is highlighted. To illustrate the idea in this topic sentence, the author provides one longer, extended illustration, which is developed with narration, and briefly mentions a few other examples in the third paragraph.

Illustrations can also take the form of complete essays. To write an illustration essay, follow the steps for writing an illustration paragraph. First, prewrite to generate ideas and to decide on your main idea. Identify in your thesis statement your idea or observation. Next, select one or more relevant examples, making sure that you have gathered a number adequate for supporting or proving

1. **penalizes:** punishes
2. **garners:** gets
3. **conservative:** traditional, restrained, or cautious

4. **stigma:** mark of disgrace
5. **avail:** use or advantage

the idea in your thesis statement. Arrange these examples in an outline according to some type of appropriate organizational pattern, such as most important to least important. As you write, include transitional words that indicate how the examples are related, and fully develop each example with details, such as narratives or descriptions.

EXERCISE 12.7   **The Illustration Essay**

Read the following essay. Then answer the questions by writing your responses on the blanks provided.

Taking It Off the Streets

By John Leo

1   If you are worried about the state of free speech in America, consider the case of longtime protester Brett Bursey. Last October the 54-year-old Bursey, carrying an antiwar sign, was arrested at Columbia Metropolitan Airport in South Carolina during a visit by President Bush. He was on public property at the time but was charged with trespassing because he was outside the zone established for demonstrators that day. The zone was on the edge of a highway, a half-mile away from the president, where neither Bush nor the media were likely to notice.

2   The Bursey case contains other oddities. Bursey charges viewpoint discrimination—he says an airport policeman specifically told him his sign ("No war for oil") was a problem for authorities. Local charges were dropped, but Bursey faces federal charges under a rarely used statute[1] that allows the Secret Service[2] to restrict access to areas where the president is visiting. The U.S. attorney's office says the sign and Bursey's protest were not issues: "The problem was where he was doing it." Federal charges against out-of-place but peaceful protesters are unusual, particularly when the charges carry maximum penalties that run to six months in jail and a $5,000 fine. Perhaps when the case comes to trial, we will learn more, including why the feds[3] bothered to file charges five months after a minor and apparently harmless act of defiance[4].

3   Serious discussion about the rights of protesters is out of fashion right now, partly because the media prefer to focus on the low-level complaints of antiwar celebrities. But there are several troubling trends, among them what seems to be a policy of more and quicker arrests, the practice of banishing protesters to far-away sites, and a tactic that Jonathan Turley of George Washington University's law school calls trap-and-arrest.

1. **statute:** law
2. **Secret Service:** government agency that protects the U.S. president
3. **feds:** federal agents
4. **defiance:** opposition or resistance to authority

4   Turley thinks the District of Columbia police deliberately encircled large numbers of protesters for mass arrests at last September's World Bank–International Monetary Fund demonstration in Washington. The goal, he thinks, was to break the protest by removing as many people as possible from the streets without giving them any chance to leave the area. Reporters and bystanders were hauled into custody. Turley said a group of protesters on bicycles, pedaling legally through the area, were guided by police into Pershing Park, penned in there, and then arrested along with everyone else. Police in cities around the country, Turley thinks, are looking for a convenient way to control protests, and they all saw what happened in D.C.

5   Keeping protesters a half-mile from the action is becoming a standard tactic and not just in anti-Bush or antiwar cases. Authorities did a job on Martha Burk and her demonstration against the all-male Augusta National Golf Club during the Masters. The sheriff put Burk and her group in a muddy pit, eight feet below street level, far from the club and well out of sight of approaching cars. Anti-Burk demonstrators were allowed closer to the gates than the pro-Burk contingent[1].

6   Colleges have adopted this technique, too. At least 20 campuses have set up "free-speech zones," effectively converting 99 percent of the campus into a giant censorship zone. The authorities usually explain that noisy protests can interfere with classes, though disallowing bullhorns[2] during certain hours would take care of this alleged[3] problem.

7   To be effective, many protests have to be site-specific. A protest against administrators needs to be mounted at the administration building, not off in some corner where officials can avoid noticing. But penning students into one or two small areas strongly appeals to administrators afflicted with an authoritarian[4] bent. At some schools, students are now being punished for handing out leaflets[5] in an unauthorized area. Twelve Florida State students were arrested for refusing to move their anti-sweatshop[6] protest to a designated zone.

8   Some colleges allow free speech outside of designated zones but not if it is "potentially disruptive." This opens the door to viewpoint discrimination, always a problem on campus. At the University of Houston, a Christmas tree in a campus plaza was taken down as potentially disruptive, and a graphic antiabortion display was forbidden though pro-lifers[7] complained that many other protests had been allowed in the plaza. Some campus "free-speech zones" are being

---

1. **contingent:** group
2. **bullhorns:** handheld devices used to increase the volume of the voice
3. **alleged:** supposed
4. **authoritarian:** favoring obedience to authority and opposing personal freedom

5. **leaflets:** printed information; fliers distributed to people
6. **sweatshop:** shop or factory that employs workers for long hours at low wages
7. **pro-lifers:** people who oppose abortion

eliminated, largely under pressure from the Philadelphia-based Foundation for Individual Rights in Education (FIRE).

9 Protecting the right to protest needn't be one of those dreaded right-vs.-left *Crossfire*[1] issues. Both sides should agree that it's OK to disagree—especially in public.*

1. What is the thesis of this essay? Write it on the blank below in your own words.

   _____

2. Does the author offer several examples or just one extended example in support of his thesis statement?

   _____

3. How many examples does the author provide to support the main idea of paragraph 7?

   _____

4. Does the author use any illustration transitional words? Do you think that he should add more? If so, where should they be added?

   _____

   _____

5. After reading this essay, do you agree with the author's thesis statement? Why or why not?

   _____

In Summary: Steps in Writing Illustrations

1. **Select relevant examples.** Make sure each example matches your main idea or thesis.

2. **Plan to include a sufficient number of examples.** You might be able to provide just one extended example, but ask yourself whether you could reinforce your point better if you provided several examples.

1. *Crossfire:* a television program with analysis and debate of social and political issues

*Source: John Leo, "Taking It Off the Streets," *U.S. News and World Report*, May 12, 2003, p. 50. Copyright © Chloe Consulting Ltd. Reprinted by permission of the author.

3. **Organize your examples.** Decide whether some of them are more important than others, and arrange them accordingly.

4. **As you write, develop each example (as appropriate) with narration or description.** Refer to Chapters 9 and 10 to review the principles of writing effective narratives and descriptions.

CHAPTER 12 REVIEW

Fill in the blanks in the following statements.

1. _____ is providing specific examples to help readers understand general or vague statements or abstract terms.

2. Using illustration to develop a paragraph may involve providing one long, extended _____ or several shorter _____.

3. A topic sentence that will need to be developed with one or more examples usually states a general _____.

4. Illustration must incorporate only those examples that develop the _____.

5. Readers will not be able to understand or agree with your point if you do not provide _____ examples.

6. If all of your examples are _____ in importance, you can arrange them in any order.

7. If some of your examples are more significant than others, you might want to present the _____ example first.

8. Common illustration _____ include *for example, for instance,* and *in one case.*

9. _____ and _____ are two modes often used to develop longer, extended examples.

10. An illustration may need several _____ for development.

11. Illustrations can also take the form of complete essays in which the idea or observation to be illustrated is stated in a _____.

Topic Ideas for Illustration Writing Assignments

Exercise 12.1 includes topic ideas you may want to develop into illustration paragraphs or essays. Here are some additional ideas:

- A bad day
- Technological improvements
- A specific habit of successful people
- High-profile athletes who break the law
- Aggressive drivers
- A quality that all effective teachers possess
- A benefit of being a volunteer
- Low-fat snacks
- A problem with cell phones
- High-paying jobs that are also fun

WebWork

Go to the Guide to Grammar and Writing Web site's information about writing illustration essays at **http://grammar.ccc.commnet.edu/grammar/composition/examples.htm.** Read the information on this page, including the sample essays. Then, on your own paper, write your answers to the questions in the "Points to Ponder" box.

Online Study Center   For additional information and practice with writing illustration paragraphs and essays, go to the Houghton Mifflin Online Study Center for this book, at **http://www.college.hmco.com/pic/dolphinwritertwo.**

13 Classification

GOALS FOR CHAPTER 13

▶ Define the term *classification*.

▶ Describe the steps in writing a classification paragraph.

▶ Write a classification paragraph.

▶ Recognize the features of a classification essay.

Sometimes you will need to show how similar things can be grouped together. Grouping things that are alike together—which is called *classifying*—often helps readers better understand both the larger thing and the relationships among its elements. The paragraph that follows, for example, classifies psychological stressors, the negative events that cause people stress:

> Psychological stressors[1] are often described as catastrophic events, life changes and strains, chronic stressors, or daily hassles. *Catastrophic events* are sudden, unexpected, potentially life-threatening experiences or traumas, such as physical or sexual assault, military combat, natural disasters, terrorist attacks, and accidents. *Life changes and strains* include divorce, illness in the family, difficulties at work, moving to a new place, and other circumstances that create demands to which people must adjust. *Chronic stressors*—those that continue over a long period of time—include circumstances such as living near a noisy airport, having a serious illness, being unable to earn a decent living, residing in a high-crime neighborhood, being the victim of discrimination, and even enduring years of academic pressure. *Daily hassles* include irritations, pressures, and annoyances that might not be significant stressors by themselves but whose cumulative[2] effects can be significant. (Adapted from Douglas Bernstein et al., *Psychology*, 6th ed. [Boston: Houghton Mifflin, 2003], p. 488)

1. **stressors:** things that cause stress

2. **cumulative:** adding up over time

The preceding paragraph groups stressors into four different categories based on their sources and then offers examples to illustrate each category.

The topic you have chosen for your paragraph will dictate a need for classification. For instance, if you need to explain a large topic, such as architectural style, the reader may grasp it more readily if you classify the major types of architectural styles. Notice how the following paragraph, for example, classifies the language we speak into five different types:

> It fascinates me how differently we all speak in different circumstances. We have levels of formality, as in our clothing. There are very formal occasions, often requiring written English: the job application or the letter to the editor—the dark-suit, serious-tie language, with everything pressed and the lint brushed off. There is our less formal out-in-the-world language—a more comfortable suit, but still respectable. There is language for close friends in the evenings, on weekends—bluejeans-and-sweatshirt language, when it's good to get the tie off. There is family language, even more relaxed, full of grammatical short cuts, family slang, echoes of old jokes that have become intimate shorthand—the language of pyjamas and uncombed hair. Finally, there is the language with no clothes on; the talk of couples—murmurs, sighs, grunts—language at its least self-conscious, open, vulnerable, and primitive. (Excerpted from Robert MacNeil, "Wordstruck," in *Patterns Plus*, ed. Mary Lou Conlin, 7th ed. [Boston: Houghton Mifflin, 2002], p. 120.)

To write effective classification paragraphs, follow the principles presented in the next section of this chapter.

Writing a Classification Paragraph

Classification focuses on the distinguishing features of various people or things and groups things that are alike together. To successfully classify a subject, you will need to apply an organizing principle, find the best order for the resulting groups, and develop your ideas with descriptive details and/or examples.

Applying an Organizing Principle, Determining a Main Idea, and Writing a Topic Sentence

Things can be classified a number of different ways. For example, think of how many ways there are to classify people. We can group people according to personality type by using categories such as the ones from the Myers-Briggs personality inventory or by grouping people according to whether they possess "Type A" characteristics or "Type B" characteristics. We can classify them according to socioeconomic class into groups that we could label lower class, middle class, or upper class. We can group them by the type of work they perform: blue collar or white collar. We can group them according to social groups: popular people, jocks, nerds, loners, and so forth. These different ways of classifying are based on an *organizing principle*, a basis for the groupings. In the previous examples, personality, socioeconomic class, line of work, and social group are the different organizing principles. When classifying things, make sure you apply only *one* organizing principle to avoid overlap among different groups. You should avoid concluding, for instance, that your groups are blue-collar workers, the middle class, and the upper class, because some of the blue-collar workers might also belong in the middle-class or upper-class categories.

When you write your topic sentence, consider naming your categories if you have just a few. For example, you could write: "The three types of rocks are igneous, sedimentary, and metamorphic." However, if there are numerous categories, you might write a more general statement: "The Myers-Briggs system has identified sixteen different personality types."

EXERCISE 13.1 **Applying Organizing Principles for Classification**

For each topic given, think of two different organizing principles and then generate three groups that would result from the application of each principle.

1. Topic: Food

Organizing Principle #1: _____   Organizing Principle #2: _____

Groups: Groups:

_____   _____

_____   _____

_____   _____

2. Topic: Films

Organizing Principle #1: _____   Organizing Principle #2: _____

Groups: Groups:

_____   _____

_____   _____

_____   _____

3. Topic: Friends

Organizing Principle #1: _____   Organizing Principle #2: _____

Groups: Groups:

_____   _____

_____   _____

_____   _____

EXERCISE 13.2 **Writing Topic Sentences for Classification Paragraphs**

For each of the following topics, use some prewriting techniques to generate ideas, and then write a topic sentence you could use for a classification paragraph.

1. Students

Topic sentence: _____

2. Neighbors

Topic sentence: _____

3. College classes

Topic sentence: _____

4. Crimes

Topic sentence: _____

5. Computer users

Topic sentence: _____

Organizing Details and Using Transitions

Once you have determined your groups, organizing a classification paragraph tends to be relatively easy. You simply devote one section of the paragraph to each group. However, you will need to determine whether these groups should be presented in a particular order. They may be equal, making their order irrelevant. However, if one group is significantly larger than others, you might consider arranging them from largest to smallest, or vice versa. If the classification is based on other quantities, such as dollar amounts, you might consider arranging them in ascending or descending order. Also, consider whether you should organize them by order of importance.

As you write, make sure you include transitional words to help readers follow your organization and train of thought. Classification paragraphs present a series of groups or categories, so they typically include transitional phrases such as

first	second	third
one category	a second kind	another type
the first group	the next group	the last group

EXERCISE 13.3 **Organizing Details in Classification Paragraphs**

Prewrite to generate ideas, and then complete each of the following topic sentences by filling in the blank. Then, on the other blanks provided, prepare an informal outline by listing the examples you would include in an appropriate order.

1. In my experience, there are _____ types of coworkers.

_____

_____

_____

_____

_____

2. Cooks fall into one of _____ categories.

_____

_____

_____

_____

_____

3. There are _____ types of lies.

_____

_____

_____

_____

_____

EXERCISE 13.4 **Recognizing Classification Transitions**

Circle all of the classification transitional words in the following paragraph.

> When most people think of domestic violence, they think of physical abuse that results in bruises or broken bones for the victim. However, physical abuse is just one kind of domestic violence; abuse occurs in three other forms as well. A second form of abuse is sexual, which includes rape or forcing the victim to unwillingly perform other physical acts. Another category of abuse is psychological, in which the abuser uses threats or taunts to instill fear in the victim and, thus, gain power over him or her. Finally, there is economic abuse, which involves the abuser's control of his or her victim's means of financial support. (The Missouri Coalition Against Domestic Violence, www.mocadv.org)

EXERCISE 13.5 **Writing a Classification Paragraph That Includes Transitions**

Choose one of the topic sentences and outlines you prepared in Exercise 13.3. Write the paragraph, including transitional words that indicate how the details are related.

Developing a Classification Paragraph

You will usually develop each group in your classification paragraph with descriptive details and examples. For example, say you are writing about intelligence, and you are classifying the different types of intelligence—such as linguistic intelligence, mathematical intelligence, musical intelligence, and so on—that have been identified by experts. As you describe each type, you will present details about the characteristics of each kind of intelligence, and you might clarify those details with illustrations of specific individuals who demonstrate these characteristics.

FOCUS ON RESEARCH

Writing a Summary

Summarizing is an important skill that you will use for incorporating source material to develop the ideas in your paragraphs and essays. In particular, you will use summaries of other sources to support your ideas in research projects such as term papers.

When you summarize a reading selection, you briefly restate, in your own words, its most important ideas. A summary usually focuses on the most general points, which include the overall main idea and some of the major supporting details. As a result, summaries are much shorter than the original material. A paragraph can usually be summarized in a sentence or two, and an entire article can be summarized in a paragraph.

To write a summary, follow these three steps:

1. Using active reading techniques, read and reread the original material until you understand it.

2. Identify the main idea and major supporting points. In particular, underline all of the topic sentences. You might also want to create an outline or map that diagrams the general and specific relationships among sentences (in a paragraph) or paragraphs (in an article or chapter).

3. Using your own words, write sentences that state the author's main idea, along with the most important major details. Your paraphrase should be accurate; it should not add anything that did not appear in the original or omit anything important from the original. It should also be objective. In other words, do not offer your own reactions or opinions; just restate the author's points without commenting on them. If you use a phrase from the original, enclose it in quotation marks to indicate that it is the author's words, not yours.

Writing Longer Classification Passages and Classification Essays

So far, this chapter has focused only on classification paragraphs. However, a classification may need several paragraphs for development. For example, read the following passage:

1 The most widely accepted approach to classifying consumer products is based on characteristics of consumer buying behavior. It divides products into four categories: convenience, shopping, specialty, and unsought products. However, not all buyers behave in the same way when purchasing a specific type of product. Thus, a single product can fit into several categories. To minimize this problem, marketers think in terms of how buyers *generally* behave when purchasing a specific item. In addition, they recognize that the "correct" classification can be deter-

mined only by considering a particular firm's intended target market. Examining the four traditional categories of consumer products can provide further insight.

2   Convenience products are relatively inexpensive, frequently purchased items for which buyers exert only minimal purchasing effort. They range from bread, soft drinks, and chewing gum to gasoline and newspapers. The buyer spends little time planning the purchase or comparing available brands or sellers. Today time has become one of our most precious assets, and many consumers therefore buy products at the closest location to preserve time for other activities. Even a buyer who prefers a specific brand will readily choose a substitute if the preferred brand is not conveniently available.

3   Shopping products are items for which buyers are willing to expend considerable effort in planning and making the purchase. Buyers spend much time comparing stores and brands with respect to prices, product features, qualities, services, and perhaps warranties. Shoppers may compare products at a number of outlets such as Best Buy, Circuit City, Sears, or Home Depot. Appliances, bicycles, furniture, stereos, cameras, and shoes exemplify shopping products. These products are expected to last a fairly long time and thus are purchased less frequently than convenience items. Although shopping products are more expensive than convenience products, few buyers of shopping products are particularly brand loyal. Most consumers, for example, are not brand loyal for computers and clothing. If they were, they would be unwilling to shop and compare among brands. Even when they are brand loyal, they may still spend considerable time comparing the features of different models of a brand. A consumer looking for a new Maytag washing machine, for example, may explore the company's website to compare the features of different washers before talking to a salesperson. Regardless of the number of brands of interest, buyers may also consult buying guides such as *Consumer Reports* or visit consumer information websites such as www.epinions.com to view others' opinions or ratings of brands and models before making an actual purchase.

4   Specialty products possess one or more unique characteristics, and generally buyers are willing to expend considerable effort to obtain them. Buyers actually plan the purchase of a specialty product; they know exactly what they want and will not accept a substitute. Examples of specialty products include a Mont Blanc pen and a one-of-a-kind piece of baseball memorabilia, such as a ball signed by Babe Ruth. When searching for specialty products, buyers do not compare alternatives; they are concerned primarily with finding an outlet that has the preselected product available. Tag Heuer, for example, issued a special Indy 500 watch designed especially for racing fans.

5   Unsought products are products purchased when a sudden problem must be solved, products of which customers are unaware, and products that people do not necessarily think of purchasing. Emergency medical services and

automobile repairs are examples of products needed quickly to solve a problem. A consumer who is sick or injured has little time to plan to go to an emergency medical center or a hospital. Likewise, in the event of a broken fan belt on the highway, a consumer will likely seek out the nearest auto repair facility to get back on the road as quickly as possible. Computer users must purchase antivirus and spyware detection software to protect their computers even though they may not want to make such purchases. In such cases, speed and problem resolution are far more important than price and other features buyers might consider if they had more time for decision making. Companies such as ServiceMaster (Rescue Rooter and Furniture Medic) and First Service (Colliers International and CMN International) are making the purchases of these unsought products more bearable by building trust with consumers through recognizable brands and superior functional performance.*

Although this passage covers five paragraphs, it develops one main idea. This main idea can be paraphrased as *Consumer products can be classified into four categories: convenience, shopping, specialty, and unsought products*. The authors develop each category with specific details.

Classifications can also take the form of complete essays. To write a classification essay, follow the same steps for writing a classification paragraph. First, prewrite to discover an organizing principle, generate ideas, and decide on your main idea. When you write your thesis statement, consider naming your categories if there are just a few. Next, determine the best order for your categories and plan to devote one paragraph to each one. As you write, include transitions that indicate how the categories are related and fully develop each one with descriptive details and examples.

EXERCISE 13.6 **The Classification Essay**

Read the following essay. Then answer the questions that follow by writing your responses on the blanks provided.

How Do I Love Thee?

1 Intimacy, passion and commitment are the warm, hot and cold vertices[1] of Sternberg's[2] love triangle. Alone and in combination they give rise to eight possible kinds of love relationships. The first is nonlove—the absence of all three

1. **vertices:** highest points; points at which the sides of angles intersect

2. **Sternberg:** R. J. Sternberg, a psychologist who published his famous triangular theory of love in 1986

*Source: From Pride/Ferrell, *Marketing*, 14th ed. (Boston: Houghton Mifflin, 2008), pp. 305–307. Copyright © 2008 by Houghton Mifflin Company. Used with permission.

components. This describes the large majority of our personal relationships, which are simply casual interactions.

Nonlove

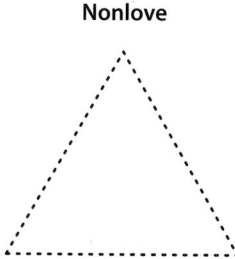

2   The second kind of love is liking. "If you just have intimacy," Sternberg explains, "that's liking. You can talk to the person, tell about your life. And if that's all there is to it, that's what we mean by liking." It is more than nonlove. It refers to the feelings experienced in true friendships. Liking includes such things as closeness and warmth but not the intense feelings of passion or commitment.

Liking

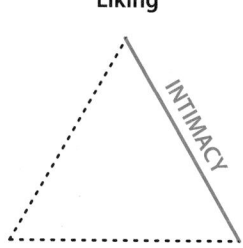

3   If you just have passion, it's called infatuated[1] love—the "love at first sight" that can arise almost instantaneously and dissipate[2] just as quickly. It involves a high degree of physiological arousal but no intimacy or commitment. It's the tenth-grader who falls madly in love with the beautiful girl in his biology class but never gets up the courage to talk to her or get to know her, Sternberg says, describing his past.

Infatuation

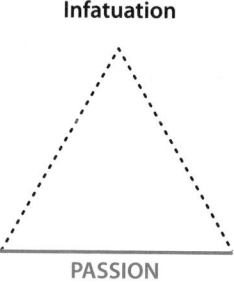

1. **infatuated:** possessed by unreasonable   2. **dissipate:** vanish; disappear
   passion or attraction

4   Empty love is commitment without intimacy or passion, the kind of love sometimes seen in a thirty-year-old marriage that has become stagnant[1]. The couple used to be intimate, but they don't talk to each other anymore. They used to be passionate, but that's died out. All that remains is the commitment to stay with the other person. In societies in which marriages are arranged, Sternberg points out, empty love may precede the other kinds of love.

Empty Love

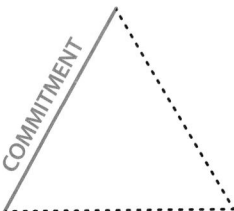

5   Romantic love, the Romeo and Juliet type of love, is a combination of intimacy and passion. More than infatuation, it's liking with the added excitement of physical attraction and arousal but without commitment. A summer affair can be very romantic, Sternberg explains, but you know it will end when she goes back to Hawaii and you go back to Florida, or wherever.

Romantic Love

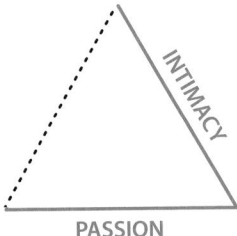

6   Passion plus commitment is what Sternberg calls fatuous[2] love. It's Hollywood love: boy meets girl, a week later they're engaged, a month later they're married. They are committed on the basis of their passion, but because intimacy

---

1. **stagnant:** not moving; motionless   2. **fatuous:** foolish; unreal

takes time to develop, they don't have the emotional core necessary to sustain the commitment. This kind of love, Sternberg warns, usually doesn't work out.

Fatuous Love

7   Companionate love is intimacy with commitment but no passion. It's a long-term friendship, the kind of committed love and intimacy frequently seen in marriages in which the physical attraction has died down.

Companionate Love

8   When all three elements of Sternberg's love triangle come together in a relationship, you get what he calls consummate love, or complete love. It's the kind of love toward which many people strive, especially in romantic relationships. Achieving consummate love, says Sternberg, is like trying to lose weight, difficult but not impossible. The really hard thing is keeping the weight off after you have lost it, or keeping the consummate love alive after you have achieved it. Consummate love is possible only in very special relationships.*

Consummate Love

*Source: Excerpted from Robert J. Trotter, "How Do I Love Thee?" in *Interactions*, Ann Moseley and Jeanette Harris, 5th ed. (Boston: Houghton Mifflin, 2003), pp. 207–210. Reprinted with permission from *Psychology Today Magazine*, copyright © 1986, Sussex Publishers, Inc.

1. What is the thesis of this essay? Write it on the blanks below in your own words.

   _____

   _____

2. What organizing principle(s) does the author apply to his topic? How many categories result from the application of this organizing principle?

   _____

3. In what order does the author present the categories?

   _____

   _____

4. Does the author use any classification transitional words? If so, where?

   _____

   _____

5. Can you think of another way to classify the topic of this essay? What categories would result from applying a different organizing principle?

   _____

In Summary: Steps in Writing Classification Assignments

1. **Select an organizing principle.** Apply just *one* principle to sort items into appropriate groups.
2. **Decide on the best order for presenting the categories.** If appropriate, arrange the groups into ascending or descending order. As you write, use transitions to help readers understand the relationships among the types.
3. **Develop each type or category with descriptive details and examples.**

Fill in the blanks in the following statements.

1. _____ is grouping like things together into categories.

2. The basis for the groupings of a classification is called the _____.

3. When you write a topic sentence for a classification paragraph, consider naming your _____ if there are just a few.

4. If all of your categories are _____ in importance, you can arrange them in any order.

5. If some of your categories are larger or more significant than others, you might want to present the _____ category first.

6. Common classification _____ include *first, second, third, one category*, and *another type*.

7. Classification paragraphs are often developed with _____ and _____.

8. A classification may need several _____ for development.

9. Classifications can also take the form of complete essays in which the topic and its categories are stated in a _____.

Topic Ideas for Classification Assignments

Exercise 13.1 includes topic ideas you may want to develop into classification paragraphs or essays. Here are some additional ideas:

- Relatives
- Goals
- Fears
- Drivers
- Change
- Parents

- Teachers
- Jobs
- Communication

Go to the Guide to Grammar and Writing Web site's information about writing classification essays at **http://grammar.ccc.commnet.edu/grammar/composition/classification.htm.** Read the information on this page, including the sample essays. Then, on your own paper, write your answers to the questions in the "Points to Ponder" box.

Online Study Center   For additional information and practice with writing classification paragraphs and essays, go to the Houghton Mifflin Online Study Center for this book, at **http://www.college.hmco.com/pic/dolphinwritertwo.**

Division

GOALS FOR CHAPTER 14

▶ Define the term *division*.

▶ Describe the steps in writing a division paragraph.

▶ Write a division paragraph.

▶ Recognize the features of a division essay.

Sometimes you will need to show how the elements of a subject that contains different things or parts can be separated from one another. Breaking a large or complex thing down into its parts—which is called *dividing*—often helps readers better understand both the larger thing and the relationships among its elements. The paragraph that follows, for example, divides the brain into three main parts:

> The vertebrate brain is divided into three major divisions: the hindbrain, mid-brain, and forebrain. The *hindbrain* is located toward the back and below the other brain regions. The cerebellum and lower brain stem structures, the medulla and pons, are located in this division. The medulla and pons are essential for maintaining life, regulating, for example, cardiac function and the sleep-wake cycle. The cerebellum is essential for maintaining the integrity of motor movement. The *midbrain* is found at the upper part of the brain stem, between the hindbrain and the forebrain. The midbrain structures control our ability to orient our ears and eyes to important events in our environment. The *forebrain* is the most evolved and complex of the brain divisions. It is the most prominent[1] and closest to the front. It is also located above the less evolved divisions. The forebrain, which is more highly developed in the human, is the division that distinguishes humans from other mammals. (Adapted from "Major Divisions of the Vertebrate Brain," http://psych.athabascau.ca/html/Psych402/Biotutorials/16/intro.shtml)

---

1. **prominent:** noticeable

Your topic will dictate whether there is a need for division. For instance, if you need to explain a complex topic, such as a machine or a large entity, to your reader, dividing it into its parts will help you present your details in an orderly way. Notice how the following paragraph, for example, divides the U.S. government into its three branches:

> The U.S. government is divided into executive, legislative, and judicial branches. In the case of the federal government, the three branches were established by the Constitution. The executive branch consists of the president, the cabinet, and the various departments and executive agencies. This branch is broadly responsible for implementing[1], supporting, and enforcing the laws made by the legislative branch and interpreted by the judicial branch. The legislative branch consists of the two houses of Congress, the Senate and the House of Representatives, and their staff. The legislature is made up of popularly elected representatives who propose laws that are sensitive to the needs and interests of their local constituents[2]. This is the branch of government empowered to make the laws that are then enforced by the executive branch and interpreted by the judicial branch. The judicial branch consists of the Supreme Court and the other federal courts, which are responsible for interpreting the laws passed by the legislative branch and enforced by the executive branch. These courts attempt to resolve conflicts impartially[3] in order to protect the individual rights guaranteed by the Constitution, within the bounds of justice, as defined by the entire body of U.S. law. (Adapted from E. D. Hirsch Jr. et al., *The New Dictionary of Cultural Literacy*, 3rd ed. [Boston: Houghton Mifflin, 2002], http://www.bartleby.com/59.)

To write effective division paragraphs, follow the principles presented in the next section of this chapter.

Writing a Division Paragraph

Division is a way of understanding a larger thing in terms of its smaller parts. To write an effective division essay, you need to determine the major and minor parts, decide on the best order for presenting those parts, and develop each part with descriptive details, examples, and possibly even an explanation of how the part works together with the other parts.

---

1. **implementing:** carrying out; putting into effect
2. **constituents:** citizens represented by an elected official

3. **impartially:** fairly; without bias toward one side or the other

Determining the Parts and the Main Idea and Writing a Topic Sentence

The first step in division is deciding what the *major* parts are. For example, if you were going to divide a bicycle into its major parts, how would you do it? You could say that a bicycle has three major parts: the frame, the wheels, and the gear and pedal mechanism. All of the bicycle's other, smaller parts can be discussed in terms of one of these major parts. The seat, for instance, is part of the frame, and the chain is part of the gear and pedal mechanism. If you are examining an organization, you could break it down into its major divisions or departments and then examine its other parts in terms of those major divisions. Doing this creates an orderly hierarchy that helps the reader more easily see how all of the parts relate to one another.

When you write your topic sentence, consider naming the major parts or at least identifying how many there are.

EXERCISE 14.1   **Determining the Parts**

Think of two different ways to divide each of the following subjects. Write the major parts of each division on the blanks provided.

   1. Classes in society

   Main Parts of Division #1: _____

   Main Parts of Division #2: _____

   2. Parts of a typical weekday

   Main Parts of Division #1: _____

   Main Parts of Division #2: _____

   3. A certain group of people or a team

   Main Parts of Division #1: _____

   Main Parts of Division #2: _____

EXERCISE 14.2   **Writing Topic Sentences for Division Paragraphs**

For each of the following topics, use some prewriting techniques to generate ideas, and then write a topic sentence you could use for a division paragraph.

   1. A historical period

   Topic sentence: _____

2. A specific body part

Topic sentence: _____

3. A major exam (e.g., the SAT, ACT, or the final exam of a course)

Topic sentence: _____

4. A place (e.g., an emergency room or an assembly line)

Topic sentence: _____

5. Periods in one's lifetime

Topic sentence: _____

Organizing the Parts and Using Transitions

To prepare to compose, create an outline that clearly groups the minor parts in terms of the major parts and reveals the relationships among all of these parts. Although you do not necessarily have to use a formal Roman-numeral outline, this format will allow you to show the relationships among all of the parts. An outline for the division of a football team, for example, might look like this:

I. Football Team
   A. Offense
      1. Quarterback
      2. Ball carriers (running back, fullback, wide receiver, tight end)
      3. Linemen (tackles, guards, center)
   B. Defense
      1. Defensive tackle
      2. Defensive ends
      3. Linebacker
      4. Cornerbacks
      5. Safeties

This outline first divides the whole team by its two major functions: offense and defense. Then it breaks those two categories into smaller parts by naming types of positions and specific players of each type.

    After you group the minor parts with the major parts, you will need to decide the order in which to present them. Sometimes the order does not matter. For example, in the paragraph about a football team, you could discuss either offense first or defense first. However, in other division paragraphs, the parts are best arranged by either time order, spatial order, or order of importance. If you are dividing the parts of a ceremony, you might want to present them in the order in which they occur, arranging them in time order. If you are dividing the parts of a machine or an organ in the body, you might want to present them in a spatial order, such as left to right or top to bottom. The earlier example of the divisions of the brain, for example, arranged the three sections from bottom to top. If you are dividing a group of some kind, you might want to use order of importance for presenting its various parts. Make sure your outline reflects the order you have chosen.

As you write, include appropriate transitional words to help the reader understand the relationships. If you use time order, include narrative transitional words (see Chapter 9 for a list of these transitional words). If you use spatial order, include spatial transitional words (see Chapter 10). If you use order of importance, you will include transitional words such as those in the following list:

first, second, third
next
last
finally
most important part
most important
above all
least important

EXERCISE 14.3 **Organizing Details in Division Paragraphs**

Prewrite to generate ideas, and then complete each of the following topic sentences by filling in the blank. Then, on the other blanks provided, prepare an informal outline by listing the parts you would include in an appropriate order.

1. The computer I use regularly is made up of _____.

_____

_____

_____

_____

_____

2. _____ is one fast-food restaurant with an efficient division of labor.

_____

_____

_____

_____

_____

3. _____ can be divided into _____ main parts.

_____

_____

_____

_____

_____

EXERCISE 14.4 **Recognizing Division Transitions**

Circle all of the division transitional words in the following paragraph.

College students can learn to control their finances by creating a budget that divides income and savings into four major sections. Using this method, you allot[1] a certain percentage of your total money to each section of the budget. The largest and most important section of the budget is dedicated to living expenses. Plan to reserve about 60 percent of your total income for rent, food, transportation costs, and utilities such as electricity and telephone service. The next major part of a budget is spending money, which should amount to about 20 percent of your income. This is money you reserve for eating out, going to movies, or doing other fun things. Third, make sure you reserve at least 10 percent of your income for unexpected or irregular expenses such as emergencies, repairs, and gifts. The final part of a budget should always be savings. Reserve at least 10 percent of your income for your future.

1. **allot:** assign; allocate

EXERCISE 14.5　Writing a Division Paragraph That Includes Transitions

Choose one of the topic sentences and outlines you prepared in Exercise 14.3. Write the paragraph, including transitions that indicate how the parts are related.

Developing the Parts in a Division Paragraph

Usually, the parts within a division essay are developed with descriptive details and examples. However, you might also need to explain how the parts work together. For example, if you were to write that essay about the football team, you would probably combine these methods of development. In your paragraph about the quarterback, you would use descriptive details to explain where he stands in the team's formation, but you would also need to explain what he does and how he does it. You might also provide an example or two of specific quarterbacks to illustrate these details.

Writing Longer Division Passages and Division Essays

So far, this chapter has focused only on division paragraphs. However, a division may need several paragraphs for development. For example, read the following passage:

1　**The U.S. Environmental Protection Agency (EPA) has two ways of analyzing the 229.2 million tons of municipal[1] solid waste generated in 2001.** The first is by material (paper and paperboard, yard trimmings, food scraps, plastics, metals, glass, wood, rubber, leather and textiles, and other); the second is by several major product categories. The product-based categories are containers and packaging; nondurable[2] goods (e.g., newspapers), durable[3] goods (e.g., appliances); food scraps; and other materials.

Materials in Municipal Solid Waste

2　A breakdown, by weight, of the municipal solid waste (MSW) materials generated in 2001 is provided in Figure ES-3. Paper and paperboard products made up the largest component[4] of municipal solid waste generated (36 percent), and yard trimming comprised the second-largest component (12 percent). Glass,

1. **municipal:** relating to a city or town
2. **nondurable:** not lasting
3. **durable:** lasting
4. **component:** part

Figure ES-3 **Municipal Solid Waste Materials Generated in 2001**

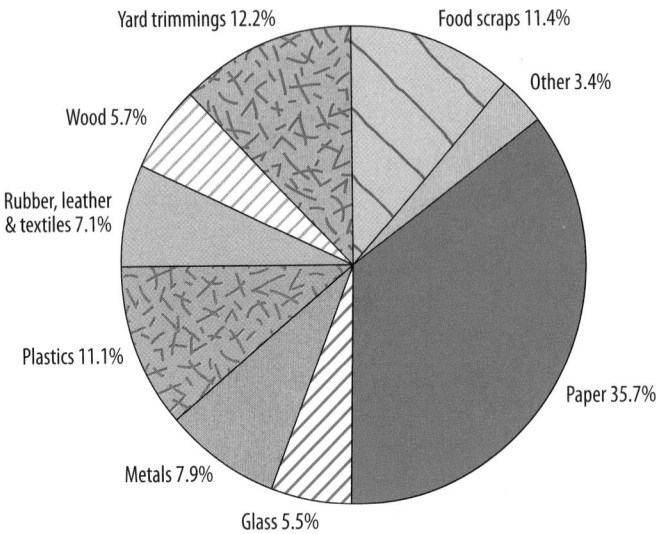

2001 Total MSW Generation — 229 Million Tons (Before Recycling)

metals, plastics, wood, and food scraps each constituted between 5 and 12 percent of the total municipal solid waste generated. Rubber, leather, and textiles combined made up about 7 percent of municipal solid waste, while other miscellaneous wastes made up approximately 3 percent of the municipal solid waste generated in 2001.

Products in Municipal Solid Waste

3 The breakdown, by weight of product categories generated in 2001, is shown in Figure ES-4. Containers and packaging comprised the largest portion of products generated, at 32.0 percent (74 million tons) of total municipal solid waste generation. Nondurable goods were the second-largest fraction, comprising[1] 26.4 percent (60 million tons). The third-largest category of products is durable goods, which comprised 16.4 percent (38 million tons) of total municipal solid waste generation.*

1. **comprising:** making up; containing

*Source: Excerpted from U.S. Environmental Protection Agency, "Municipal Solid Waste in the United States: 2001 Facts and Figures Executive Summary," http://www.epa.gov/epaoswer/non-hw/muncpl/pubs/msw-sum01.pdf.

Figure ES-4 **Products in Municipal Solid Waste in 2001**

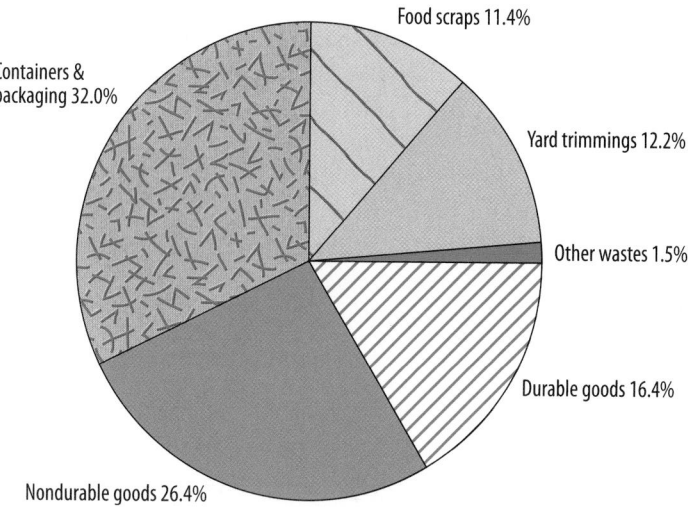

Products Generated in MSW — 2001
(Total Weight = 229 million tons)

Food scraps 11.4%

Containers & packaging 32.0%

Yard trimmings 12.2%

Other wastes 1.5%

Durable goods 16.4%

Nondurable goods 26.4%

Although this passage covers three paragraphs, it develops just one topic sentence, which is highlighted with bold print. Solid waste, or garbage, in the United States is then divided two different ways, by material and by product. Note how this information is summarized in two pie charts. Also, headings function as organizational markers, which are discussed in Chapter 11.

Divisions can also take the form of complete essays. To write a division essay, follow the same steps for writing a division paragraph. First, prewrite to discover the subject's major parts, to generate ideas, and to decide on your main idea. Next, determine the best order for the major parts and plan to devote one paragraph to each one. As you write, include transitions—such as narrative, spatial, or order-of-importance transitions—that indicate how the parts are related and fully develop your explanation of each part with descriptive details and examples.

Note-Taking Methods

If you do not use an organized system to keep up with the source material you collect during research, you run the risk of not being able to find what you need when you begin composing. Therefore, as you search for facts, quotations, and other material to incorporate into your paragraphs and essays, you will need to develop a way to collect and manage the information you find. There are several methods for taking notes, each with its advantages and disadvantages.

The Photocopy/Highlight Method

Many students photocopy or print copies of entire articles, and then they underline or highlight the information that they plan to use to develop a paragraph or essay. The advantages of this method include

- Time. It takes less time to print pages or run copies than to write down the information you need.
- Convenience. Having the entire source available later during the composition stage can be beneficial, for you may need to refer to it again.
- Accuracy. Because you have the original sentence or passage, you are less likely to make a mistake when using the information to develop the ideas in your own paper.

However, this is perhaps the most disorganized of the three note-taking methods, for each time you need a particular fact or detail, you will have to shuffle through a pile of articles in search of that piece of information. Thus, searching for that information might slow down your composition process.

The Note Card Method

This method involves writing specific facts, quotations, and other kinds of information on note cards and then labeling each card by topic or by corresponding section of the composition's outline. Although it is a much more organized method because the cards can be shuffled to follow the order of the outline, it can be more time-consuming. It also requires the careful transfer of information in order to prevent inaccuracies.

A Combination Method

You may want to consider using a system that combines the photocopy/highlight and note card methods so that you will obtain the advantages of both of these methods. To combine them, follow these steps:

1. Photocopy or print the page or article that contains the information you will need to include in your own paragraph or essay.
2. Underline or highlight the specific facts or details you need.
3. With scissors, cut out this specific passage and paste it to a note card.
4. On the note card, write the topic of the information, or, even better, write down the section of the outline to which the information corresponds. Also, do not forget to include bibliographic information (author, title, publication, publication date, page numbers, and so on) for the original source.
5. Prior to composing, follow the topics of your outline to put your note cards into the order in which you will need them.

EXERCISE 14.6 The Division Essay

Read the following essay. Then answer the questions that follow by writing your responses on the blanks provided.

The Good-News Generation

1 Ours is a four-generation family. I am a "silent" or a "mature," born before 1946 ("duty, tradition, loyalty" are the watchwords to professional generation watchers, who like to find three nouns for each group). My esteemed[1] spouse is a baby boomer[2] ("individuality, tolerance, self-absorption"), our first two daughters are generation X-ers[3] ("diversity, savvy, pragmatism") and our youngest daughter is a "millennial," a member of the cohort[4] born between 1977 and 1994. One of the best researchers and generation watchers, Ann Clurman of the Yankelovich Partners, suggests "authenticity[5], authorship, and autonomy[6]" as the three nouns for the emerging millennials, also known as generation Y or the "echo boomers."

2 The comic overtones of dividing and labeling everyone this way are hard to miss, but there is some sense to it, too. The sharp break between the silents and the boomers, obvious to all, has fueled the search for clean dividing lines between the generations that came after.

3 Now the focus is almost entirely on millennials, 78 million strong and the largest birth cohort in American history. Speaking at the American Magazine Conference last week in the Palm Springs, Calif., area, Clurman described millennials this way: They are family oriented, viscerally[7] pluralistic[8], deeply committed to authenticity and truth-telling, heavily stressed, and living in a no-boundaries world where they make short-term decisions and expect paradoxical[9] outcomes. (The sense of paradox means that every choice results in some good consequences, some bad: Air bags save lives but kill people, too.)

4 By pluralistic, Clurman means that distinctions of race, ethnicity, and gender are of little interest to millennials—they tend to overlook differences and treat everyone the same. Part of the fallout is that opposition to gay marriage, strong among older Americans, is low among millennials. Authenticity and integrity[10] are prime values. Millennials want very much to succeed in life, says Clurman, but "integrity trumps success." (Enron should have hired millennial executives.)

1. **esteemed:** respected; favorably regarded
2. **baby boomer:** American born during the late 1940s to the early 1960s
3. **generation X-ers:** Americans born during the early 1960s to the late 1970s
4. **cohort:** group
5. **authenticity:** trustworthiness; genuineness
6. **autonomy:** independence
7. **viscerally:** profoundly
8. **pluralistic:** tolerant of different ethnic, religious, and cultural groups
9. **paradoxical:** seemingly contradictory
10. **integrity:** living according to a strict code of ethics

5   Yankelovich and other researchers have been picking up a renewed emphasis on family for years. The yearning for a good marriage is a dominant value among millennials, Clurman says, and 30 percent of those surveyed say they want three or more children. Indeed, one research company, Packaged Facts and Silver Stork, recently predicted a 17 percent increase in the U.S. birthrate over the next 10 years.

6   Clurman says that as a group, boomer parents are spending a lot of time getting close to their millennial children. These are better relationships than the gen X-ers had with boomer parents, or than boomers had with their own mothers and fathers. According to Gallup, more than 90 percent of teens say they are very close to their parents. In 1974, over 40 percent of boomers said they would be better off without their parents. J. Walker Smith, president of Yankelovich, says the drive toward reconnection with family and community was showing up in the data even before 9/11[1] and is exceptionally strong today.

7   Brandchannel.com, an online marketing site run by Interbrand, issued a gen Y report last week that echoes Yankelovich. Gen Y is not turning out to be the edgy, cynical[2], ironic[3] cohort many expected, the report said. In addition to millennials' closeness to their parents, statistics on sexual activity, violence, and suicide rates are down, and concern with religion and community are up. Evidence on drinking and drugs is more mixed, but smoking, drinking, and drug use among eighth, tenth, and twelfth graders fell simultaneously in 2002 for the first time. The millennial affection for the authentic over the glitzy[4] marketing product is marked by the rise of Avril Lavigne[5], "an ordinary looking, midriff-free, nondancing singer hailed as the anti-Britney[6]," reports Brandchannel.com. Yankelovich makes the same point about Lavigne. Smith says the millennials will watch over-the-top cultural products like reality TV and the movie *Kill Bill*, but they stand apart from them and look around for more genuine, less exploitative[7] material.

8   Millennials are apt[8] to trust parents, teachers, and police. Apparently they are likely to trust presidents, too. A Harvard poll released last week reported that President Bush has a 61 percent favorability rate among American college students. This may not mean much. The millennials are not a very politically active generation. But they are clearly able to resist programming by their professors, 90 percent of whom seem convinced that Bush is either Hitler[9] or a moron[10].

1. **9/11:** September 11, 2001, the day terrorists attacked the United States	7. **exploitative:** using others for selfish ends
2. **cynical:** believing that people are selfish	8. **apt:** likely
3. **ironic:** saying the opposite of what one really means	9. **Hitler:** German dictator who founded the Nazi Party and was defeated during World War II
4. **glitzy:** showy; flashy	
5. **Avril Lavigne:** a Canadian singer	10. **moron:** idiot; stupid person
6. **Britney:** Britney Spears, an American singer	

The millennials are a very interesting generation. Now if they could just walk one block without carrying a bottle of water and making four phone calls. . . .*

1. What is the thesis of this essay? Write it on the blank below in your own words.

   _____

2. Into what four parts does the author divide today's American population?
   1. _____
   2. _____
   3. _____
   4. _____

3. Upon what does the author base his division of the population?

   _____

4. What are three main distinguishing characteristics that set millennials apart from the other generations?

   _____

5. According to the author, of which generation are you a part? Do you agree with the author's description of that generation? Why or why not?

   _____

In Summary: Steps in Writing Division Assignments

1. **Divide the subject into its major parts.** Group minor parts with their major parts.
2. **Create an outline that shows the relationships of major and minor parts.** If appropriate, arrange the parts using time order, spatial order, or order of importance. As you write, include transitions that reveal how the parts are related.
3. **Develop each part with descriptive details, examples, and/or an explanation of how the parts work together.**

*Source: John Leo, "The Good-News Generation," *U.S. News & World Report,* Nov. 3, 2003. Copyright Chloe Consulting Ltd. Reprinted by permission of the author.

CHAPTER 14 REVIEW

Fill in the blanks in the following statements.

1. _____ is breaking a large or complex thing down into its parts.

2. The first step in division is deciding what the _____ are.

3. When you write a topic sentence for a division paragraph, consider naming the _____ or telling how many there are.

4. To prepare to compose, create an _____ that clearly groups the minor parts in terms of the major parts and reveals the relationships among all of these parts.

5. Often the parts of a division paragraph are best arranged by either _____, _____, or _____.

6. Common order-of-importance _____ include *first, second, third, next, most important,* and *least important.*

7. Division paragraphs are often developed with _____ and _____.

8. A division may need several _____ for development.

9. Divisions can also take the form of complete essays in which the topic and its major parts are stated in a _____.

Topic Ideas for Division Writing Assignments

Exercises 14.1 and 14.2 include topic ideas you may want to develop into division paragraphs or essays. Here are some additional ideas:

- A ceremony or special event
- A machine, tool, or piece of equipment
- A certain population
- Analysis of an artistic work
- A specific area
- Parts of a particular document, such as a résumé

■ The parts of a baseball field (see the diagram) or some other sports-playing area:

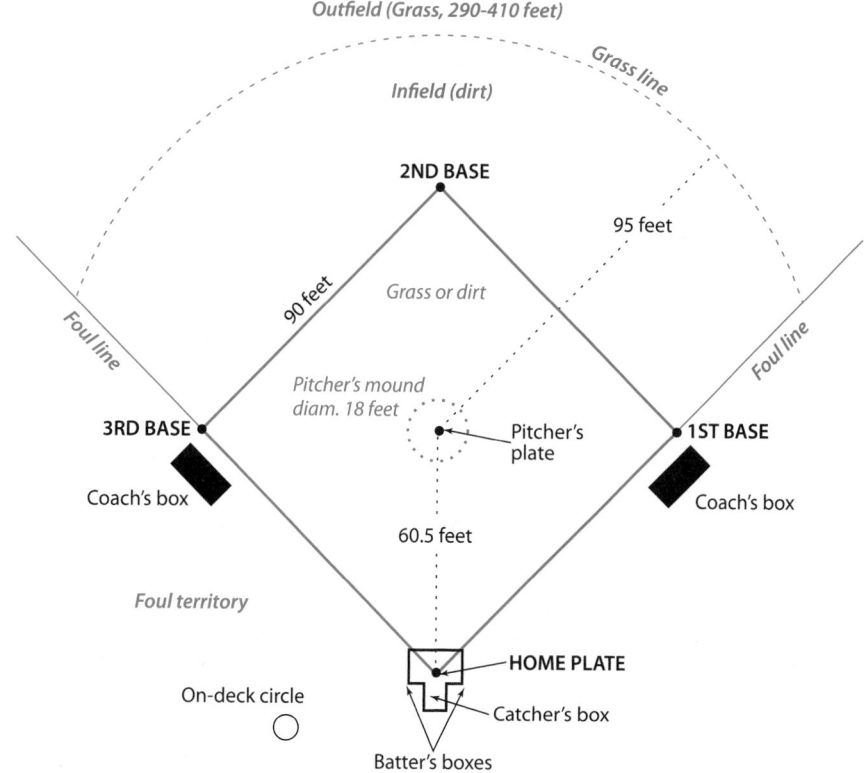

Outfield (Grass, 290–410 feet)

Grass line

Infield (dirt)

2ND BASE

95 feet

90 feet

Grass or dirt

Foul line

Foul line

Pitcher's mound
diam. 18 feet

3RD BASE   Pitcher's   1ST BASE
                  plate

Coach's box   Coach's box

60.5 feet

Foul territory

HOME PLATE

On-deck circle

Catcher's box

Batter's boxes

WebWork

The outlining stage of the writing process is especially important when writing division paragraphs and essays, for the writer must thoroughly understand the relationships among all of the parts before he or she can clearly explain those relationships to the reader. For more practice with outlining, study the outline about a library and its resources at **http://grammar.ccc.commnet.edu/grammar/composition/brainstorm_outline.htm.** Then create a different outline that reveals all of the major and minor parts of a library you frequent.

Online Study Center   For additional information and practice with writing division paragraphs and essays, go to the Houghton Mifflin Online Study Center for this book, at **http://www.college.hmco.com/pic/dolphinwritertwo.**

15

Comparison/Contrast

GOALS FOR CHAPTER 15

▶ Define the terms *comparison* and *contrast*.

▶ Describe the steps in writing a comparison/contrast paragraph.

▶ Write a comparison/contrast paragraph.

▶ Recognize the features of a comparison/contrast essay.

When you *compare* two things, you examine the similarities between them. When you *contrast* two things, you examine the differences between them. Comparison, contrast, or a combination of both is useful for developing ideas in compositions. A study of how two people, places, things, or ideas are alike or different is a good way to help your readers understand something about the two subjects. For example, read the following paragraph:

Studying alone and studying with a group both have their advantages and disadvantages. If you study alone, you can often concentrate better on the task at hand, for you will not run the risk of socializing instead of learning, which often happens in a study group. Studying alone also allows you to focus only on the material you do not yet know. In a study group, on the other hand, you might have to waste valuable time going over information that you have mastered but your group members have not. However, studying in a group can often deepen your level of learning, for the opportunity to teach others results in reinforcement and clarification[1] of what you already know. When you study alone, you do not get this kind of opportunity. Plus, studying with a group gives you the added benefit of having access to people who might be able to answer your questions about the material. Study groups tend to provide a supportive atmosphere, too, so you might be more motivated to study in a group than by yourself.

---

1. **clarification:** making something clearer or easier to understand

This paragraph contrasts studying alone with studying in a group. After reading this paragraph, we understand the main advantages and disadvantages of the two study methods.

You can also help the reader understand an idea by offering a brief comparison called an *analogy*. An analogy explains one subject in terms of another subject that the reader already understands. Here is an example of an analogy:

> Every teacher should have secretarial assistance. Can you imagine a business executive being told that he or she will be supervising 30 to 150 people every day and receiving no secretarial help? Or that he or she cannot fire employees who disrupt or fail to perform? And finally, that trips to the executive restroom will be limited? Classroom teachers work under these conditions every day. (Adapted from David L. Rose, Canton, Michigan, "Small Classes Help Students, Teachers" [Letter to the Editor], *USA Today*, Oct. 14, 2003, 11A.)

In this analogy, the author compares teachers with business executives. These comparisons help readers see his point about teachers' inadequate working conditions. When you can relate a new subject to something your readers already know, you can increase their understanding of the new subject.

Comparison and contrast are also useful for persuading readers to favor or choose one thing over another.

> When evaluating applicants for admission, the majority of colleges and universities in the United States now accept scores from both the Scholastic Aptitude Test (SAT) and the American College Testing Program college entrance exam (ACT), so which one should prospective students take? Because of several differences between the two exams, students may get better results with the ACT. The questions on the SAT are not entirely multiple choice, while the questions on the ACT are. When a student can select from a list of provided answers, he or she often has a better chance of answering a question correctly. In addition, the SAT tends to include many tricky distracters, or wrong answer choices. The ACT, on the other hand, is more straightforward with fewer distracters[1], so the correct answer may not be as difficult to spot. What is more, the SAT includes penalties for wrong answers in order to discourage guessing. The ACT, though, has no such penalties. Finally, the ACT tests more knowledge of specific content, whereas the SAT is known for testing critical thinking and problem-solving skills. Because the ACT is based more on school curriculum than the SAT is, it includes material that is more likely to be familiar to students.

This paragraph compares two different college entrance exams and focuses on the advantages of the ACT. Therefore, it is designed to persuade readers that the ACT may be the better choice of the two.

---

1. distracters: incorrect answer choices on multiple-choice tests

To write effective comparison/contrast paragraphs, follow the principles presented in the next section.

Writing a Comparison/Contrast Paragraph

Comparison and contrast are ways of understanding something in relation to its similarities to or differences from something else. To write an effective comparison/contrast paragraph, you need to determine your points of comparison, decide on the best order for presenting those parts, and develop each point with descriptive details and examples.

Determining the Points of Comparison and the Main Idea and Writing a Topic Sentence

To write an effective comparison/contrast paragraph, it is important, first of all, to decide *why* you are comparing and/or contrasting your two subjects. Do you want readers to understand one of the subjects by seeing how it resembles something with which they are already familiar? Do you want to show that the two subjects are more different than readers think they are? Do you want to prove that one of the subjects is better than or preferable to the other subject? Your answers to these questions will lead you to decide on your purpose, which will affect how you formulate your topic sentence. For example, the following topic sentence focuses on how two subjects are very different:

> Riding a motorcycle and driving a car are two completely different experiences.

This topic sentence suggests that an informative and relatively objective comparison will follow. If you want to persuade your reader that one is better than the other, though, the topic sentence would need to change:

> Riding a motorcycle *is better than* driving a car.

After you write a working topic sentence, decide which features of the two subjects would be most appropriate to proving your main point. In proving the first topic sentence given, you would probably need to examine the different aspects of the two driving experiences, such as level of sensory stimulation, sense of freedom, vehicle performance, fun, and relative danger or risk. A discussion of the two vehicles' varying levels of environmental impact, though, would probably not be relevant to this thesis.

In the paragraph about the SAT and the ACT exams, the writer wants to persuade the reader that the ACT is the better choice. In order to accomplish that, the writer compares the question format, the number and type of answer choices, the consequences of wrong answers, and the content of each test.

After deciding on the right points of comparison, you will need to make sure that you examine both subjects in terms of those points. So in a paragraph about riding a motorcycle and driving a car, you would need to discuss the sensory stimulation and sense of freedom that a rider experiences on a motorcycle, and then you would need to devote equal attention to the sensory stimulation and freedom to be had while driving a car. You would not compare the sensory stimulation of a motorcycle ride with the sense of freedom in a car ride. Doing so would be "comparing apples and oranges," as the saying goes, and you would not truly be contrasting the two subjects. To avoid this type of faulty comparison, it is important to outline your ideas, the topic of the next section.

EXERCISE 15.1 **Determining Points of Comparison**

For each of the following topics, determine three points of comparison and write those points on the blanks provided. Then write down the main idea that would arise from your comparison of these points.

1. Topic: Two places I have lived

Points of comparison: _____

_____

_____

Main idea: _____

2. Topic: My family life and a friend's family life

Points of comparison: _____

_____

_____

Main idea: _____

3. Topic: East versus West (or North versus South)

Points of comparison: _____

_____

_____

Main idea: _____

EXERCISE 15.2   **Writing Topic Sentences for Comparison/Contrast Paragraphs**

For each of the following topics, use some prewriting techniques to generate ideas, and then write a topic sentence you could use for a comparison/contrast paragraph.

1. Two competing products (e.g., Coke and Pepsi)

   Topic sentence: _____

2. Two kinds of love

   Topic sentence: _____

3. A famous celebrity (athlete, actor, musician) of the past versus a famous modern celebrity

   Topic sentence: _____

4. Two restaurants I like

   Topic sentence: _____

5. Two instructors of mine

   Topic sentence: _____

Organizing Points of Comparison and Using Transitions

Organization is especially important in comparison/contrast paragraphs because when you are juggling two different subjects and examining several features of each of those subjects, a reader can become lost easily if the composition is not clearly organized. So after you have chosen your points of comparison, you must give careful thought to how you will arrange your discussion of these points to help readers follow your ideas. There are two major patterns to choose from when organizing the points of a comparison/contrast paragraph.

Whole-by-Whole Pattern of Organization. The first pattern, whole-by-whole, looks at all of the points of comparison for one whole subject, and then it turns to a discussion of those same points of comparison for the other subject. An outline of this pattern looks like this:

I. Comparison of Subject A and Subject B
   A. Subject A
      1. Point of comparison #1
      2. Point of comparison #2
      3. Point of comparison #3

B. Subject B
    1. Point of comparison #1
    2. Point of comparison #2
    3. Point of comparison #3

The advantages of this pattern are mostly for the writer because he or she has to concentrate on only one subject at a time. However, it often asks more of readers, who are burdened with the task of remembering what was said about the first subject as they read about the second subject. Often, this pattern also requires readers to make necessary connections or distinctions between the two subjects on their own. The second pattern of organization, however, eliminates these problems.

Point-by-Point Pattern of Organization. In a point-by-point organizational pattern, the writer alternates back and forth between his two subjects, arranging his or her composition according to the points of comparison. An outline of this pattern looks like this:

I. Comparison of Subject A and Subject B
    A. Point of comparison #1
        1. Subject A
        2. Subject B
    B. Point of comparison #2
        1. Subject A
        2. Subject B
    C. Point of comparison #3
        1. Subject A
        2. Subject B

This pattern usually makes it easier for the reader to see the similarities and/or differences between two subjects. Also, it allows the writer to make clearer, more explicit connections for the reader about the two subjects. However, it does require the writer, who is switching back and forth from one subject to the other, to be more attentive to thought progression. In addition to dividing the information into distinct paragraphs, another way to prevent the reader from getting lost is to use clear transitions to signal similarities, differences, or the movement from one subject to another. The following lists include many of the common comparison and contrast transitional words:

Comparison transitional words:

also	similarly	similar to
too	in like manner	in the same way
likewise	just like, just as	along the same line

Contrast transitional words:

however	nevertheless	in contrast
but	on the one hand/on the other hand	conversely
yet	unlike	even though
although	rather	still
instead	on the contrary	nonetheless
in opposition	actually	whereas
in spite of	despite	in reality
just the opposite	while	as opposed to
though	unfortunately	

EXERCISE 15.3   **Organizing Details in Comparison/Contrast Paragraphs**

Prewrite to generate ideas, and then complete each of the following topic sentences by filling in the blank. Then, on the other blanks provided, prepare an informal outline by listing the points you would include in an appropriate order.

1. My expectations about _____ were a lot different from my actual experience.

   _____

   _____

   _____

   _____

2. A comparison of _____ and _____ reveals that _____ is better.

   _____

   _____

   _____

   _____

3. Many people believe that _____ and _____ are similar, but they are really quite different.

   _____

   _____

   _____

   _____

EXERCISE 15.4 **Recognizing Comparison/Contrast Transitions**

Circle all of the comparison/contrast transitional words in the following paragraph.

American and British varieties of English definitely have many similarities in grammar, vocabulary, and spelling. Yet there are a number of differences that distinguish the two dialects. British and American English differ in their use of present perfect verbs. A speaker of American English would probably say, "I just had lunch." A speaker of British English, though, would be more likely to say, "I've just had lunch." Possession is also expressed a little differently in the two dialects. Most American English speakers would say, "Do you have a car?" However, most British English speakers would say, "Have you got a car?" Prepositions are used differently, too. In American English, one would say, "I play on a softball team." In contrast, the British English version would be "I play in a softball team." ("Differences Between American and British English," http://esl.about.com/library/weekly/aa110698.htm).

EXERCISE 15.5 **Writing a Comparison/Contrast Paragraph That Includes Transitions**

Choose one of the topic sentences and outlines you prepared in Exercise 15.3. Write the paragraph, including transitions that indicate how the points are related.

Developing the Points in a Comparison/Contrast Paragraph

Because comparison/contrast paragraphs examine the features of two subjects to show how they are alike and/or different, you will often use descriptive details and examples to develop each point of comparison. For example, if you were to write the paragraph about riding a motorcycle versus driving a car, you would want to add specific descriptive details when you compared sensory stimulation. You would want to mention the wind in your hair, the smells, and the sounds. When you compared the relative sense of freedom to be had on or in each vehicle, you might want to provide examples of specific rides from your experience. These kinds of details help the reader understand each point better.

Writing Longer Comparison/Contrast Passages and Comparison/Contrast Essays

So far, this chapter has focused only on comparison/contrast paragraphs. However, a comparison/contrast may need several paragraphs for development. For example, read the following passage:

> The common stereotype of the diligent[1], hard-working German and the laid back, TV-watching American is rather wrong. **It is my experience that Americans are generally much more hard working than Germans.** For example, it is not uncommon to meet people who work two 40-hour jobs, or who work full time while also taking a full time course load at a college. Both are completely nonexistent in Germany (there are rules against working too much, intended to protect workers; two full-time jobs are not allowed). Many Germans work only 35 hours a week, others 37.5, all take long vacations, and I estimate that over the whole year, the average German with a job works about two thirds the hours of the average working American.
>
> In the U.S., it is also quite common that people who are not paid by the hour work much longer than the 40 hours per week that they are obliged[2] to. In spite of the fact that many large and successful employers freely lay off workers to increase profits and appease[3] Wall Street[4], employees in the U.S. exhibit a rather strange loyalty to their employers. They often own stock of the very company they work for and really want "their" company to succeed, almost like a team sport. In Germany, where it is taboo[5] for a successful company to lay off any workers, many workers are still not very loyal to their employer: basically, the employer is the enemy who forces you to come to work every day.
>
> Even in their time off, Americans often volunteer for charities or at schools, join their children at sports games, or work out at a gym. In Germany, it seems to be much more common to relax by spending time in a pub or going for a walk. Americans watch a lot more TV, though, while Germans like to join various sports and hobby clubs, so maybe the time off is a tie. (Axel Boldt, "A Subjective Comparison of Germany and the United States," July 10, 2003, http://math-www.uni-paderborn.de/~axel/us-d.html).

Although this passage covers three paragraphs, it develops just one topic sentence, which is highlighted with bold print. The passage presents three points of

1. **diligent:** marked by perseverance and painstaking effort
2. **obliged:** required
3. **appease:** satisfy

4. **Wall Street:** the controlling financial interests of the United States
5. **taboo:** forbidden

comparison: amount of time spent at work, workers' loyalty to employers, and common leisure activities. Each point is discussed in a separate paragraph and developed with specific details and examples.

Comparisons can also take the form of complete essays. To write a comparison/contrast essay, follow the steps for writing a comparison/contrast paragraph. First, prewrite to discover points of comparison, generate ideas, and decide on your main idea. Next, determine whether you will use the whole-by-whole or point-by-point method of comparison. Then decide on the best order for the points of comparison and plan to devote one paragraph to each point. As you write, include comparison/contrast transitions that indicate how the points and details are related and fully develop your explanation of each point with descriptive details and examples.

Writing a First Draft Using Outline and Notes

After you have completed your research, you are ready to write a first draft of your composition. However, do not make the mistake of simply stringing together all of the information you found in your sources and then calling your paper complete. Instead, think of source material as *layers of development*, which you learned about in Chapter 4 of this text. A layer of development provides more specific information about a general idea in the sentence that came before it. In compositions that do not include source material, these layers often take the form of specific details or examples from the writer's observations and experiences. In compositions that do include source materials, layers of development can also take the form of data or statistics, expert opinion, specific facts, or direct quotations.

If source material is used as layers of development, then it stands to reason that the writer still needs to complete all of the steps in the writing process in order to complete a composition containing information from other sources. From generating ideas and an outline to writing a rough draft, the steps for a research paper are the same as those for any other kind of composition. The difference, though, is that as the writer is composing the paragraphs of the body in a research paper, he or she keeps the stack of note cards containing source material close at hand. Then, during composition, information from the cards is integrated to develop each paragraph.

Another way to understand how source material should be used in a composition is to remember that every sentence in a research paper functions in one of three ways. A sentence states an idea or observation of the writer's, states an idea or information obtained from another source, or offers the writer's reaction to that information from another source. The paper's thesis statement and topic sentences should be of the first type. In addition, some of the development for topic sentences should be of the first type. However, development of topic sentences can also be of the second and third types.

EXERCISE 15.6   **The Comparison/Contrast Essay**

Read the following essay. Then answer the questions that follow by writing your responses on the blanks provided.

Mr. Fix-It and the Home-Improvement Committee

1 The most frequently expressed complaint women have about men is that men don't listen. Either a man completely ignores her when she speaks to him, or he listens for a few beats, assesses what is bothering her, and then proudly puts on his Mr. Fix-It cap and offers her a solution to make her feel better. He is confused when she doesn't appreciate his gesture of love. No matter how many times she tells him that he's not listening, he doesn't get it and keeps doing the same thing. She wants empathy[1], but he thinks she wants solutions.

2 The most frequently expressed complaint men have about women is that women are always trying to change them. When a woman loves a man she feels responsible to assist him in growing and tries to help him improve the way he does things. She forms a home-improvement committee, and he becomes her primary focus. No matter how much he resists her help, she persists—waiting for any opportunity to help him or tell him what to do. She thinks she is nurturing him, while he feels he's being controlled. Instead, he wants her acceptance.

3 These two problems can finally be solved by first understanding why men offer solutions and why women seek to improve. Let's pretend to go back in time, where by observing life on Mars and Venus—before the planets discovered one another or came to Earth—we can gain some insights into men and women.

Life on Mars

4 Martians value power, competency, efficiency, and achievement. They are always doing things to prove themselves and develop their power and skills. Their sense of self is defined through their ability to achieve results. They experience fulfillment primarily through success and accomplishment.

5 Everything on Mars is a reflection of these values. Even their dress is designed to reflect their skills and competence. Police officers, soldiers, businessmen, scientists, cab drivers, technicians, and chefs all wear uniforms or at least hats to reflect their competence and power.

6 They don't read magazines like *Psychology Today, Self,* or *People.* They are more concerned with outdoor activities, like hunting, fishing, and racing cars. They are interested in the news, weather, and sports and couldn't care less about romance novels and self-help books.

1. **empathy:** identification with and understanding of another's feelings

7   They are more interested in "objects" and "things" rather than people and feelings. Even today on Earth, while women fantasize about romance, men fantasize about powerful cars, faster computers, gadgets, gizmos, and new more powerful technology. Men are preoccupied with the "things" that can help them express power by creating results and achieving their goals.

8   Achieving goals is very important to a Martian because it is a way for him to prove his competence and thus feel good about himself. And for him to feel good about himself he must achieve these goals by himself. Someone else can't achieve them for him. Martians pride themselves in doing things all by themselves. Autonomy[1] is a symbol of efficiency, power, and competence.

9   Understanding this Martian characteristic can help women understand why men resist so much being corrected or being told what to do. To offer a man unsolicited[2] advice is to presume that he doesn't know what to do or that he can't do it on his own. Men are very touchy about this, because the issue of competence is so very important to them.

10   Because he is handling his problems on his own, a Martian rarely talks about his problems unless he needs expert advice. He reasons: "Why involve someone else when I can do it by myself?" He keeps his problems to himself unless he requires help from another to find a solution. Asking for help when you can do it yourself is perceived as a sign of weakness.

11   However, if he truly does need help, then it is a sign of wisdom to get it. In this case, he will find someone he respects and then talk about his problem. Talking about a problem on Mars is an invitation for advice. Another Martian feels honored by the opportunity. Automatically he puts on his Mr. Fix-It hat, listens for a while, and then offers some jewels of advice.

12   This Martian custom is one of the reasons men instinctively offer solutions when women talk about their problems. When a woman innocently shares upset feelings or explores out loud the problems of her day, a man mistakenly assumes she is looking for some expert advice. He puts on his Mr. Fix-It hat and begins giving advice; this is his way of showing love and of trying to help.

13   He wants to help her feel better by solving her problems. He wants to be useful to her. He feels he can be valued and thus worthy of her love when his abilities are used to solve her problems.

14   Once he has offered a solution, however, and she continues to be upset, it becomes increasingly difficult for him to listen because his solution is being rejected, and he feels increasingly useless.

15   He has no idea that by just listening with empathy and interest he can be supportive. He does not know that on Venus talking about problems is not an invitation to offer a solution.

---

1. **autonomy:** independence   2. **unsolicited:** not asked for

Life on Venus

16 Venusians have different values. They value love, communication, beauty, and relationships. They spend a lot of time supporting, helping, and nurturing one another. Their sense of self is defined through their feelings and the quality of their relationships. They experience fulfillment through sharing and relating.

17 Everything on Venus reflects these values. Rather than building highways and tall buildings, the Venusians are more concerned with living together in harmony, community, and loving cooperation. Relationships are more important than work and technology. In most ways, their world is the opposite of Mars.

18 They do not wear uniforms like the Martians (to reveal their competence). On the contrary, they enjoy wearing a different outfit every day, according to how they are feeling. Personal expression, especially of their feelings, is very important. They may even change outfits several times a day as their mood changes.

19 Communication is of primary importance. To share their personal feelings is much more important than achieving goals and success. Talking and relating to one another is a source of tremendous fulfillment.

20 This is hard for a man to comprehend. He can come close to understanding a woman's experience of sharing and relating by comparing it to the satisfaction he feels when he wins a race, achieves a goal, or solves a problem.

21 Instead of being goal oriented, women are relationship oriented; they are more concerned with expressing their goodness, love, and caring. Two Martians go to lunch to discuss a project or business goal; they have a problem to solve. In addition, Martians view going to a restaurant as an efficient way to approach food: no shopping, no cooking, and no washing dishes. For Venusians, going to lunch is an opportunity to nurture a relationship, for both giving support to and receiving support from a friend. Women's restaurant talk can be very open and intimate, almost like the dialogue that occurs between therapist and patient.

22 On Venus, everyone studies psychology and has at least a master's degree in counseling. They are very involved in personal growth, spirituality, and everything else that can nurture life, healing, and growth. Venus is covered with parks, organic gardens, shopping centers, and restaurants.

23 Venusians are very intuitive. They have developed this ability through centuries of anticipating the needs of others. They pride themselves in being considerate of the needs and feelings of others. A sign of great love is to offer help and assistance to another Venusian without being asked.

24 Because proving one's competence is not as important to a Venusian, offering help is not offensive, and needing help is not a sign of weakness. A man, however, may feel offended because when a woman offers advice he doesn't feel she trusts his ability to do it himself.

25 A woman has no conception of this male sensitivity because for her it is another feather in her hat if someone offers to help her. It makes her feel loved and cherished. But offering help to a man can make him feel incompetent, weak, and even unloved.

26   On Venus it is a sign of caring to give advice and suggestions. Venusians firmly believe that when something is working it can always work better. Their nature is to want to improve things. When they care about someone, they freely point out what can be improved and suggest how to do it. Offering advice and constructive criticism is an act of love.

27   Mars is very different. Martians are more solution oriented. If something is working, their motto is don't change it. Their instinct is to leave it alone if it is working. "Don't fix it unless it is broken" is a common expression.

28   When a woman tries to improve a man, he feels she is trying to fix him. He receives the message that he is broken. She doesn't realize her caring attempts to help him may humiliate him. She mistakenly thinks she is just helping him to grow.

Give Up Giving Advice

29   Without this insight into the nature of men, it's very easy for a woman unknowingly and unintentionally to hurt and offend the man she loves most.

30   For example, Tom and Mary were going to a party. Tom was driving. After about twenty minutes and going around the same block a few times, it was clear to Mary that Tom was lost. She finally suggested that he call for help. Tom became very silent. They eventually arrived at the party, but the tension from that moment persisted the whole evening. Mary had no idea of why he was so upset.

31   From her side she was saying "I love and care about you, so I am offering you this help."

32   From his side, he was offended. What he heard was "I don't trust you to get us there. You are incompetent."

33   Without knowing about life on Mars, Mary could not appreciate how important it was for Tom to accomplish his goal without help. Offering advice was the ultimate insult. As we have explored, Martians never offer advice unless asked. A way of honoring another Martian is *always* to assume he can solve his problem unless he is asking for help.

34   Mary had no idea that when Tom became lost and started circling the same block, it was a very special opportunity to love and support him. At that time he was particularly vulnerable and needed some extra love. To honor him by not offering advice would have been a gift equivalent to his buying her a beautiful bouquet of flowers or writing her a love note.

35   After learning about Martians and Venusians, Mary learned how to support Tom at such difficult times. The next time he was lost, instead of offering "help" she restrained herself from offering any advice, took a deep relaxing breath, and appreciated in her heart what Tom was trying to do for her. Tom greatly appreciated her warm acceptance and trust.

36   Generally speaking, when a woman offers unsolicited advice or tries to "help" a man, she has no idea of how critical and unloving she may sound to him. Even though her intent is loving, her suggestions do offend and hurt. His

reaction may be strong, especially if he felt criticized as a child or he experienced his father being criticized by his mother.

37   For many men, it is very important to prove that they can get to their goal, even if it is a small thing like driving to a restaurant or party. Ironically he may be more sensitive about the little things than the big. His feelings are like this: "If I can't be trusted to do a small thing like get us to a party, how can she trust me to do the bigger things?" Like their Martian ancestors, men pride themselves on being experts, especially when it comes to fixing mechanical things, getting places, or solving problems. These are the times when he needs her loving acceptance the most and not her advice or criticism.

Learning to Listen

38   Likewise, if a man does not understand how a woman is different, he can make things worse when he is trying to help. Men need to remember that women talk about problems to get close and not necessarily to get solutions.

39   So many times a woman just wants to share her feelings about her day, and her husband, thinking he is helping, interrupts her by offering a steady flow of solutions to her problems. He has no idea why she isn't pleased.

40   For example, Mary comes home from an exhausting day. She wants and needs to share her feelings about the day:

She says, "There is so much to do; I don't have any time for myself."

Tom says, "You should quit that job. You don't have to work so hard. Find something you like to do."

Mary says, "But I like my job. They just expect me to change everything at a moment's notice."

Tom says, "Don't listen to them. Just do what you can do."

Mary says, "I *am!* I can't believe I completely forgot to call my aunt today."

Tom says, "Don't worry about it, she'll understand."

Mary says, "Do you know what she is going through? She needs me."

Tom says, "You worry too much, that's why you're so unhappy."

Mary angrily says, "I am not always unhappy. Can't you just listen to me?"

Tom says, "I *am* listening."

Mary says, "Why do I even bother?"

41   After this conversation, Mary was more frustrated than when she arrived home seeking intimacy and companionship. Tom was also frustrated and had no idea what went wrong. He wanted to help, but his problem-solving tactics didn't work.

42   Without knowing about life on Venus, Tom didn't understand how important it was just to listen without offering solutions. His solutions only made things worse. You see, Venusians never offer solutions when someone is talking. A way of honoring another Venusian is to listen patiently with empathy, seeking truly to understand the other's feelings.

43   Tom had no idea that just listening with empathy to Mary express her feelings would bring her tremendous relief and fulfillment. When Tom heard about the Venusians and how much they needed to talk, he gradually learned how to listen.

44   When Mary now comes home tired and exhausted their conversations are quite different. They sound like this:

Mary says, "There is so much to do. I have no time for me."

Tom takes a deep breath, relaxes on the exhale, and says, "Humph, sounds like you had a hard day."

Mary says, "They expect me to change everything at a moment's notice. I don't know what to do."

Tom pauses and then says, "Hmmm."

Mary says, "I even forgot to call my aunt."

Tom says with a slightly wrinkled brow, "Oh, no."

Mary says, "She needs me so much right now. I feel so bad."

Tom says, "You are such a loving person. Come here. Let me give you a hug."

45   Tom gives Mary a hug and she relaxes in his arms with a big sigh of relief. Then she says, "I love talking with you. You make me really happy. Thanks for listening. I feel much better."

46   Not only Mary but also Tom felt better. He was amazed at how much happier his wife was when he finally learned to listen. With this new awareness of their differences, Tom learned the wisdom of listening without offering solutions while Mary learned the wisdom of letting go and accepting without offering unsolicited advice or criticism.

47   To summarize the two most common mistakes we make in relationships:

1. A man tries to change a woman's feelings when she is upset by becoming Mr. Fix-It and offering solutions to her problems that invalidate her feelings.

2. A woman tries to change a man's behavior when he makes mistakes by becoming the home-improvement committee and offering unsolicited advice or criticism.*

1. What is the thesis of this essay?

_____

_____

*Source: Excerpted from John Gray, "Mr. Fix-It and the Home-Improvement Committee," in *Men are From Mars, Women Are From Venus.* Copyright © 1992 by John Gray. Reprinted by permission of HarperCollins Publishers.

2. The author includes many points of comparison. What are three of these points?

   _____

3. Does the author organize his information using a whole-by-whole or point-by-point pattern?

   _____

4. List three comparison/contrast transitions the author uses in this essay.

   _____

5. Do you agree with the author's explanation of the differences between men and women? Do you think that his points of comparison adequately account for a couple's communication problems? Explain your answer.

   _____

In Summary: Steps in Writing Comparison/Contrast Essays

1. **Determine a main idea and points of comparison.** Decide on the purpose of your comparison, and then select relevant points of comparison. Make sure you apply these points to both subjects.
2. **Choose an organizing pattern for the points of comparison.** Use either a whole-by-whole or point-by-point pattern for arranging ideas, and include transitions to help the reader follow these ideas.
3. **Develop each point of comparison.** Use descriptions, examples, or any other kind of details that explain each point.

Fill in the blanks in the following statements.

1. When you _____ two things, you examine the similarities between them.
   When you _____ two things, you examine the differences between them.

2. An _____ is a brief comparison that explains one subject in terms of another subject the reader already understands.

3. The first step in comparison/contrast is determining the _____ of your comparison.

4. After you write your topic sentence, decide on the best _____, the features of the two subjects that would be most appropriate to proving your main point.

5. Two major comparison/contrast patterns of organization are the _____ _____ pattern and the _____ pattern.

6. Common comparison/contrast _____ include *also*, *similarly*, *however*, and *on the contrary*.

7. Comparison/contrast paragraphs are often developed with _____ and _____.

8. A comparison may need several _____ for development.

9. Comparisons can also take the form of complete essays in which the topic and its major parts are stated in a _____.

Topic Ideas for Comparison/Contrast Assignments

Exercises 15.1 and 15.2 include topic ideas you may want to develop into comparison/contrast paragraphs or essays. Here are some additional ideas:

- Two historical figures
- Living in a house versus living in an apartment
- Two different forms of public transportation
- Two different areas of one town or city
- A film and the book on which it is based

- Two jobs I have held

- A familiar place during two different times of day

- Customs surrounding a particular holiday (e.g., Christmas) in two different countries

- Two types of music

- Country versus city

- Past versus present

- The two people in the accompanying photograph:

Source: © Shalom Ormsby/Getty Images

WebWork

Go to the *Guide to Grammar and Writing* Web site's information about writing comparison/contrast essays at **http://grammar.ccc.commnet.edu/grammar/composition/comparison.htm.** Read the information on this page, including the sample essays. Then, on your own paper, write your answers to the questions in the "Points to Ponder" box.

Online Study Center For additional information and practice with writing comparison/contrast paragraphs and essays, go to the Houghton Mifflin Online Study Center for this book, at **http://www.college.hmco .com/pic/dolphinwritertwo.**

Cause/Effect

> ### GOALS FOR CHAPTER 16

▶ Define the terms *cause* and *effect*.

▶ Describe the steps in writing a cause/effect paragraph.

▶ Write a cause/effect paragraph.

▶ Recognize the features of a cause/effect essay.

People like to understand why something happened. We ask questions such as *Why did the Vietnam War occur?* and *Why did a teenager take a gun to school and shoot several of his classmates?* When we ask questions like these, we are trying to determine the *causes* of, or reasons for, an occurrence. We also like to understand the consequences of the things that happen. So we ask such questions as *How did the September 11, 2001, terrorist attacks change America?* and *What will happen if children watch too much television?* These types of questions lead to an analysis of the *effects*, or results, of an occurrence.

Paragraphs and essays often develop an idea by explaining causes, discussing effects, or doing both. The following paragraph, for example, explores causes only:

Why do young men want to put off getting married as long as possible? A new study conducted by Rutgers University revealed that men have a number of reasons for dragging their feet when it comes to walking down the aisle. For one thing, these days they can obtain sex and affection outside of marriage; furthermore, their committed partners often agree to co-habit, so they get the benefits of having a wife without actually getting married. Another reason men tend to postpone marriage is their fear of divorce and its consequences. Because men believe that a break-up of a marital relationship will cost them both emotionally and financially, they are reluctant to marry. Finally, many men say that they aren't eager to marry because being a husband will require them to make too many changes and compromises. (Karen S. Peterson, "Why Men Drag Their Feet Down the Aisle," *USA Today*, June 26, 2002.)

This paragraph gives three causes for men's reluctance to get married.
This next example focuses only on effects:

Having access to the Internet at home has improved my life in many ways. One benefit is the ability to stay connected to my family and friends via e-mail messages. Because it is so easy to send a quick e-mail just to say hello or to report a piece of news, I am better able to stay in touch with loved ones who live either nearby or far away. I also am grateful for all of the information I get via the Internet. I can research everything from possible vacation spots to definitions of words to driving directions to prescription drugs; therefore, I can stay better informed about things that affect me personally. I can also read newspapers and magazines online, so it is easy to stay informed about current events. In addition, the Internet has made it very convenient to make arrangements for things that I used to do over the phone. For example, I can book an airplane flight online, and I can reserve a library book, too, that I have been wanting to read. Last year, I did most of my Christmas shopping online as well. Having the ability to get the things I need with just a few clicks of the mouse has definitely saved me a lot of time and aggravation.

This paragraph explores several different effects of having Internet access at home.
To write effective cause/effect paragraphs, follow the principles presented in the next section.

Writing a Cause/Effect Paragraph

Explaining causes is a way to help readers understand *why* something happened, and explaining effects is a way to help readers understand the *consequences* of something. To write an effective cause/effect paragraph, you need to generate ideas about the relationships between your cause(s) and/or effect(s), determine your topic sentence, organize your causes and/or effects based on their relationships, and develop each cause or effect with descriptive details and examples.

Generating Ideas, Determining the Main Idea, and Writing a Topic Sentence

After you have selected an occurrence or phenomenon to examine, you will need to generate some ideas about its causes, effects, or both. As you begin to explore your topic, you might find it useful to create a diagram, a visual representation of the relationships among the causes and effects. A student who chose to write about cheating among college students, for example, created the accompanying diagram.

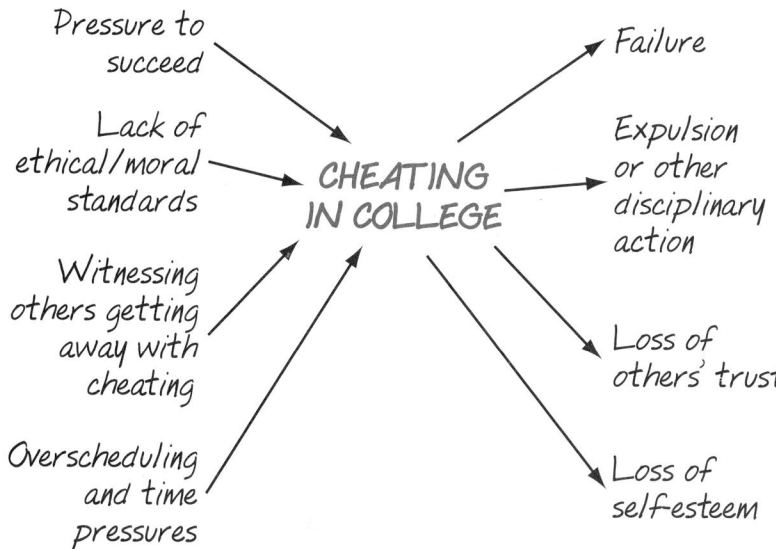

The causes are listed on the left, and the arrows indicate that each one leads to cheating. Arrows drawn outward from the subject indicate its various effects. This diagram focuses only on *immediate* causes and effects, those that are the direct reasons for and the direct consequences of the occurrence. Depending on the topic, it may also be appropriate to present some of the *remote* causes, or ultimate roots of a situation, and/or the remote effects, or long-term consequences. Adding some of these remote causes and effects might change parts of the diagram as follows:

Unstable job market and increased competition → Pressure to succeed → CHEATING IN COLLEGE → Loss of self-esteem → Decline in achievement

Thus, to truly do justice to your subject, you may need to discuss a *chain reaction* of causes or effects rather than just the immediate causes alone.

As you continue prewriting to generate ideas, spend some time thinking about the relationships in your diagram, adding to them or altering them as appropriate. For example, the student who created the diagram about cheating may want to consider whether "lack of ethical/moral standards" and "witnessing others getting away with cheating" are two separate causes, just one cause, or one chain reaction of causes. Beware of oversimplifying complex factors or consequences; for example, you would be out on a limb if you assert that consumption of fast food is the number one cause of obesity in the United States. Other contributing factors may be just as important. So spend some time thoroughly evaluating each cause or effect to make sure that the relationships are complete, reasonable, and logical. Then, when you think your diagram accurately reflects these relationships, you can determine your main idea.

The main idea of a cause/effect paragraph or essay usually states some point about the relationships you discover in your diagram. Are there multiple causes for one occurrence, or is there a chain reaction of events that ultimately leads to the occurrence? Is one cause more to blame than others? Are there several effects of a particular occurrence, or does this occurrence set off one chain reaction of immediate and remote effects? What conclusion can you draw from the relationships among all of the causes and/or effects? Studying your diagram will help you draw this conclusion and then write a topic sentence that incorporates this conclusion. From the preceding revised diagram, for example, you might draw the conclusion that, ironically, cheating actually prevents one from achieving the very goal that made him or her cheat in the first place. So a topic sentence might read:

> Although the pressure to succeed in a competitive and unstable job market leads college students to cheat, they run the risk of robbing themselves of that professional success when they stoop to dishonesty.

This topic sentence focuses on one specific cause and one specific effect. If you wanted to present a broader, more comprehensive look at the subject, you might write one of the following topic sentences:

> College students resort to cheating for three main reasons. *(causes only)*

> Before they resort to cheating, college students should be aware of the severe consequences of academic dishonesty. *(effects only)*

> Many different factors are driving today's college students to academic dishonesty, but giving in to the temptation to cheat holds serious consequences. *(causes and effects)*

EXERCISE 16.1 **Generating Cause/Effect Diagrams**

For each of the following topics, draw a diagram of the cause-and-effect relationships in the space provided.

1. The stress in my life

2. Dropping out of high school

3. Becoming a pet owner

EXERCISE 16.2 **Writing Topic Sentences for Cause/Effect Paragraphs**

For each of the following topics, use some prewriting techniques to generate ideas, and then write a topic sentence you could use for a cause/effect paragraph.

1. An important decision I made

Topic sentence: _____

2. A significant change in my physical appearance

Topic sentence: _____

3. Success

Topic sentence: _____

4. A relationship that ended

   Topic sentence: _____

5. The popularity of a current fad or trend

   Topic sentence: _____

Organizing Causes and/or Effects and Using Transitions

Creating a diagram of cause-and-effect relationships like the one in the previous section will help you not only discover ideas but also organize them. The relationships you discover among the causes and effects will assist you in determining the best arrangement of your details. If you were going to develop the topic sentence *College students resort to cheating for three main reasons,* your informal outline for the paragraph might look like this:

   1. Topic sentence
   2. Pressure to succeed in a competitive environment
   3. Lack of firm moral/ethical standards
   4. Time pressure

When you are deciding on the best order for the information, it is important to evaluate the order of each cause and effect in case they are somehow related. Look for time order or causal order among reasons or consequences that initially look as though they are separate. If you are exploring the effects of cheating, for example, you might decide that failure leads to loss of self-esteem, so you would need to discuss failure (an immediate effect) *before* you discuss loss of self-esteem (a remote effect). In the case of separate, unrelated factors or effects, consider whether some are more important than others; if so, arrange them using order of importance. For instance, you might decide that the lack of moral/ethical standards is the most significant cause of cheating in college, so you would need to discuss that reason *first*, instead of second.

   As you write, be sure to add transitions that help the reader discern the cause-and-effect relationships. Some of the most common cause-and-effect transitional words are:

so	as a consequence
therefore	due to
as a result	hence
thus	for this reason
because of	one cause, a second cause, and so on
in response	one reason, another reason, and so on
consequently	

EXERCISE 16.3 **Organizing Details in Cause/Effect Paragraphs**

Prewrite to generate ideas, and then complete each of the following topic sentences by filling in the blank. Then, on the other blanks provided, prepare an informal outline by listing the points you would include in an appropriate order.

1. _____ has affected me and my family in a number of ways.

_____

_____

_____

_____

2. For _____ reasons, I decided to _____.

_____

_____

_____

_____

3. I decided to _____ because _____, but _____ was the end result instead.

_____

_____

_____

_____

EXERCISE 16.4 **Recognizing Cause/Effect Transitions**

Circle all of the cause/effect transitions in the following paragraph.

When I was just twenty-two years old, I suffered from a social phobia, or fear of being around others in social situations. I was shy in high school, but my insecurities and fear of being embarrassed in public began to grow after I had to give a speech in one of my classes. I was so nervous that I stuttered, and my classmates laughed at me. As a result, I began to feel unreasonably anxious if I faced any situation in which I had to speak to strangers or even interact with a large group of people. In response, my hands would sweat, my heart would race, I would have trouble speaking, and if I did manage to get the words out, my voice would tremble. As these physical signs would increase in severity, my anxiety would escalate. Consequently, my mind and body would be trapped in a vicious cycle, each one perpetuating[1] the negative responses of the other. I decided, therefore, to avoid all situations that could trigger this cycle. I began to avoid the social situations I feared, and I stopped going out and interacting with people, even those I knew. When attending my college classes became too painful and I dropped all of my courses, I knew I would have to do something. So I began seeing a therapist who helped me overcome my anxiety. I finally learned to break the cycle of fear and live a more normal life.

EXERCISE 16.5 **Writing a Cause/Effect Paragraph That Includes Transitions**

Choose one of the topic sentences and outlines you prepared in Exercise 16.3. Write the paragraph, including transitions that indicate how the causes and/or effects are related.

Developing the Points in a Cause/Effect Paragraph

Whether the explanation of a cause-and-effect relationship has been scientifically proven (such as the effects of laser eye surgery) or is based on educated opinion (such as the causes of cheating in college), readers will expect writers to provide them with plenty of evidence to support that explanation. This evidence can be in the form of examples, observations, facts, statistics, expert testimony, or even personal experiences. So you will often use the other modes, particularly narration, description, illustration, and process, to develop your ideas.

Writing Longer Cause/Effect Passages and Cause/Effect Essays

So far, this chapter has focused only on cause/effect paragraphs. However, an explanation of causes or effects may need several paragraphs for development. For example, read the following passage:

> **Work has become life, for both sexes; therefore, life has been compressed into ever smaller compartments.** Both men and women are working more hours than

1. **perpetuating:** causing to continue

they did twenty years ago, with moonlighting[1] for extra money more common and taking work home routine. In research completed by the Families and Work Institute, fathers of children under eighteen reported that they work some fifty-one hours a week, and mothers about forty-one hours. That's ninety-two hours a week in a family with two full-time breadwinners, more than double what used to be enough to keep a middle-class family middle class.

The big squeeze hasn't affected the overall amount of time working parents spend with children. The Families and Work Institute survey showed that because today's employed fathers spend more time with the kids than their own dads did—and because working mothers, despite the increase in hours worked since 1977, haven't cut the time they spend with children—kids are getting more parental face time from employed parents than they did two decades ago.

Our collective guilt and compulsion[2] to keep-up-with-the-Joneses has got every parent running from soccer fields to swim lessons to the slumber-party dropoff. And so, the tiniest box of all the little boxes we're splitting our lives into is the one reserved for the novelty formerly known as personal time. It's down to about an hour-and-a-half per day for working fathers and about an hour a day for working moms. And that, I'll bet, counts driving time as personal, so long as the radio is on and the cell phone isn't.*

Although this passage covers three paragraphs, it develops just one topic sentence, which is highlighted with bold print. The passage explains why working parents have so little personal time these days. A diagram of these relationships might look like the one shown here.

There are two main causes for the end result, and each cause is discussed in a separate paragraph. Note that the author explains how the causes and effects are related by using words such as *therefore, so,* and *because.* Each point is developed with statistics or specific examples.

Explanations of causes and/or effects can also take the form of complete essays. To write a cause/effect essay, follow the same steps for writing a cause/effect paragraph. First, prewrite to generate ideas, diagram relationships, and decide on your main idea. Next, decide on the best order for the causes and/or effects

1. **moonlighting:** working a second job   2. **compulsion:** irresistible impulse to act

*Source: Adapted from Marie Cocco, "Work Ethic Has Led to Overwork." Copyright © 1998, *Newsday.* Reprinted with permission.

based on their relationships and plan to devote one paragraph to each cause or effect. As you write, include cause/effect transitions that indicate how the causes and effects are related and fully develop your explanation of each cause or effect with the other modes of development, such as narration, description, illustration, and process.

EXERCISE 16.6 **The Cause/Effect Essay**

Read the following essay. Then answer the questions that follow by writing your responses on the blanks provided.

Our Energy Conundrum[1]

1   The average driver who pulls into a gas station these days and barks, "Fill 'er up!" focuses primarily on the surging price of gas and gives little or no thought to where it comes from or why the price is so high. Some may understand the surging demand that comes from a billion Chinese and a billion Indians who have joined the oil market as consumers—not only to fuel their cars and planes but as an ingredient in fertilizers, pesticides, medicines, paints, and plastics. Guess how many barrels of oil we import a day? A million? Five million? No, the staggering answer is . . . 12 million barrels a day, and we're heading for 20 million barrels a day by 2025. The price increases over the past year mean that we consumers will send oil producers an additional $50 billion this year—on top of the $120 billion we sent last year.

2   What makes this so maddening is that we're sending all these dollars to countries that use a good chunk of them to promote anti-American ideas, to spread radical Islam, and to finance the jihadists[2] who are waging the war of terrorism against us. Some of these same countries are also using this largess[3] to develop weapons of mass destruction. As if all that weren't enough, we're also spending hundreds of billions of dollars on a U.S. military presence to protect this Middle East energy source. It is a tax on consumers here—not to mention the fact that, yes, these same Middle East oil producers have enmeshed us in two wars over the past two decades. Their capricious[4] governments are increasingly vulnerable to religious fundamentalists[5] and Islamist terrorists, who, any day, could devastate the world's economy by sabotaging production.

1. **conundrum:** difficult problem
2. **jihadists:** people who want to expand the Islam religion through political or military struggle
3. **largess:** gifts or generosity
4. **capricious:** prone to impulsively changing one's mind
5. **religious fundamentalists:** people who believe in the literal interpretation of their sacred texts, which they consider the only source of truth

What Is Plagiarism?

As you prepare to incorporate source material as layers of development in your composition, you will need to understand what the term *plagiarism* means. Plagiarism is the intentional or unintentional use of someone else's ideas or words without giving proper credit to that individual and/or clearly acknowledging the original source.

Intentional plagiarism, the most blatant form, occurs when a writer knowingly transfers someone else's sentences or paragraphs into his or her own paper without providing any information about where they came from. Word processing and the Internet allow writers to copy and paste others' words into their documents, so computers have made it easier to plagiarize.

However, a writer can also be guilty of unintentional plagiarism. This occurs when he or she does not properly indicate where borrowed material begins or ends or when he or she fails to provide source information. For example, if a writer does not express someone else's thoughts in his or her own words and ends up using too much of

the wording in the original source, plagiarism can result. Likewise, a writer who forgets to acknowledge a source will be inadvertently plagiarizing.

What are the consequences of plagiarism? The practice of using someone else's words as your own is illegal and unethical. It is a lot like lying; you may not go to jail for telling a lie or plagiarizing a passage, but you will cast serious doubt upon your own character and credibility for committing either one of these moral transgressions. Plagiarism will undermine your own ideas and arguments because, if you are found to have "stolen" the ideas of others, readers will view you as an untrustworthy source of information. What is more, most academic institutions are now imposing serious penalties for students who cheat by plagiarizing, so make sure you always give credit where credit is due.

In the next three chapters, you will learn how to properly acknowledge other writers and sources using a common system of documentation known as MLA style.

3   How dumb are we, anyway?

4   There is much talk these days about energy independence—a fantasy. Any program to reduce our 60 percent dependence on foreign oil will take anywhere from five to 10 years. And neither the Republican answer—more production—nor the Democratic answer—more conservation—will solve the problem. Any coherent[1] energy program will require us to do both. It is also fantasy to imagine that we can rely on alternative power sources from waves or windmills or solar panels. That kind of power is weak, intermittent,[2] and expensive—costing roughly twice the cost of the electrical power produced by either coal or gas.

5   Most Americans believe they're entitled to cheap fuel, regardless of how much they consume. As gas prices rise, the American public looks for someone to blame, even though gas is cheaper today by at least a third than it was 25 years

1. **coherent:** orderly and logical   2. **intermittent:** stopping and starting

ago, if you adjust the peak prices then for inflation and for the drop in the dollar. Our gasoline tax is only 43 cents a gallon, compared with $4 in most of Europe, making a gallon of gas cheaper than a bottle of water. Is it any wonder so few Americans don't bother to conserve? When fuel prices did go up, drivers switched to smaller, less wasteful cars, and we began a program of energy efficiency. That was great, but when prices fell, we went back to the gas guzzlers, and now, with just 5 percent of the world's population, we use a quarter of the world's oil.

6   So what are the options? Higher fuel taxes and tighter controls by business. CAFE, the corporate average fuel efficiency standards imposed on carmakers, have barely risen in 20 years. By some estimates, reasonably phased higher standards could save us about a million barrels of oil a day.

7   On the production side, we are going to have to start building nuclear power plants, particularly since new nuclear technologies are safer and cleaner than ever. We are also going to have to look to find places to drill, such as the Arctic National Wildlife Refuge, which has become a symbolic issue to environmentalists. The refuge is far from the picture postcard of green forests and snow-capped mountains its defenders would have us believe. It's the Alaskan tundra,[1] and drilling there would involve only a minuscule[2] portion of the 18.5 million acres that are being set aside for conservation. Drilling there makes sense.

8   This isn't to say that we should overlook the environmental consequences of fuel consumption, particularly when you think about the fact that as China and India explode economically and are able to buy cars, we may have to face the possibility that the number of cars by the year 2050 will go from 800 million today to as high as 3.25 billion then—an unimaginable threat to our environment and a surefire guarantee of global warming.

9   Any energy program we come up with will involve some cost or controversy. But this is one of the great national issues facing the nation, and there is no justifiable excuse for avoiding the kind of informed debate that must take place if we're to put a coherent policy in place before too much more time elapses.

10   The failure of our elected officials in both parties to come to grips with this vital issue long before now is a national disgrace. Continued failure is not an option.*

1. State the main idea of this essay in your own words.

_____

_____

1. **tundra:** a cold, treeless area   2. **minuscule:** tiny

Source: "Our Energy Conundrum," by Mortimer B. Zuckerman, *U.S. News & World Report,* April 25, 2005, p. 72. Copyright 2005, U.S. News & World Report, L. P. Reprinted with permission.

2. According to the author, why are gas prices rapidly increasing?

_____

_____

_____

3. According to the author, what are some serious negative effects of Americans' dependence on Middle Eastern oil sources?

_____

_____

4. What are the author's solutions to our "energy conundrum"?

_____

_____

5. Do you agree with all of the author's solutions? Can you think of any better solutions?

_____

In Summary: Steps in Writing Cause-Effect Essays

1. **Create a diagram of cause-and-effect relationships.** Use this diagram to generate ideas and to explore the topic so that you can draw a conclusion that will become your thesis.
2. **Organize the cause-and-effect relationships into an outline.** Evaluate what seem to be separate causes and effects for time order or causal relationships, and order them accordingly. If different causes and effects are unrelated, decide whether they should be arranged by order of importance.
3. **As you write, develop each cause or effect with sufficient evidence.** Use narration, description, illustration, or the other modes to offer readers plenty of evidence in support of your explanations.

CHAPTER 16 REVIEW

Fill in the blanks in the following statements.

1. When you try to understand why something happened, you are trying to determine the _____ of, or reasons for, an occurrence. When you analyze the _____, or results, of an occurrence, you are trying to understand the consequences of that occurrence.

2. As you generate ideas about causes, effects, or both, you might find it useful to create a _____, a visual representation of the relationships among the causes and effects.

3. _____ causes and effects are those that are the direct reasons for and the direct consequences of an occurrence.

4. _____ causes and effects are the ultimate roots or long-term consequences of an occurrence.

5. The _____ you discover among the causes and effects will assist you in determining the best arrangement for your details.

6. Common cause/effect _____ include *so, therefore, as a result,* and *one cause.*

7. Cause/effect paragraphs are often developed with the other _____ _____, such as narration, description, illustration, and process.

8. An explanation of causes or effects may need several _____ for development.

9. Explanations of causes and/or effects can also take the form of complete essays in which the topic and main point are stated in a _____.

Topic Ideas for Cause/Effect Assignments

Exercises 16.1 and 16.2 include topic ideas you may want to develop into cause/effect paragraphs or essays. Here are some additional ideas:

■ Moving to a new town (or choosing not to move)

■ A time when NOT getting what you wanted turned out to be a good thing

- The current popularity of a sport

- An addiction or obsession

- Pollution

- A specific law or proposed law

- A hobby or interest

- Joining a particular organization

- A selfless act

- How the situation in the accompanying photograph happened:

Source: © Eleanor Bentall/Corbis

WebWork

Go to the *Guide to Grammar and Writing* Web site's information about writing cause/effect essays at **http://grammar.ccc.commnet.edu/grammar/composition/cause_effect .htm.** Read the information on this page, including the sample essays. Then, on your own paper, write your answers to the questions in the "Points to Ponder" box.

Online Study Center   For additional information and practice with writing cause/effect paragraphs and essays, go to the Houghton Mifflin Online Study Center for this book, at **http://www.college.hmco.com/pic/dolphinwritertwo.**

17 CHAPTER

Definition

GOALS FOR CHAPTER 17

▶ Define the term *definition*.

▶ Describe the steps in writing a definition paragraph.

▶ Write a definition paragraph.

▶ Recognize the features of a definition essay.

The definition mode involves explaining what a term means. Writers include shorter definitions, those that require only a sentence or two, to make sure readers will understand the meaning of a term that may be unfamiliar. For example, if you were writing about computers for a general audience, you would want to briefly define the technical terms you include.

Definitions can also be extended, requiring a whole paragraph to develop. Abstract or general terms, new terms, and terms that have changed meaning, for example, often require longer definitions and explanations. Take a look at the following example, which defines the abstract term *love*:

> If you look up the word *love* in the dictionary, the definitions you read will probably describe it as a feeling or emotion. However, these definitions are inadequate when it comes to explaining what true love really is. I think the best definition I have ever seen was in Dr. M. Scott Peck's 1978 classic self-help book *The Road Less Traveled*. In it, Peck says that love is "the will to extend one's self for the purpose of nurturing one's own or another's spiritual growth." According to this definition, love is not an emotion that sweeps us off our feet; instead, it is a conscious choice to set aside one's own self-interests to act in ways that will benefit others. Parents do this, of course, when they stop whatever they are doing to nurture their children. People in romantic relationships do it when they listen to each other and provide emotional support.

This paragraph defines the term by giving an expert's opinion, by telling what love is *not*, and by providing two examples as illustration.

The following example defines the new term *retronym*:

> The word *retronym* is such a new word that only one dictionary—the current *American Heritage Dictionary*—is the only one that includes it so far. This reference defines it as "a word or phrase created because an existing term that was once used alone needs to be distinguished from a term referring to a new development or variation." In other words, some new invention caused us to have to adjust the way we used to describe something that pre-dated the new invention. For example, the invention of the electric guitar required us to create the retronym *acoustic guitar* to distinguish it from those that are plugged in. E-mail required us to invent the term *snail mail* to refer to paper mail sent via the post office and the term *voice mail* to refer to messages left on a voice recorder. The creation of skim milk, one-percent milk, and two-percent milk led to the retronym *whole milk*. And the many other retronyms include terms like *manual transmission, wood-burning fireplace, two-parent family,* and *natural childbirth*. (Lyrysa Smith, "Taking a Backward Glance at the History of Useful Retronyms," *The Charlotte Observer*, NC, Nov. 30, 2003, p. 4G.)

Writing a Definition Paragraph

Defining a term involves explaining it so that readers can understand it. To write an effective definition paragraph, you need to determine how you will define the term in your topic sentence and then select other modes—such as narration, illustration, or process—that you can use to generate, organize, and develop your ideas.

Determining a Topic Sentence

If you decide that you will need to write an extended definition to explain your subject to your reader, your first step will be to determine your main point about your subject before you begin to write. Your topic sentence will probably provide a general definition of the term you have chosen. For example, a topic sentence for a paragraph defining the word *hero* might read:

> A hero is someone who sacrifices himself or herself for the good of others.

The main idea of a definition paragraph can also be implied. That is, you can present all of your developing details and then allow the reader to draw a conclusion about the meaning of the term.

EXERCISE 17.1   **Writing Topic Sentences for Definition Paragraphs**

For each of the following topics, use some prewriting techniques to generate ideas, and then write a topic sentence you could use for a definition paragraph.

1. A term used by a particular group (such as a social group, ethnic group, family) to which you belong

   Topic sentence: _____

2. What it means to be "cool"

   Topic sentence: _____

3. Genius

   Topic sentence: _____

4. Marriage

   Topic sentence: _____

5. Evil

   Topic sentence: _____

Generating Ideas

After writing a general definition for your topic sentence, the next step is to determine the most effective methods of development. Definitions are usually developed with one or more of the other modes. So your first step is asking the question *What would be the best way to explain this term to the reader?* One or more of the following modes are useful in developing a definition paragraph:

- **Tell a story.** For instance, you could define what *fear* is by narrating the story of a time when you were lost in a cave and could not find your way out.

- **Provide descriptive details.** Another way to define the word *fear* is to describe the body's response when the mind is fearful.

- **Give examples.** Illustration is a very common method of development for definition. The previous paragraph about retronyms, for instance, provides numerous examples that illustrate the meaning of the term.

- **Classify or divide.** You could also classify the parts of the subject into categories or divide it into its parts to help define what it is. For example, you could define what blood is by dividing it into its different components and describing each one.

- **Explain how something is done.** Process analysis can help to define a term by explaining how the subject works. You could define *conflict resolution*, for example, by describing each step in the process of resolving a conflict.

- **Explain causes and effects.** You could explain the reasons for the topic's existence or discuss the consequences of its existence. A paragraph that defines *employee morale*, for example, could explain what produces high or low morale; it might also explore the effects of high or low morale.

- **Compare or contrast.** You could offer an analogy, comparing the term or idea you are defining or explaining to something with which the reader is already familiar. Or you could use contrast, explaining what the term *does not* mean. For example, if you are defining what *sexual harassment* is, you might want to distinguish what it is *not*. Contrast can also involve explaining how the thing or idea being defined is different from something else. The previous paragraph about love, for instance, contrasts a true definition of *love* to incorrect notions of what the word means.

Which modes seem appropriate for developing each of the topic sentences below?

Adolescence is the period in one's life when one's personal values begin to come into conflict with society's values.

If you are in a Catch-22 situation, you are in a no-win situation.

Depression is a mental condition characterized by an inability to concentrate, along with feelings of sadness and hopelessness.

Any one of these three topic sentences could be developed with a narrative that includes descriptive details; for example, the writer could relate a personal story, or he or she could tell a tale about someone else to help readers understand the meaning of the term.

In addition, the first topic sentence could be developed with comparison/ contrast, for personal values could be contrasted with society's values. Cause/ effect would be another suitable mode of development because the writer could explore the reasons why these values conflict or could explain the consequences.

A writer might illustrate the second topic sentence with either one long example or a series of examples. Also, he or she could explain how the term *Catch-22* originated from Joseph Heller's novel of the same name.

The third topic sentence could be illustrated with descriptive details, causes or effects, or even classification, for the writer could group different types of depression into categories based on their severity or symptoms.

After selecting the appropriate modes for your topic, spend some time prewriting to generate ideas for each of these modes. For example, if you are going to write about bullies by using illustration, brainstorm the names of people you would label bullies. If you are going to define the term *forgiveness* by using process, list all of the steps that one would have to take in order to forgive.

EXERCISE 17.2 **Determining Modes of Development for Definition Topic Sentences**

For each of the following topic sentences, briefly explain on the blanks provided which two modes would best develop the main idea.

1. My definition of the word *success* has changed over time.

_____

_____

_____

2. Most of us know at least one individual who is in the grip of an obsession, an unnatural fixation upon a certain person, thing, or activity.

_____

_____

_____

3. A true friend is someone who knows all about you and likes you anyway.

_____

_____

_____

4. Possessing wisdom is much different from being knowledgeable.

_____

_____

_____

5. Cyberdating is a new trend in romance that involves meeting potential mates via the Internet.

_____

_____

_____

Organizing a Definition Paragraph and Using Transitions

You may choose to use just one of the other modes for developing your ideas, or you might combine several different modes. If you will be using multiple modes to define or explain your subject, you will need to decide on the best order in which to present them and then create an outline that reflects this order. Often, one of the modes will provide the organizing structure for the entire paragraph, whereas another mode or modes will be used to provide layers of development. For example, for the topic sentence

> Adolescence is the period in one's life when one's personal values begin to come into conflict with society's values.

you might organize the entire paragraph using comparison/contrast. Then you could develop each point of comparison with examples or narratives.

As you write, be sure to add transitions that help the reader discern the relationships among the details. The transitions you include will depend upon the specific modes you have chosen to develop your ideas. However, because illustration is a common mode for defining ideas, you are likely to use illustration transitional words such as *for example* and *for instance*.

EXERCISE 17.3   **Organizing Details in Definition Paragraphs**

Prewrite to generate ideas, and then complete each of the following topic sentences by filling in the blank. Then, on the other blanks provided, prepare an informal outline by listing the details you would include in an appropriate order.

1. Prejudice is _____.

_____

_____

_____

_____

2. To understand _____, one must understand the meaning of

the term _____.

_____

_____

_____

_____

3. _____ is the one term that underlies the whole _____
philosophy (or religion).

_____

_____

_____

_____

EXERCISE 17.4   **Recognizing Transitions in a Definition Paragraph**

Circle all of the transitional words in the following paragraph.

> What is a *weblog*, or *blog*, for short? Think about a "normal" Web site. It usually has a home page, with links to lots of sub-pages that have more detail. A blog, on the other hand, is much simpler. A blog is normally a single page of entries. There may be archives of older entries, but the "main page" of a blog is all anyone really cares about. A blog is organized in reverse-chronological order, from most recent entry to least recent. The entries in a blog usually come from a single author, and they are usually stream-of-consciousness. There is no particular order to them, so a blog is a lot like an online journal or diary. The author can talk about anything and everything. However, many blogs have a focus. For example, if a blogger is interested in technology, the blogger might go to the Consumer Electronics Show and post entries of the things he or she sees there. If a blogger is interested in a certain disease, he/she might post every news article and every piece of research he/she finds on the disease. If a blogger is interested in economic issues, he/she might post links to articles that discuss the economy and then offer commentary on them. (Adapted from Marshall Brain, "How Blogs Work," http://computer.howstuffworks.com/blog1.htm)

EXERCISE 17.5   **Writing a Definition Paragraph That Includes Transitions**

Choose one of the topic sentences and outlines you prepared in Exercise 17.3. Write the paragraph, including transitions that indicate how the details are related.

Developing the Details in a Definition Paragraph

Once you have selected the appropriate mode (or modes) for developing your definition, you will follow the specific guidelines for that mode to provide the necessary details. For example, if you use illustration to develop your definition, remember the principles of writing effective illustration. If you use cause/effect, remember that set of principles, and so on.

Writing Longer Definition Passages and Definition Essays

So far, this chapter has focused only on definition paragraphs. However, a definition may need several paragraphs for development. For example, read the following passage:

Who are our heroes, and how can they make us happier? Heroes are a fading memory in our times, but we still can recall a little about them. We know, at least, that what sets the hero apart is some extraordinary achievement. Whatever this feat[1], it is such as to be recognized at once by everyone as a good thing; and somehow, the achieving of it seems larger than life. The hero, furthermore, overcomes the ordinary and attains greatness by serving some great good. His example very nearly rebukes[2] us, telling us that we fail, not by aiming too high in life, but by aiming far too low. Moreover, it tells us we are mistaken in supposing that happiness is a right or an end in itself. The hero seeks not happiness, but goodness, and his fulfillment lies in achieving it. In truth, the question is less about heroes than about the framework of belief in which they can, and cannot, flourish[3]. In the end, it concerns what we ourselves believe in and what we ask of life. What the hero gives us is a completely fresh, unfailed way of looking at life and, perhaps, the answer to our pervasive[4], mysterious unhappiness. Heroes, by their example, remind us that to pursue happiness for its own sake is the surest way to lose it.

Modern experience certainly bears this out. If nothing else, then, the hero yanks us out of the old rut and bids us to reexamine our values and goals. At the same time, he shows us by his own example that higher purposes in life, far from being an illusion, are the key to our richest potentials. Already, this is much more than the how-to books can promise.

1. **feat:** achievement
2. **rebukes:** scolds; criticizes

3. **flourish:** do well; prosper; thrive
4. **pervasive:** present everywhere

Real heroism requires courage. It entails[1] peril[2] or pain. The dictionary says heroes are "distinguished by valor[3] or enterprise in danger, or fortitude[4] in suffering." Plainly, heroism also has a selfless quality. The hero's deed is ennobled[5] not by courage alone, but by the call to duty or by service to others. In this, it gains a larger symbolic value that can inspire and bind a whole nation. **The hero acts for what is common and precious to all, and thereby replenishes[6] the strength of our shared convictions.***

Although this passage covers three paragraphs, it develops just one topic sentence, which is highlighted with bold print. The passage explores several characteristics of heroes: a hero achieves some great feat, causes others to reexamine their values and goals, and is both selfless and courageous. Then it ties all of these qualities together in one statement of definition at the end of the third paragraph.

Definitions can also take the form of complete essays. To write a definition essay, follow the steps for writing a definition paragraph. First, write a thesis statement that offers a general definition of the term. Next, decide on the best modes to develop this idea, and generate ideas. Then follow the guidelines for the mode or modes you have chosen to organize and develop your points and details. As you write, include transitions that indicate how the details are related.

 **EXERCISE 17.6** **The Definition Essay**

Read the following essay. Then answer the questions that follow by writing your responses on the blanks provided.

What Is Terrorism?

1 Since the terrible events of September 11, 2001, with the attacks on the World Trade Center and the Pentagon, the subject of terrorism has exploded on the world stage. President George W. Bush has declared a war against terrorism. The vast resources of the United States and other countries have been directed toward ending terrorism in America and around the world. Yet, in spite of these developments, it is clear that countries are not only divided about what to do about terrorism, but even about how to define it.

1. **entails:** requires; includes
2. **peril:** danger
3. **valor:** bravery
4. **fortitude:** strength

5. **ennobled:** made noble (having high moral character)
6. **replenishes:** restores

**Source:* Excerpted from George Roche, "A World Without Heroes," reprinted from *USA Today Magazine,* November 1998. Copyrighted by the Society for the Advancement of Education.

Integrating Source Material

When you incorporate source material into your writing, you can use either direct quotations or paraphrases. A *direct quotation* provides the exact wording of the original source, so it is enclosed in quotation marks:

> Anna Quindlen writes, "According to the National Association of Home Builders, the average American home has doubled in size in the past century. This is not because families are larger. Quite the contrary. The three-car-garage-and-great-room-trend—a great room being a living room on steroids—reflects family life that has devolved into individual isolation, everyone with his own TV and computer, centrally cooled to a frosty edge or heedlessly heated." ("A Shock to the System," Anna Quindlen, *Newsweek*, Aug. 25, 2003, p. 68.)

A *paraphrase* rewords the information in the original source, so it is not enclosed in quotation marks:

> Anna Quindlen points out that even though American families have not gotten any larger, the average American home is now twice the size it was 100 years ago. She says that

this trend of building huge houses reveals that even members of the same family are becoming more isolated from one another, for everyone has his or her own space apart from everyone else.

Is it better to use more direct quotations or more paraphrases when you integrate source material? In general, it is actually better to use more paraphrases for two reasons:

1. **Paraphrasing allows you to include only the essential information.** Although it is true that you can remove parts of quotations and indicate the omission with ellipses dots (. . .), a paraphrase allows you to incorporate just the pertinent facts or ideas, without including any unnecessary words.

2. **Paraphrases are usually easier for the reader of your paper to read.** Because paraphrases are in the same wording and style as the rest of your paper, they tend to flow better with the rest of the text. Also, readers do not have to do the extra mental work required to shift from your voice to a different voice, as they do when they read direct quotations.

2   By its nature, the term "terrorism" is bound up in political controversy. It is a concept with a very negative connotation[1]. Because terrorism implies the killing and maiming[2] of innocent people, no country wants to be accused of supporting terrorism or harboring terrorist groups. At the same time, no country wants what it considers to be a legitimate use of force to be considered terrorism. An old saying goes, "One person's terrorist is another person's freedom fighter."

---

1. **connotation:** suggestion of meaning   2. **maiming:** injuring

3   Today, there is no universally accepted definition of terrorism. Countries define the term according to their own beliefs and to support their own national interests. International bodies, when they craft a definition, do so in the interests of their member states. Academics striving to define terrorism are also subject to their own political points of view.

4   European countries and the United States tend to define terrorism narrowly, making sure that it only applies to acts of non-governmental organizations. For example, Title 22 of the U.S. Code defines terrorism as "premeditated[1], politically motivated violence" against "noncombatant[2] targets by subnational groups" usually with the goal to influence an audience.

5   The U.S. Department of Defense uses a definition that highlights another element of the Western concept of terrorism. Terrorism is "the calculated use of violence or the threat of violence to inculcate fear; intended to coerce[3] or to intimidate governments or societies in the pursuit of goals that are generally *political, religious,* or *ideological.*" In other words, terrorism is violence designed to advance some cause by getting a government to change its policies or political behavior.

6   Contrast these definitions with one produced by Iranian religious scholar Ayatulla Taskhiri in a paper delivered at a 1987 international terrorism conference called by the Organization of the Islamic Conference. After a review of Islamic sources concerning terrorism, Taskhiri defined it as follows: "Terrorism is an act carried out to achieve an inhuman and corrupt objective[4] and involving threat to security of any kind, and in violation of the rights acknowledged by religion and mankind."

7   This is a much broader definition of terrorism. Under this definition, nation states themselves could be guilty of terrorism. Any inhuman or corrupt objective coupled with an act that threatens security and rights regardless of the motivation could be considered terrorism. Later in his paper, Taskhiri accuses the United States of being the "mother of international terrorism" by oppressing[5] peoples, strengthening dictatorships[6], and supporting the occupation of territories and savage attacks on civilian areas.

8   The United States would likely reject this definition and Taskhiri's charges and could point out that many states under this definition would also be chargeable with terrorism. Nevertheless, the definition points out the wide gulf in perceptions about what is terrorism and who is guilty of it.

1. **premeditated:** planned beforehand
2. **noncombatant:** not fighting
3. **coerce:** force someone to act a certain way
4. **objective:** goal

5. **oppressing:** keeping down by use of force or authority
6. **dictatorships:** governments ruled by one individual (a dictator)

9   Consider some additional definitions of terrorism.

■ "All criminal acts directed against a State intended or calculated to create a state of terror in the minds of particular persons or persons in the general public." (League of Nations, 1937)

■ "Act of terrorism = Peacetime Equivalent of War Crime." (Alex P. Schmid of United Nations Office for the Prevention of International Terrorism. He is the author of many books on terrorism, including *Terrorism and the Media*, 1992.)

■ "Terrorism is the premeditated, deliberate, systematic murder, mayhem[1], and threatening of the innocent to create fear and intimidation[2] in order to gain a political or tactical advantage, usually to influence an audience." (James M. Poland, professor of criminal justice at California State University, Sacramento. He has written extensively on terrorism and hostage crisis intervention.)

10   While there is no universal definition of terrorism, various experts point out that there are common elements to most terrorist acts.

11   Acts of terrorism usually are committed by groups who do not possess the political power to change policies they view as intolerable. Middle Eastern terrorism intensified in the 1970s in response to defeats of Arab nations in wars with Israel over the Palestine[3] issue. Convinced that further wars were futile[4], a number of countries, including Egypt, sought peace with Israel. This enraged groups within those countries dedicated to the defeat of Israel, who then turned to terrorism.

12   Terrorists choose targets and actions to maximize the psychological effect on a society or government. Their goal is to create a situation in which a government will change its policies to avoid further bloodshed or disruption. For these reasons, terrorists often choose methods of mass destruction, such as bombings, and target transportation or crowded places to increase anxiety and fear.

13   Terrorists plan their acts to get as much media exposure as possible. Media coverage magnifies the terrorist act by spreading fear among a mass audience and giving attention to the terrorist cause. The attacks on Israeli athletes at the 1972 Olympics assured a worldwide television audience, as did crashing planes into the World Trade Center.

14   Terrorists often justify their acts on ideological[5] or religious grounds arguing that they are responding to a greater wrong or are promoting a greater good. For example, Leon Trotsky, a communist leader during the Russian Revolution,

1. **mayhem:** violent disorder
2. **intimidation:** stimulating fear
3. **Palestine:** "the Holy Land," a source of conflict with Israel

4. **futile:** useless
5. **ideological:** relating to a set of beliefs

justified the use of terror by the Red Army as a necessary evil to promote the worldwide cause of workers and as a response to the military actions of counter-revolutionaries[1] and Western powers.*

1. What is the thesis of this essay?

_____

_____

2. What are the two primary modes of development used in paragraphs 4–7?

_____

3. What is the main mode of development used in paragraphs 12–13?

_____

4. In addition to cause/effect, what mode of development is used in paragraphs 11, 13, and 14?

_____

5. In your opinion, which of the various definitions of terrorism offered in this essay seems to be the most accurate? Why? Illustrate your answer with a specific example of a terrorist attack.

_____

In Summary: Steps in Writing Definition Essays

1. **Determine your main idea.** Write a general definition of your term to serve as your topic sentence or thesis statement.
2. **Decide on your modes of development and generate ideas.** Choose one or more modes for developing your definition, and then prewrite to generate ideas.
3. **Organize and develop ideas.** Follow the guidelines for the specific mode(s) you have chosen to organize and explain your ideas.

1. **counterrevolutionaries:** people who want to get rid of a political or social system set up by a previous overthrow of a government

*Source: Adapted from *Terrorism in America*, 3d ed., Constitutional Rights Foundation, 2006. www.crf-usa.org.

Fill in the blanks in the following statements.

1. The definition mode involves explaining _____.

2. A definition may be short, requiring only a sentence or two to develop. Or a definition can be _____, requiring a whole paragraph or more to develop.

3. _____ or general terms, _____ terms, and terms that have changed _____ often require longer definitions.

4. The topic sentence of a definition paragraph usually provides a general _____ of the term you have chosen.

5. After writing a general definition for a topic sentence, the writer must determine which of the other _____ will most effectively develop that idea.

6. Often, one mode will provide the organizing _____ for the entire paragraph, whereas another mode or modes are used to provide _____.

7. Because illustration is a common mode for defining ideas, you are likely to use illustration _____ such as *for example* and *for instance*.

8. A definition may need several _____ for development.

9. Definitions can also take the form of complete essays in which the topic and main point are stated in a _____.

Topic Ideas for Definition Assignments

Exercise 17.1 includes topic ideas you may want to develop into definition paragraphs or essays. Here are some additional ideas:

- True love
- Conscience
- Imagination
- Pornography

- Racism

- A word related to one of your hobbies or interests

- A word that is overused or abused

- An emotion (fear, anger, sorrow, and so on)

- A value (responsibility, loyalty, neatness, and so on)

Go to the *Guide to Grammar and Writing* Web site's information about writing definition essays at **http://grammar.ccc.commnet.edu/grammar/composition/ definition.htm.** Read the information on this page, including the sample essay. Then, on your own paper, write your answers to the questions in the "Points to Ponder" box.

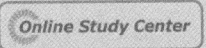 For additional information and practice with writing definition paragraphs and essays, go to the Houghton Mifflin Online Study Center for this book, at **http://www.college.hmco.com/pic/dolphinwritertwo.**

18

Argument

GOALS FOR CHAPTER 18

▶ Define the term *argument*.

▶ Describe the steps in writing an argument paragraph.

▶ Write an argument paragraph.

▶ Recognize the features of an argument essay.

There will be many occasions when you will need to convince a reader to do something or to change his or her belief about something. You may need to write an academic research paper arguing that online learning is as effective as traditional classroom-based learning. You may have to write a memo or report to convince your boss to implement a certain change at work. Or you may want to write a letter to your newspaper's editor to convince citizens to vote for a particular candidate for public office or to oppose a proposed change for your community. This type of writing is called argument because you are *arguing* a certain position. Argument writing attempts to persuade the reader to accept a certain viewpoint.

The following paragraph, for example, argues against home schooling:

There are compelling[1] reasons to oppose home teaching both for the sake of the children involved and for society. Home schooling is an extension of the misguided notion that "anyone can teach." That notion is simply wrong. Recently, some of our best and brightest college graduates, responding to the altruistic[2] call to "Teach for America," failed as teachers because they lacked training. Good teaching is a complex act that involves more than simply loving children. Research on student achievement overwhelmingly supports the "common-sense" logic that the most important factor affecting student learning is teacher

1. **compelling:** forceful; requiring attention

2. **altruistic:** caring unselfishly about the needs of others

335

competency[1]. While some parents may be competent to teach very young children, that competence will wane[2] in more advanced grades as the content and complexity increases. Plus, schools serve important functions far beyond academic learning. Attending school is an important element in the development of the "whole child." Schools, particularly public schools, are the one place where "all of the children of all of the people come together." Can there be anything more important to each child and thus to our democratic society than to develop virtues and values such as respect for others, the ability to communicate and collaborate[3] and an openness to diversity and new ideas? Such virtues and values cannot be accessed on the Internet. The isolation implicit[4] in home teaching is anathema[5] to socialization and citizenship. (Adapted from "Home Is No Place for School," Dennis L. Evans, *USA Today*, Sept. 3, 2003, p. 11A. Reprinted by permission of the author.)

In this paragraph, the author provides two reasons why home schooling is a bad idea. First, the writer argues that parents are not necessarily good teachers. Second, he argues that home-schooled children cannot learn socialization and citizenship.

Writing an Argument Paragraph

Arguing for or against something involves offering convincing reasons in support of your position. To write an effective argument paragraph, you need to consider your audience's needs and goals, write a persuasive topic sentence, select relevant reasons and acknowledge opposing arguments, and develop your reasons with sufficient logical or emotional evidence.

Thinking About Your Audience

Many of the other modes of development usually focus on either the writer and his or her thoughts and experiences (narration, description) or the subject itself (comparison/contrast, cause/effect, definition, and so on). Argument writing, in contrast, focuses on the *reader*. Because the whole purpose of persuasive writing is to persuade, or convince, the reader, the whole essay revolves around the kinds of reasons and evidence the reader will need in order to accept the idea in the writer's topic sentence.

Thus, the first step in planning an argument paragraph is to carefully consider the targeted reader. Whether this is one person or many, remember that

1. **competency:** ability or skill
2. **wane:** decrease
3. **collaborate:** work together

4. **implicit:** implied or understood though not directly expressed
5. **anathema:** a curse

arguments are not directed at people who agree with the writer; writing a paragraph for those who already concur with the thesis would be a waste of time. Instead, argument paragraphs are directed at readers who either disagree with the writer's viewpoint or have not yet made up their minds.

Once you have determined exactly who needs to be persuaded to accept your opinion, then spend some time thinking about that reader's needs, goals, and potential objections. At this point, at least informally analyze your readers. What do they probably believe now? What do you think their goals and priorities are? To what parts of your argument will they object? Can you think of ways to overcome these objections? As you plan and write your paragraph, you will return often to this analysis to guide you in making decisions about *what* to include and *how* to include it.

EXERCISE 18.1   **Considering Your Audience**

For each of the following argument topic sentences, consider who the best audience would be. On the blanks provided, identify the most likely audience and briefly describe their needs, goals, and potential objections.

1. You should not get married until you are at least thirty years old.

   _____

   _____

   _____

2. All motorcycle riders should wear helmets.

   _____

   _____

   _____

3. The legal driving age should be raised to eighteen.

   _____

   _____

   _____

4. I deserve an increase in my hourly wage.

   _____

   _____

   _____

5. My absence from class should be excused.

_____

_____

_____

Determining Your Topic Sentence, Relevant Reasons, and Opposing Arguments

Your analysis of your readers will affect, first of all, your choice of a topic sentence and supporting reasons. It will also help you determine how to refute those readers' objections to your ideas.

The Persuasive Topic Sentence. Persuasive topic sentences usually have several important characteristics:

1. Persuasive topic sentences clearly state the behavior or belief they want the reader to adopt after reading the paragraph. And, to reflect their persuasive purpose, these types of topic sentences often include words and phrases such as _should, must, ought to,_ and _have to._ For example, read the following thesis statements:

    > When you go shopping for a new car, you should not even consider buying a sport-utility vehicle.
    > The United States government has to change its policies about Mexican immigration.
    > Even fans of the actress must admit that her performance in the film was very poor.

    Each of these statements clearly states the change in belief or behavior that the writer is advocating.

2. Persuasive topic sentences are also assertive. They do not include tentative or hedging words and phrases such as "I believe that" or "_maybe_ we should." They take a stand, and they confidently ask the reader to accept that stand as true and valid.

3. Persuasive topic sentences often include the agent of the action; in other words, they state exactly who should make or bring about this change.

In the preceding statements, drivers, the United States government, and the actress's fans are the ones being asked to alter either a belief or a behavior.

4. Persuasive topic sentences ask the reader to make changes that are logical and reasonable. Again, a consideration of your audience will guide your composition of your topic sentence. Although you might want them to make a very big change, you must consider whether or not you should argue for that big change or for some intermediate, shorter-term change that will, you hope, ultimately lead to the bigger change. For instance, will an audience that believes immigration laws are fine the way they are think that it is reasonable for you to ask them to support opening the border between America and Mexico? Probably not. And no matter how eloquent and well-reasoned your argument, you might not be able to convince them. So you might have to adjust your thesis statement to argue an idea that is more within the realm of possibility. You would argue instead that current immigration policies need some adjustments.

EXERCISE 18.2   **Writing Topic Sentences for Argument Paragraphs**

For each of the following topics, use some prewriting techniques to generate ideas, and then write a topic sentence you could use for an argument paragraph.

1. Attendance requirements for college courses

Topic sentence: _____

2. Beauty pageants

Topic sentence: _____

3. The legal drinking age

Topic sentence: _____

4. The speed limit on highways

Topic sentence: _____

5. Smoking cigarettes

Topic sentence: _____

Supporting Reasons. Just as a consideration of your reader determined your thesis statement, your analysis of your audience should guide your choice of supporting points. Often, there are many different reasons that support a particular opinion. However, not all of these reasons may be *relevant* to your target audience. So in the planning stages of writing your paragraph, you will need to decide which reasons most closely match your readers' priorities and goals.

For example, if you intend to argue to drivers that they should not buy a sport-utility vehicle, you would need to consider these readers' priorities. Typical motorists want a vehicle that is safe, trustworthy, stylish, fun to drive, and affordable. Thus, they will respond to reasons that relate to accident statistics, costs, driving ease, and image. These readers would be less likely to be convinced by reasons—such as environmental issues—that are unrelated to their main concerns, so the writer can leave those points out.

EXERCISE 18.3   **Selecting Relevant Supporting Reasons**

For each of the argument topic sentences you wrote for Exercise 18.2, identify the target audience on the corresponding blank, and then list two or three supporting reasons that would be relevant to that audience.

1. Audience: _____

   Supporting reasons:

   _____

   _____

   _____

2. Audience: _____

   Supporting reasons:

   _____

   _____

   _____

3. Audience: _____

   Supporting reasons:

   _____

   _____

   _____

4. Audience: _____

Supporting reasons:

_____

_____

_____

5. Audience: _____

Supporting reasons:

_____

_____

_____

Opposing Arguments. One special feature of argument paragraphs is acknow-ledgment of the opposing arguments, which is also known as making *conces-sions*. When you make a concession, you mention one or more of your opponent's arguments, and then you go on to refute each argument by explaining how your position is stronger, more logical, or more valid. Making concessions to the op-posing arguments indicates to your reader that you understand the entire issue, not just your side of it. It also allows you to expose the weaknesses in opposing reasons by explaining how they are flawed.

Argument writers do not explain an opposing argument in detail. They merely mention it and then go on to refute it. Concessions can be dealt with in one section of the paragraph, but they are often most effective when you match each concession to one of your supporting points and use the supporting point as a refutation of the opposing argument. For example, if you assert that sport-utility vehicles are not as safe as motorists think they are, someone who disagrees with you could point out all of their safety features or cite accident statistics that show that the occupants of an SUV often suffer fewer injuries than the oc-cupants of a car. To refute these arguments, you could point to statistics about rollover accidents, which are more common and more deadly in SUVs than in other types of vehicles. The following example, which includes a concession in italic type, shows one way of doing this:

> *You might think that you are safer in a large, heavy SUV than you are in a more lightweight car.* However, statistics show that you are more likely to be involved in a dangerous rollover accident in an SUV.

If you decide to include the argument that SUVs are not an economical choice, someone who disagrees with you might point out that these vehicles are larger and that their price per square foot is comparable to other vehicles. In turn, you could counter with information about upkeep costs such as gasoline, maintenance, and insurance. The following example includes both the concession (in italic type) and the response:

> *Car shoppers may argue that the price of an SUV is not that much higher than the price of many cars.* They probably do not realize, however, that the day-to-day cost of maintaining an SUV is quite a bit higher.

Notice that both of these concessions to the opposing argument are mentioned very briefly in just one sentence. Notice also that the transitional word *however* signals the end of the concession and the beginning of the author's argument. Other contrast transitional words, such as *but, on the other hand,* and *nevertheless*, are also appropriate in signaling this shift. Concessions themselves often begin with words and statements such as *admittedly, of course, it is true that*, and *I concede that.*

As you get in the habit of incorporating concessions in your argument paragraphs, choose your words carefully to avoid insulting or offending readers. Remember that they either disagree with you or are undecided and that they are likely to believe many of the opposing arguments you are going to refute. So when you make concessions, use language that is sensitive to the reader. Do not suggest that the opposing argument (and thus the reader who believes it) is uninformed or ignorant. It is probably best to avoid using aggressively judgmental words such as *ridiculous* or *silly* when you mention an opposing argument. Instead, gently refute each one with logical, well-reasoned explanations of your own viewpoints.

EXERCISE 18.4   **Determining Concessions**

For each of the supporting reasons you listed in Exercise 18.3, write a concession on the blanks provided.

1. _____

_____

_____

2. _____

_____

_____

3. _____

_____

_____

4. _____

_____

_____

5. _____

_____

_____

Organizing an Argument Paragraph and Using Transitions

After you decide on the reasons you will offer in support of your argument, your next major consideration will be the order in which to present these reasons. Order of importance is the most common pattern for arranging reasons. So rank each of your reasons in importance, and then let your analysis of your readers guide you in your decision about whether to discuss them in order of most important to least important, or of least important to most important. If your readers are very busy decision-makers, consider beginning with your strongest, most important reason, the one that will be most likely to persuade them. If you are reasonably sure that your readers will be willing to read the entire paragraph, giving your argument careful consideration, consider saving your strongest reason for last so it will be the one they remember best after they have finished reading.

As you write, do not forget to include transitions that help readers follow you from one point to the next. Some common argument transitional words are

first, second, third
one reason, another reason, and so on
most important
for one thing
next
last
finally
another
in addition
furthermore
also

⯌ **EXERCISE 18.5** **Organizing Reasons in Argument Paragraphs**

Prewrite to generate ideas, and then complete each of the following topic sentences by filling in the blank. Then, on the other blanks provided, prepare an informal outline by listing the reasons you would include in an appropriate order.

1. _____ should not be mandatory.

_____

_____

_____

2. _____ should be outlawed once and for all.

_____

_____

_____

3. _____ is a complete waste of money.

_____

_____

_____

⯌ **EXERCISE 18.6** **Recognizing Argument Transitions**

Circle all of the argument transitional words in the following paragraph.

Although people are using both legal and technical means to try to rid cyberspace[1] of the unsolicited[2] e-mail advertisements known as "spam," this annoyance will probably never be completely eradicated[3]. The only effective way to combat the problem is to strike at its roots by convincing would-be spammers of the harm done in the process of sending out millions of bulk e-mail mes-

1. **cyberspace:** the electronic medium of computer networks

2. **unsolicited:** not asked for
3. **eradicated:** wiped out; eliminated

sages. Do not become a spammer, for if you do, you will be damaging American society in a number of ways. First of all, spam harms American businesses by requiring them to drain corporate budgets to combat the problem. Employees lose time and money when they must slog[1] through unwanted e-mail on the job, so businesses are forced to spend hundreds of thousands of dollars to install spam filters and other barriers. These expenses threaten the very existence of companies, as well as the jobs they provide for American citizens. Secondly, spam threatens the very usefulness of the Internet, one of the most valuable communication tools of the computer age. About 40 percent of e-mail is now spam, and that proportion continues to grow every day. This amount of electronic junk mail is already wreaking havoc[2] with many servers that cannot cope with the high volume. It is causing Internet service providers to raise the prices they charge consumers. Also, spam is leading many people, who are tired of being force-fed advertisements that are fraudulent[3] or pornographic, to abandon the Internet altogether. Many of them are parents who do not want their children exposed to the obscene content of many spam messages. So please do not contribute to what is already a serious problem by becoming a spammer yourself! (Jonathan Krim, "Spam's Cost to Business Escalates," *Washington Post*, March 13, 2003. © 2003, *Washington Post*, reprinted with permission.)

EXERCISE 18.7 **Writing an Argument Paragraph That Includes Transitions**

Choose one of the topic sentences and outlines you prepared in Exercise 18.5. Write the paragraph, including transitions that indicate how the reasons are related.

Developing Your Reasons with Evidence

As you develop each reason that supports your thesis, be aware of the two kinds of evidence you can offer and plan to include the kind that is more likely to convince your reader. The first type is *logical* evidence, which includes facts, statistics, expert opinion, and examples. This type of evidence consists of the hard data and observable facts that will appeal to your readers' reason and intellect. If you want to argue against buying a sport-utility vehicle, for instance, you can provide accident statistics that show this type of vehicle is unsafe. You can also

1. **slog:** work at for long hours
2. **wreaking havoc:** causing disorder or chaos

3. **fraudulent:** false and deceitful

provide specific cost information that reveals exactly how much more money your readers will have to spend on gasoline every week if they buy an SUV.

The second type of evidence is *emotional*. This evidence appeals to readers' needs and feelings, such as the need for fun or friendship and the desire to be a good parent. Think of television commercials, which attempt to sell people many products—from perfume to beer to peanut butter—by appealing to their desires to be attractive, well liked, loving to our children, and so on. These types of arguments can be effective in argument essays, too. For example, you could argue that by buying an SUV, motorists make the road more dangerous for everyone; this particular argument appeals to readers' concern for their fellow man. However, beware of basing entire academic arguments on emotional evidence. Readers of academic and professional arguments will expect the majority of your evidence to be factual and logical.

As you incorporate both logical and emotional kinds of evidence in support of your argument, make sure you avoid *logical fallacies*, arguments that are flawed in various ways because they are based on careless thinking or on deliberate attempts to distract the reader. Some of these fallacies are based on a lack of sufficient evidence. For example, a writer may simply repeat a point over and over without ever offering any real proof in support of it. Or the writer may jump to conclusions on the basis of very little evidence. Other fallacies arise from flawed relationships. For example, a writer might claim that one thing led to another without considering the other factors that could have been at work, or he might carelessly compare two things that are really more different than they are alike. Still other fallacies take the form of personal attacks against those who believe the opposing arguments or try to persuade the reader on the basis of what other people—such as celebrities—believe. Alert readers will detect such fallacies, which weaken arguments.

Writing Longer Arguments and Argument Essays

So far, this chapter has focused only on argument paragraphs. However, an argument may need several paragraphs for development. For example, read the following passage written by the president of the American Association of Colleges for Teacher Education:

> The American Association of Colleges for Teacher Education (AACTE) supports the creation of a common national test to assess teacher candidates' readiness to teach for two reasons.

First, all teacher candidates, whether graduates from education schools or from alternative programs, should be held to the same standards. As the demand for more highly qualified teachers has risen, policymakers have responded by promoting a range of alternative routes to certification. Those who emerge from such routes often are held to different standards and exempted[1] from the expectations and assessments[2] set for others who follow more traditional teacher-preparation routes.

AACTE demands that all candidates for teaching meet the same standards, as set by federal law, and promotes the use of a common assessment to test all prospective teachers' knowledge of content and pedagogy[3]. The efforts to subvert[4] the law and create an alternative class of teachers must end.

Second, the hundreds of tests currently being used to assess teacher candidates vary widely and prevent meaningful comparison of the quality of candidates entering the teaching field across states, within and between demographic[5] groups or for other purposes. Uniform[6] use of a national test would allow for more appropriate pass-rate-data reporting across states and institutions—as required by Title II of the Higher Education Act—and would enable policymakers and practitioners to measure and evaluate more effectively what and how well candidates are learning. (Reprinted with permission. Copyright by the American Association of Colleges for Teacher Education, 2003.)

Although this passage covers four paragraphs, it develops just one topic sentence, which is highlighted with bold print. The passage presents two reasons in support of the main idea. Each point is introduced with a transition and developed with logical evidence.

Arguments can also take the form of complete essays. To write an argument essay, follow the steps for writing an argument paragraph. First, consider your reader(s) and write a thesis statement that clearly states what you want that reader to do or to believe. Then generate a list of supporting reasons and concessions. Next, determine the best order for your reasons and plan to discuss each one in a separate paragraph. As you write, include argument transitions and fully develop each reason with either logical or emotional evidence.

1. **exempted:** freed from an obligation or requirement
2. **assessments:** tests
3. **pedagogy:** the art or profession of teaching
4. **subvert:** destroy; ruin; overthrow
5. **demographic:** related to a particular group within a population
6. **uniform:** always the same; consistent

Documenting Sources

In Chapter 17, you learned how to incorporate direct quotations and paraphrases from other sources into your writing. Now you are ready to learn how to properly acknowledge — or *document* — the source material you include in support of your ideas. There are several different systems of documentation, including MLA (Modern Language Association) style, APA (American Psychological Association) style, and the *Chicago Manual of Style* system. In this text, you will focus on MLA style, the system used most often for papers in the humanities.

MLA style has two main components: (1) citations in the text, enclosed in parentheses, that provide the author's name and page number (for print sources) of the original source, along with (2) a works-cited list that provides complete bibliographic information for all of the sources cited in the paper. The following examples provide typical citations for direct quotations and paraphrases:

DIRECT QUOTATION:

"Americans have been careless and casual with our natural resources for a long time" (Quindlen 68).

PARTIAL QUOTATION:

Most environmentalists would agree that "we cannot simply create larger quantities of waste and dump it into the environment and pretend that it doesn't matter" (Gore 55).

PARAPHRASE:

According to one U.S. senator, protecting natural resources should be one of the government's highest priorities (Kohl).

To distinguish source material from your own ideas, make sure to clearly identify source material at both its beginning and its end. In the case of a direct quotation, the quotation mark will indicate the beginning of the material, and the parenthetical citation will indicate the end. Paraphrases are often introduced with the author's name to indicate where the source material begins. In that case, the author's name is not repeated in the citation:

In his book *Earth in the Balance,* Al Gore tries to increase awareness about how waste is affecting the environment (55).

For more information about integrating source material into your paragraphs, see *Purdue University's MLA Formatting and Style Guide* at http://owl.english.purdue.edu/owl/resource/557/01/

EXERCISE 18.8 **The Argument Essay**

Read the following essay, which was written soon after the space shuttle *Columbia* broke apart while reentering Earth's atmosphere on February 1, 2003. Then answer the questions that follow by writing your responses on the blanks provided.

To Reach for the Stars

1 We all share the pain and grief of the families of the seven astronauts who died aboard the shuttle *Columbia*. We mourn with the men and women of NASA[1], who must not only contend with the loss of their seven colleagues and friends but must also work as quickly as possible to find the cause of the disaster.

2 Within hours of the tragedy, tough questions were being asked. What caused this disaster to occur? Who's responsible? And how do we prevent it from happening again? Is space travel worth the loss of life?

3 There are other questions as well, some of which are naive[2] or ill-informed. I'm talking about questions such as should the *Columbia* disaster mean the end of the shuttle program and the international space station—and the end of manned space missions altogether? And should we even be spending money on space when there are so many other priorities here on Earth?

4 A few critics argue we can't afford to spend money on space, and we can't afford the risk. I believe they're wrong on both points. We can't afford not to.

5 In terms of economics, NASA spending is less than 1 percent of the entire federal budget. And, unlike so many other government programs, the NASA budget has actually declined over the past decade. In fact, it was slashed 40 percent during that period.

6 Given those constraints[3], consider the technologies and medical advances the space program has developed that we now rely upon in everyday life: global positioning satellite systems (GPS), weather radar, ATM technology, radiation-blocking sunglasses, smoke detectors, wind-shear-prediction technology, cordless power tools, robotic surgery, body-imaging technology, and implantable heart aids.

7 In addition, there is the work being done with protein crystal growth, which is helping scientists make progress in treating patients recovering from open-heart surgery and those suffering from diabetes, AIDS, and the flu.

8 Then there are those who support spending money on space but argue that there's no need to send humans there—that the work in space should all be done

---

1. **NASA:** National Aeronautics and Space Administration

2. **naive:** lacking in experience or sophistication

3. **constraints:** restrictions

robotically. They argue that manned missions are more about sentimentality[1] than practicality. They miss the point, as well.

9   We must not only travel in space, but we must inhabit it, as well. Space exploration is an extension of our biological imperative[2]. As the last man to walk on the moon, retired Navy Capt. Gene Cernan, said so eloquently[3] last week, "We don't have any choice. Curiosity is the essence of human existence. . . . We have an insatiable[4] desire to learn about the unknown, and there is no greater unknown than the universe which surrounds us." Space exploration is the grandest opportunity to raise our level of knowledge and extend the reach of mankind. And no matter how advanced our computers may become, technology alone will never possess the judgment and creativity of man.

10   Space is not only the ultimate emerging economic market but also offers us a wonderful example of international cooperation. In fact, sixteen countries work together on the international space station. And in these complicated times, space continues to inspire all of us on planet Earth.

11   There is no doubt that we face numerous challenges. We face war or the likelihood of military intervention abroad. Our economy is stubbornly weak, and so is the stock market. But none of this should ever cause us to avert[5] our eyes from the stars. In fact, these heightened challenges make it even more important for us to continue to develop and explore space, to continue to advance mankind in defiance[6] of those who would destroy it.

12   NASA has many tough questions to answer, some of them appropriate, some of them well off the mark. But NASA will answer all of them in time. I hope the agency will continue to be as open as in the first days after this tragedy. Facing the critics and finding the answers is the best way to honor the seven astronauts who sacrificed their lives to further our knowledge. But the *Columbia* disaster should not impede[7] our progress and commitment to space. Arguing against investing in space is essentially arguing against investing in our future.*

   1. What is the thesis of this essay?

   _____

1. **sentimentality:** the use of emotion rather than reason
2. **imperative:** obligation; duty
3. **eloquently:** expressively
4. **insatiable:** impossible to satisfy
5. **avert:** turn away
6. **defiance:** refusal to obey
7. **impede:** slow or prevent progress

*Source: Adapted from "To Reach for the Stars," by Lou Dobbs, *U.S. News and World Report*, Feb. 17, 2003, p. 50. Reprinted by permission of the author.

2. List three reasons the author provides in support of his thesis.

_____

_____

_____

_____

_____

3. List two concessions the author makes.

_____

_____

_____

_____

4. Give an example of logical evidence the author provides to support his thesis.

_____

_____

5. Give an example of emotional evidence the author provides to support his thesis.

_____

_____

_____

6. Did the author convince you to agree with his thesis? Why or why not?

_____

In Summary: Steps in Writing Argument Essays

1. **Consider your reader.** An analysis of your reader will drive all of the other decisions you will make as you plan and write your paragraph or essay.
2. **Write a persuasive main idea statement that takes your audience into consideration.** Write a reasonable, assertive topic sentence or thesis statement that clearly expresses what you want your reader to do or to believe.

3. **Match your supporting reasons to your reader's priorities and goals.** Include only those reasons that are relevant to your reader.

4. **Incorporate concessions.** Anticipate and acknowledge the opposing viewpoints and then go on to refute them.

5. **Determine the best order for your reasons.** Decide whether you should arrange your reasons from most important to least important, or vice versa. Include transitions to help the reader follow you from one point to the next.

6. **Develop each reason with either logical or emotional evidence.** Use your analysis of your reader to decide which facts, statistics, expert testimony, examples, or emotional appeals will be most effective.

CHAPTER 18 REVIEW

Fill in the blanks in the following statements.

1. When you try to convince a reader to do something or to change his or her belief about something, you are _____ a certain position.

2. Whereas the other modes of development focus on the writer's thoughts or experiences or on the subject itself, argument writing focuses on the _____.

3. The first step in planning an argument paragraph is to carefully consider the _____, _____, and _____ of the targeted reader.

4. Persuasive _____ clearly state the behavior or belief they want the reader to adopt after reading the paragraph, and they often include words and phrases such as *should*, *must*, *ought to*, and *have to*.

5. Persuasive topic sentences are also _____; they do not include tentative or hedging words or statements such as "I believe that."

6. Persuasive topic sentences often include the _____, the person or group who should make or bring about the change.

7. Persuasive topic sentences ask the reader to make changes that are logical, _____, and within the realm of possibility.

8. In the planning stages of writing an argument paragraph, the writer needs to decide which reasons are most _____ to the target audience.

9. Acknowledging the opposing arguments is known as making _____.

10. _____ words and phrases such as *however, but, on the other hand,* and *nevertheless* often signal the end of a concession and the beginning of the author's argument.

11. When writers make concessions, they should use language that is _____ to the readers to avoid insulting or offending them.

12. _____ is the most common pattern for arranging reasons in an argument paragraph.

13. Common argument _____ include *first, second, third, most important,* and *finally.*

14. The two kinds of evidence you can offer in an argument paragraph are _____ evidence and _____ evidence.

15. _____ evidence, which includes facts, statistics, expert opinion, and examples, consists of the hard data and observable facts that will appeal to your readers' reason and intellect.

16. _____ evidence appeals to readers' needs and feelings, such as the need for fun or friendship or the desire to be a good parent.

17. _____ are arguments that are flawed because they are based on careless thinking or on deliberate attempts to distract the reader.

18. An argument may need several _____ for development.

19. Arguments can also take the form of complete essays in which the topic and main point are stated in a _____.

Topic Ideas for Argument Assignments

Exercises 18.1 and 18.2 include topic ideas you may want to develop into argument paragraphs or essays. Here are some additional ideas:

- Junk food in schools
- Violence on television or in video games
- Reciting the Pledge of Allegiance in public schools
- Same-sex marriage

- Watching television

- Professional athletes' salaries

- A rule or practice that is not fair to everyone

- Something that should be banned

- Something that should be changed

WebWork

Go to the *Guide to Grammar and Writing* Web site's information about writing argument essays at **http://grammar.ccc.commnet.edu/grammar/composition/argument.htm**. Read the information on this page, including the sample essay.

Online Study Center   For additional information and practice with writing argument paragraphs and essays, go to the Houghton Mifflin Online Study Center for this book, at **http://www.college.hmco.com/pic/dolphinwritertwo.**

Combining Modes of Development

GOALS FOR CHAPTER 19

▶ Write a paragraph that is developed with at least two modes.

▶ Recognize different modes of development in longer passages and essays.

In Chapters 9–18 of this text, you examined each of the major modes of development by itself. Although these modes can be used in isolation, they are very often combined to develop one main idea. For example, read the following paragraph:

Organ donation remains a topic that altogether too many people still refuse to discuss, perhaps thinking it morbid to contemplate their mortality[1]. **But once you've confronted the possibility that a loved one may need an organ transplant, it's a no-brainer to tell the surgeons to begin harvesting your organs the instant your heart monitor shows a flat line.** My sister Julie contracted hepatitis from a dental procedure years ago. Her liver was damaged and continued to deteriorate before her condition was detected. If she did not respond to drug therapy to halt the progression of the disease, the doctors said she would need a liver transplant to survive. As my sister's only full-blooded relative, I told her she could have a segment of my liver for transplantation if a whole liver from a suitable donor could not be located. Thankfully, neither of us had to undergo the knife. Julie responded to the drug therapy and today is healthy, although she must take a host of expensive medications for the rest of her life. I was pro-organ donation before the scare over my sister, but the experience deepened my resolve to promote giving this gift. I even talked with my children to explain there were other youths they could save if tragedy ever befell[2] our family, and they agreed that I should sign the consent forms if the worst ever happens. (Adapted from "Become an Organ Donor" by Randy Ludlow, *The Cincinnati Post*, July 14, 2001. Reprinted by permission.)

1. **mortality:** death   2. **befell:** happened to

355

To develop the idea in the topic sentence, which is highlighted with bold print, this author chose two modes of development: narration and cause/effect. He tells the story about his sister Julie, who came close to needing a liver transplant. Then he goes on to explain the effects of this experience in the last two sentences. The ordeal of his sister's illness strengthened his belief in the importance of organ donation, which led him to convince his children to become organ donors.

The preceding paragraph uses first one mode and then another to organize and develop the topic sentence. In other paragraphs that combine two or more modes of development, you might want to use one mode to provide the structure for the entire paragraph while another mode is used to provide layers of development. For example, read the following paragraph:

> Migraine headaches are of two general types: classic and common. The *classic* type begins with an intense constriction of the blood vessels in the brain, dramatically diminishing the supply of blood. Depending on which part of the brain is affected most, the person may show various neurological symptoms, such as distortion of vision, numbness of parts of the body, or speech and coordination problems. When the blood vessels then become distended to compensate for the diminished blood supply, severe pain occurs. The nerves become so sensitive that the blood, as it courses through the vessels with each heartbeat, produces a characteristic pulsating or throbbing pain. With *common* migraine headaches, the first phase is less severe, and neurological symptoms may not be evident. The pain is also less intense than in classic migraine headaches. (Excerpted from David Sue et al., *Understanding Abnormal Behavior*, 8th ed. [Boston: Houghton Mifflin, 2006], p. 224.)

This paragraph uses three modes of development. Classification organizes the whole paragraph, cause/effect is used to develop the first category of migraines, and comparison/contrast is used to develop the second category.

Some Common Combinations

Although there are many different combinations of the various modes, some combinations tend to arise more frequently than others:

Narration and **description.** When you tell a story, it is natural to include details about the people, places, and things involved. Narration is often combined with cause/effect, too. As you saw in the example paragraph about organ donation, it is natural to explain the results of a particular experience.

Comparison/contrast and **description, illustration,** or **narration.** You learned in Chapter 15 that comparisons are often developed with descriptive details or examples. Narration, too, can be used to help readers understand similarities or differences. For example, for the topic sentence *Although my two closest friends are very different people, they have both helped me through difficult times,* you could tell stories about the difficult times and explain how each friend helped in a different way.

Definition and **illustration.** As you saw in Chapter 17, illustration is often used to develop a definition. However, many of the other modes, too, are useful in explaining what a term means. To develop the topic sentence *Courage is not the absence of fear but deciding to act in spite of your fear,* for example, you could give examples of specific individuals who were afraid but acted anyway.

Division and **description.** As you divide something into its parts, it is natural to provide descriptive details about each part. If you want to help readers understand the different parts of a city such as New York, for example, it would make sense to divide it into its different areas and then describe what you would see and hear in each area.

Argument and **effects.** Providing reasons in support of an argument often involves explaining the consequences of something. For example, if you argued that *Children should be limited to watching an hour of television per day,* you would need to explain the effects of excessive viewing on young minds. Likewise, arguing the idea that *Americans should drive hybrid electric cars* would involve explaining the effects of driving these cars.

Writing a Paragraph Using a Combination of Modes

When you write a paragraph that combines two or more modes, you begin by evaluating your topic sentence and selecting the modes that are most appropriate for explaining this idea. Then you follow the guidelines of the modes you have chosen to generate, organize, and develop your ideas.

Evaluating Your Topic Sentence and Selecting Appropriate Modes

After you have written your topic sentence, study it to determine all of the possible ways you could develop it. Some topic sentences will clearly indicate which methods to use. For example, if your topic sentence is *Although losing weight was difficult for me, the struggle was worth it in the end,* you would need to use process or narration to tell about the struggle and then explain the effects of achieving that weight loss.

However, many topic sentences will not suggest any one particular mode of development. For example, if your topic sentence is *The person I admire most is my Aunt Carol,* you could provide reasons, or you could describe the qualities about her that you admire, or you could give examples of admirable things she has done, or you could tell a story about her. You could even compare her with other admirable people with whom readers would be familiar. There are many possibilities.

Other topic sentences will clearly require at least one particular primary mode of development, but they will allow you to choose from various secondary modes of development. For example, if your topic sentence is *Private ownership of handguns should be outlawed*, you will obviously choose argument as your primary mode of development, and your reasons will give the paragraph its overall structure. However, how will you develop each reason? You could use cause/effect, explaining the consequences of continuing to allow private ownership of guns. Or you could compare U.S. handgun accident and murder rates with those of other countries in which guns are banned. You could also relate a brief anecdote about an accident or murder that occurred because of easy accessibility to guns.

EXERCISE 19.1   **Selecting Appropriate Modes of Development**

Read each of the following topic sentences. On the blanks provided, briefly explain which modes would best develop the sentence.

1. Colds and flu are both respiratory illnesses, but the flu is a much more serious disease.

   _____

   _____

   _____

2. You can learn to break your habit of procrastinating on difficult or unpleasant tasks.

   _____

   _____

   _____

3. Most of my friends fall into one of three categories.

   _____

   _____

   _____

4. The police officers in this town deserve a raise.

   _____

   _____

   _____

5. As William Shakespeare put it, jealousy is a "green-eyed monster."

_____

_____

_____

Organizing a Combination Paragraph and Using Transitions

When you use more than one mode of development, it is particularly important to organize and outline your ideas before writing to avoid confusing the reader. A topic sentence such as *The person I admire most is my Aunt Carol* can result in a very disorganized paragraph if you do not first spend some time finding the best order for all of your ideas. First, determine which mode will provide the structure for the entire paragraph or will come first. Outline the paragraph's main points using that pattern. For example, you might choose to develop the point about your Aunt Carol by describing her admirable qualities. Description, then, would be your primary organizational mode, and the beginnings of your informal outline might look like this:

1. Hard-working and independent
2. Courageous
3. Caring and generous

This outline indicates that the overall paragraph will be organized with the three traits you admire.

Next, decide on secondary modes to organize and develop your layers of development. Then expand your outline by adding details related to these other modes:

1. Hard-working and independent

   – Give details about the business she runs

2. Courageous

   – Tell story about the time she went to Rome by herself

3. Caring and generous

   – Give examples of the charitable work she does

As you write, do not forget to include transitions that help readers follow you from one point to the next.

EXERCISE 19.2   Organizing Paragraphs Developed with Different Modes

Prewrite to generate ideas, and then complete each of the following topic sentences by filling in the blanks. Then, on the other blanks provided, identify the modes of development you would use, and prepare an informal outline by listing the points and details you would include in an appropriate order.

1. _____ should have been one of the _____ days of my life, but it was actually one of the _____.

Modes of development: _____

Outline:

_____

_____

_____

_____

_____

2. _____ is an individual whom I greatly admire.

Modes of development: _____

Outline:

_____

_____

_____

_____

_____

3. If you want to change the world for the better, you should _____

_____.

Modes of development: _____

Outline:

_____

_____

_____

_____

_____

 **EXERCISE 19.3** **Recognizing Transitions in a Paragraph Developed with Different Modes**

Circle all of the transitional words in the following paragraph.

The Walt Disney World Magic Kingdom amusement park is divided into seven main areas. The first area is Main Street, which leads to all other areas. As you walk down this street, which is lined with shops and restaurants, you will be heading toward the beautiful blue-and-white Cinderella's Castle, which is in the center of the park. The second area is Tomorrowland, which is to your right as you stand facing the castle. This is where you will find rides like Buzz Lightyear's Space Ranger Spin on your right, the futuristic[1] roller coaster Space Mountain directly in front of you, and the Tomorrowland Indy Speedway go-karts to your left. The next area you reach is Mickey's Toontown Fair, the newest section of the park. Here, you will be able to ride the Barnstormer mini-roller coaster and tour the homes of Mickey and Minnie Mouse. From there, you will enter the fourth area, Fantasyland, the section that contains some of the park's most beloved rides. First, ride The Many Adventures of Winnie the Pooh. Then get on Snow White's Scary Adventures, Dumbo the Flying Elephant, and Cinderella's Golden Carrousel. Finally, ride Peter Pan's Flight and It's a Small World. Next, you will move into the fifth area, Liberty Square, where the ghosts at The Haunted Mansion await you. In the sixth area, Frontierland, you will find favorite thrill rides like Splash Mountain and Big Thunder Mountain Railroad. Last, head for Adventureland, home to the popular Pirates of the Caribbean, the Jungle Cruise, and The Magic Carpets of Aladdin. After you pass through Adventureland, you will find yourself on Main Street again, ready to go around again!

 **EXERCISE 19.4** **Writing a Combination Paragraph That Includes Transitions**

Choose one of the topic sentences and outlines you prepared in Exercise 19.2. Write the paragraph, including transitions that indicate how the details are related.

Developing the Details in a Combination Paragraph

Once you have selected the modes you will use to develop your topic sentence, you will follow the specific guidelines for those modes to provide the necessary

1. **futuristic:** expressing a vision of the future

details. For example, if you use illustration to develop your main idea, remember the principles of writing effective illustration. If you use narration, remember that set of principles, and so on.

Combining Modes in Longer Passages and Essays

So far, this chapter has focused only on paragraphs that combine modes. However, a passage of several paragraphs might also be developed with two or more modes. For example, read the following passage:

> In the summer, my wife and I bike down to the lake nearly every afternoon for a swim. It is a dogleg[1] Adirondack[2] lake, with three beaver lodges, a blue heron, some otter, a family of mergansers[3], the occasional loon. A few summer houses cluster at one end, but mostly it is surrounded by wild state land. During the week we swim across and back, a trip of maybe forty minutes—plenty of time to forget everything but the feel of the water around your body and the rippling, muscular joy of a hard kick and the pull of your arms.
>
> But on the weekends, more and more often, someone will bring a boat out for waterskiing, and make pass after pass up and down the lake. And then the whole experience changes, changes entirely. Instead of being able to forget everything but yourself, and even yourself except for the muscles and the skin, you must be alert, looking up every dozen strokes to see where the boat is, thinking about what you will do if it comes near. It is not so much the danger—few swimmers, I imagine, ever die by Evinrude[4]. It's not even so much the blue smoke that hangs low over the water. It's that the motorboat gets in your mind. You're forced to think, not feel—to think of human society and of people. The lake is utterly different on these days, just as the planet is utterly different now. (From *The End of Nature* by William McKibben, copyright © 1989 by William McKibben. Used by permission of Random House, Inc.)

These two paragraphs develop one main idea, which is implied. This idea might be stated: *People and their machines destroy the experience of being in nature for others.* To develop this idea, the author uses contrast (swimming in the lake on weekdays versus swimming in the lake on weekends), description (details about the lake), and effects (how the boat changes the experience).

Complete essays are often developed with more than one mode. To write an essay using a combination of modes, follow the steps for writing a paragraph.

---

1. **dogleg:** bent
2. **Adirondack:** part of the Adirondack Mountains of New York
3. **mergansers:** ducks
4. **Evinrude:** a brand of boat motor

First, write your thesis statement. Next, decide on the best modes to develop this idea and generate ideas. Then follow the guidelines for the mode or modes you have chosen to organize and develop your points and details. As you write, include transitions that indicate how the details are related.

EXERCISE 19.5 **Recognizing Modes in an Essay**

Read the following essay written by Helen Keller (1880–1968), who was blind and deaf all of her life. Then answer the questions that follow by writing your responses on the blanks provided.

Three Days to See

1   I have often thought it would be a blessing if each human being were stricken blind and deaf for a few days at some time during his early adult life. Darkness would make him more appreciative of sight; silence would teach him the joys of sound.

FOCUS ON RESEARCH

Preparing the Works-Cited List

The works-cited section is the second element (in addition to citations in the text) of MLA style. This page, which appears at the end of a paper begins with the centered title *Works Cited*. It then lists entries, arranged by author (last name first) in alphabetical order, for each source that was cited in the text. (If there is no named author, the entry begins with the article or book title or Web site name.) Each entry includes specific details about the source in a particular order. Examples of typical entries follow:

BOOK:

Gore, Al. *Earth in the Balance*. Boston: Houghton Mifflin, 1992.

ENCYCLOPEDIA:

"Environmentalism." *Merriam-Webster's Collegiate Encyclopedia*. 2000.

MAGAZINE:

Quindlen, Anna. "A Shock to the System." *Newsweek* 25 Aug. 2003: 68.

WEB SITE:

U.S. Senator Herb Kohl. 2003. U.S. Senate. <http://http://kohl.senate.gov/pri_fam_ environment.html>.

For complete information about formatting works-cited entries for different kinds of sources, see Purdue University's MLA Formatting and Style Guide at http://owl.english.purdue.edu/owl/ resource/557/01. Click on the pages titled "Works Cited" for samples.

2   Now and then I have tested my seeing friends to discover what they see. Recently I asked a friend, who had just returned from a long walk in the woods, what she had observed. "Nothing in particular," she replied.

3   How was it possible, I asked myself, to walk for an hour through the woods and see nothing worthy of note? I who cannot see find hundreds of things to interest me through mere touch. I feel the delicate symmetry[1] of a leaf. I pass my hands lovingly about the smooth skin of a silver birch, or the rough, shaggy bark of a pine. In spring I touch the branches of trees hopefully in search of a bud, the first sign of awakening Nature after her winter's sleep. Occasionally, if I am very fortunate, I place my hand gently on a small tree and feel the happy quiver of a bird in full song.

4   At times my heart cries out with longing to see all these things. If I can get so much pleasure from mere touch, how much more beauty must be revealed by sight. And I have imagined what I should most like to see if I were given the use of my eyes, say, for just three days.

5   I should divide the period into three parts. On the first day, I should want to see the people whose kindness and companionship have made my life worth living. I do not know what it is to see into the heart of a friend through that "window of the soul," the eye. I can only "see" through my finger tips the outline of a face. I can detect laughter, sorrow, and many other obvious emotions. I know my friends from the feel of their faces.

6   How much easier, how much more satisfying it is for you who can see to grasp quickly the essential qualities of another person by watching the subtleties[2] of expression, the quiver of a muscle, the flutter of a hand. But does it ever occur to you to use your sight to see into the inner nature of a friend? Do not most of you seeing people grasp casually the outward features of a face and let it go at that?

7   For instance, can you describe accurately the faces of five good friends? As an experiment, I have questioned husbands about the color of their wives' eyes, and often they express embarrassed confusion and admit that they do not know.

8   Oh, the things that I should see if I had the power of sight for just three days!

9   The first day would be a busy one. I should call to me all my dear friends and look long into their faces, imprinting upon my mind the outward evidences of the beauty that is within them. I should let my eyes rest, too, on the face of a baby, so that I could catch a vision of the eager, innocent beauty which precedes the individual's consciousness of the conflicts which life develops. I should like to see the books which have been read to me, and which have revealed to me the deepest channels of human life. And I should like to look into the loyal, trusting eyes of my dogs, the little Scottie and the stalwart[3] Great Dane.

---

1. **symmetry:** balance; equality on both sides

2. **subtleties:** things that are difficult to detect

3. **stalwart:** strong

10   In the afternoon I should take a long walk in the woods and intoxicate[1] my eyes on the beauties of the world of Nature. And I should pray for the glory of a colorful sunset. That night, I think, I should not be able to sleep.

11   The next day I should arise with the dawn and see the thrilling miracle by which night is transformed into day. I should behold with awe the magnificent panorama[2] of light with which the sun awakens the sleeping earth.

12   This day I should devote to a hasty glimpse of the world, past and present. I should want to see the pageant of man's progress, and so I should go to the museums. There my eyes would see the condensed[3] history of the earth—animals and the races of men pictured in their native environment; gigantic carcasses[4] of dinosaurs and mastodons[5] which roamed the earth before man appeared, with his tiny stature[6] and powerful brain, to conquer the animal kingdom.

13   My next stop would be the Museum of Art. I know well through my hands the sculptured gods and goddesses of the ancient Nile[7]-land. I have felt copies of Parthenon[8] friezes[9], and I have sensed the rhythmic beauty of charging Athenian[10] warriors. The gnarled, bearded features of Homer[11] are dear to me, for he, too, knew blindness.

14   So on this, my second day, I should try to probe into the soul of man through his art. The things I knew through touch I should now see. More splendid still, the whole magnificent world of painting would be opened to me. I should be able to get only a superficial[12] impression. Artists tell me that for a deep and true appreciation of art one must educate the eye. One must learn through experience to weigh the merits of line, of composition, of form and color. If I had eyes, how happily would I embark[13] on so fascinating a study!

15   The evening of my second day I should spend at a theater or at the movies. How I should like to see the fascinating figure of Hamlet, or the gusty[14] Falstaff[15] amid colorful Elizabethan[16] trappings! I cannot enjoy the beauty of rhythmic movement except in a sphere restricted to the touch of my hands. I can vision only dimly the grace of a Pavlova[17], although I know something of the delight of rhythm, for often I can sense the beat of music as it vibrates through

1. **intoxicate:** stimulate or excite
2. **panorama:** view of an entire surrounding area
3. **condensed:** made smaller or more compact
4. **carcasses:** dead bodies
5. **mastodons:** extinct animals resembling elephants
6. **stature:** height
7. **Nile:** a river in Egypt
8. **Parthenon:** a temple of the goddess Athena in Athens, Greece
9. **friezes:** decorative parts of a wall
10. **Athenian:** from Athens, Greece
11. **Homer:** an ancient Greek poet
12. **superficial:** on or near the surface
13. **embark:** set out on a journey
14. **gusty:** given to sudden outbursts
15. **Hamlet and Falstaff:** characters in plays by William Shakespeare
16. **Elizabethan:** related to the reign of Britain's Queen Elizabeth I (1558–1603)
17. **Pavlova:** Russian ballerina

the floor. I can well imagine that cadenced[1] motion must be one of the most pleasing sights in the world. I have been able to gather something of this by tracing with my fingers the lines in sculptured marble; if this static[2] grace can be so lovely, how much more acute[3] must be the thrill of seeing grace in motion.

16   The following morning, I should again greet the dawn, anxious to discover new delights, new revelations of beauty. Today, this third day, I shall spend in the workaday world, amid the haunts of men going about the business of life. The city becomes my destination.

17   First, I stand at a busy corner, merely looking at people, trying by sight of them to understand something of their daily lives. I see smiles, and I am happy. I see serious determination, and I am proud. I see suffering, and I am compassionate.

18   I stroll down Fifth Avenue. I throw my eyes out of focus, so that I see no particular object but only a kaleidoscope[4] of color. I am certain that the colors of women's dresses moving in a throng[5] must be a gorgeous spectacle of which I should never tire. But perhaps if I had sight I should be like most other women—too interested in styles to give much attention to the splendor of color in the mass.

19   From Fifth Avenue I made a tour of the city—to the slums, to factories, to parks where children play. I take a stay-at-home trip abroad by visiting the foreign quarters. Always my eyes are open wide to all the sights of both happiness and misery so that I may probe deep and add to my understanding of how people work and live.

20   My third day of sight is drawing to an end. Perhaps there are many serious pursuits to which I should devote the few remaining hours, but I am afraid that on the evening of that last day I should again run away to the theater, to a hilariously funny play, so that I might appreciate the overtones[6] of comedy in the human spirit.

21   At midnight permanent night would close in on me again. Naturally in those three short days I should not have seen all I wanted to see. Only when darkness had again descended upon me should I realize how much I had left unseen.

22   Perhaps this short outline does not agree with the program you might set for yourself if you knew that you were about to be stricken blind. I am, however, sure that if you faced that fate you would use your eyes as never before. Everything you saw would become dear to you. Your eyes would touch and em-

---

1. **cadenced:** having rhythm or a steady beat
2. **static:** not moving
3. **acute:** sharp
4. **kaleidoscope:** a tube-shaped instrument that produces colored designs
5. **throng:** crowd
6. **overtones:** qualities

brace every object that came within your range of vision. Then, at last, you would really see, and a new world of beauty would open itself before you.*

1. What sentence states the thesis of this essay? Where is it located?

   _____

2. What mode provides structure for the entire essay?

   _____

   _____

   _____

3. Which two modes organize most of the layers of development in this essay?

   _____

   _____

4. Helen Keller became blind and deaf when she was just an infant, yet she describes the world as though she has seen it with her own eyes firsthand. How must she have learned the details about the things she describes, and what do her descriptions say about the power of that method?

   _____

   _____

   _____

   _____

5. If you were going to permanently lose your sense of sight in three days, what things would you want to make sure you looked at before you went blind? Does Helen Keller convince you to place more value in your ability to see these things?

   _____

In Summary: Steps in Combining Modes

1. **Evaluate your main idea and decide on appropriate modes of development.** Choose one or more modes for developing your topic sentence or thesis statement, and then prewrite to generate ideas.

*Source: From "Three Days to See" by Helen Keller, *Reader's Digest,* April 2002, pp. 60A-60E. Reprinted with permission from the March 1933 *Reader's Digest,* and by kind permission of the Helen Keller Foundation for Research and Education, www.helenkellerfoundation.org.

2. **Organize your ideas.** Follow the guidelines for the specific modes you have chosen to create an outline. You may want to use one mode for the structure of the entire paragraph and the other mode to develop the details.

3. **As you write, develop your details according to the specific guidelines for each mode.** Include transitions to help the reader understand the relationships among the details.

CHAPTER 19 REVIEW

Fill in the blanks in the following statements.

1. Modes can be used in isolation, or they can be _____ to develop one main idea.

2. Often, one mode provides the structure for the entire _____ while another mode is used to provide _____.

3. Narration and _____ are two modes that are often combined.

4. Comparison/contrast is often combined with _____, _____, and/or narration.

5. _____ is often used to develop a definition.

6. Division and _____ are a common combination.

7. An explanation of _____ is often used to develop an argument.

8. To decide which modes of development are suitable, evaluate the _____ of your paragraph.

9. A combination of different modes might develop a passage of several _____.

10. Complete essays are often developed with more than one mode; the _____ will help you choose appropriate modes.

Topic Ideas for Assignments That Combine Modes

Here are some topic ideas you could develop into paragraphs or essays using a combination of modes:

- Becoming physically fit
- A favorite possession
- A childhood memory
- A holiday, custom, or tradition
- A change for the worse (or better)
- A new fad or trend
- A relationship that is important to you

WebWork

Go to the *Guide to Grammar and Writing* Web site at **http://grammar.ccc.commnet .edu/grammar/composition/organization.htm** and read the section called "Why You Want Organization" in the essay entitled "Principles of Organization." Discuss with a small group of your classmates the modes the author uses to develop his point in this section. Does the author's use of these different modes help you understand his main idea?

Online Study Center For additional information and practice with using a combination of modes, go to the Houghton Mifflin Online Study Center for this book, at **http://www.college.hmco.com/pic/dolphinwritertwo.**

Reading Selections

Mother Tongue

By Amy Tan

1   I am not a scholar of English or literature. I cannot give you much more than personal opinions on the English language and its variations in this country or others.

2   I am a writer. And by that definition, I am someone who has always loved language. I am fascinated by language in daily life.

3   I spend a great deal of my time thinking about the power of language—the way it can evoke an emotion, a visual image, a complex idea, or a simple truth. Language is the tool of my trade. And I use them all—all the Englishes I grew up with.

4   Recently, I was made keenly aware of the different Englishes I do use. I was giving a talk to a large group of people, the same talk I had already given to half a dozen other groups. The talk was about my writing, my life, and my book *The Joy Luck Club*, and it was going along well enough, until I remembered one major difference that made the whole talk sound wrong. My mother was in the room. And it was perhaps the first time she had heard me give a lengthy speech, using the kind of English I have never used with her. I was saying things like "the intersection of memory and imagination" and "There is an aspect of my fiction that relates to thus-and-thus"—a speech filled with carefully wrought grammatical phrases, burdened, it suddenly seemed to me, with nominalized[1] forms, past perfect tenses, conditional phrases, forms of standard English that I had learned in school and through books, the forms of English I did not use at home with my mother.

5   Just last week, as I was walking down the street with her, I again found myself conscious of the English I was using, the English I do use with her. We were talking about the price of new and used furniture, and I heard myself saying this: "Not waste money that way." My husband was with us as well, and he didn't notice any switch in my English. And then I realized why. It's because over the twenty years we've been together I've often used the same kind of English with him, and sometimes he even uses it with me. It has become our language of intimacy, a different sort of English that relates to family talk, the language I grew up with.

Language Barriers

6   You should know that my mother's expressive command of English belies how much she actually understands. She reads the *Forbes*

---

1. **nominalized:** functioning as a noun

report, listens to *Wall Street Week,* converses daily with her stockbroker, reads Shirley MacLaine's books with ease—all kinds of things I can't begin to understand. Yet some of my friends tell me they understand fifty percent of what my mother says. Some say they understand eighty to ninety percent. Some say they understand none of it, as if she were speaking pure Chinese. But to me, my mother's English is perfectly clear, perfectly natural. It's my mother tongue. Her language, as I hear it, is vivid, direct, full of observation and imagery. That was the language that helped shape the way I saw things, expressed things, made sense of the world.

7   Lately I've been giving more thought to the kind of English my mother speaks. Like others, I have described it to people as "broken" or "fractured" English. But I wince[1] when I say that. It has always bothered me that I can think of no way to describe it other than "broken," as if it were damaged and needed to be fixed, as if it lacked a certain wholeness and soundness. I've heard other terms used, "limited English," for example. But they seem just as bad, as if everything is limited, including people's perceptions of the limited-English speaker.

8   I know this for a fact, because when I was growing up, my mother's "limited" English limited my perception of her. I was ashamed of her English. I believed that her English reflected the quality of what she had to say. That is, because she expressed them imperfectly, her thoughts were imperfect. And I had plenty of empirical[2] evidence to support me: the fact that people in department stores, at banks, and in restaurants did not take her seriously, did not give her good service, pre-tended not to understand her, or even acted as if they did not hear her.

9   My mother has long realized the limitations of her English as well. When I was a teenager, she used to have me call people on the phone and pretend I was she. In this guise, I was forced to ask for information or even to complain and yell at people who had been rude to her. One time it was a call to her stockbroker in New York. She had cashed out her small portfolio[3], and it just so happened we were going to New York the next week, our first trip outside California. I had to get on the phone and say in an adolescent voice that was not very convincing, "This is Mrs. Tan."

10   My mother was standing in the back whispering loudly, "Why he don't send me check, already two weeks late. So mad he lie to me, losing me money."

11   And then I said in perfect English on the phone, "Yes, I'm getting rather concerned. You had agreed to send the check two weeks ago, but it hasn't arrived."

12   Then she began to talk more loudly. "What he want, I come to New York tell him front of his boss, you cheating me?" And I was trying to calm her down, make her be quiet, while telling the stockbroker, "I can't tolerate any more excuses. If I don't receive the check immediately, I am going to have to speak to your manager when I'm in New York next week." And sure enough, the following week, there we were in front of this astonished stockbroker, and I was sitting there red-faced and quiet, and my mother, the real Mrs. Tan, was shouting at his boss in her impeccable broken English.

---

1. **wince:** flinch in pain or distress
2. **empirical:** based on observation

3. **portfolio:** a group of stocks or investments held by an investor

Blending Old and New

13 Lately I've been asked, as a writer, why there are not more Asian-Americans represented in American literature. Why are there few Asian-Americans enrolled in creative writing programs? Why do so many Chinese students go into engineering? Well, these are broad sociological questions I can't begin to answer. But I have noticed in surveys—in fact, just last week—that Asian-American students, as a whole, do significantly better on math achievement tests than on English tests. And this makes me think that there are other Asian-American students whose English spoken in the home might also be described as "broken" or "limited." And perhaps they also have teachers who are steering them away from writing and into math and science, which is what happened to me.

14 Fortunately, I happen to be rebellious and enjoy the challenge of disproving assumptions made about me. I became an English major my first year in college, after being enrolled as pre-med. I started writing nonfiction as a freelancer the week after I was told by my boss at the time that writing was my worst skill and I should hone[1] my talents toward account management.

15 But it wasn't until 1985 that I began to write fiction. At first I wrote what I thought to be wittily crafted sentences, sentences that would finally prove I had mastery over the English language. Here's an example from the first draft of a story that later made its way into *The Joy Luck Club,* but without this line: "That was my mental quandary in its nascent[2] state." A terrible line, which I can barely pronounce.

16 Fortunately, for reasons I won't get into here, I later decided I should envision a reader for the stories I would write. And the reader I decided on was my mother, because these were stories about mothers. So with this reader in mind—and in fact she did read my early drafts—I began to write stories using all the Englishes I grew up with: the English I spoke to my mother, which for lack of a better term might be described as "simple"; the English she used with me, which for lack of a better term might be described as "broken"; my translation of her Chinese, which could certainly be described as "watered down"; and what I imagined to be her translation of her Chinese if she could speak in perfect English, her internal language, and for that I sought to preserve the essence, but neither an English nor a Chinese structure. I wanted to capture what language ability tests could never reveal: her intent, her passion, her imagery, the rhythms of her speech, and the nature of her thoughts.

17 Apart from what any critic had to say about my writing, I knew I had succeeded where it counted when my mother finished reading my book and gave me her verdict: "So easy to read." ■

---

1. **hone:** focus on, direct one's attention to

2. **nascent:** emerging, coming into existence

Vocabulary

Answer the following questions about some of the vocabulary words in the reading selection. Circle the letter of the correct answer.

1. What does *keenly* (paragraph 4) mean?

    a. faintly
    b. reluctantly
    c. intensely
    d. unexpectedly

2. What does *wrought* (paragraph 4) mean?

    a. formed
    b. planned
    c. imagined
    d. pulled apart

3. What does *belies* (paragraph 6) mean?

    a. reveals
    b. expands
    c. disguises
    d. reduces

4. What does *guise* (paragraph 9) mean?

    a. crime
    b. appearance
    c. comedy
    d. decision

5. What does *impeccable* (paragraph 12) mean?

    a. strange
    b. flawless
    c. imperfect
    d. loud

6. What does *quandary* (paragraph 15) mean?

    a. decision
    b. idea
    c. dilemma
    d. exercise

Checking Comprehension

Circle the letter of the correct answer.

1. When giving her talk on her book, *The Joy Luck Club*, what made Amy Tan suddenly aware of the kind of language she was using?

   a. her mother's presence
   b. the presence of a large, non-English speaking population in the audience
   c. the presence of her aunts, who are characters in the book
   d. her husband's presence

2. When Tan was young, how did she feel about the way her mother spoke English?

   a. She did not have any feelings about it; everyone in her neighborhood spoke the same way.
   b. She was happy that her mother was bilingual.
   c. She was ashamed of the way her mother spoke English.
   d. Readers cannot tell from the way the selection is written.

3. What did Tan's mother think of her own ability to converse in English?

   a. She thought that her English was perfect.
   b. She recognized the limitations of her English.
   c. She thought that she knew most English verbs until Tan told her she was using them incorrectly.
   d. Tan does not describe how her mother felt.

4. Tan describes her first attempt at fiction as "terrible," so she changed the way she approached writing her stories. What did she do?

   a. She envisioned a reader for her stories, and that person was her mother.
   b. She went to a creative writing class.
   c. She joined a writer's group.
   d. She started recording stories of her youth in a journal.

Mode and Skill Check

Circle the letter of the correct answer or write your answer on the blank provided.

1. What is the topic of this selection?

   a. the problems of immigrants in America
   b. the joys of writing
   c. the different types of "Englishes"
   d. mothers and daughters

2. On the following blank, write the thesis of this selection in your own words.

_____

3. What are the dominant modes of development used in this selection?

    a. description, process, and definition
    b. comparison/contrast and argument
    c. division and cause/effect
    d. classification, illustration, and narration

4. What mode develops paragraph 13?

    a. cause/effect
    b. illustration
    c. narration
    d. classification

5. Paragraphs 9–12 are developed with

    a. comparison/contrast.
    b. cause/effect.
    c. definition.
    d. narration.

Questions for Discussion and Writing

1. How many different "Englishes" do you speak? Describe the way the language you speak changes when you converse with friends or family members or at work or in class. Contrast your speech patterns in two of these settings.

2. Tan writes about the power of language to "evoke an emotion, a visual image, a complex idea, or a simple truth" (paragraph 3). When have you witnessed this power first-hand? Illustrate your own experiences with several examples.

3. In the future, do you think that being bilingual will be more important or less important in America? Argue for or against the need to speak more than one language.

Winning the War on Drugs

By Dave Barry

1   Recently, I had a simple, foolproof idea for eliminating the drug problem in this country. It came to me while I was making spaghetti sauce.

2   I use an ancient Italian spaghetti sauce recipe that has been handed down through many generations of ancient Italians, as follows:

1. Buy some spaghetti sauce.
2. Heat it up.

3   Sometimes I add some seasoning to the sauce, to give it a dash of what the Italians call joie de vivre[1] (literally, ingredients). I had purchased, from the supermarket spice section, a small plastic container labeled "Italian Seasoning." My plan was to open this container and sprinkle some seasoning into the sauce.

4   Already I can hear you veteran consumers out there chortling in good-natured amusement.

5   "You complete moron," you are chortling. "You actually thought you could gain access to a product protected by modern packaging?"

6   Yes, I did, and I certainly learned my lesson. Because it turns out that Italian seasoning has joined the growing number of products that, For Your Protection, are packaged in containers that you cannot open unless you own a home laser cannon.

7   This trend started with aspirin. Years ago—ask your grandparents—aspirin was sold in bottles that had removable caps. That system was changed when consumer-safety authorities discovered that certain consumers were taking advantage of this loophole by opening up the bottles and—it only takes a few "bad apples" to spoil things for everybody—ingesting aspirin tablets.

8   So now aspirin bottles behave very much like stinging insects in nature movies, defending themselves against consumer access via a multilevel security system:

1. There is a plastic wrapper to keep you from getting at the cap.
2. The cap, which is patented by the Rubik's Cube[2] company, cannot be removed unless you line an invisible arrow up with an invisible dot while rotating the cap counterclockwise and simultaneously pushing down and pulling up.
3. In the unlikely event that you get the cap off, the top of the bottle is blocked by a taut piece of extremely feisty foil made from the same impenetrable material used to protect the Space Shuttle during atmospheric re-entry.
4. Underneath the foil is a virtually unremovable wad of cotton the size of a small sheep.
5. As a final precaution, there is no actual aspirin underneath the cotton. There is only a piece of paper listing dangerous side effects, underneath which is . . .

1. **joie de vivre:** French for "love of life," enjoyment of life

2. **Rubik's Cube:** a mechanical puzzle invented in 1974, the goal of which is to match each six sides so that they display the same color

Source: From *Dave Barry Is from Mars and Venus* by Dave Barry, copyright © 1997 by Dave Barry. Used by permission of Crown Publishers, a division of Random House, Inc.

6. . . . a second piece of paper warning you that the first piece of paper could give you a paper cut.

9 Even this may not be enough security for the aspirin of tomorrow. At this very moment, packaging scientists are working on an even more secure system, in which the entire aspirin container would be located inside a live sea urchin[1].

10 With aspirin leading the way, more and more products are coming out in fiercely protective packaging designed to prevent consumers from consuming them. My Italian Seasoning container featured a foil seal and a fiendish plastic thing that I could not remove with my bare hands, which meant, of course, that I had to use my teeth. These days, you have to open almost every consumer item by gnawing on the packaging. Go to any typical consumer household and you'll note most of the products—food, medicine, compact discs, appliances, furniture—are covered with bite marks, as though the house is infested with crazed beavers. The floor will be gritty with little chips of consumer teeth. Many consumers are also getting good results by stabbing their products with knives. I would estimate that 58 percent of all serious household accidents result from consumers assaulting packaging designed to improve consumer safety.

11 Anyway, I finally gnawed my seasoning container open, no doubt activating a tiny transmitter that triggered an alarm in some Spice Security Command Post (WHEEP! WHEEP! WHEEP! INTRUDER GAINING ACCESS TO ITALIAN SEASONING IN SECTOR 19!). While I was stirring my spaghetti sauce, it occurred to me that if we want to eliminate the drug problem in this country, all we have to do is:

1. Make all drugs completely legal and allow them to be sold in supermarkets ("Crack[2]? Aisle 6, next to the Sweet 'n Low.").
2. Require that the drugs be sold in standard consumer packaging. My reasoning is that if physically fit, clear-headed consumers can't get into these packages, there's no way that strung-out junkies[3] could.

12 Eventually, they would give up trying to get at their drugs and become useful members of society, or at least attorneys.

13 I realize that some of you may have questions about this plan. Your most likely concern is: "If dangerous and highly addictive narcotics are sold freely in supermarkets, will the packages be required to have Nutritional Facts labels, like the ones that now helpfully inform consumers of the protein, carbohydrate, vitamin A, vitamin C, calcium, and iron content of products such as Cool Whip Lite?"

14 Of course they will. Even though, if my plan works as expected, an addict would be unable to consume his heroin purchase, he still has a vital right to know, as an American consumer, that if he did consume it, he'd be getting only a small percentage of his Minimum Daily Requirement of dietary fiber.

15 This is just one of the many benefits we enjoy as residents of this Consumer Paradise. My head aches with pride. ■

---

1. **sea urchin:** a small, spiny ocean creature
2. **crack:** short for "crack cocaine," a purified form of cocaine that is smoked in a pipe and is extremely addictive
3. **junkies:** a term for narcotics addicts, especially those who are using cocaine

Vocabulary

Answer the following questions about some of the vocabulary words in the reading selection. Circle the letter of the correct answer.

1. What does *chortling* (paragraph 4) mean?

   a. crying
   b. chuckling
   c. sneezing
   d. screaming

2. What is a *loophole* (paragraph 7)?

   a. a gap in the law
   b. a loose knot
   c. a set of instructions
   d. an office supply

3. What does *taut* (paragraph 8) mean?

   a. shiny
   b. tent-like
   c. stretched tight
   d. loose

4. What does *fiendish* (paragraph 10) mean?

   a. evil
   b. round
   c. effective
   d. tiny

5. If someone is *gnawing* on something (paragraph 10), he or she is

   a. stepping on it.
   b. chewing on it.
   c. cutting it.
   d. burning it.

Checking Comprehension

Circle the letter of the correct answer.

1. What occurrence brought on Barry's rant about modern packaging?

   a. His attempt to open an aspirin packet.
   b. His inability to find the aspirin he wanted in the grocery store.

c. His attempt to open an Italian Seasoning container.

d. His attempt to get into the drugstore in his neighborhood.

2. What product, according to Barry, ushered in this era in which many items are sealed for the consumer's protection?

a. aspirin

b. spices

c. cold medicine

d. compact discs

3. According to Barry, what do most people do to open difficult packaging?

a. They use a home laser cannon.

b. They use their teeth or knives.

c. They burn the packaging.

d. They soak the packaging in water.

4. Which of the following, according to Barry, would eliminate the drug problem in this country?

a. make drugs legal

b. sell drugs in the supermarket

c. require that drugs be sold in standard consumer packaging

d. all of the above

Mode and Skill Check

Circle the letter of the correct answer or write your answer on the blank provided.

1. What is the topic of this selection?

a. the causes of drug addiction

b. using packaging to eliminate the drug problem

c. the dangers of taking aspirin

d. a spaghetti sauce recipe

2. On the line below, write the thesis of this selection in your own words.

_____

3. What mode develops paragraph 8?

a. narration

b. comparison/contrast

c. description

d. cause/effect

4. Which of the following is a reason Barry gives to support his thesis?

   a. Making drugs legal would allow the government to better control their ingredients.
   b. Selling drugs in standard consumer packaging would prevent people from opening and using them.
   c. Consumer packaging is responsible for more injuries than the products they contain.
   d. Selling drugs in supermarkets would encourage people to become more health-conscious.

5. Which of the following paragraphs includes a concession to the opposing argument?

   a. paragraph 1
   b. paragraph 2
   c. paragraph 7
   d. paragraph 13

6. Does Barry really believe that drug addicts would give up "trying to get at their drugs and become useful members of society" if drugs were sold in supermarkets and put in childproof containers?

   a. yes
   b. no
   c. He is undecided.
   d. Readers cannot tell from this selection.

Questions for Discussion and Writing

1. Although Dave Barry writes with humor about consumer packaging, he does make some serious points about the subject. Why has consumer packaging become so complex and difficult to open? In your opinion, is this level of security necessary? Barry mentions one drawback of difficult-to-open packaging: injuries resulting from using knives to remove products. Are there additional drawbacks?

2. Do you think that there is any merit to Barry's contention that the drug problem could be eliminated by legalizing drugs and selling them in the supermarket? Why or why not?

3. Do you have any pet peeves? If so, what are they? Write about what bothers you in a brief essay, using humor if you wish.

What's the Matter with Moviegoers?

By Whitney Matheson

1 Repeat this about 120 times, and you'll have re-created my last three trips to the multiplex[1]. Summer movie season is barely under way, and already I'm feeling defeated.

2 It started with *X2*[2], where a loud talker behind me commented on nearly every scene—five minutes before it happened. Days later, at a screening of *The Dancer Upstairs,* nasty throat-clearing grunts and blaring cell phone rings obliterated my concentration.

3 Last weekend my lousy luck continued with *The Matrix Reloaded,* marred by nearby 'tweens[3] who hooted at anything remotely resembling a love scene. (To top it off, one of them was heavily scented with some sort of men's fragrance, which caused by nose to run for 138 minutes. Not pretty.)

4 People have been going to the movies for what, 100 years? You'd think by now we'd all know you *can't* carry on a full-volume conversation during a film. You *don't* wave your arms in the air and wave 'em like you just don't care. You *shouldn't* tote a wailing newborn to *The Pianist.*

5 Forgive me if I'm sounding crotchety, but I'm desperate to reclaim my movie season; there are few summertime activities I love more. And I don't just go for the free air-conditioning (although that's certainly part of it)—I go because there's something exhilarating about experiencing a film with dozens of strangers.

6 Let me be clear—I'm not looking for utter silence and robotic behavior, just a little peace and understanding. Some of my best theater memories include laughing hysterically during *Jackass* and *There's Something About Mary*; jumping six inches, along with everyone else, on opening night of *The Sixth Sense*; and feeling a collective hush over the crowd during *Dead Man Walking.*

7 It's great to boo when the bad guy wins and clap when the good one prevails. But, at a movie theater, there's a thin line between community and corruption.

8 Why are some people acting so insanely? Part of it could be because today's kids—and many adults—don't spend as much time in public, social environments as their parents did. Most days after school, they scream at video and computer games in their bedrooms. They can talk on cell phones in restaurants and on the street, so why not in a multiplex?

9 If, say, Spike Jonze[4] were to make a movie about going to the movies, he wouldn't have a lick of trouble coming up with characters. Theaters are full of Kramers, Screeches and Fonzies[5] to drive us up the wall, and I guess they always will be.

---

1. **multiplex:** movie theater with multiple screens
2. **X2:** a film based on the X-Men comic book characters
3. **'tweens:** children who are not small children, but not old enough to be considered teenagers
4. **Spike Jonze:** an actor and director known for his quirky roles and directing style
5. **Kramer, Screech, and Fonzie:** characters from television sitcoms

Source: "What's the Matter with Moviegoers?" by Whitney Matheson, *USA Today,* May 27, 2003. Reprinted with permission.

10   For instance, Keith Richards[1] could headline as . . .

11   **Mr. Emphysema:** Just when you thought it was safe to leave your surgical mask at home, you end up seated next to this phlegm-throwing theatergoer who has already hacked up half a lung by the opening credits.

12   And then there's . . .

13   **Chewy:** Is it absolutely necessary to smack your lips after every bite? Chewy seems to think so. During the next two hours, you hear him munching popcorn at record volume, slurping every last drop out of his Mountain Dew and crunching on a bag of Doritos he brought from home.

14   And don't forget:

15   **The Cellmaster:** Yeah, there's nothing worse than, during a crucial scene in *The Hours*, being jarred by a telephone ring to the tune of *Livin' La Vida Loca*.

16   **Madam Spasm:** Well, a swift kick in the kidneys sure livens up a trip to the big picture show. When Spasm's legs get tired, she likes to place them on the armrest beside you and act like there's nothing wrong. Lovely.

17   So, the question remains: What can we do to improve the American moviegoing experience? Talking to offenders can work, but it can also make matters worse.

18   Personally, I prefer subtlety, such as giving a sideways glare or moving to the kick-free back row. But I'm open to more suggestions.

19   And if none of them works, then hey, there's always the drive-in. ■

Vocabulary

Answer the following questions about some of the vocabulary words in the reading selection. Circle the letter of the correct answer.

1. In paragraph 2, *obliterated* means

   a. enhanced.
   b. destroyed.
   c. engaged.
   d. depended.

2. To *mar* something (paragraph 3) is to

   a. ruin it.
   b. enhance it.
   c. make it more attractive.
   d. devour it.

3. The writer describes herself as *crotchety* (paragraph 5). What does that mean?

   a. happy-go-lucky
   b. sinister
   c. grumpy
   d. old

1. **Keith Richards:** a member of the rock bank *The Rolling Stones*

4. A synonym for *crucial* (paragraph 15) is

a. important.
b. intelligent.
c. stupid.
d. last.

5. In paragraph 18, *subtlety* means

a. openness.
b. difficulty to detect.
c. obscurity.
d. substitution.

Checking Comprehension

Circle the letter of the correct answer.

1. The author is not looking for "utter silence and robotic behavior" in the movies, just

a. happiness and joy.
b. some silence and politeness.
c. peace and understanding.
d. laughter and good times.

2. Of the following, which is not one of the modern-day items that the author lists as contributing to kids' talking in movie theaters?

a. cell phones
b. video games
c. wide-screen televisions
d. computer games

3. If there was a movie made about impolite moviegoers, Keith Richards could headline as who, according to the author?

a. Mr. Emphysema
b. Chewy
c. The Cellmaster
d. Madam Spasm

4. If the American moviegoing experience does not improve, what does the author suggest as an alternative?

a. renting movies
b. staying home altogether
c. wearing ear plugs
d. going to the drive-in

5. According to the author, what is one cause of kids "acting so insanely" in public, and specifically, in movie theaters?

   a. Kids today are hard of hearing.
   b. Kids today do not spend as much time in public, social environments as their parents did.
   c. Kids today are just loud for no reason.
   d. Kids today are allowed to talk in school.

Mode and Skill Check

Circle the letter of the correct answer or write your answer on the blank provided.

1. What is the topic of this selection?

   a. movies
   b. politeness
   c. rude moviegoers
   d. *The Matrix Reloaded*

2. What is the predominant mode of development used in paragraphs 9–19?

   a. narration
   b. description
   c. cause/effect
   d. classification

3. Into how many categories has the author divided moviegoers?

   a. two
   b. three
   c. four
   d. five

4. Which of the following is not one of the categories that the author uses to describe moviegoers?

   a. Mr. Emphysema
   b. The Cellmaster
   c. Loud Talker
   d. Madame Spasm

5. On the line below, write the thesis of this selection in your own words.

   _____

Questions for Discussion and Writing

1. Think of another category of rude moviegoer not mentioned by the author. Write an essay describing that person and his or her behavior. How do you deal with this type of person?

2. Write an essay in which you classify the annoying people you know at work, school, or home.

3. Do you think that any of the behaviors outlined by the author in this selection are acceptable? If so, why? Write an essay defending your position.

And on the Seventh Day We Rested?

By Nancy Gibbs

1 Once upon a time, in the "Dominion of New Haven," it was illegal to kiss your children on Sunday. Or make a bed or cut your hair or eat mince pies or cross a river unless you were a clergyman riding your circuit[1]. If you lived in Connecticut in 1650, there was no mistaking Sunday for just another shopping day; regardless of whether you'd go to hell for breaking the Sabbath[2], you could certainly go to jail. Centuries later, the sense that Sunday is special is still wired in us, a miniature sabbatical during which to peel off the rest of the week and savor ritual, religious or otherwise: Sunday worship, Sunday football, Sunday papers, Sunday brunch, the day you call your mother, the night the family gathers around the TV to watch, once upon a time, *The Wonderful World of Disney*[3] and, now, *The Simpsons*[4].

2 The idea that rest is a right has deep roots in our history. Blue laws[5] were a gift as much as a duty, a command to relax and reflect. That tension, explains Sunday historian Alexis McCrossen, has always been less between sacred and secular than between work and respite[6]; America does not readily sit still, even for a day. The Civil War and a demand for news begat the Sunday paper; industrialization[7] inspired progressives to argue that libraries and museums should open on Sundays so working people could elevate themselves. Major league baseball held its first Sunday game in 1892 (the Cincinnati Reds beat the St. Louis Browns, 5–1). Joseph Pulitzer

1. **circuit:** district or territory
2. **Sabbath:** day of rest and worship
3. *The Wonderful World of Disney:* a television event on Sunday nights whereby Walt Disney would air movies or specials
4. *The Simpsons*: an animated television comedy series

5. **blue laws:** laws regulating commercial business on Sundays
6. **respite:** short period of rest and relief
7. **industrialization:** a time in American history when industry became more mechanized

Source: "And On the Seventh Day We Rested?" by Nancy Gibbs, *Time*, August 2, 2004. Reprinted by permission of *Time*.

realized the Sunday paper was less about news than about fun, comics, and book reviews, and soon the theaters were open too, as well as amusement parks and fairs.

3   Over time, Sunday has gone from a day we could do only a very few things to the only day we can do just about anything we want. The U.S. is too diverse, our lives too busy, our economy too global, and our appetites too vast to lose a whole day that could be spent working or playing or power shopping. Pulled between piety and profit, even Christian bookstores are open. Children come to Sunday school dressed in their soccer uniforms; some churches have started their own leagues just to control the schedule. Politicians recite their liturgies[1] in TV studios. Post offices may still be closed, but once you miss that first Sunday e-mail from the boss, it becomes forever harder not to log on and check in. Even the casinos are open.

4   If your soul has no Sunday, it becomes an orphan, Albert Schweitzer[2] said—which raises a question for our times: What do we lose if Sunday becomes just like any other day? Lawmakers in Virginia got to spend part of their summer break debating that question, thanks to a mistake they made last winter when they inadvertently revived a "day of rest" rule; hotels and hospitals and nuclear power plants would have had to give workers a weekend day off or be fined $500. After a special legislative session was convened to fix the error, Virginia's workers, like the rest of us, are once more potentially on call 24/7. Meanwhile, Rhode Island just became the 32nd state to let liquor stores open every Sunday; until this month, they could do so only in December, perhaps because even George Washington's eggnog recipe called for brandy, whiskey, and rum. Social conservatives[3] may want to honor the Fourth Commandment[4], but businesses want the income, states need the tax revenues, and busy families want the flexibility.

5   With progress, of course, comes backlash from those who desperately want to preserve the old ways. Mom-and-pop[5] liquor stores in New York fought to keep the blue laws to have more time with their families. Car dealers in Kansas City, Mo., pushed for a law to make them close on Sundays so they could have a day off without losing out to competition. Chick-Fil-A, a chain of more than 1,100 restaurants in 37 states, closes on Sundays because its founder, Truett Cathy, promised employees time to "worship, spend time with family and friends, or just plain rest from the work week," says the chain's website. "Made sense then, still makes sense now." Pope John Paul II even wrote an apostolic[6] letter in defense of Sunday: "When Sunday loses its fundamental meaning and becomes merely part of a 'weekend,'" he wrote, "people stay locked within a horizon so limited that they can no longer see 'the heavens.'"

6   In an age with no free time, we buy it through hard choices. Do we skip church so we can sleep in or skip soccer so we can go to church or find a family ritual—cook together, read together, a Parcheesi[7] challenge—that we treat as sacred? That way, at least some part of Sunday faces in a different direction, whether toward heaven or toward one another. ■

1. **liturgies:** forms for public religious worship
2. **Albert Schweitzer:** an author, theologian, missionary, humanitarian, and medical doctor
3. **conservatives:** people who favor traditional views and values
4. **The Fourth Commandment:** "Remember the Sabbath day, keep it holy."
5. **mom-and-pop:** related to small, family-owned businesses
6. **apostolic:** relating to an apostle; a missionary of the Christian church
7. **Parcheesi:** a popular board game; also called the Royal Game of India

Vocabulary

Answer the following questions about some of the vocabulary words in the reading selection. Circle the letter of the correct response.

1. In paragraph 1, what does *sabbatical* mean?

   a. work day
   b. homework
   c. time off
   d. time at church

2. What does *secular* (paragraph 2) mean?

   a. not spiritual
   b. immaterial
   c. unresolved
   d. filled with despair

3. *Piety* (paragraph 3) means

   a. wickedness.
   b. fun.
   c. devoutness.
   d. unhappiness.

4. To *convene* something (paragraph 4) means to

   a. call together.
   b. end.
   c. disband.
   d. disorganize.

Checking Comprehension

Circle the letter of the correct answer.

1. In the early days of America, what could happen to a citizen if he or she broke the Sabbath?

   a. He or she could go to jail.
   b. He or she could be fined.
   c. He or she could be deported.
   d. Nothing would happen.

2. According to the author, the main function of blue laws was to

   a. force Americans to go to religious services.
   b. force Americans to get together with family.
   c. force Americans to rest.
   d. make sure nobody made any money on the Sabbath.

3. Who said, "If your soul has no Sunday, it becomes an orphan"?

   a. Nancy Gibbs
   b. Alexis McCrossen
   c. Paul Revere
   d. Albert Schweitzer

4. Which state was the thirty-second to allow liquor stores to stay open every Sunday?

   a. Virginia
   b. Rhode Island
   c. New York
   d. Connecticut

5. Why did car dealers in Kansas City, Missouri, push to stay closed on Sunday?

   a. They wanted to spend more time with their families.
   b. They did not want to be the only type of franchise open on Sunday.
   c. They did not want to lose out to the competition.
   d. They wanted an extra day off.

Mode and Skill Check

Circle the letter of the correct answer or write your answer on the blank provided.

1. What is the topic of this selection?

   a. Sundays
   b. work
   c. modern life
   d. Americans and rest

2. On the line below, write the thesis of this selection in your own words.

   _____

3. What is the predominant mode used in this selection?

   a. argument
   b. description
   c. cause/effect
   d. comparison/contrast

4. Is the author for or against blue laws?

   a. for
   b. against
   c. You cannot tell from the selection.
   d. She is undecided.

5. Which of the following paragraphs begin with a time order transition?

    a. paragraphs 1 and 2
    b. paragraphs 2 and 3
    c. paragraphs 1 and 3
    d. paragraphs 3 and 4

Questions for Discussion and Writing

1. Do you work on Sunday, or does your state still enforce blue laws? Whatever your situation, write an essay describing how either working or having blue laws has affected your life—for better or worse.

2. Do you think that businesses that stay open on Sunday are fair to their employees? Why or why not?

3. Write an essay arguing for or against blue laws.

At Large: Giving Teachers Guns a Simple but Stupid Idea

By Leonard Pitts Jr.

1   In the wake of the recent spate of shootings at U.S. schools, a Wisconsin state legislator has proposed a novel[1] solution: Let's arm the teachers.

2   You can hardly be surprised at Republican Rep. Frank Lasee's interest in this issue: One of those shootings took place in his state. There, on Sept. 29, a 15-year-old boy shot Weston High School principal John Klang to death. Still, Lasee's proposed solution has raised eyebrows. As others debate solutions ranging from heightened security to increased vigilance against bullying, Lasee has cut through the namby and the pamby[2]. He wants to pass legislation that would allow properly trained teachers and administrators to carry concealed handguns on school property.

3   And I just have to say: Of all the ideas I've ever heard, that's . . . certainly one of them.

4   Naturally, you'd expect criticism of such, ahem, bold thinking, and you would not be disappointed. The *Capital Times* newspaper compared Lasee to "the village idiot[3]" who fights a fire by dousing[4] it with gasoline. The paper seemed concerned that this

1. **novel:** new or unusual
2. **namby-pamby:** a slang term used to describe someone who is wishy-washy on a situation

3. **the village idiot:** a term used to describe someone in a town or city who is the butt of jokes and ridicule
4. **dousing:** wetting or drenching

Source: Miami Herald by Leonard Pitts Jr. Copyright 2006 by the *Miami Herald*. Reproduced with permission of *Miami Herald* in the format textbook via Copyright Clearance Center.

characterization unfairly stigmatized village idiots.

5   Meantime, the *Duluth News-Tribune* observed that having guns in school would make them even more readily available to disturbed, violence-prone children. The executive director of a Wisconsin anti-violence group called the idea "perverse[1]."

6   Even Lasee's cousin, State Senate President Alan Lasee, dubbed the idea "goofy," leading one to hope all the guns are properly secured at the next Lasee family reunion.

7   Anyway, you get the drift. The consensus says, bad idea. Really bad idea.

8   Me, I think Frank Lasee is simply an agent of the zeitgeist[2] and no one knows it yet. Or hasn't anyone else noticed our recent surplus of really bad ideas whose commonality and selling point is that they are simple. Workability? That's optional. Rationality: Overrated. What we want are ideas that can be explained on bumper stickers. If they require position papers, we're not interested.

9   Think I'm kidding? Consider a few actual ideas recently floated, debated, or enacted by actual elected representatives.

10   Terrorism a threat? Bomb Mecca[3].

11   Terrorists won't talk? Torture them.

12   Illegal immigration a problem? Fence off the country.

13   FEMA[4] a failure? Change its name.

14   We have become ever more impatient with the complexities and convolutions that characterize our most intractable[5] problems, ever more intolerant of solutions that require patience, long-term thinking, and the coordination of multiple strategies. Like overweight people looking for a fat-burning pill, we want magic solutions that require no investment of time, tears, or tolerance.

15   So sure, if school shootings are a threat, let's arm the teachers. Because, as everyone knows, the real problem in this country is that there just aren't enough people with guns. At the very least, arming teachers will sure discourage cheating. Indeed, why stop there?

16   Arm the bus drivers. That'll teach some punk to try to slip on with an expired transfer.

17   Arm the waiters. Bet folks won't be so quick to whine about their soup being cold.

18   Heck, arm the editors. Presto! Suddenly everybody's able to make their deadlines.

19   Lasee's proposal is emblematic of the simple, simplistic, simple-minded schemes that bubble to the surface of the national discourse[6] with troubling frequency these days.

20   They are not just dumb, they're frightening, suggesting as they do that we are becoming a people too obtuse, too impatient, or too both, to grapple[7] the complexities and gray shades of this life.

21   As George Clinton[8] used to say, "Think! It ain't illegal yet."

22   Which would be a really good idea. And hey, look at that! It fits on a bumper sticker, too. ∎

---

1. **perverse:** directed away from what is right or good
2. **zeitgeist:** the ideas prevalent in a time and place
3. **Mecca:** the most holy city of the religion of Islam
4. **FEMA:** the Federal Emergency Management Agency
5. **intractable:** difficult, stubborn
6. **discourse:** discussion of a subject
7. **grapple:** struggle
8. **George Clinton:** the leader of the music group Parliament Funkadelic

Vocabulary

Answer the following questions about some of the vocabulary words in the reading selection. Circle the letter of the correct answer.

1. What does the phrase *spate of* (paragraph 1) mean?

a. increase in
b. decrease in
c. interest in
d. violence of

2. What does *vigilance* (paragraph 2) mean?

a. misunderstanding
b. attention to
c. discouragement
d. disorganization

3. What does the word *stigmatized* (paragraph 4) mean?

a. put to sleep
b. praised
c. ignored
d. labeled as undesirable

4. What does *surplus* (paragraph 8) mean?

a. disappearance
b. donation
c. excess
d. lack

5. What does *convolutions* (paragraph 14) mean?

a. simplicities
b. complications
c. emotions
d. parts

6. What does the phrase *emblematic of* (paragraph 19) mean?

a. symbolic of
b. related to
c. different from
d. better than

7. What does *obtuse* (paragraph 20) mean?

a. intelligent
b. sensitive
c. foolish
d. complicated

Checking Comprehension

Circle the letter of the correct answer.

1. According to Leonard Pitts, what was the reason that a Wisconsin state legislator suggested arming teachers?

a. to combat violence in the state senate
b. to prevent shootings in U.S. schools
c. to punish a teacher who was arrested for carrying a gun at a Wisconsin school
d. to give teachers something they requested

2. Of the following, which is not one of the ideas recently proposed, debated, or enacted by elected representatives, according to Pitts?

a. bombing Mecca
b. torturing terrorists
c. building a fence to keep illegal immigrants out
d. all of the above are examples

3. In your opinion, what does Pitts think about the idea of arming teachers?

a. He thinks it is a great idea.
b. He is not sure how he feels about it.
c. He is against this idea.
d. He thinks that they should be given knives instead of guns.

Mode and Skill Check

Circle the letter of the correct answer or write your answer on the blank provided.

1. What is the topic of this selection?

a. violence in schools
b. Frank Lasee
c. guns in America
d. dumb ideas

2. On the following blank, write the thesis of this selection in your own words.

_____

3. What are the predominant modes of development used in this selection?

a. description and narration
b. comparison/contrast and classification
c. argument and illustration
d. illustration and division

4. Do you think Pitts is an advocate for gun control?

a. yes
b. no
c. He is undecided.
d. Readers cannot tell from this selection.

5. What modes develop paragraphs 4–7?

a. comparison/contrast and illustration
b. narration and description
c. division and process
d. illustration and cause/effect

Questions for Discussion and Writing

1. How do you feel about arming teachers? Do you, as Representative Frank Lasee feels, that arming teachers will combat school violence? Write a brief essay discussing your opinion.

2. Do some research online and find an idea that has been debated or enacted that you think is ridiculous or outlandish. (Review the ideas listed by Pitts in paragraphs 10–13 to remind you of some recent ones.) Write a paragraph or two describing it and why you think it is an outlandish idea. Be creative!

3. Do you agree or disagree with Pitts' statement that people are increasingly "intolerant of solutions that require patience, long-term thinking, and the coordination of multiple strategies" (paragraph 14)? If you disagree with Pitts, illustrate your opinion with specific examples. If you agree with Pitts, explain what you believe to be the reasons for this growing intolerance.

No Need to Stew: A Few Tips to Cope with Life's Annoyances

By Ian Urbina

1   When Seth Shepsle goes to Starbucks, he orders a "medium" because "grande"—as the coffee company calls the size, the one between big and small—annoys him.

2   Meg Daniel presses zero whenever she hears a computerized operator on the telephone so that she can talk to a real person. "Just because they want a computer to handle me doesn't mean I have to play along," she said.

3   When subscription cards fall from magazines Andrew Kirk is reading, he stacks them in a pile at the corner of his desk. At the end of each month, he puts them in the mail but leaves them blank so that the advertiser is forced to pay the business reply postage without gaining a new subscriber.

4   Life can involve big hardships, like being fired or smashing up your car. There is only so much you can do about them. But far more prevalent—and perhaps in the long run just as insidious—are life's many little annoyances.

5   These, you can do something about.

6   To examine the little weapons people use for everyday survival is to be given a free guidebook on getting by, created by the millions who feel that they must. It is a case study in human inventiveness, with occasional juvenile and petty passages, and the originators of these tips are happy to share them.

7   "They're an integral part of how people cope," said Prof. James C. Scott, who teaches anthropology and political science at Yale University, and the author of "Weapons of the Weak," about the feigned[1] ignorance, foot-dragging, and other techniques Malaysian[2] peasants used to avoid cooperating with the arrival of new technology in the 1970's. "All societies have them, but they're successful only to the extent that they avoid open confrontation."

8   The slow driver in fast traffic, the shopper with fifty coupons at the front of the checkout line, and the telemarketer calling at dinner all inflict life's thousand little lashes. But some see these infractions[3] as precious opportunities, rare chances for retribution[4] in the face of forces beyond our control.

9   Wesley A. Williams spent more than a year exacting his revenge against junk mailers. When signing up for a no-junk-mail list failed to stem the flow, he resorted to writing at the top of each unwanted item: "Not at this address. Return to sender." But the mail kept coming because the envelopes had "or current resident" on them, obligating mail carriers to deliver it, he said.

10   Next, he began stuffing the mail back into the "business reply" envelope and sending it back so that the mailer would have to pay the postage. "That wasn't exacting a heavy enough cost from them for bothering me," said Mr. Williams, 35, a middle school science teacher who lives in Melrose, N.Y., near Albany.

---

1. **feigned:** not real; pretended
2. **Malaysia:** a country in southeast Asia, a peninsula bordering Thailand and the northern third of the island of Borneo, bordering Indonesia, Brunei, and the South China Sea, south of Vietnam
3. **infractions:** violations of rules
4. **retribution:** revenge

Source: "No Need to Stew: A Few Tips to Cope with Life's Annoyances," by Ian Urbina, *The New York Times*, March 15, 2005. Copyright © 2005 by The New York Times Co., Reprinted with permission.

11   After checking with a postal clerk about the legality of stepping up his efforts, he began cutting up magazines, heavy bond paper, and small strips of sheet metal and stuffing them into the business reply envelopes that came with the junk packages.

12   "You wouldn't believe how heavy I got some of these envelopes to weigh," said Mr. Williams, who added that he saw an immediate drop in the amount of arriving junk mail. A spokesman for the United States Postal Service, Gerald McKiernan, said that Mr. Williams's actions sounded legal, as long as the envelope was properly sealed.

13   Sometimes, small acts of rebellion offer big doses of relief.

14   I've come to realize that I'm almost addicted to the sick little pleasure I get from lashing out at these things," said Mr. Kirk, 24, a freelance writer from Brooklyn who collects and returns magazine inserts.

15   When ordering a pizza from Domino's, Mr. Kirk says he always requests a "small," knowing that he will be corrected and told that medium is the smallest available size. "It makes me feel better to point out that their word games aren't fooling anyone," he said.

16   The Internet offers a booming trade to help with this type of annoyance-fighting behavior. For example, shared passwords to free Web sites are available at www.bugmenot.com to help people avoid dealing with long registration forms. To coexist with loud cellphone talkers, the Web offers hand-held jammers that, although illegal in the United States, can block all signals within a 45-foot radius.

17   Mitch Altman, a 48-year-old inventor living in San Francisco, said that in the last three months he has sold about 30,000 of his key-chain-size zappers called TV-B-Gone, which can be used discreetly to switch off televisions in public places. "When you go to a restaurant to talk with friends, why should you have to deal with the distraction of a ceiling-mounted television?" Mr. Altman said.

18   Some Web sites specialize in arming people against online annoyances. The site www.slashdot.org posted the name and the mailing address of one of the worst known spammers[1], encouraging people to sign the spammer up for catalogs and other junk mail to be sent to the spammer's home. Mr. McKiernan of the Postal Service said that tactic also appeared to be legal, but might constitute harassment.

19   Some groups are more frustrated than others. In 2002, Harris Interactive, a market research group based in Rochester, conducted a phone survey called the Daily Hassle Scale that asked 1,010 people to rank the aggravations they faced in a typical day. The survey found that poor people and African-Americans suffer the most stress from the everyday annoyances such as noisy neighbors, telemarketers, and pressure at work, but it did not explain why.

20   Sometimes, the resistance to these frustrations is organized.

21   Work slowdowns[2] are methods commonly used by labor unions to apply pressure without actually striking. During the Solidarity movement[3] in Poland, people expressed their disapproval of the government-run news media by taking a walk with their hats on backward at exactly 6 p.m. when the state news program started. When the

1. **spammer:** a company or individual who advertises a product via junk e-mail messages on the Internet
2. **work slowdowns:** instances where workers do not work to their full capacity in order to protest work conditions, pay issues, or contract disputes, among others
3. **Solidarity movement:** an anti-communist movement led by a Polish federation of trade unions

government noticed the trend, it issued curfews[1], but people then put their televisions in their windows facing outward so that only the police walking the streets would see the broadcasts.

22   "You have to remember, in Poland during those years showing up drunk at work was seen as a patriotic act because people hated the bosses so much," Professor Scott said.

23   But even on less coordinated levels, shared frustration is often the augur of countercultural[2] trends. Mr. Shepsle said he took great solace[3] in discovering his irritations with Starbucks' lingo[4] summed up on a popular T-shirt in Chicago. The shirt, which mocks the pretentiousness[5] of a certain Chicago neighborhood, features two names. Next to Lincoln Park it says "Tall, Grande, Venti." Next to Wicker Park it says "Small, Medium, Large."

24   "It's nice to know I'm not alone," said Mr. Shepsle, 28, who works for a theater company in Manhattan.

25   Most people participate in this sort of behavior on some level, Professor Scott said, adding that his own habit was to write "England" rather than "United Kingdom" on letters he sends to his British friends. He described this as his way of disregarding British claims to Wales and Scotland.

26   "As a tactic, it doesn't amount to much except a way to provide a tiny and private sense of satisfaction," he said. "But that's something." ■

Vocabulary

Answer the following questions about some of the vocabulary words in the reading selection. Circle the letter of the correct response.

1. In paragraph 4, what does *prevalent* mean?

   a. disorganized
   b. widespread
   c. rare
   d. powerless

2. What does *insidious* (paragraph 4) mean?

   a. sinister
   b. joyful
   c. lethargic
   d. romantic

3. In paragraph 7, the author uses the word *integral*. What does that word mean in this context?

   a. not necessary
   b. connected

1. **curfews:** laws requiring people to be in their homes by a certain hour
2. **countercultural:** in opposition to the values of the established culture
3. **solace:** source of comfort
4. **lingo:** language
5. **pretentiousness:** self-importance or showing off

c. essential

d. unimportant

4. As used in paragraph 23, what does *augur* mean?

a. prediction

b. announcement

c. oration

d. reading

Checking Comprehension

Circle the letter of the correct answer.

1. How does Andrew Kirk deal with subscription cards from magazines?

a. He burns them.

b. He shreds them.

c. He collects them and then sends them back to the advertiser.

d. He throws them out.

2. In what country was "feigned ignorance, foot-dragging, and other techniques" the result of new technology coming to that country?

a. India

b. Pakistan

c. China

d. Malaysia

3. What was the result of the Harris Interactive phone survey called the Daily Hassle Scale?

a. The survey found that poor people and African-Americans suffer the most stress from everyday annoyances.

b. The survey found that the elderly fall prey to phone scams.

c. The survey found that women are particularly susceptible to telemarketers' sales pitches.

d. The survey study was inconclusive.

4. In what country did people express their disapproval of the government-run news media by walking with their hats on backward?

a. China

b. Malaysia

c. Poland

d. Russia

Mode and Skill Check

Circle the letter of the correct answer or write your answer on the blank provided.

1. What is the topic of this selection?

   a. magazine blow-in cards
   b. people who cannot cope
   c. coping with life's annoyances
   d. junk mail

2. On the following blank, write the thesis of this selection in your own words.

   _____

3. What is the predominant mode used in this selection?

   a. narration
   b. description
   c. illustration
   d. argument and comparison/contrast

4. Choose three examples of how people deal with life's petty annoyances and write your answers on the following blanks.

   1. _____
   2. _____
   3. _____

Questions for Discussion and Writing

1. What annoys you? How do you handle this annoyance? Write an essay about your coping skills.

2. Go online and visit the two sites listed in this selection—www.bugmenot .com and www.slashdot.org. Compare and contrast these two sites. Which one do you like better and why? Which one offers the best tips for combating life's little annoyances?

3. Are there better ways than revenge, rebellion, and resistance to deal with the minor annoyances of everyday life? What are they?

'Like,' Like, Covers It All

By Lenore Skenazy

1 Like, what gives?

2 And while we're at it: What gives about like?

3 The word "like" has been around a long time, but now it is taking over our language. On this linguists agree, parents despair, and teenagers are, like, duh.

4 But I'm a "like, duh" addict myself. And when I stop to listen to my everyday chatter—and that of my middle-aged friends—we all use "like," like, all the time.

5 Is this simply verbal Botox[1]—the hope that if we say "like" enough we'll all seem incredibly young and vapid? Or is "like" truly a new part of speech, crucial to the way we communicate these days—and maybe even not that bad?

6 It's, like, both.

7 In the sentence above, for instance, "like" is a hedge. It's my way of saying, "The rest of this column may not quite prove my points, so don't sue me when you get to the bottom." Used this way, "like" lets me—and everyone else who uses it—get off easy while sounding cool.

8 In this respect, it reflects directly on the beatniks[2] who first popularized the term. The beats used "like" to sound jazzy, to riff out loud. They reveled in being inarticulate. Perhaps, suggests communication consultant Sims Wyeth, that's because they were high.

"Like, wow, man," sounds a lot more profound if you're wasted.

9 Nowadays, "like, wow, man" just sounds silly (and wasted). But "like" itself has evolved to sound deliciously conspiratorial, even intimate.

10 If you, for instance, tell me that your boss is, "like, nuts," you are winking at me with the word "like." You hope that I will telepathically[3] understand just what you mean: That your boss is *totally* nuts, without you putting it that baldly.

11 This way, "like" creates an instant bond: I am expected to understand what you are saying without your coming right out and saying it. And that's one thing I really like about like: It may sound teenaged but it also sounds like we're best friends, having a ball because we understand one another so utterly. "Like" turns any conversation into a slumber party.

12 But, of course, there are also a whole lot of other ways people use like, some far more annoying. The one that *Webster's New World Dictionary* most recently added is a replacement for "said." "He's like, 'Are you going to the party?' and I'm like, 'No way!'"

13 The biggest problem with this use is that the listener cannot be entirely sure that the speaker actually said, "No way!" or if she nodded along while secretly thinking, "No way! I'm going to pretend I have to baby-sit!"

1. **Botox:** an injection given by a cosmetic surgeon to smooth out lines and wrinkles on one's face
2. **beatnik:** term given to counter-culture members of society in the time after World War II. Most often associated with writers and musicians

3. **telepathically:** to understand something by reading someone's mind

Source: "'Like,' Like, Covers It All," by Lenore Skenazy, *New York Daily News*, June 22, 2003. Reprinted by permission of the author.

14   So "like" can be maddeningly imprecise. That's generally why linguists—and parents—dislike it. If your son tells you that the pen was, like, going to explode anyway, you are left to determine just how much his biting the pen had to do with its destruction. He's hoping the "like" will absolve him from the fact that he's telling a lie. After all, he didn't say the pen was *really* about to explode. He said it was, *like*, about to explode.

15   Another way your son could explain this scenario would be to say, "The pen was, like—" and make a funny face or gesture as if he's holding a toxic pen. That way he leaps from telling you what happened to pantomiming[1] his version. And very likely, unless the pen exploded on your brand-new white sofa, it will make you laugh.

16   This is one way "like" has become absolutely perfect for our TV-centric society. It turns any sentence into a sitcom. "We were at the funeral, and my brother was like—" grimace, grimace. You can just picture Elaine on *Seinfeld* explaining events this way. "Like" opens the door for shtick. Then it lets you in on the joke.

17   And so, imprecise, evasive, and overused though it may be, what's not to like about, like, "like"? ■

Vocabulary

Answer the following questions about some of the vocabulary words in the reading selection. Circle the letter of the correct answer.

1. A *linguist* (paragraph 3) is

    a. someone who studies the dictionary.
    b. someone who studies language.
    c. someone who studies tongues.
    d. someone who studies Russian.

2. To be *vapid* (paragraph 5) is to be

    a. uninteresting.
    b. savvy.
    c. disinterested.
    d. lovely.

3. To *revel* in something (paragraph 8) means to

    a. enjoy or bask in it.
    b. have distaste for it.
    c. discourage it.
    d. encourage it.

1. pantomiming: to communicate without using words

4. In paragraph 9, what does *conspiratorial* mean?

    a. conniving
    b. distracting
    c. overwhelming
    d. distasteful

5. A *scenario* (paragraph 15) is

    a. a problem.
    b. a sequence of events.
    c. a joke.
    d. an area.

6. *Shtick* (paragraph 16) is

    a. a piece of wood.
    b. a target.
    c. an entertainment routine.
    d. a member.

Checking Comprehension

Circle the letter of the correct response.

1. According to Lenore Skenazy, how do parents feel about the use of the word *like*?

    a. They like it.
    b. They think it is cool.
    c. They dislike it.
    d. They do not care one way or the other.

2. Who first popularized the term *like*, according to the author?

    a. teens
    b. parents
    c. linguists
    d. beatniks

3. According to the author, "like" turns any conversation into

    a. a slumber party.
    b. a young, happening conversation.
    c. instant understanding.
    d. idle chatter.

4. Skenazy says that "like" turns any sentence into

a. a slumber party.
b. a sitcom.
c. an episode of *Seinfeld*.
d. a moment for MTV.

Mode and Skill Check

Circle the letter of the correct answer or write your answer on the blank provided.

1. The author's tone in this selection is

a. sad.
b. bemused.
c. serious.
d. sarcastic.

2. What can you infer about how the author feels about the word *like* from this selection?

a. Linguistically, she does not think it adds anything to conversation, but it creates bonds between people who understand how it is being used.
b. She thinks it, like, stinks.
c. She does not really care about the word *like*.
d. She is waiting to hear if linguists endorse its use in language.

3. What is the topic of this selection?

a. conversation
b. parents and teenagers
c. the English lexicon
d. the word *like*

4. On the following blank, write the thesis of this selection in your own words.

_____

5. Overall, the mode used in this selection is

a. narration.
b. description.
c. definition/explanation.
d. argument.

Questions for Discussion and Writing

1. Does the way that someone communicates verbally give you an instant impression of who he or she is and what he or she is like? Write an essay in which you explain how a verbal tic or a certain word usage that indicates to you the character or personality of someone else.

2. Is there a word or expression that you use all the time? If so, what is it and what does that word or expression convey about you?

3. Similarly, is there a word or expression an older person in your life uses a lot? If so, what is it, and what does that word or expression mean for his or her generation?

Most Divorced Dads Deserve to See Their Kids

By Connie Schultz

1   Divorce seems to suck every drop of common sense right out of us. How else to explain the latest child-custody arrangement—called "birdnesting"—reported by *The Wall Street Journal?*

2   Birdnesting allows the kids to live in one house all the time while the parents take turns sleeping over. That way, say the few who support it, it's the parents who suffer, not the kids.

3   Granted, there are those who feel that all divorcing parents should suffer. And suffer. And suffer.

4   These are often the same married folks who inexplicably are drawn to murder mysteries where the spouses are chopped into chunks and then sold as shrink-wrapped Spam[1], but who am I to suggest hidden motives? Besides, as a single mother myself, I've been far too busy ripping apart the fabric of American family life; I haven't got time to worry about which unraveling threads the unhappily married ones are pulling.

5   Birdnesting forces two adults who can no longer stand the sight of each other to share a household and live their lives in suspended animation[2].

6   Imagine trying to get on with your life when you are still sharing a bathroom and cat-litter duty with the person who brings out the worst in you. Your children are teased into stoking their most heartbreaking

1. **Spam:** the trademarked name for canned chopped meat that is pressed into a loaf

2. **suspended animation:** a temporary interruption of vital functions that looks like death

fantasy—that Mom and Dad will get back together. And, inevitably, they decide it is their castle, breeding in the little darlings a sense of entitlement to rival Richard Grasso[1].

7   Who, I wondered, would support this? I read on and found my answer: Fathers, that's who.

8   In their relentless effort to matter in their kids' lives, some fathers would willingly sacrifice their privacy and any semblance of independence for the chance to be regularly involved in their children's lives.

9   I know fathers like this, men who are divorced but desperate to be steeped in the daily mess of life with their kids. They want to help their children with their math homework, remind them that even Spider-Man changes his underwear, and promise that tomorrow morning they'll not only serve Pop-Tarts, but the ones with frosting. Oftentimes, the only impediment to forging this kind of relationship is the bitterness of divorce.

10   We hear a lot about deadbeat dads, the ones who fail to support their children financially, and those who drop out of their kids' lives. We talk—and write—a lot less about the fathers who are jerked around by bitter ex-wives who feel the only power they have left is their ability to manipulate visitation.

11   Talk about a loaded word: visitation. The first time I used that word with one divorced friend, his face fell.

12   "I do not *visit* my daughters," he said. "I don't babysit them, either. I drive two and a half hours one-way so that I can bring them home to our house, our home, the one they share with me."

13   When I apologized, he shook his head sadly. "I hate the word 'visitation.' I hate what it suggests about me as a father, and my relationship with my daughters. And I hate what it communicates to them."

14   Divorce under the best of circumstances is the hardest thing many of us will ever go through until it comes time for us to die. Even when it's best for the children that parents part, the pain is searing.

15   Wounds can heal, though, if they aren't constantly ripped open, which is what happens every time a child's time with a parent becomes a tool for revenge. While most courts now favor shared parenting arrangements, the mother remains the primary caregiver in the majority of divorces. Mom's the one with the power, and it is heartbreaking to watch children suffer when she decides the only way to make her ex-husband pay is to steal away their time with him.

16   A man's failure as a husband does not automatically disqualify him for fatherhood. If he is not a physical or emotional threat, then he has the right to spend time with his kids. And they have the right, the need, to know him as someone other than the man Mom loves to hate.

17   We should always keep in mind that kids grow up. When they do, they figure out for themselves if their relationship with their father failed—and why.

18   There's not a mother alive who wants to be on the receiving end of that blame. ∎

---

1. **Richard Grasso:** the former chairman of the New York Stock Exchange, known for the large compensation package he received for doing that job

Vocabulary

Answer the following questions about some of the vocabulary words in the reading selection. Circle the letter of the correct answer.

1. What does the word *inexplicably* (paragraph 4) mean?

   a. unexplainably
   b. understandably
   c. unfortunately
   d. unknowingly

2. What does *entitlement* (paragraph 6) mean?

   a. mystery
   b. claim
   c. grief
   d. fear

3. What does the word *relentless* (paragraph 8) mean?

   a. unrealistic
   b. useless
   c. steady and persistent
   d. stopping and starting

4. What does *semblance* (paragraph 8) mean?

   a. belief
   b. desire
   c. appearance
   d. rejection

5. What is an *impediment* (paragraph 9)?

   a. assistance
   b. an obstacle
   c. a beginning
   d. a clue

6. What does the word *searing* (paragraph 14) mean?

   a. burning
   b. decreasing
   c. not real
   d. mild

Checking Comprehension

Circle the letter of the correct answer.

1. According to the selection, what is "birdnesting"?

a. an arrangement in which children of divorce live with their grandparents

b. a shared-custody arrangement in which children split their time between their parents' homes

c. an arrangement that allows kids to live in one house all the time while the parents take turns sleeping over

d. an arrangement in which children spend six months with one parent and six months with the other parent

2. According to Connie Schultz, who are the biggest proponents of birdnesting?

a. fathers

b. mothers

c. courts

d. children

3. Who are "deadbeat" dads?

a. dads who have passed away

b. dads who will not coach their children's sports teams

c. dads who are uninvolved

d. dads who do not support their children financially

4. How does Schultz feel about dads who will do anything to stay involved in their children's lives?

a. She supports them.

b. She does not support them.

c. She thinks that they should have time limits placed on their involvement.

d. Readers cannot tell from the selection.

Mode and Skill Check

Circle the letter of the correct answer or write your answer on the blank provided.

1. What is the topic of this selection?

a. divorced dads

b. children of divorce

    c. "birdnesting"
    d. custody battles

2. On the following blank, write the thesis of this selection in your own words.

_____

3. What is the predominant mode of development used in this selection?

    a. description
    b. comparison/contrast
    c. argument
    d. illustration

4. Do you think Schultz is an advocate for birdnesting?

    a. yes
    b. no
    c. She is undecided.
    d. Readers cannot tell from this selection.

5. What mode develops paragraphs 6 and 15?

    a. process
    b. classification
    c. comparison/contrast
    d. cause/effect

Questions for Discussion and Writing

1. What do you think of the concept of "birdnesting"? Do you think it benefits children? Divorced parents? Why or why not?

2. If a father does not support his children financially after a divorce, what should be done? Why? Write a brief essay exploring your viewpoint.

3. What long-term effects does divorce have on children? Do some research on the Internet to find information about the topic and write a brief essay.

Don't LOL[1], but Texting Turns Me Off

By Ana Veciana-Suarez

1   I've never been fast enough on the trigger, and in the world of modern-day communications, where Instant and Immediate are the new buzzwords, that lack of speed is, like, so last millennium.

2   It's taken me a few years to get up to snuff[2] with "killer apps[3]." Not because I'm a Luddite[4], but because I cherish my alone space and find its boundaries constantly threatened. Nonetheless, I've dragged myself into the virtual world of faceless contact and 24-7 availability—whining all the way.

3   True, some stuff I find useful. E-mail, for instance. How did I ever live without it? Now I zap spam, monitor messages on my wireless, and organize my in box in a way no one could have predicted five years ago.

4   Then again, the very mention of e-mail just goes to show how old—and outdated—I am. My teenage children, those with nimble thumbs and the attention span of a swarming gnat, think e-mail dates to the Stone Age[5]. (Isn't that how Fred Flintstone communicated with Barney[6]? Ha, ha. Or, is that LOL?)

5   That's because my kids are into text messaging. Me, I can't even see the letters without my reading glasses. So unfair.

6   Yet that's the reality. The 15-year-old no more gets into the car than he begins pawing away at his cell phone. Anything worth saying has been abbreviated into one-letter words.

7   The worst part? I can't even eavesdrop on his conversations.

8   Don't waste your pity on me, though. Last week I felt slightly better about that expiration date stamped on my forehead after my 25-year-old confessed that he sometimes is forced to call one of the younger brothers to help him figure out tech stuff. This may be the first time in history when the oldsters—read: anybody out of high school—are taking their cue from those in braces.

9   A recent report confirms that yes, indeed, no matter how fast we learn we're still behind the times. That e-mail account I'm so fond of? Going the way of the postage stamp, at least among teenagers.

10   According to comScore Media Metrix, teen e-mail use has been dropping in the past year even though the average time they spent online actually increased. In April, it was down 8 percent from the same month last year. In the meantime, the rest of us slowpokes continue to use e-mail faithfully and fervently, but if the past predicts the future, it won't be for long.

11   E-mail has lost its luster because it's *slo-o-oo-ow*. Teens are abandoning it for the faster, briefer text messaging and instant

1. **LOL:** abbreviation for "laughing out loud"
2. **up to snuff:** having acceptable quality
3. **"killer apps":** computer industry jargon for programs that entice a person to buy the computer system they run on
4. **Luddite:** someone opposed to technological or industrial innovation
5. **the Stone Age:** an early historical period in which tools and weapons were made of stone rather than metal
6. **Fred Flintstone and Barney:** two Stone Age characters in the cartoon television series *The Flintstones*

Source: Miami Herald by Ana Veciana-Suarez. Copyright 2006 by *Miami Herald*. Reproduced with permission of *Miami Herald* in the format Textbook via Copyright Clearance Center.

messaging, though even the latter is losing ground to MySpace[1]. (If you don't know what MySpace is, or have never been on the site, rush yourself to Tech E.R.)

12   E-mail, it turns out, is also too complicated, too formal, too uncertain. In comparison, texting—it's a verb, by the way—pops up on your phone screen immediately and with a few, quick strokes, voila[2]! you can reply with your own message. What's more, texting makes you instantly and irreversibly accessible.

13   Which is fine, if you don't need time to collect your thoughts or sort your feelings or compose a sweet turn of phrase. In fact, this kind of instant communication is perfect for those who don't suffer from foot-in-mouth disease[3] or for those who can think on their feet, or should I say, on their thumbs.

14   For the rest of us, for those who savor their own company and think solitude is an endangered species, the tsunami[4] of instant communication can only mean one thing: quantity, not quality.

15   I'm beginning to think the off button is the best invention since *churros*[5] and hot chocolate. ■

Vocabulary

Answer the following questions about some of the vocabulary words in the reading selection. Circle the letter of the correct answer.

1. What does the word *nimble* (paragraph 4) mean?

  a. stiff
  b. clumsy
  c. quick
  d. thick

2. What does *fervently* (paragraph 10) mean?

  a. enthusiastically
  b. reluctantly
  c. quickly
  d. without energy

3. What does *luster* (paragraph 11) mean?

  a. bravery
  b. effectiveness
  c. bad reputation
  d. glory

1. **MySpace:** an online social networking site
2. **voila:** a French exclamation meaning "There!"
3. **foot-in-mouth disease:** the tendency to make remarks that are embarrassing or without tact
4. **tsunami:** a large ocean wave
5. *churros*: thick fritters made from dough

4. What does *irreversibly* (paragraph 12) mean?

   a. barely
   b. slowly
   c. permanently
   d. at a distance

5. What does *savor* (paragraph 14) mean?

   a. dislike
   b. enjoy
   c. avoid
   d. steal

Checking Comprehension

Circle the letter of the correct answer.

1. Why has it taken the author a few years to get accustomed to using new technology?

   a. She cherishes her alone time and thinks that it will be threatened by additional technological communication.
   b. She is thrifty and will not spend the money to get new devices.
   c. She just learned to use her cell phone and does not want to learn anything else.
   d. She figures that her kids have everything; why should she, too?

2. Which of the following statements about teen e-mail usage is true, according to this selection?

   a. Teens do not use e-mail at all.
   b. Teens use cell phones more than e-mail to communicate.
   c. Teens' e-mail usage has been dropping even though the average time they spend online is increasing.
   d. Teens' e-mail usage is increasing.

3. According to Ana Veciana-Suarez, why has e-mail lost its luster?

   a. It is not cool anymore.
   b. It is slow.
   c. Not too many kids have hand-held devices.
   d. Teens prefer talking on the phone to e-mailing each other.

Mode and Skill Check

Circle the letter of the correct answer or write your answer on the blank provided.

1. What is the topic of this selection?

   a. text messaging
   b. e-mailing
   c. Luddites
   d. the Internet

2. On the following blank, write the thesis of this selection in your own words.

   _____

3. What are the predominant modes of development used in this selection?

   a. narration and division
   b. illustration and cause/effect
   c. comparison/contrast and classification
   d. description and argument

4. Do you think Veciana-Suarez likes e-mail as a communication tool?

   a. yes
   b. no
   c. She is undecided.
   d. Readers cannot tell from this selection.

5. Paragraphs 11 and 12 are developed with

   a. classification and narration.
   b. description and process.
   c. division and illustration.
   d. cause/effect and comparison/contrast.

Questions for Discussion and Writing

1. Would you consider yourself a "Luddite" or someone who is technologically savvy? Why? Illustrate the topic sentence of your paragraph with specific examples.

2. What are the advantages and disadvantages of using text messaging to communicate?

3. Which technological device that you own has made your life easier overall? Why?

The Deeper Truth of Good and Evil

By Marc Gellman

1   We cannot choose the news, but we can choose which news items surprise us most. Recently, within the span of a week, we were presented with striking examples of radical human depravity and radical human goodness. Which one surprised you most?

2   The first story was the execution of Saddam Hussein[1]. This was a story of the full achievement of radical evil. Unfortunately, the crude, coarse, and vengeful manner of his hanging obscured the main spiritual point, which is that here was a man who was responsible directly and indirectly for the death of hundreds of thousands of beings through aggressive war, brutal torture, terrorism, and the genocidal gassing of thousands of innocent people. Saddam was not merely a thug[2] or a simply bad man. He pushed the envelope of radical evil and his remorseless cruelty was unrelenting. His story causes us to ask, "How could a person do such evil?"

3   The second story was about Wesley Autrey and it is the story of the full achievement of human goodness. On Jan. 2, [2007] Autrey, a fifty-year-old construction worker, was taking his two daughters, Syshe, four, and Shuqui, six, to their mother's home before he went to work. Around 1 p.m., they were waiting for the subway train at 137th Street and Broadway in Manhattan, when Cameron Hollopeter, twenty, suffered a seizure and fell onto the subway tracks. The No. 1 train was fast approaching and, leaving his daughters in the care of strangers, Autrey jumped onto the tracks and covered Hollopeter with his body in a space less than two feet deep, as the train roared over them. The passing train covered Autrey's blue knit cap with grease, but otherwise miraculously left both men untouched. Autrey refused medical help, because, he said, nothing was wrong. He did visit Hollopeter in the hospital before heading to his night shift. "I don't feel like I did something spectacular; I just saw someone who needed help," Autrey said. "I did what I felt was right." His story causes us to ask, "How could a person do such goodness?"

4   My question is, which story stumps you more? Are you more bewildered by how a dictator can feed people into wood choppers feet first, or are you more bewildered by how a father with two young daughters could jump onto electrified subway tracks to save a total stranger? Both achievements are obviously remote, but they present a deep spiritual challenge to us all. I believe we can be surprised by great evil or by great goodness. I do not believe we can be surprised by both goodness and evil equally. One of them must strike us as a truer reflection of human nature than the other. Which is it for you?

5   Thomas Hobbes[3] wrote the epigram for all who believe that people are, at root, basi-

---

1. **Saddam Hussein:** former Iraqi dictator who was hanged for his crimes in 2007
2. **thug:** criminal

3. **Thomas Hobbes:** an English philosopher who lived in the 1600s

Source: "The Deeper Truth of Good and Evil," copyright © 2007 by Marc Gellman. Published by *Newsweek.com.* All rights reserved. Used with permission.

cally evil: "Man is a wolf to men" (*homo hominis lupis*). For Hobbes and also for Nietzsche[1] and Schopenhauer[2] and Freud[3], the naturally aggressive and predatory[4] nature of human beings is fundamental and decisive. The task of government, and all alert citizens, is therefore to structure a series of protections against the hostile incursions[5] of others. Hobbes would have totally understood Saddam, but would have been utterly bewildered by Wesley Autrey. Perhaps Hobbes wrote the truth of your own heart.

6   On the other side of this defining moral question about human nature are Plato[6], Aristotle[7], the Bible, Buddha, Thomas Aquinas[8], John Dewey[9], and Anne Frank[10] who believed that people are basically good and kind and compassionate unless that good nature is distorted by fear, ignorance, illusion, and sin. This tradition would obviously be impressed, but not surprised, by Wesley Autrey's leap, and would be utterly dumbstruck by the evil

Saddam produced without a tear or regret. The world offers ample evidence for both ways. The story of Saddam Hussein and the story of Wesley Autrey are both true. The question is not which one is true. The question is which one you believe reflects the deepest truth of human nature. Your answer, I deeply believe, will not only change you but will also change the world.

7   I don't believe Hobbes's wolf story. I believe the wolf story of the Native American people I told a graduating class last spring and told you soon after. It is the story of a chief telling his grandchildren that there was a war going on inside him between two wolves, one the wolf of kindness and the other the wolf of cruelty. His grandchildren asked him which wolf would win the fight, and he said to them, "The wolf that will win is the wolf you feed." Now that is a wolf story that does not surprise me. ■

1. **Nietzsche:** a German philosopher who lived in the 1800s
2. **Schopenhauer:** a German philosopher who lived from 1788 to 1860
3. **Freud:** an Austrian neurologist and psychiatrist who is best known for his theories about the unconscious mind
4. **predatory:** living by exploiting or destroying others
5. **incursions:** entering or invading another's territory or space
6. **Plato:** a philosopher who lived in ancient Greece
7. **Aristotle:** an ancient Greek philosopher who was a student of Plato
8. **Thomas Aquinas:** an Italian scholar and theologian in the scholastic tradition; he was canonized a saint and is considered by many in the Catholic faith as the Church's greatest theologian
9. **John Dewey:** an American philosopher, psychologist, and educational reformer who was born in 1859 and died in 1952
10. **Anne Frank:** a European Jewish girl who wrote of hiding from the Nazis in her posthumously published work, *The Diary of Anne Frank*. She died in 1945 after being captured by the Nazis and sent to a death camp.

Vocabulary

Answer the following questions about some of the vocabulary words in the reading selection. Circle the letter of the correct answer.

1. What does *depravity* (paragraph 1) mean?

   a. goodness
   b. insanity
   c. humor
   d. evil

2. What does *genocidal* (paragraph 2) mean?

   a. harmless
   b. favoring long prison sentences
   c. lasting for a long period of time
   d. trying to exterminate an entire group

3. What does *remorseless* (paragraph 2) mean?

   a. without regret
   b. without fear
   c. without joy
   d. without pain

4. What is an *epigram* (paragraph 5)?

   a. a brief saying
   b. a poem that rhymes
   c. a beautiful song
   d. a long speech

5. What does it mean to be *dumbstruck* (paragraph 6)?

   a. limited
   b. shocked
   c. energized
   d. inspired

6. What does *ample* (paragraph 6) mean?

   a. unreliable
   b. scarce
   c. plentiful
   d. in the form of numbers

Checking Comprehension

Circle the letter of the correct answer.

1. What was Wesley Autrey's accomplishment, as related by Marc Gellman?

    a. He pried open a New York City subway car's door to save his daughter from being crushed.
    b. He threw his body over a man who was lying on a New York City subway track, saving that man's life.
    c. He pushed a man out of the way of a speeding taxi cab.
    d. He donated a kidney to a dying man.

2. Which of the following is *not* one of the people whom Gellman uses to illustrate those who believe in "the predatory nature of human beings" as being "fundamental and decisive" (paragraph 5)?

    a. Thomas Hobbes
    b. John Dewey
    c. Nietzsche
    d. Freud

3. Which of the following, according to Gellman, thought that "people are basically good and kind and compassionate unless that good nature is distorted by fear, ignorance, illusion, and sin" (paragraph 6)?

    a. Anne Frank
    b. Thomas Aquinas
    c. Plato
    d. all of the above

4. According to Gellman, what would Thomas Hobbes's reaction to Autrey's actions have been?

    a. He would have been utterly bewildered.
    b. He would have applauded him.
    c. He would not have been surprised.
    d. Readers cannot tell from the information Gellman gives.

Mode and Skill Check

Circle the letter of the correct answer or write your answer on the blank provided.

1. What is the topic of this selection?

    a. good and evil
    b. philosophers

c. Wesley Autrey
d. acts of bravery

2. On the following blank, write the thesis of this selection in your own words.

_____

3. What are the predominant modes of development used in this selection?

a. description, narration, and illustration
b. illustration, comparison/contrast, and cause/effect
c. process, division, and classification
d. argument and definition

4. Does Gellman think that people are inherently and basically good?

a. yes
b. no
c. He is undecided.
d. Readers cannot tell from this selection.

5. Paragraph 3 is developed with

a. definition.
b. comparison/contrast and process.
c. description and classification.
d. narration and cause/effect.

Questions for Discussion and Writing

1. In your opinion, are people inherently good or evil? Why do you believe what you do? Write a paragraph or brief essay to explore your viewpoint, using examples to support your main idea.

2. Now that you know Wesley Autrey's story, what do you think you would do in a similar situation? Could you risk your life to save a total stranger? Why or why not?

3. What does Gellman mean when he writes in paragraph 7 that "the wolf that will win is the wolf you feed"? In what specific ways have you observed people feeding the "wolf of kindness" and the "wolf of cruelty"?

Handbook

Parts of Speech

Every word in every sentence acts as a particular part of speech (a classification). A word can function as different parts of speech depending on its *context*, that is, the other words around it. For example, the word *left* can be a noun, verb, adjective, or adverb:

Turn **left** at the stop sign. (adverb)
She writes with her **left** hand. (adjective)
I **left** her a message. (verb)
I live in the first house on the **left.** (noun)

In each sentence, the context determines the part of speech (the function) of this particular word.

Nouns

A **noun** is a word that names a person, place, thing, or idea: *doctor, building, fruit, hate.* Nouns are either common or proper. *Common nouns* refer to general people, places, or things: *girl, pharmacy, car. Proper nouns* name one specific person, place, thing, or idea, so they are capitalized:

George Washington
Zion National Park
Volvo

Collective nouns are those that refer to a group of people or things *(team, class, crowd, group, company, audience, family, jury, gang, faculty).*

To identify nouns in a sentence, ask yourself if a word names a person, place, thing, or idea.

proper noun   *common noun*

Cashews are crunchy **nuts.**

proper noun   *common noun*

Nelson Mandela is my **hero.**

Also, look for the words *a*, *an*, and *the* (called *articles*, a kind of adjective), which appear in front of nouns.

common noun   *common noun*

The *dog*   ate   **a** *treat.*

proper noun   *common noun*

A *Ferrari*   is   **a** fast *car.*

NOTE: Adjectives, such as the word *fast* in the second sentence, will often separate *a*, *an*, or *the* from the noun.

Nouns can be individual words, or they can be *verbals*, verb forms that can act as nouns. For example, read the following sentences:

I really hate **cooking.**
Running is his hobby.

In the first sentence, the verbal *cooking* (a *gerund*) functions as the direct object of the sentence. In the second sentence, the verbal **running** (a *gerund*) is the subject. Verbals are explained further in The Basic Sentence section of this Handbook.

EXERCISE 1

Circle all of the nouns in each of the following sentences.

1. Carlos drank a teaspoon of the cough syrup.

2. Shopping is one of my favorite activities.

3. Paris is called the city of lights.

4. My son has long, beautiful eyelashes.

5. Alcoholic drinks make some people very depressed.

6. Jack likes antique cars.

7. The library is Mike's favorite hangout.

8. *Huckleberry Finn* is Mark Twain's most famous book.

9. Dictionaries explain the meanings of words.

10. The shopping mall was crowded.

For practice in identifying nouns in sentences, go to http://www.college .hmco.com/pic/dolphinwritertwo.

Pronouns

A **pronoun** is a word that is used in the place of a noun. For example, if you write one sentence that says, "John left the theater," the next sentence you write could substitute a pronoun instead of repeating the name *John*: "*He* did not like the movie." *He* is the pronoun used in place of the name *John*.

There are different kinds of pronouns. One kind refers to one or more specific people or things:

I	you	she	they
me	yourself	her	them
myself	yourselves	herself	themselves
it	we	he	their
itself	us	him	
	ourselves	himself	

She took **him** to see **them.**
He did **it himself.**

I, he, she, it, we, you, and *they* are the **personal pronouns.**

Other pronouns are called *indefinite* because they do not refer to any particular person, place, or thing:

any	everybody	one	something
anybody	everyone	no one	several
anyone	everything	nothing	some
anything	few	somebody	
both	many	someone	

Everybody knows what will happen.
He longs to tell **someone** her secret.

Another kind of pronoun points out people, places, things, or ideas by referring to a specific noun. These are called **demonstrative pronouns.**

this
that
these
those

Those are the nicest shoes I have ever seen.
That is my house.

NOTE: The pronouns *this, that, these,* and *those* also function as adjectives when they precede a particular noun. For example, in the sentence "These boots belong to Susan," the word *these* is an adjective that answers the question *Which boots?* For more on adjectives, see the next page and The Basic Sentence section of this Handbook.

Some pronouns, called **interrogative pronouns,** introduce questions:

who   what
whom   whose
which

Which is yours?
Who is coming to the movies with us?

Some of these pronouns also function as adjectives:

Which car is yours?

And, finally, still other pronouns introduce dependent clauses, which you will learn more about in the Subordination section of this Handbook. These are the **relative pronouns:**

that   whose
what   whoever
which   whichever
who   whatever
whom

He is the one **who loves to fish.**
Her flight, **which leaves at 7:00,** will last two hours.

For more about pronouns, see The Basic Sentence section of this Handbook.

⭐ **EXERCISE 2**

Circle all of the pronouns in the following sentences.

1. He asked her about the assignment.

2. I told him to take care of himself.

3. Did you go to the opera by yourself?

4. Nobody likes that.

5. Anybody can come to the party.

6. To whom should I address the question?

7. Who lives here?

8. This is the new magazine I told her about.

9. Make sure somebody gives you the instructions.

10. Someone will win the money.

For practice identifying pronouns in sentences, go to http://www.college
.hmco.com/pic/dolphinwritertwo.

Adjectives

Adjectives modify (describe or limit) either nouns or pronouns. They tell *how
many*, *what kind*, or *which one*.

> **four** dogs
> **blue** shirt
> **those** trees
> a **snowy** evening
> **few** participants

Some adjectives introduce questions:

> **Which** one is the wrong answer?
> **Whose** coat is this?

An adjective can appear before or after the noun or pronoun it modifies:

> I will have **another** slice of **juicy** steak.
> She is a woman **possessed**.
> He is **strong** and **rugged**.

One special class of adjectives includes the words *a, an,* and *the,* which are called
articles. These words precede and point out specific people, places, things, or ideas.

> She ate **a** piece of candy.
> Tell me **the** story again.
> She drank **an** ounce of medicine to relieve **the** coughing.

Adjectives can be individual words, or they can be phrases:

> He made the decision **to go to Paris.**
> **Trying to skip,** she tripped and fell.

EXERCISE 3

Circle all of the adjectives in each of the following sentences.

1. Bill likes to take exciting, adventurous vacations.

2. Learning a new language can be a difficult task.

3. We decided to stay home and have a nice, relaxing evening.

4. She planned a backyard reception.

5. Please pass me a salt shaker.

6. The depressed student stopped attending his favorite classes.

7. Doing laundry is the biggest chore.

8. You can get some delicious white wine at that casual restaurant.

9. You sound thrilled!

10. Franklin Roosevelt had a severe case of polio.

For practice identifying adjectives in sentences, go to http://www.college.hmco.com/pic/dolphinwritertwo.

Comparative and Superlative Forms of Adjectives

Most adjectives have two additional forms. One of them, the **comparative** form, is used to compare two things. The other, the **superlative** form, is used to compare three or more things.

Adjective	*Comparative*	*Superlative*
pretty	prettier	prettiest
young	younger	youngest
smart	smarter	smartest
dull	duller	dullest
hungry	hungrier	hungriest

You usually add *–er* to the end of the adjective to create the comparative form. You add *-est* to the end to create the superlative form. However, some adjectives keep the same form and add the word *more* to create the comparative and *most* to create the superlative.

Adjective	*Comparative*	*Superlative*
grateful	more grateful	most grateful
foolish	more foolish	most foolish
determined	more determined	most determined
gorgeous	more gorgeous	most gorgeous

Still other adjectives are irregular and change forms altogether:

Adjective	*Comparative*	*Superlative*
good	better	best
bad	worse	worst

little	less	least
much, many, some	more	most
far	farther	farthest

Verbs

Verbs express *action* performed by (active verb) or received by (passive verb) the sentence's subject or describe the *state of being* of the subject (linking verb):

The girl **dove** into the pool. (active verb)
The ball **was thrown** by the boy. (passive verb)
I **am** a mother. (linking verb)
He **was** angry. (linking verb)

Most verbs that indicate a state of being are forms of the verb *to be:*

am
is
are
was
were
be
been
being

Verbs can be in the *present tense,* meaning that the action or state of being is occurring now (at the present time):

He **likes** to eat hamburgers.
They **are** excited about the new neighborhood.
She **teaches** high school English.

Verbs can also be in the *past tense,* meaning that the action or state of being occurred in the past:

He **liked** to eat hamburgers when he was a child.
They **were** excited about the new neighborhood last year.
She **taught** high school English five years ago.

Sometimes, we create the past tense by adding *-d* or *-ed* to the end of the base form of the verb. For other verbs (such as *break/broke* and *fly/flew),* the form of the word changes.

To create different tenses, one or more helping, or auxiliary, verbs are added to the base form to create verb phrases (verbs consisting of more than one word):

is	were	will
are	has	shall
am	had	could
be	have	would
was	might	

She **has spoken** to him twice.
We **might be going** to Puerto Rico.
They **will have been** in Madrid for six months this June.

EXERCISE 4

Circle the verb or verb phrase in each of the following sentences.

1. I am arriving at ten tomorrow.

2. We are happy.

3. Mei loves her cooking class.

4. I am upset about that turn of events.

5. Pat might be coming, too.

6. Kellie has decided on beige for her new carpet.

7. She has been in publishing for twenty years.

8. I swam for three hours.

9. Carmen will be asking you for a ride.

10. We jumped off the side of the ship.

For practice identifying verbs in sentences, go to http://www.college.hmco .com/pic/dolphinwritertwo.

Adverbs

Adverbs modify verbs, adjectives, and other adverbs by telling *when, where, how,* or *to what degree* an action occurred. Many adverbs end in *-ly (certainly, hungrily, really),* but not all of them do. Adverbs can appear anywhere in a sentence.

She **unhappily** does her homework. (does *how?*)
The rooster crowed **loudly.** (crowed *how?*)

We are having a party **tomorrow**. (are having a party *when?*)
We should go **home**. (go *where?*)
They were **very** surprised. (surprised *to what degree?*)

Prepositional phrases can also act as adverbs.

We threw her **into the pool**. (threw *where?*)
I want your answer **by next week**. (want *when?*)

NOTE: Answers to the question *What?* are direct objects, not adverbs.

direct object adverb

She stubbed her *toe* **on the bed post.**

The question *stubbed what?* is answered by *toe*, which is the direct object. The question *stubbed where?* is answered by *on the bed post*, which is the adverb. For more on direct objects, see The Basic Sentence section of this Handbook.

EXERCISE 5

Circle all of the adverbs in each of the following sentences.

1. She landed hard.

2. Jim will see us on Tuesday.

3. The cat ran up the tree quickly.

4. I dropped the groceries onto the floor.

5. The news made me sob uncontrollably.

6. You clearly understand the details of this project.

7. Francine will call you in a second.

8. Unfortunately, I was late for dinner.

9. Happily we began a new phase in our relationship.

10. Pierre sent the article to her.

For practice identifying adverbs in sentences, go to http://www.college .hmco.com/pic/dolphinwritertwo.

Conjunctive adverbs are transitional words that explain the close relationship between complete sentences or independent clauses joined by a semicolon.

We went to the theatre. However, the show had already started.
We went to the theatre; however, the show had already started.

Conjunctive adverbs help you show relationships such as the following:

Comparison: likewise, similarly, nevertheless
Addition: furthermore, moreover, additionally, also, further
Contrast: however, instead, nonetheless, otherwise, although
Time: meanwhile, finally, next, then, still
Result: accordingly, hence, consequently, therefore

Like adjectives, many adverbs have comparative and superlative forms. Usually, you add the word *more* to form the comparative and *most* to form the superlative.

Adverb	*Comparative*	*Superlative*
bravely	more bravely	most bravely
quick	more quickly	most quickly
rudely	more rudely	most rudely

Of all the people I spoke to, Ellen behaved **most rudely.**
This shrub grows **more quickly** than that shrub does.

Prepositions

Prepositions are words that are combined with a noun or pronoun, called an *object,* to form a *prepositional phrase,* a modifier. Many prepositions are single words that show position or time orientation:

about	before	but	into	over
above	behind	by	like	past
across	below	despite	near	through
after	beneath	down	of	to
against	beside	during	off	toward
along	between	except	on	under
among	beyond	for	onto	underneath
around	in	unlike	until	up
from	on	upon	at	with
without	out	outside		

Others are phrases:

according to	ahead of	along with
as far as	as well as	aside from
because of	in back of	in case of
in front of	in spite of	instead of
on account of	together with	with respect to

A **prepositional phrase** consists of a preposition, its object (which is always a noun or a pronoun), and the object's modifiers. For example, look at this prepositional phrase:

preposition   *object*

behind <u>the short</u> bush

           modifiers

In sentences, prepositional phrases can function as either adjectives or adverbs.

Adverb: The plate broke **into a million pieces.** (broke *how?*)
Adjective: The man **with the red coat** is my father. (*which* man?)

EXERCISE 6

In the following sentences, circle the prepositions and underline the objects of prepositions.

1. Chan went to the performance Friday.

2. He is not from New York.

3. According to Frank, that program began during Clinton's presidency.

4. Until now, there has been no warning.

5. Despite my best intentions, the pie burned in the oven.

6. That question is beyond my grasp.

7. Between the two of you, you should be able to figure this out.

8. Look for the advice columns in the front of the magazine.

9. What is a little debate among colleagues?

10. The cafeteria is inside the first door on your right.

For practice identifying prepositions in sentences, go to http://www.college .hmco.com/pic/dolphinwritertwo.

Conjunctions

Three kinds of **conjunctions** connect and show relationships between words, phrases, or clauses. The seven **coordinating conjunctions** that can link any type of equal elements together are

    and   yet
    but   so

or   for
nor

not this **but** that (words)
for love **or** for money (phrases)
We are out of mustard, **so** we cannot have hotdogs. (clauses)

Other conjunctions come in pairs; they are called **correlative conjunctions**.

both/and   not/but
neither/nor   whether/or
either/or   not only/but also

Both the parents **and** the children look forward to summer vacation.
Either you are with us, **or** you are against us.

Subordinating conjunctions connect dependent clauses to independent clauses.
A *clause* is a group of words with a subject and a verb (whereas a *phrase* is simply a group of words). An *independent clause* can stand alone as a complete sentence, but a *dependent clause* cannot. The following list contains some subordinating conjunctions that begin dependent clauses. These conjunctions link dependent and independent clauses and show their relationship to one another.

after   because   since   where
although   before   so that   whereas
as   if   unless   wherever
as if   in order that until   while
as (long) as whenever   when   than

sub. conjunction

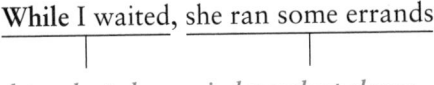

While I waited, she ran some errands.

dependent clause   independent clause

sub. conjunction

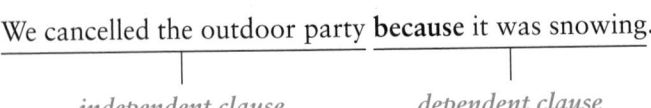

We cancelled the outdoor party **because** it was snowing.

independent clause   dependent clause

NOTE: You probably noticed that some of the words in the list of subordinating conjunctions can also be prepositions. To tell them apart, determine whether the word is part of a phrase or a clause.

She finished **before** dinner. (preposition)
She finished **before** we ate breakfast. (conjunction)

EXERCISE 7

Circle all of the conjunctions in each of the following sentences.

1. She was thinking about a career change but decided to remain in medicine.

2. Before I make a decision, let me think for a few minutes.

3. Because life is so crazy, I am going to get a planner to keep track of my appointments.

4. Whenever you think of Paris, think of me.

5. Fred will go with you as long as you promise to leave by ten.

6. Diego will have steak, and you will have chicken.

7. Neither Chris nor Isabel will bring enough money.

8. We do not have a lot of property, yet we still have to mow the grass two times a month.

9. The law will make a difference in people's lives, so you should support it.

10. We will come early or not at all.

For practice identifying conjunctions in sentences, go to http://www.college .hmco.com/pic/dolphinwritertwo.

Interjections

Interjections are words or phrases that express emotion or surprise. Mild interjections are followed by a comma; those expressing stronger emotions are followed by an exclamation point.

> **Oh,** you scared me.
> **Darn!** We lost again.
> **Hey!** He looks great.

Because of their informality, strong interjections are rarely appropriate in academic and professional writing.

For practice identifying different parts of speech in sentences, go to http:// www.college.hmco.com/pic/dolphinwritertwo.

The Basic Sentence

Now that you have reviewed the eight parts of speech, you can begin to see how words are put together to form sentences. Once you learn about basic sentences, you can begin to understand how to make your own sentences interesting, sophisticated, and grammatically correct.

A **simple sentence** is defined as one independent clause. An independent clause is a group of words that can stand alone as a separate sentence because it contains both a subject (a noun or pronoun that causes or receives [with passive verb] the action or is in some state of being) and a verb and expresses a complete thought. A simple sentence can also contain other parts of speech, such as adverbs or prepositions, but it includes just one subject-verb relationship (although the subject or verb may be compound).

Key Terms

Simple sentence = one independent clause
Independent clause = a group of words that can stand alone as a separate sentence; contains subject and verb
Subject = a noun or pronoun that causes or receives (when verb is passive) the action or is in some state of being
Verb* = a word that expresses action or describes a state of being

---

subject   verb

  We   ate   soup.

      subject   verb

The candidate spoke from the podium.

Subjects

The **subject** of a sentence is always a noun or a pronoun. So when you are trying to identify the subject, find all of the nouns and pronouns first. Next, find the verb, the word or words that express action or a state of being. (Verbs are discussed in detail later in this Handbook.) Then ask yourself, *Who or what is performing the action or expressing some state of being?* For example, look at the following sentence:

She yelled her greeting across the field.

*The next section of this Handbook will cover verbs in more detail.

There are two nouns and one pronoun in this sentence.

pronoun   *noun*   *noun*

She yelled her **greeting** across the **field.**

Therefore, the subject of the sentence is either *she, greeting,* or *field.* Now, what is the action being performed? The past-tense verb in this sentence is *yelled.* Who is doing this yelling? It is *she,* so *she* is the subject of the sentence.

Can you identify the subjects in the following sentences?

The microwave broke yesterday.

English is my favorite subject.

I cannot find my clarinet.

In the preceding sentences, the subjects are *microwave, English,* and *I.*

Locations of Subjects

You have probably noticed that subjects often appear at or near the beginning of sentences. However, they can also follow the verb:

     verb   *subject*

Here is an **apple.** (In this sentence, *here* is an adverb, not the subject.)

          verb *subject*

In the car sat the **dog.**

In questions, too, the subject may follow the verb or part of the verb:

verb *subject* *verb*

Can   **you**   go with us tomorrow?

To determine the subject in questions, you can mentally rearrange the sentence so that it is a statement:

subject   *verb*

You   can go with us tomorrow.

Now, it is easier to see that the subject is *you.*

In sentences that make commands or requests, the subject may not be stated. Instead, it is implied:

Go get my raincoat.
Please come to my party.

The subject of both of these sentences is *you.* Although the word does not appear in either sentence, it is understood that the person to whom the sentence is directed is to perform the action.

EXERCISE 8

Circle the subject in each of the following sentences. If the subject is implied, write the implied subject beside the sentence.

1. *American Idol* is my favorite television show.

2. Holly is a good neighbor.

3. You should arrive before the other guests.

4. Does Ikea carry furniture, too?

5. Please do not go into that room!

6. Alexis has many cats.

7. What did he think of my research paper?

8. The brake light on my car is out.

9. Here is my money.

10. Mind your manners.

For practice identifying the subjects of sentences, go to http://www.college .hmco.com/pic/dolphinwritertwo.

Simple and Complete Subjects

So far, you have been identifying just the simple subject of a sentence. The **simple subject** is a single noun or pronoun. A **complete subject,** on the other hand, is the subject along with all of its modifiers (the articles and adjectives that limit or describe it).

Our fabulous trip included a visit to Disney World.

In this sentence, *trip* is the simple subject, and *our fabulous trip* is the complete subject.

A desire to save lives led him to become a paramedic.

In this sentence, *desire* is the simple subject, and *a desire to save lives* is the complete subject. Note that a verbal or a verbal phrase (gerund or infinitive) can be the subject of a sentence:

Exploring the South Pole was an incredible achievement.

To learn about verbal phrases, see the Parts of Speech and The Basic Sentence sections of this Handbook.

 **EXERCISE 9**

Circle the complete subject in each of the following sentences.

1. The two rambunctious children rolled around on the floor.
2. My cell phone has not been charged in weeks.
3. Learning to swim was one of her major goals.
4. Do you not want to go with me?
5. Going to Brazil is one of my dreams.
6. This wonderful day would not have been possible without your support.
7. Rescue Heroes are my son's favorite action figures.
8. Cooking gourmet meals is my favorite activity.
9. A West Highland Terrier is a great dog.
10. Owning a horse requires a lot of money.

For practice identifying complete subjects in sentences, go to http://www
.college.hmco.com/pic/dolphinwritertwo.

Compound Subjects

A **compound subject** consists of two or more subjects joined by a coordinating conjunction such as *and, or,* or *nor.* A simple compound subject does not include modifiers.

      subject   *subject*

The **dentist** and his **wife** are going to Barcelona.

  subject   *subject*

Francisco or I will pick you up.

      subject   *subject*

Neither the **cat** nor the **dog** can swim.

EXERCISE 10

Circle all of the simple compound subjects in the following sentences.

1. In the catalog are pants and blouses.
2. Neither my son nor my daughter will eat broccoli.

3. Do you or Louise want a kitten?

4. At the side of my bed are books and an alarm clock.

5. Seeing the Taj Mahal and visiting Bangladesh are on our agenda.

6. Where are Ray and Mayako vacationing this year?

7. Watching movies and reading are my favorite activities.

8. Glenn or Mary Anne left the lights on.

9. Bad driving, speeding, and snow are to be blamed for many accidents.

10. Fishing and hiking are enjoyable summer activities.

For practice identifying compound subjects in sentences, go to http://www.college.hmco.com/pic/dolphinwritertwo.

Subjects Versus Objects of Prepositions

Often, it can be easy to confuse a subject with the object of a preposition. The object of a preposition cannot be the subject of a sentence, so you might want to identify all prepositional phrases before you decide what the subject is.

One of the girls in the class is on the gymnastics team.

The pronoun and nouns in this sentence are *one, girls, class,* and *team.* To identify the ones that are objects of prepositions, draw parentheses around all of the prepositional phrases.

One of the girls in the class is on the gymnastics team.

Now it is much easier to see that *one* is the simple subject of the sentence. Refer back to the Parts of Speech section of this Handbook for a list of typical prepositions.

EXERCISE 11

In each of the following sentences, put parentheses around all of the prepositional phrases and then circle the simple subject.

1. The flight to Cape Cod was very smooth.

2. Driving in a rainstorm is dangerous.

3. Three of my siblings go to this church.

4. Several of you can come with us.

5. The man with the cane walks along the river on Tuesdays.

6. Riding to school in the snowstorm was treacherous.

7. On the spine of the book is a drawing of a garden.

8. In the nest lay a blue robin's egg with yellow flecks.

9. I danced with joy on the dance floor.

10. In one second, the man in the box will reappear.

For practice identifying subjects in sentences with prepositional phrases, go to http://www.college.hmco.com/pic/dolphinwritertwo.

Other Elements of Simple Sentences

As mentioned earlier, a simple sentence must contain both a subject and a verb. It can also include other sentence elements such as a direct object, an indirect object, modifiers, and appositives.

Verbs

A **verb** is defined as a word or phrase that expresses action or a state of being. Verbs are discussed in detail in the next section of this Handbook. Note, however, that verbs—like subjects—can be **compound.**

They **ate** a picnic lunch and **played** Frisbee.

In this simple sentence, the subject, *They,* performs two actions, so there are two verbs.

EXERCISE 12

Circle all of the verbs in the following sentences. Watch for compound verbs, and make sure you circle all verbs.

1. Los Angeles is a very large city.

2. They danced for hours and ate a nice dinner to celebrate.

3. Maria lives next to a nuclear power plant.

4. We laughed and chatted throughout the meeting.

5. What is the answer to his query?

6. I walked very carefully on the icy sidewalk.

7. These are very small houses.

8. Her children play and scamper much of the time.

9. We surfed and swam through the waves.

10. Think about coming with me.

For practice identifying verbs in sentences, go to http://www.college.hmco .com/pic/dolphinwritertwo.

Direct Objects

A simple sentence may or may not include a direct object. A **direct object** is a noun or pronoun that answers the question *whom?* or *what?* for an active verb (when the subject performs the action).

> *verb   direct object*
>
> He **lost** his **watch.**   (lost *what?*)

To find the direct object in a sentence, you will need to locate the verb first.

> She wrote the letter with tears in her eyes.

In this sentence, the verb is *wrote*. Next ask *who* wrote to find the subject (*she*). Now ask the question wrote *what?* The answer is *letter,* which is the direct object.

> We thanked her for the generosity.

In this sentence, the verb is *thanked*. Ask *who* thanked to find the subject (*she*). When you next ask the question thanked *whom?* the answer is *her,* which is the direct object.

Direct objects can be compound, just as subjects and verbs can.

> *direct object   direct object*
>
> He sings **jazz**   and   **opera.**

> *direct object   direct object*
>
> She set the **package** and the **keys** on the table.

EXERCISE 13

Circle the direct object(s) in each of the following sentences.

1. You sang that song beautifully.

2. She made a wonderful salad.

3. Carrie loves movies.

4. The lawyer settled the case.

5. I studied English in college.

6. Esteban enjoys cooking and wrestling.

7. The church collected money for the new air conditioner.

8. Please mail this letter.

9. Lee sent an e-mail message to me.

10. Check your voice mail for messages.

For practice identifying direct objects in sentences, go to http://www.college.hmco.com/pic/dolphinwritertwo.

Indirect Objects

A simple sentence may or may not include an indirect object. An **indirect object** answers the question *to whom, for whom, to what,* or *for what?* for an active verb. You must have a direct object in a sentence in order to have an indirect object.

> *indirect object   direct object*
>
> He gave his **friend**   a   *present.*   (gave a present *to whom?*)

To find the indirect object, locate the verb first.

> My brother gave me his car.

In this sentence, the verb is *gave.* Next find the subject, *brother.* To find the direct object, you ask *brother gave what?* The answer is *car.* To find the indirect object, ask *gave to whom?* The answer is *me,* which is the indirect object.

Like direct objects, indirect objects can be compound:

> *indirect object   indirect object   direct object*
>
> My grandfather left his **children** and his **grandchildren** his *money.*

EXERCISE 14

Circle the indirect object(s) in each of the following sentences.

1. I sold my uncle my car.

2. Jorge wrote Fran a song.

3. Yuan told me the answer.

4. Michael prepared Gemma and Bob breakfast.

5. I gave her twenty dollars.

6. The nurse handed the patient a Band-Aid.

7. Please give me and Paul your e-mail address before Friday.

8. They sent the teacher a dozen roses.

9. We found the cat a home.

10. The diner left the waiter a big tip.

For practice identifying indirect objects in sentences, go to http://www
.college.hmco.com/pic/dolphinwritertwo.

Modifiers

A simple sentence may include **modifiers** (descriptive words), which are adjectives, adverbs, and prepositional phrases. You learned in the section about parts of speech that adjectives, which modify nouns or pronouns, can be single words or phrases (groups of words):

adjective

She stopped speaking to her **disloyal** friend.   (*Disloyal* describes the noun *friend.*)

adjective

The cast **of the play** took a bow.   (The prepositional phrase *of the play,* acting as an adjective, answers the question *which cast?*)

Adverbs, which modify verbs, adjectives, or other adverbs, can also be single words or phrases:

adverb

He speaks **quickly.**   (The adverb *quickly* answers the question *speaks how?*)

adverb

She studied **until dinner.**   (The prepositional phrase *until dinner,* acting as an adverb, answers the question *studied when?*)

adverb

He was **very** tired.   (*Very* is an adverb that modifies the adjective *tired.*)

For more on adjectives and adverbs, see The Basic Sentence section of this Handbook.

EXERCISE 15

Circle the adjectives and underline the adverbs in the following sentences.

1. A hard rain fell this evening.

2. The old receptionist works slowly.

3. The overworked mom fell asleep on the couch.

4. Quickly, I ran past the deserted side alley.

5. This cell phone works well.

6. Unfortunately, I cannot attend the glamorous party.

7. A smart student studies every day.

8. Five unhappy taxpayers attended the board meeting and wisely voiced dissenting opinions.

9. Do you have a carefully prepared will?

10. The weekly magazine includes extremely important articles on finance.

For practice identifying adjectives and adverbs in sentences, go to http://www.college.hmco.com/pic/dolphinwritertwo.

Appositives

Sentences might also include appositives. An **appositive** is a noun or noun phrase that follows a noun or pronoun and renames it.

appositive

Our neighbor, **Mr. Franklin,** rides a moped. (*Mr. Franklin* renames *neighbor*)

An appositive phrase includes the appositive and all of its modifiers:

appositive phrase

John, **the worst player on our team,** scored the winning basket.

In this sentence, *player* is the appositive that renames *John,* and the other words in the appositive phrase modify the word *player.*

EXERCISE 16

Circle the appositive or appositive phrase in each of the following sentences.

1. Marc Anthony, my favorite singer, was performing at the concert.
2. F. Scott Fitzgerald, a member of the "Lost Generation," wrote many wonderful novels.
3. My best friend, Alison, attends daily religious services.
4. *Trading Spaces,* a home improvement show, has been on television for many years.
5. December 7, the day of the Pearl Harbor attack, is a sad anniversary.
6. Pinot noir, an Oregon wine, became very popular because of the movie *Sideways.*
7. My favorite movie, *Vertigo,* stars Jimmy Stewart and Kim Novak.
8. Saturday, the Jewish Sabbath, is a day for going to temple.
9. *The Apprentice,* the Donald Trump reality TV show, has declined in popularity.
10. Do you, an exercise fiend, recommend spin aerobics classes?

For practice identifying appositives in sentences, go to **http://www.college .hmco.com/pic/dolphinwritertwo.**

Avoiding Sentence Fragments

To be complete, a sentence must contain a subject and a verb. When either is lacking, a sentence fragment results. Notice how both of the following examples lack subjects:

Made her sad.
Found my keys in the car.

Adding subjects, though, will make them complete:

subject

The romantic **movie** made her sad.

subject

I found my keys in the car.

The following examples lack verbs:

Only one of the dishes.
Mr. Kaplan, my favorite neighbor.

Adding verbs will make them complete:

verb

Only one of the dishes **broke.**

verb

Mr. Kaplan, my favorite neighbor, **is moving.**

For more information about avoiding other types of sentence fragments, see The Basic Sentence and the Subordination sections of this Handbook.

For practice identifying sentence fragments, go to http://www.college.hmco .com/pic/dolphinwritertwo

Verbs

In the previous sections of this Handbook, you learned that a verb is the word (or words) in a sentence that expresses action or a state of being. In this section, you will examine in more detail the various features of verbs. Knowing how to use verbs correctly will strengthen your writing significantly.

Active Verbs, Passive Verbs, and Linking Verbs

There are three kinds of verbs—active verbs, passive verbs, and linking verbs. In sentences with **active verbs,** the subject is performing an action of some kind.

She **thought** about the book.
He **studied** night and day.
They **swam** in the ocean.

In sentences with **passive** verbs, the subject is receiving the action.

The ball **was thrown** to the boy.
Those records **were misplaced** years ago.
The robber **was captured** by the police.

To learn more about active and passive verbs, see later on in this section.

Linking verbs express some state of being. They are called *linking* because they connect the subject with an adjective that describes it or a noun or pronoun that renames it.

am	appear
is	seem
are	become
was	grow
were	remain

I **am** amazed. (*amazed* describes *I*)
That man **is** a sales representative. (*sales representative* renames *man*)
They **appear** elated after the trip to Chile. (*elated* describes *they*)

NOTE: Forms of the verb *to be*—such as *am, is, are, was,* and *were*—can also be helping, or auxiliary, verbs that are used to form tenses or passive verbs. Helping verbs are discussed later in this section.

Linking verbs can also relate to the senses:

look	sound
smell	feel
taste	

Her meatloaf **smells** wonderful.
I **feel** grouchy.
The chocolate cake **tastes** like heaven.

NOTE: You can test for a linking verb relating to the senses by substituting *is* or *are*: *I am grouchy.*

> **EXERCISE 17**

In each of the following sentences, circle the verb and write on the blank whether it is an *active verb,* a *passive verb,* or a *linking verb.*

_____ 1. She eats chicken every night.

_____ 2. That novel was written in the nineteenth century.

_____ 3. That song sounds beautiful.

_____ 4. I was class president last year.

_____ 5. Li walks to work every day.

_____ 6. Donald was honored at the reception.

_____ 7. I am happy today.

_____ **8.** She sings in a Broadway show.

_____ **9.** Mary grows tired at about five o'clock.

_____ **10.** The visitor was greeted by the family.

For practice identifying kinds of verbs in sentences, go to http://www.college
.hmco.com/pic/dolphinwritertwo.

Verb Tense

Tense indicates the time in which the verb's action or state of being occurs. Two
of the basic tenses, or simple tenses, are the present tense and the past tense.
(The other is the future tense, which is discussed later in this section.) **Present-
tense verbs** indicate that the action or state of being is occurring right now or is
ongoing:

> I **am** tired.
> They **adore** each other.
> He **wants** to begin a new life.
> She **cooks** dinner on Mondays.

The form of a present-tense verb often changes based on whether the subject is
singular (meaning that it refers to just one person or thing) or *plural* (referring to
more than one thing):

Singular	*Plural*
I ask	we ask
you ask	you ask
he, she, it asks	they ask

Notice that the singular form that goes with *he, she* and *it* has an *-s* on the end.
The other forms do not. This is the case with many verbs that are *regular,* that
is, conform to predictable patterns. Here are a few more regular verbs that add
an *-s* to certain forms:

> I stop, he stops
> You ride, she rides
> I speak, it speaks

Past-tense verbs indicate that the action or state of being happened completely
in the past:

> I **was** tired after the trip.
> They **adored** each other.

He **wanted** to start a new life.
She **cooked** dinner on Mondays last year.

To form the past tense of regular verbs, you add *-ed*, *-d*, or *-ied*, depending on how the base form of the verb ends. Here are some examples:

Base Form	Past Tense
wink	winked
learn	learned
start	started
stop	stopped
rub	rubbed

When the base form of the verb ends in a consonant, you will usually add *-ed* to form the past tense. Sometimes, however, forming the past tense requires doubling the final consonant of the verb and then adding *-ed*, as you can see in the last two examples in the preceding list.

For regular verbs that end in *-e*, you will usually add just a *-d*, as you can see in the following examples.

Base Form	Past Tense
like	liked
hope	hoped
change	changed
file	filed

For regular verbs that end in *-y*, you will usually drop the *-y* and add *-ied*, as shown in the following examples.

Base Form	Past Tense
cry	cried
carry	carried
satisfy	satisfied

EXERCISE 18

In each of the following sentences, write on the blank the correct form of the verb in parentheses.

1. Yesterday, I _____ to see you. (*want*)

2. When she lived there, she _____ his shirts. (*iron*)

3. In her twenties, she _____ in New York City. (*live*)

4. Connie _____ the piano while Sam sings. (*play*)

5. Last night, she _____ a shutout. (*pitch*)

6. At this moment, I _____ you would go away. (*wish*)

7. The dog _____ constantly when she is alone. (*whine*)

8. Every evening he _____ to do one hundred pushups. (*try*)

9. I _____ some chicken last night. (*boil*)

10. Right now, I _____ an answer. (*desire*)

For practice using the correct forms of past- and present-tense verbs, go to http://www.college.hmco.com/pic/dolphinwritertwo.

Helping Verbs

The past tense and the present tense are two of the basic tenses. A third basic tense is the **future tense,** which indicates an action or state of being that will occur in the future. To indicate the future tense, as well as more specific types of tenses, helping, or auxiliary, verbs are added to the main verb. Some **helping verbs** are

is	be	may	would
am	can	might	has
are	could	must	have
was	do	shall	
were	does	should	
been	did	will	

The following lists show examples of verbs in the present, past, and future tenses:

Present Tense	*Past Tense*	*Future Tense*
like	liked	will like
hope	hoped	will hope
change	changed	will change
file	filed	will file
cry	cried	will cry
carry	carried	will carry
satisfy	satisfied	will satisfy

Using different combinations of helping verbs and main verbs allows speakers and writers of English to indicate very specifically different times when actions occur. In addition, users of these twelve different verb tenses, which are summarized in the following table, can indicate the relationship of actions that occurred at different times and can express actions in progress.

Present	I work He works They work
Past	I worked He worked They worked
Future	I **will** work He **will** work They **will** work
Present Perfect	I **have** worked He **has** worked They **have** worked
Past Perfect	I **had** worked He **had** worked They **had** worked
Future Perfect	I **will have** worked He **will have** worked They **will have** worked
Present Progressive	I **am** working He **is** working They **are** working
Past Progressive	I **was** working He **was** working They **were** working
Future Progressive	I **will be** working He **will be** working They **will be** working
Present Perfect Progressive	I **have been** working He **has been** working They **have been** working
Past Perfect Progressive	I **had been** working He **had been** working They **had been** working
Future Perfect Progressive	I **will have been** working He **will have been** working They **will have been** working

Other helping verbs express different qualities of the action (such as ability, possibility, or necessity) or are used to form questions.

> She **can work** tomorrow.
> They **do** not **work** as hard as she does.
> **Do** you **work** on Tuesdays?
> He **could be** at work.
> You **should have been working**.
> **May** I **work** with you?

The main verb combined with a helping verb or verbs is called a **verb phrase**.

EXERCISE 19

Circle the verb phrases in the following sentences.

1. She has been corresponding with me for the last few years.

2. Will he be joining you in Florida?

3. She will assist you with your job search.

4. Are you planning a big wedding?

5. I can carry your backpack.

6. They have cooked a big feast.

7. Should we travel on Sunday?

8. Did Jim believe that theory?

9. Luisa is wrapping the gift now.

10. Shall we chat?

For practice identifying verb phrases in sentences, go to http://www.college.hmco.com/pic/dolphinwritertwo.

Irregular Verbs

So far, you have focused only on regular verbs, the verbs that change forms according to predictable patterns. However, there is another category of verbs called *irregular verbs.* **Irregular verbs** are those verbs that change form in different tenses and when forming the *past participle,* the form of the verb that is used with the helping verbs *has, have,* or *had* to form the perfect tenses. Whereas the past-participle form of regular verbs is usually the same as the past-tense form (he *worked*, he has *worked*), the past-participle form of irregular verbs is different from the past-tense form (it *flew*, it has *flown*). The following list includes some common irregular verbs:

Base Form	Present Tense	Past Tense	Past Participle
arise	arises	arose	arisen
be	is	was/were	been
bear	bears	bore	borne
begin	begins	began	begun
bite	bites	bit	bitten/bit
blow	blows	blew	blown
break	breaks	broke	broken
bring	brings	brought	brought
buy	buys	bought	bought
catch	catches	caught	caught
choose	chooses	chose	chosen
come	comes	came	come
creep	creeps	crept	crept
dive	dives	dived/dove	dived
do	does	did	done
draw	draws	drew	drawn
dream	dreams	dreamed/dreamt	dreamt
drink	drinks	drank	drunk
drive	drives	drove	driven
eat	eats	ate	eaten
fall	falls	fell	fallen
fight	fights	fought	fought
fly	flies	flew	flown
forget	forgets	forgot	forgotten
forgive	forgives	forgave	forgiven
freeze	freezes	froze	frozen
get	gets	got	got/gotten
give	gives	gave	given
go	goes	went	gone
grow	grows	grew	grown
hang	hangs	hung	hung
hide	hides	hid	hidden
know	knows	knew	known
lay	lays	laid	laid
lead	leads	led	led
lie	lies	lay	lain
light	lights	lit	lit
lose	loses	lost	lost

prove	proves	proved	proved/proven
ride	rides	rode	ridden
ring	rings	rang	rung
rise	rises	rose	risen
run	runs	ran	run
see	sees	saw	seen
seek	seeks	sought	sought
set	sets	set	set
shake	shakes	shook	shaken
sing	sings	sang	sung
sink	sinks	sank	sunk
sit	sits	sat	sat
speak	speaks	spoke	spoken
spring	springs	sprang	sprung
steal	steals	stole	stolen
sting	stings	stung	stung
strike	strikes	struck	struck
swear	swears	swore	sworn
swim	swims	swam	swum
swing	swings	swung	swung
take	takes	took	taken
tear	tears	tore	torn
throw	throws	threw	thrown
wake	wakes	woke/waked	woken/waked/woke
wear	wears	wore	worn
write	writes	wrote	written

EXERCISE 20

In each of the following sentences, write on the blank the correct form of the verb in parentheses.

1. Have you _____ to her before today? (*speak*)

2. Last year, the bus company _____ better pay for its drivers. (*seek*)

3. That bridge _____ before the pavement did. (*freeze*)

4. She was grouchy when she _____ from her nap. (*arise*)

5. I have _____ out that old sweater. (*throw*)

6. She has _____ up his letter. (*tear*)

7. I have been _____ wrong. (*prove*)

8. The cat could not swim, so it _____. (*sink*)

9. I _____ you everything I had. (*give*)

10. The thief _____ that car yesterday. (*steal*)

For practice using the correct forms of irregular verbs, go to http://www.college.hmco.com/pic/dolphinwritertwo.

Verbals

As you are learning to identify verbs in sentences, you will need to watch for words called **verbals** that are parts of verbs but function as other parts of speech in sentences. There are three kinds of verbals: *infinitives, gerunds,* and *participles.*

An **infinitive** is composed of the word *to* plus the base form of a verb. Infinitives often act as nouns in sentences (but can also serve as adjectives or adverbs):

> He wanted **to drive.** (The infinitive *to drive* is the direct object that answers the question *wanted what?*)
>
> **To write** was her only goal. (*To write* is the subject of the sentence.)

Infinitive phrases, which serve as the same parts of speech that infinitives do, include the infinitive and its modifiers and objects.

> He wanted **to drive all day long.** (direct object)
> **To write a best-selling novel** was her only goal. (subject)

A **gerund,** which is a verb form with *-ing* on the end, functions as a noun.

> **Losing** was not easy. (*Losing* is the subject of this sentence.)
> He loved **swimming.** (*Swimming* is the direct object.)

A gerund phrase includes the gerund and its modifiers, objects, and/or complements. It serves the same function that a single gerund does.

> **Losing the race** was not easy. (subject)
> He loved **swimming in the pool.** (direct object)

Participles are verb forms that end in *-ing* (like gerunds) or *-ed.* They function as adjectives in sentences. Since present participles and gerunds both end in *-ing,* you have to examine a word's role in a sentence to determine which verbal it is.

> **Dancing,** he fell and broke his leg. (*Dancing* is an adjective that describes *he.*)
> Turn off the **running** water. (*Running* is an adjective that describes *water.*)
> He was a fugitive **hunted** in three states. (*Hunted* is an adjective that modifies *fugitive.*)

As you can see in the third example just listed, a participle phrase consists of a participle and its modifiers and objects. Modifiers in participle phrases can be prepositional phrases:

Dancing on the slippery floor, he fell and broke his leg.
I saw her **walking home quickly during the storm.**

EXERCISE 21

In each of the following sentences, circle the verbal and write on the blank whether it is an *infinitive*, a *gerund*, or a *participle*.

_____ **1.** The girl swimming in the lake almost drowned.

_____ **2.** Swimming is my passion.

_____ **3.** To attend college is my goal.

_____ **4.** He wanted to stay.

_____ **5.** He was an accountant courted by every major firm in Chicago.

_____ **6.** Speaking well is a goal of mine.

_____ **7.** Driving can be dangerous.

_____ **8.** A person driving slowly in the left lane should move over.

_____ **9.** She wants to learn Spanish.

_____ **10.** They regret selling their van.

For practice identifying verbals in sentences, go to http://www.college.hmco .com/pic/dolphinwritertwo.

Avoiding Sentence Fragments

Verbals cannot stand alone; they must be attached to an independent clause or they become sentence fragments. For example, read the following sentences:

sentence fragment

Dancing and singing songs. The performers put on a show.

sentence fragment

He set a goal. **To complete his master's degree.**

In both of these examples, the fragment must be attached to the independent clause (simple sentence) next to it.

For information about avoiding other kinds of sentence fragments, see later on in this section and the Subordination section of this Handbook.

For practice recognizing sentence fragments, go to http://www.college.hmco.com/pic/dolphinwritertwo.

Writing Better Sentences

You can write better, more interesting sentences of your own by paying more attention to your choice of verbs. In particular, avoid using too many passive verbs, choose strong verbs over weaker ones, and make sure the tense of your verbs is consistent.

Passive Versus Active Voice

We can write sentences in either of two basic ways. The first uses the **active voice,** in which the subject of the sentence is the performer of the action, and the verb is active. Active verbs can have direct and indirect objects that receive the action.

subject	*active verb*	*direct object*
Jin	pruned	the hedge.

The active voice is clear and direct. In **passive-voice** sentences, on the other hand, the subject is the *receiver* of the action, and the verb is passive. The object of the preposition is the performer of the action.

subject	*passive verb*	*object of preposition*
The hedge	was pruned	by Jin.

In this version, the reader has to wait until the end of the sentence to find out who performed the action. This type of sentence is less interesting and less energetic than an active-voice sentence. It also includes more words.

However, the passive voice is appropriate in some sentences. If you do not know who the performer of the action is, use a passive verb to show action done to the subject:

The dishwasher was turned off sometime during dinner.

If you do not want to reveal who was responsible for performing an action, then the passive voice will suit your purpose:

Mistakes were definitely made.

The passive voice should be used intentionally rather than accidentally. In most instances, if the subject is known, the active voice is the better, more interesting choice.

EXERCISE 22

On the blanks provided, rewrite each of the following sentences, changing passive verbs to active verbs.

1. All of the hotdogs were eaten by the men.

_____

2. The cello was played by Marisa.

_____

3. The quiz was taken by all of the students.

_____

4. The sauce was cooked by Mario.

_____

5. The damage was done by the storm.

_____

6. The bowling party was enjoyed by the guests.

_____

7. The decorations were made by the children.

_____

8. The show *Teen Titans* is watched by my son.

_____

9. The picture was drawn by me.

_____

10. The house was painted by Mike.

_____

For practice rewriting sentences with passive verbs, go to http://www.college .hmco.com/pic/dolphinwritertwo.

Strong Verbs Versus Weak Verbs

Clear, interesting writing always includes strong active verbs. The more descriptive the verb, the sharper the image it produces in the reader's mind. Compare these next two sets of examples:

Weak: At our tag sale, we **will have** free baked goods.
Strong: At our tag sale, we **will give away** free baked goods.

Weak: He **comes** in every morning.
Strong: He **saunters** in every morning.

In the second sentence of the first set of examples, a more action-oriented verb brings more vitality to the sentence. In the second sentence of the second set of examples, a more specific verb conveys more information about *how* the subject moves.

As you write, you may tend to choose weaker verbs because they are the first ones that occur to you. Using *to be* and *to have* verbs, in particular, often drains the life from a sentence.

Weak: He **was** all over the room.
Strong: He **paced** the room.

Weak: He **has** a great love for beagles.
Strong: He **adores** beagles.

Notice how the second sentence of each pair conveys the same information as the first sentence, but with more action and energy. Beware, too, of writing too many sentences that begin with *there is/are* or *it is*. Although this can sometimes be an appropriate way to begin a sentence, the sentence will automatically include a weak *to be* verb. Notice how each revision improves the sentence:

Weak: There are many reasons why I am against the idea.
Strong: I oppose the idea for many reasons.

Weak: It is important that we stop spending so much time on the computer.
Strong: We must stop spending so much time on the computer.

When you begin to see sentences in your own writing that begin with *there is/are* or *it is*, try to rewrite them to eliminate those phrases and substitute stronger verbs.

As you are evaluating the strength of your verbs, be aware that the best potential verb can be lurking elsewhere in the sentence as another part of speech:

We **have been having** quite a few calls of complaint.

This sentence relies on a weak *to have* verb. But notice the word *calls,* which is functioning as the direct object, as well as the word *complaint,* which is hiding as the object of a preposition at the very end of the sentence. Either one of these words could be revised as a better verb for this sentence:

People **are calling** often to complain.
Callers **are complaining** often.

Now look at the sentence that follows. Which word in this sentence would actually work better as the verb?

We will have a short meeting to get prepared.

If you said that the word *meeting* should be the verb, you are right. We could rewrite this sentence to read: *We will meet briefly to get prepared.*

Also, ask yourself if you are overusing adjectives and adverbs in place of strong verbs. For example, read the next sentence:

He walked quickly into the room.

The adverb *quickly* tells how he walked, but you could replace the phrase *walked quickly* with one strong verb, such as *strode, jogged,* or *trotted.* Here is another example:

Her eyes were very pretty and shiny in the sunlight.

You could substitute strong verbs for the weak verb *were* and the adjectives *pretty* and *shiny:*

Her eyes shone and sparkled in the sunlight.

EXERCISE 23

On the blank provided, rewrite each of the following sentences to include a stronger verb.

1. There was a hot breeze blowing through the window.

_____

2. I am very fond of you.

_____

3. We took a plane ride to Dublin.

_____

4. There were sharks swimming in the tank.

_____

5. There are a lot of things that we will discuss at the town board meeting.

_____

6. She cried hard and very loudly when she saw that sad movie.

_____

7. It is important that you try to understand what I am saying.

_____

8. He was dishonest when he completed his test.

_____

9. The star looked bright and glowing in the dark sky.

_____

10. There are many reasons for you to agree to this proposal.

_____

For practice rewriting sentences to include stronger verbs, go to http://www.college.hmco.com/pic/dolphinwritertwo.

Consistency in Verb Tense

As you write, you will want to make sure that you use verb tenses consistently. Mixing past and present tenses inappropriately is confusing to readers. Note the shift in verb tense in the following sentence:

    present tense   *past tense*

    We **shop** at Food Emporium, and I **bought** tomatoes.

The first verb, *shop*, should also be in the past tense (*shopped*) to match the second verb. We may shift tenses like this in casual conversation, but we should not write this way. If you start out in the past tense, remain in the past tense throughout the sentence and/or paragraph. If you start out in the present tense, remain in the present tense.

EXERCISE 24

In each of the following sentences, underline the two verbs. Then correct the second verb so that its tense matches that of the first verb. Write the corrected verb on the blank following the sentence.

1. Last summer, we went on vacation but Sally stays home. _____

2. After we left the house, the phone rings. _____

3. Every morning, I dress in a suit and chose a tie. _____

4. During the class, Ang takes notes, but Rory looked out the window. ____

5. Mark reads the map, and Abbie fiddled with the radio. _____

6. Javier bought many stocks, but Carrie invests in junk bonds. _____

7. Last year, we added on to our house and renovate our kitchen. _____

8. Each spring, she plants flowers and sowed grass seed. _____

9. Every time you try something new, you became stressed out. _____

10. We scheduled a meeting time, but my friend does not show up. _____

For practice correcting errors in verb tense consistency, go to http://www .college.hmco.com/pic/dolphinwritertwo.

Modifiers: Adjectives, Adverbs, and Prepositional Phrases

In previous sections of this Handbook, you learned that **modifiers** are either adjectives or adverbs. In this section, you will explore both kinds of modifiers in more detail.

Adjectives

Adjectives are words that describe or limit nouns. They tell *how many, what kind,* or *which one*:

blue pants	(*what kind?*)
fourth verse	(*which one?*)
that man	(*which one?*)
five students	(*how many?*)
several reasons	(*how many?*)

The **articles**—*a*, *an*, and *the*—are special kinds of adjectives that point out nouns.

> **the** door
> **a** dog
> **an** angel

Adjectives can come before the noun, or, in a sentence with a linking verb, they can follow the verb (these are called *predicate adjectives*):

> She looks **gorgeous.**
> He is **short, slim,** and **attractive.**

EXERCISE 25

Circle the adjectives in each of the following sentences.

1. She wore a huge, fuzzy coat.
2. The glistening moon shone.
3. A loud, noisy police siren woke up everyone.
4. Was that big tree cut down?
5. Are those diamond earrings rare?
6. The president looks young and vigorous.
7. Mrs. Polk is an old woman.
8. The speedy car raced.
9. Mr. Desmond is a science teacher.
10. The black terrier drools.

For practice identifying adjectives in sentences, go to http://www.college.hmco.com/pic/dolphinwritertwo.

Phrases That Function as Adjectives

Adjectives can be single words, or they can be phrases. Prepositional phrases, which you learned about in the section on parts of speech, can function as adjectives:

> the man **in the window**   (the phrase describes *man*)
> fudge **with marshmallows**   (the phrase describes *fudge*)
> the shoe **on the floor**   (the phrase describes *shoe*)

Participle phrases, too, function as adjectives in sentences. A participle is a verbal, a verb form that ends in *-ed* (past participle) or *-ing* (present participle).

> **Skipping slowly,** the child headed for the swing.
> The hamburger **topped with cheese and onions** was delicious.
> The cat **hissing its head off** belongs to me.

Notice that phrases that function as adjectives can come either before or after the noun they modify. See previous parts of this section of this Handbook for more on participles.

EXERCISE 26

Circle the phrases that function as adjectives in each of the following sentences.

1. Everyone in the room was clapping.
2. The boy next to me was crying.
3. Running quickly, the basketball players raced down the court.
4. That dessert covered in nuts and ice cream is her favorite.
5. The little girl lost in the mall was frightened.
6. Humming softly, she dusted the furniture.
7. The man in the front seat of the car is my brother.
8. The mushrooms drenched in garlic and olive oil look delicious.
9. Stopped for running a red light, the man looked nervous.
10. That hamster hiding in the cage is Ben's.

For practice identifying phrases functioning as adjectives, go to http://www.college.hmco.com/pic/dolphinwritertwo.

Avoiding Sentence Fragments

Prepositional and participle phrases cannot stand alone; they must be attached to an independent clause or they become sentence fragments. For example, read the following sentences:

> *sentence fragment*
> **Dialing the phone slowly.** Joe attempted to remember the number.

> *sentence fragment*
> She sat beside her ailing husband. **Through the whole day.**

Both of these sets of sentences must be combined to eliminate the fragments. For information about avoiding other kinds of sentence fragments, see previous parts of this section and the Subordination section of this Handbook.

For practice recognizing sentence fragments, go to http://www.college.hmco .com/pic/dolphinwritertwo.

Comparative and Superlative Forms of Adjectives

Most adjectives have two additional forms. One of them, the **comparative** form, is used to compare two things. The other, the **superlative** form, is used to compare three or more things.

Adjective	*Comparative*	*Superlative*
pretty	prettier	prettiest
young	younger	youngest
smart	smarter	smartest
dull	duller	dullest
hungry	hungrier	hungriest

Thus, we would say, for example, that the rose is *prettier* than the daisy. But we would say that the rose is the *prettiest* flower in the whole bouquet.

As you can see in the preceding list, we usually add *-er* to the end of the adjective to form the comparative form. We add *-est* to the end to form the superlative form. However, other (usually longer) adjectives stay the same and add the word *more* to form the comparative and *most* to form the superlative.

Adjective	*Comparative*	*Superlative*
grateful	more grateful	most grateful
foolish	more foolish	most foolish
determined	more determined	most determined
gorgeous	more gorgeous	most gorgeous

Still other adjectives are irregular and change forms altogether:

Adjective	*Comparative*	*Superlative*
good	better	best
bad	worse	worst
little	less	least
much, many, some	more	most
far	further	furthest

EXERCISE 27

On the blank in each sentence, write the correct form of the adjective in parentheses.

1. We are _____ to you than they are. (*grateful*)

2. I am the _____ person I know. (*determined*)

3. We have the _____ money of all of our friends. (*little*)

4. You looked the _____ of all. (*foolish*)

5. Which of the four sisters do you think is _____? (*pretty*)

6. Miguel is the _____ person I have ever met. (*gorgeous*)

7. My cat is _____ than my dog. (*calm*)

8. She is usually _____ than Bob is. (*happy*)

9. That is the _____ thing I have ever seen. (*bad*)

10. Bill Clinton is the _____ man alive, in my opinion. (*smart*)

For practice using the correct forms of adjectives in sentences, go to http://www.college.hmco.com/pic/dolphinwritertwo.

Punctuating Adjectives

When you describe a noun with more than one adjective, you may need to separate the adjectives with a comma:

It was a **cold, windy** day.
The **thin, bare** tree swayed in the wind.

However, no comma is necessary in this sentence:

Let us get some **delicious Chinese** food.

To decide whether or not to include a comma, you mentally insert the word *and* between the two adjectives. If the sentence still makes sense, you will need to add a comma.

It was a cold **and** windy day.
The thin **and** bare tree swayed in the wind.

Both of these sentences require a comma between the two adjectives.

You can also try to reverse the two adjectives. If the sentence still makes sense, insert a comma:

It was a **windy, cold** day.

Notice that the adjectives in one of the previous sentences cannot be reversed; you would not write this:

Let us get some **Chinese delicious** food.

EXERCISE 28

In each of the following sentences, circle the regular adjectives (but not the articles) and add a comma between them if necessary. If no comma is necessary, write *No comma needed* beside the sentence.

1. The balloon rose into the light blue sky.

2. We need a dependable inexpensive car.

3. He ate every bite of the hot delicious meal.

4. I bought a long thin French bread.

5. The abused scared dog ended up in the pound.

6. The bright red ball disappeared in the woods.

7. The midterm chemistry exam was difficult.

8. The patients appreciated the gentle soft touch of the dentist.

9. He could not climb the barbed wire fence.

10. The tall graceful Gothic church rose up over the skyline.

For practice punctuating adjectives in sentences, *go to* http://www.college .hmco.com/pic/dolphinwritertwo.

Adverbs

Adverbs are words that describe or limit verbs, adjectives, or other adverbs. They tell *where, when, how,* and *to what degree*:

Please put it **there**.	(put *where?*)
They will call **tomorrow**.	(will call *when?*)
She cried **loudly**.	(cried *how?*)
It is **very** lovely.	(lovely *to what degree?*)

Many adverbs end in *-ly (gracefully, terribly, poorly),* but others do not *(soon, later, so, here).*

Adverbs can appear anywhere in a sentence:

Recently I saw Jack.
He is **usually** late.
I picked up the crumbs **carefully**.

EXERCISE 29

Circle the adverbs in the sentence.

1. I am usually on time.
2. Unfortunately, he married yesterday.
3. They will call her later.
4. I will be outside tomorrow.
5. Merry blew the horn noisily.
6. We speak too quickly.
7. I am incredibly tired.
8. They are extremely kind people.
9. Put that very large cake there.
10. She does her homework carefully.

For practice identifying adverbs in sentences, go to http://www.college.hmco .com/pic/dolphinwritertwo.

Phrases That Function as Adverbs

Adverbs, like adjectives, can be single words, or they can be prepositional phrases, which you learned about in the section on parts of speech.

The meeting begins **at five o'clock.**	(begins *when?*)
He raced **around the track.**	(raced *where?*)
She jumped **with glee.**	(jumped *how?*)

EXERCISE 30

Circle the phrases that function as adverbs in each of the following sentences. Beware of phrases that are functioning as adjectives, and do not circle those by mistake.

1. My shoes are under the dresser.
2. Patrice starts violin lessons on Friday.
3. We went to the mall.
4. The power plant is beside the lake.

5. I clapped my hands with joy.

6. She attends church on Sundays.

7. He sings with enthusiasm.

8. I drove to the store.

9. On Thursdays, we go to the river.

10. She was writing on the blackboard.

For practice identifying prepositional phrases functioning as adverbs, go to http://www.college.hmco.com/pic/dolphinwritertwo.

Comparative and Superlative Forms of Adverbs

Like adjectives, some adverbs can have comparative and superlative forms. Usually, we add the word *more* to form the comparative and *most* to form the superlative.

Adverb	*Comparative*	*Superlative*
slowly	more slowly	most slowly
eagerly	more eagerly	most eagerly
politely	more politely	most politely

Of all the people I questioned, Fred responded **most eagerly.**
Traffic is moving **more slowly** today than it did yesterday.

Avoiding Double Negatives

Certain adverbs that express the negative should not be used together in the same sentence. These words include

no	never
not	hardly
none	barely
nothing	scarcely

Notice how double negatives are corrected in the following sentences:

Double negative:	I have **hardly never** been on time.
Corrections:	I have **hardly** ever been on time.
	I have **never** been on time.

Double negative:	There is **not no** jelly for the sandwich.
Corrections:	There is **not** any jelly for the sandwich.
	There is **no** jelly for the sandwich.

Using Adjectives and Adverbs Correctly

Certain adjectives and adverbs are easily confused if you are unsure about which is which. The words *good* and *well, bad* and *badly,* and *real* and *really* are the three pairs that are most often misused in sentences.

The adverbs in these pairs are *well, badly,* and *really.* (Note that *well* can be an adjective, too: the *well* child.) The last two are easy enough to remember because they both end in *-ly,* like many other adverbs.

You read **well** last night.	(**not** you read *good*)
He sings **badly.**	(**not** he sings *bad*)
She is **really** exhausted.	(**not** she is *real* exhausted)

The adjectives are *good, bad,* and *real.* They all describe nouns, but they are sometimes misused with linking verbs:

He feels **bad** about that.	(**not** he feels *badly*)
The chicken smells **good.**	(**not** the chicken smells *well*)

Notice how the meaning changes in the following sentences depending on whether you use an adjective or an adverb:

He smells bad.
He smells badly.

In the first sentence, the adjective *bad,* which follows a linking verb, communicates that the subject is the source of a foul odor. In the second sentence, the word *smells* is an active verb, and the word *badly* is an adverb. Therefore, the sentence indicates that the subject's nose is not functioning properly.

EXERCISE 31

Rewrite each of the following sentences to correct adverb errors. Check for the correct use of comparative and superlative forms, double negatives, and adjectives incorrectly used as adverbs. If the sentence needs no correction, write *No correction needed* beside it.

1. He speaks good.

_____

2. There is not nothing to say.

_____

3. She is real stressed.

_____

4. He acts bad when others question him.

_____

5. She sings poor.

_____

6. The dinner tasted good.

_____

7. There is hardly any milk left.

_____

8. That is not no way to talk about your sister!

_____

9. He types very bad.

_____

10. He was not pitching good last Tuesday.

_____

For practice correcting adverb and adjective errors, go to **http://www.college**
.hmco.com/pic/dolphinwritertwo.

Avoiding Dangling and Misplaced Modifiers

In a sentence, an adjective modifier must be placed next to the word it describes.
If a modifier is not next to the word it describes, it is called a **misplaced modifier**:

> Debbie saw a turtle **driving down the street.**

In this sentence, the phrase *driving down the street* modifies *turtle* because that is
the closest word to the phrase. Therefore, this sentence is saying that the *turtle*
was driving down the *street*. Actually, though, it was Debbie who was doing
the driving. To correct this sentence, rewrite it so that the modifier is next to the
word it is supposed to modify:

> **Driving down the street,** Debbie saw a turtle.

Misplaced modifiers can be phrases or single words. The word *only,* for example, is commonly misplaced:

> When he reached for a cookie, he **only** found crumbs.

In this sentence, the word *only* is modifying the verb, but it should be modifying the word *crumbs*. So it needs to be moved:

When he reached for a cookie, he found **only** crumbs.

If the word the modifier is supposed to be describing is not in the sentence at all, the error is called a **dangling modifier.**

Working hard for two weeks, the project was finally finished.
At four years old, my grandfather began my reading instruction.

In the first sentence, the modifier *working hard for two weeks* is incorrectly describing *project*. It was not the project that worked hard but rather the person or people who completed it. In the second sentence, the modifier *at four years old* is incorrectly describing *grandfather*. It was not the grandfather who was four years old but rather the speaker of the sentence. To correct these errors, rewrite the sentences to add the missing information:

Working hard for two weeks, **the group** finally finished the project.
At four years old, I began reading instruction with my grandfather.

EXERCISE 32

Underline each dangling or misplaced modifier in the following sentences. If a sentence does not contain a dangling or misplaced modifier, write *C* for *Correct* beside it.

1. Lying in the road, Tom saw his newspaper.
2. Growling and snarling, I backed away from the dog.
3. Hua found his coat lying on the floor.
4. The students pacing in the cage looked at the lion.
5. After breaking a leg, a cast was needed.
6. Calling daily, the telemarketers soon became very annoying.
7. Spread with garlic butter, Renee enjoyed every bite of the bread.
8. Driving home from church, the rain was heavy.
9. My friends stuck in traffic missed the whole first quarter of the game.
10. Being a nurse in a busy emergency room, stress is inevitable.

Writing Better Sentences

There are three ways to improve your writing using adjectives and adverbs:

1. Use them to add descriptive detail.
2. Do not overuse them.
3. Do not use them instead of strong verbs.

Adjectives and adverbs help create mental images in your readers' minds. Notice the difference between the following sets of sentences:

Our living room was cool.

Our air-conditioned, chilly living room was cool and inviting on a hot summer day.

The leaves fell down to earth.

The red, yellow, and gold leaves fell gently to earth.

The second sentence of each pair, which includes more adjectives and adverbs, provides more descriptive details that help readers form a sharper mental picture. Especially when you are describing something, such as an object, a person, or a place, make sure you are adding adjectives and adverbs to bring your description to life.

However, beware of overusing adjectives and adverbs. You do not want to load your sentences with too many of them, for an excess can slow the pace of your sentences and bog down your ideas with unnecessary information.

Too many modifiers:	The young lady was very lovely looking and very desirable to young men her own age.
Revision:	The men desired the lovely young lady.
Too many modifiers:	He quickly threw the ball hard, fast, and with a lot of power to first base.
Revision:	He threw the ball hard and fast to first base.

Check to make sure that your adjectives or adverbs offer essential information and that they are not simply repeating each other.

If you have a tendency to use too many modifiers, you might also be using adjectives and adverbs to convey meaning that could be more effectively delivered by strong verbs.

Too many adjectives:	We went for miles and miles down the long, lonely stretch of deserted highway.
Revision:	The lonely highway **stretched** for miles before us.

Too many adjectives: He was in the deep snow, struggling to walk.

Revision: He **trudged** through deep snow.

EXERCISE 33

Rewrite each of the following sentences to add modifiers, eliminate modifiers, or strengthen verbs as appropriate.

1. He is an enthusiastic singer and dancer, full of joy.

_____

2. The Judges are a gleeful, happy, laughing, fun-loving family.

_____

3. He sang merrily, with great happiness and joy on his face.

_____

4. Full of energy and life, the little boy jumped in a lively manner.

_____

5. Michael and I are in admiration of the one with the trophy in his hands.

_____

For practice revising sentences to use adjectives and adverbs more effectively, go to http://www.college.hmco.com/pic/dolphinwritertwo.

Subject-Verb Agreement

The Basics of Subject-Verb Agreement

Earlier in this Handbook, you learned that a basic sentence contains both a subject and a verb. This subject and verb must agree in number; that is, if the subject is singular (one person, place, thing, or idea), then the verb in the sentence must also be in its singular form. If the subject is plural (more than one person, place, thing, or idea), then the verb in the sentence must also be plural.

     singular singular

The **alarm**   **buzzes** at seven.

plural plural

The alarms buzz at seven.

The third person singular forms of regular verbs (see earlier in this section of this Handbook) end in *-s*.

She reads.
The flag waves.
The audience applauds.

Irregular verbs (such as *to be* and *to have*) have different singular and plural forms.

I am.
They are.

He has.
We have.

EXERCISE 34

In each of the following sentences, underline the simple subject(s). Then circle the verb that agrees with that subject.

1. The baby (cry, cries) all the time.

2. The printer (mangle, mangles) the paper.

3. The marchers (walk, walks) to the park.

4. I (play, plays) with my dogs every evening.

5. (Do, does) you e-mail often?

6. Darlene (perform, performs) at Stage One every weekend.

7. Loud noises (make, makes) me jump.

8. Michael and Roy (build, builds) houses for a living.

9. We (sleep, sleeps) during our commute.

10. Persian rugs (cost, costs) a lot of money.

For practice making subjects and verbs agree, go to http://www.college.hmco.com/pic/dolphinwritertwo.

Trickier Subject-Verb Agreement Situations

Basic subject-verb agreement is relatively straightforward. However, you will need to write sentences that will present you with trickier subject-verb agreement situations. They might be tricky because the subject is more difficult to find, or they may be tricky because you may not be sure whether the subject is singular or plural. The remainder of this section covers the kinds of sentences that will make choosing the correct verb a little more challenging.

Intervening Prepositional Phrases

Sometimes a prepositional phrase will separate the subject and the verb of a sentence, causing confusion about what the subject of such a sentence really is. As you learned earlier, the object of a preposition cannot be the subject of a sentence. Therefore, before you attempt to determine the right verb, you may want to physically or mentally cross out the prepositional phrase or phrases that intervene between the subject and the verb.

> *One* of the boys **plays** catch every day.

In this example, it might be tempting to conclude that *boys* is the subject of the sentence. But *boys* is the object in a prepositional phrase, and *one* is actually the subject. If you use the plural form of the verb (*play*) to make it agree with *boys*, then your sentence will contain a subject-verb agreement error. The singular subject *one* must be matched with the singular verb *plays*.

Cross out the intervening prepositional phrases in the following sentences and decide whether the subjects and verbs agree.

> People with a good sense of humor **is** exactly what we need.
> The wrinkles in her face **makes** her look wise.
> Men in tuxedoes **are** very handsome.

In the first sentence, the subject is *people* (not *sense* or *humor*, which are objects of prepositions). The subject is plural and the verb *is* is singular, so the sentence contains a subject-verb agreement error. The verb should be *are*. In the second sentence, *wrinkles* is the subject, and *face* is the object of the preposition. The singular verb *makes* does not agree with the plural subject, so it should be changed to *make*. In the last sentence, both the subject (*men*) and the verb (*are*) are plural, so the sentence is correct.

EXERCISE 35

In each of the following sentences, draw parentheses around prepositional phrases that intervene between the subject and the verb. Then circle the verb that agrees with the subject.

1. Children in daycare (learn, learns) prereading skills.

2. The bottles of ketchup (is, are) almost empty.

3. The price of oranges (has, have) increased.

4. The interest on his investments (give, gives) him extra income.

5. Gray hair on your head (looks, look) distinguished.

6. The women in the club (loves, love) to read.

7. The scent of the roses (is, are) wonderful.

8. This shelf of books (needs, need) dusting.

9. People with determination (go, goes) far in life.

10. A litter of puppies (make, makes) a mess.

For practice making subjects and verbs agree in sentences with intervening prepositional phrases, go to http://www.college.hmco.com/pic/dolphin writertwo.

Inverted Word Order

Another type of sentence that makes the subject more difficult to discern is one with inverted word order. In a sentence with inverted word order, the subject comes *after* the verb. In sentences that begin with *there* or *here,* for example, the subject follows the verb (not the order of a regular sentence):

> *verb   subject*
> Here **are** two *sandwiches* for your lunch.

The subject of this sentence is the plural *sandwiches.* The word *here* is an adverb, and the word *lunch* is the object of a preposition. Therefore, if you were to write *Here **is** two sandwiches for your lunch,* the sentence would be incorrect.

In questions, too, inverted word order can make determining the subject more challenging:

> *verb subject*
> Where **are** my *socks?*

In this sentence, the verb (*are*) must agree with the plural subject *socks. Where* is an adverb. Therefore, writing *Where **is** my socks?* would be incorrect.

Finally, there are other cases of inverted word order:

> *verb   subject*
> In the cooler **were** two *sodas* on ice.

In the cooler and *on ice* are prepositional phrases, so cross them out. Then you can see that *sodas* (plural) is the subject, so the verb must be plural, too.

EXERCISE 36

In each of the following sentences, underline the subject and then select the verb that agrees with that subject.

1. There (is, are) banging sounds coming from the attic.

2. On a hook (hangs, hang) the key.

3. Under the dresser (is, are) two pairs of socks.

4. Here (is, are) the dictionary.

5. Where (is, are) my shoes?

6. (Is, Are) there any cookies left?

7. In the closet (was, were) an umbrella.

8. In my car (was, were) two booster seats.

9. On the driveway (sits, sit) four cats.

10. There (goes, go) my friend.

For practice making subjects and verbs agree in sentences with inverted word order, go to http://www.college.hmco.com/pic/dolphinwritertwo.

Indefinite Pronouns

In the remaining tricky sentences, the subject is not necessarily difficult to find, but you may wonder whether some of the indefinite pronouns are singular or plural. As you learned in the section about parts of speech, indefinite pronouns do not refer to any particular person, place, or thing.

> **Everybody** loves cake.
> **Anybody** can come.

The indefinite pronouns become more specific when a prepositional phrase is added.

> **One** *of my friends* won the blue ribbon.
> **No one** *in the class* is prepared for the lecture.

However, many indefinite pronouns are either singular or plural, regardless of the phrases that modifies them. The singular indefinite pronouns are

one	nobody	nothing	each
anyone	anybody	anything	either
someone	somebody	something	neither
everyone	everybody	everything	

singular   *singular*
Each *of my children* **loves** me in a different way.

singular   *singular*
Everyone *in Richmond* **wants** a ticket.

The plural indefinite pronouns include

both	many
few	several

plural   *plural*
Both of my arms **were** fractured.

plural   *plural*
Several of his assertions **are** good ones.

But perhaps the trickiest of the indefinite pronouns are the ones that can be either singular or plural, depending on the noun or pronoun to which they refer (which is in the prepositional phrase following the subject). These pronouns are

all	most
any	none
more	some

Notice the difference in the following examples:

singular *singular*
Most of the *pie*   **is** gone.

plural *plural*
Most of my *friends* **know** how to paint.

singular *singular*
All of the *book*   **is** dull.

plural *plural*
All of her *relatives*   **plan** to attend the party.

EXERCISE 37

In each of the following sentences, circle the verb that agrees with the subject.

1. Each of the singers (is, are) happy to be here.

2. Everyone on our team (owns, own) a car.

3. Most of the students (arrive, arrives) on time.

4. One of his daughters (do, does) not eat meat.

5. Some of the paint (were, was) peeling.

6. Several of the cats (has, have) distemper.

7. Most of the work (is, are) complete.

8. Both of her sons (go, goes) to Rotary Club meetings every year.

9. Neither of us (support, supports) his proposal.

10. Some of the members (has not, have not) attended in a while.

For practice choosing verbs that agree with indefinite pronoun subjects, go to http://www.college.hmco.com/pic/dolphinwritertwo.

Compound Subjects

You have learned that a compound subject consists of two or more subjects joined by a coordinating conjunction (*and, or, either/or, neither/nor*). The use of this conjunction determines whether you use the singular form of the verb or the plural form of the verb. If the word *and* joins the two subjects, they are plural, and you use the plural form of the verb:

The stars *and* the moon **are** twinkling tonight.
My son *and* I **love** to surf.

However, if the subjects are joined by *or, either/or,* or *neither/nor,* the verb agrees with the subject that is closest to the verb:

singular subject   plural subject

The **nanny** *or*   the **children** always **eat** the pizza.

singular subject   plural subject

Either **Michael** *or* his **brothers clean** the yard every day.

plural subject   singular subject

Neither the **monkeys** *nor* the **elephant is** in this particular show.

EXERCISE 38

In each of the following sentences, circle the verb that agrees with the correct subject.

1. Either the cheerleaders or the mascot (get, gets) the team excited.
2. Neither the beach nor the lake (is, are) an option for us.
3. The parents and their children (attend, attends) tennis camp.
4. Elena and her son (enjoy, enjoys) opera.
5. Neither the painters nor the plumber (has, have) arrived yet.
6. Mittens or a pair of gloves (is, are) necessary in cold weather.
7. May and her family (move, moves) every few years.
8. Cash or checks (is, are) acceptable forms of payment.
9. Neither Jim nor his parents (is, are) willing to give an inch.
10. The editor or the proofreaders (find, finds) errors in manuscripts.

For practice choosing verbs that agree with compound subjects, go to http://www.college.hmco.com/pic/dolphinwritertwo.

Singular Nouns That End in *-s*

Some nouns end in *-s* as do plural nouns, but they are nevertheless considered singular. The following list includes some examples of these words.

physics	series
news	politics
sports	measles
economics	

The news **is** not positive.
The series **starts** tonight on NBC.

Collective Nouns

Collective nouns are those that refer to a group of people or things (*team, class, crowd, group, company, audience, family, jury, gang, faculty*). If the subject of the sentence is a collective noun and if the group is acting together as one unit, then use a singular verb:

The squad **practices** every evening.
The audience always **snickers** at that joke.

However, if the members of the group are acting individually, use a plural verb.

The family **go** to different parts of the house after dinner.

Sums of money and measurements are also thought to be singular when they are considered one unit.

Ten *dollars* for a gourmet lunch **is** a high cost.
Fourteen *miles* **is** the length of the path.

Titles and Other Proper Nouns

Titles of poems, novels, short stories, plays, films, and other works are always considered to be singular.

Tom Sawyer **is** Mark Twain's best book.
The Jetsons **is** my favorite cartoon.

A proper noun, such as the name of a person, place, or thing, is also considered to be singular.

Wendy's **is** open until ten o'clock.
The southeast United States **lies** in the tornado's path.
Disney Studios **is** releasing the feature this summer.

EXERCISE 39

In each of the following sentences, circle the verb that agrees with the subject.

1. Physics (is, are) a challenging discipline for me.
2. The Academy Awards (is, are) the biggest event during the awards season.
3. The faculty (meets, meet) once a month.
4. Two weeks (is, are) not a long time.
5. Twenty pounds (is, are) her weight loss goal.
6. Congress (is, are) in session now.
7. That group (take, takes) a short dinner break every night.
8. The editorial staff (make, makes) decisions about marketing, too.
9. Economics (is, are) an interesting subject.
10. The *Times* (arrive, arrives) on my driveway every day.

For practice making verbs agree with singular nouns that end in -s, collective nouns, and proper nouns, go to http://www.college.hmco.com/pic/dolphin writertwo.

Pronouns and Pronoun Agreement

In the section about parts of speech, you learned that a pronoun is a word that is used in place of a noun or another pronoun (called its *antecedent*). In this section, you will learn how to choose the correct pronouns for your sentences.

Pronoun Case

The **case** of a pronoun refers to the form it takes as determined by its function in a sentence. A pronoun that functions as a subject or refers back to the subject (in a sentence with a linking verb) is in the **subjective case.** The subjective pronouns are

I	we
he	they
she	who
you	whoever

In the following sentences, the subjective pronouns are functioning as subjects:

You and **I** should have dinner.
Who is at the door?

In these sentences the pronouns follow a linking verb and rename the subject, so they are also in the subjective case:

The winner was **he.**
It is **I** at the door.

Subjective pronouns also follow the words *than* or *as* in a comparison:

You are smarter than **I.** (The verb *am* is implied after the word *I* because *than I am* is a dependent clause.)
We are as capable at tennis as **they.**

We do not usually speak this formally, though, so you will often hear "You are stronger than *me.*" However, this usage is incorrect in writing.

In the next set of examples, the pronouns are a subject followed by a noun appositive (*players*) and an appositive renaming the subject, so they, too, are subjective:

We players are having a fund drive.
The volunteers—Ann, Jin, and **I**—will gather the newspapers.

See earlier in this section of this Handbook for more on appositives.

The **objective pronouns** function as direct objects, indirect objects, or objects of prepositions, or they refer back to objects. The objective pronouns are

me	us
him	you
her	them
it	whom, whomever

direct object

I saw **her** at the gym this morning.

indirect object

The child gave **me** a big wave.

object of preposition

To **whom** did you send the e-mail message?

direct object with appositive (boys)

They sent **us** boys to the auditorium.

Therefore, if you figure out the role that the pronoun is playing in the sentence, you can determine whether you should use the subjective or objective case. For example, look at the following sentence. What part of speech is the pronoun in question?

Mr. Meyer and (I, me) presented the information to the class.

This sentence has a compound subject, and the pronoun is the second half of that subject. Therefore, we must choose the subjective case pronoun, *I*. Now read another example:

For (he, him) and (I, me), this is a wonderful day.

In this sentence, the two pronouns are objects of the preposition *for*. Thus, we must use the objective case pronouns, *him* and *me*. Here is one final example:

(We, Us) students want to go home now.

In this sentence, the pronoun is the subject and is followed by an appositive, *students*, so we must use the subjective *we*. If you pretend that the word *students* is not there, you can see that *We want to go home now* is correct.

Of all of these pronouns, *who* and *whom* tend to be two of the most confusing. The difference between these two words is discussed later in this Handbook.

EXERCISE 40

In each of the following sentences, circle the correct pronoun.

1. She and (I, me) enjoy dancing.

2. Ling and (I, me) do not know each other.

3. The relationship between Alison and (I, me) is just beginning.

4. (We, Us) members have a right to ask for a vote.

5. (She, Her) and (I, me) will be going to Montreal in June.

6. The rat bit (me, I).

7. I phoned (her, she) last night.

8. The time off was necessary for (she, her) and (I, me).

9. Felipe gave (me, I) a present for my birthday.

10. They told (us, we) the story.

The **possessive pronouns** indicate possession, or ownership. The possessive pronouns are

my	our
mine	ours
your	your
yours	yours
his	their
her	theirs
hers	
its	

Julie has finished writing **her** paper.
Hernando gave me **his** granola bar, and I gave him **my** pear.

For practice choosing the correct pronoun case, go to http://www.college
.hmco.com/pic/dolphinwritertwo.

Pronoun Consistency

When you write, you take a certain **point of view,** or perspective. In the *first-person* point of view, you use the pronouns *I* and *we* because you describe the events from your own perspective. In the *second-person* point of view, you use the pronoun *you* because you are usually directing the reader to do something. In instructions, for example, you would write "you do this" and "you do that." In the *third-person* point of view, you stick with *he, she, they,* and *it,* and you avoid the first- and second-person pronouns.

If you start out in one point of view, remain consistently within that point of view, and do not shift from one to another. Notice how the point of view changes in the following sentences:

> *first person*   *second person*
>
> When **I** applied for my passport, **you** had to stand in line for hours.

>   *first person*   *first person*
>
> Although **we** dislike getting winded, **we** signed up for a class at the gym
>   *second person*
>
> because **you** have to take it.

> *second person*   *first person*
>
> **You** do not want to feed the cat until **we** find out if it has a home.

To remain consistent, change the *you* to *I* in the first sentence and the *you* to *we* in the second sentence. In the third sentence, you can change the *you* to *we* or the *we* to *you.*

EXERCISE 41

In each of the following sentences, cross out the pronoun that is incorrect, and write the correct pronoun above it, also making any other necessary changes.

1. They know about her inability to make a decision, so you do not ask for her opinion.

2. She is going to the spa because you need to relax.

3. If you know that dog is mean, one should avoid it at all costs.

4. We like swimming in the lake, but you really need to watch out for the electric eels in the water.

5. Although we do not know how to sing, we signed up for singing class so I can learn the basics about breathing and phrasing.

For practice revising sentences containing inconsistent pronouns, go to http://www.college.hmco.com/pic/dolphinwritertwo.

Clear Pronoun Reference

Another pronoun problem is unclear reference. A pronoun always refers to a noun or another pronoun, and this word is called its **antecedent.** If a pronoun's antecedent is not clear, confusion can result:

Bob told his father that **he** had acted like a jerk.

In this sentence, does the pronoun *he* refer to Bob or to his father? Is Bob criticizing his father's behavior, or is Bob assessing his own actions? Because there are two possible antecedents for the pronoun, the meaning of this sentence is in question. To correct it, you would probably have to rewrite the sentence:

Bob said to his father, "I acted like a jerk."

Here is another sentence that contains an unclear reference:

The girl on the bicycle ran into a tree, but **it** was barely damaged.

In this sentence, the pronoun *it* could refer to the bicycle or to the tree. To correct the unclear reference, rewrite the sentence:

The girl ran into the tree, but her bicycle was barely damaged.

Possessive pronouns, too, can be unclear:

She let her daughter wear **her** mink coat to the opera.

Does the mink coat belong to the mother or the daughter? The pronoun *her* does not make the meaning clear. Here is one way to correct the problem:

She wore her mother's mink coat to the opera.

Also, do not use a pronoun that has no antecedent:

I took my car to be fixed, and **they** said I need a new starter.

Who is *they* in this sentence? Readers can infer that this pronoun refers to the mechanics who examined the car, but they cannot be sure. To correct the unclear reference, rewrite the sentence, eliminating the unclear pronoun altogether if necessary:

I took my car to be fixed, and the mechanics said I need a new starter.

 **EXERCISE 42**

Rewrite each of the following sentences to eliminate unclear pronoun reference.

1. Rick told his neighbor that his car needed to be fixed.

2. The watermelon hit the floor, but it was dented only slightly.

_____

3. He let his son use his car.

_____

4. I had an appointment, but they told me I would have to wait.

_____

5. Barbara told her daughter that she needed a manicure.

_____

6. Juan took his son to the sporting goods store so that he could buy a jersey.

_____

7. Jim told his brother that his car needed an oil change.

_____

8. Colleen put her toe through her stocking, but it was not that big.

_____

9. Hiroko wanted to buy the new toy for her son, but they said it was not in stock.

_____

_____

10. I made a motion to the board, but they said it was not made at the right time.

_____

For practice eliminating unclear pronoun reference, go to http://www.college.hmco.com/pic/dolphinwritertwo.

Pronoun Agreement

A pronoun must agree with, or match, the gender and the number of its antecedent. **Gender** refers to whether the antecedent is masculine (*he/him/his*), feminine (*she/her/her*), or neuter (*it/it/its*). In the following sentences, notice how the gender of the pronoun matches the gender of the italicized antecedent:

His *wife* gave **her** vow.
The *man* driving the car said **he** was exhausted.
The *tree* has lost most of **its** leaves.

Number refers to whether the antecedent is singular or plural. If the antecedent is singular, use a singular pronoun, and if the antecedent is plural, use a plural pronoun:

singular   singular

The *professor* dropped **his** pencil.

plural   plural

The *men* are packing **their** bags right now.

singular   singular

Her *hair* has lost **its** sheen.

Basic pronoun agreement is relatively straightforward. However, you will need to write sentences that will present you with trickier pronoun-agreement situations. They are usually tricky because you may not be sure whether the antecedent is singular or plural. The remainder of this section covers the kinds of sentences that make choosing the correct pronoun a little more challenging.

Indefinite Pronouns

Earlier in this Handbook, you learned that the indefinite pronouns can make subject-verb agreement trickier. When an indefinite pronoun is an antecedent, choosing the pronoun that agrees with it is more challenging. However, you can apply what you have already learned about indefinite pronouns to pronoun agreement.

Most of the indefinite pronouns are singular:

one	nobody	nothing	each
anyone	anybody	anything	either
someone	somebody	something	neither
everyone	everybody	everything	

Therefore, you will use a singular pronoun to match an antecedent that is one of the indefinite pronouns in the preceding list. When you know the gender of the antecedent, choose the appropriate singular pronoun:

Each of the men broke **his** promise.
Neither of the boys knows where **he** stands.

To avoid gender bias when the gender of the indefinite pronoun is either unknown or mixed, writers often use the phrases *he or she* and *his or her:*

Everyone thinks **he or she** would love to win lots of money.
One of the students forgot to write **his or her** name on the application.

In spoken conversation, you may hear (and say), "Each of the men broke *their* promises" and "Everybody paid *their* dues on time." However, both of these sentences contain pronoun-agreement errors, so we do not write this way. If you think that writing *he or she* and *his or her* is cumbersome, then rewrite the sentence with a plural subject. Then you can use *they* or *their* as the pronoun:

All *people* think **they** would love to win lots of money.

The indefinite pronouns that are plural include

both	many
few	several

You use plural pronouns with these subjects:

Both of the ladies wore **their** red coats.
Few remembered what **they** were supposed to bring to the dinner.

Finally, remember that some indefinite pronouns can be singular or plural, depending on the noun or pronoun to which they refer. These pronouns are

all	most
any	none
more	some

Most of the *books* are missing **their** spines.
Most of the *soil* had lost **its** ability to absorb water.

EXERCISE 43

In each of the following sentences, underline the antecedent. Then circle the pronoun that agrees with that antecedent.

1. Somebody left (his or her, their) paper on the seat.

2. Everybody misses (his or her, their) train connection now and then.

3. Neither of the boys found (his, their) hockey stick.

4. Everyone thinks that (he or she is, they are) a good conversationalist.

5. Most of them like to think that (he or she is, they are) right.

6. Her dog has lost (her, its) hair.

7. Anyone who attends must bring (their, his or her) raincoat.

8. One of the Boy Scouts has lost (his, their) radio.

9. Each of the women got (her, their) pedicure.

10. Everybody in our town acknowledges (his or her, their) neighbors.

For practice making pronouns agree with indefinite pronoun antecedents, go to http://www.college.hmco.com/pic/dolphinwritertwo.

Compound Subjects

As with subject-verb agreement, if the word *and* joins two antecedents, they are plural, and you use the plural form of the pronoun:

Troy *and* the rest of the team brought in presents for **their** coach.
The man *and* the woman looked at **their** schedules.

However, if the antecedents are joined by *or, either/or,* or *neither/nor,* the pronoun agrees with the antecedent that is closest to it:

　　　　　　plural antecedent　　*singular antecedent singular pronoun*
Neither the **dogs**　　*nor*　　the **cat**　　would stop **its** crying.

Collective Nouns

Collective nouns are those that refer to a group of people or things (*team, class, crowd, group, company, audience, family, jury, gang, faculty*). If the antecedent is a collective noun and if the group is acting together as one unit, then use a singular pronoun:

The *flock* fixed **its** attention on the group of photographers.

However, if the members of the group are acting individually, use a plural pronoun:

The *flock* scattered in different directions to save **their** own hides.

EXERCISE 44

In each of the following sentences, underline the antecedent. Then circle the pronoun that agrees with that antecedent.

1. The jury has reached (its, their) verdict.

2. The audience clapped (its, their) hands wildly.

3. The Congress will reveal (its, their) decision later today.

4. The faculty are concerned about (its, their) pay raises.

5. The family (are, is) vacationing at Yellowstone Park this year.

6. The town council decided to let the citizens know about (its, their) qualifications.

7. The school board makes (its, their) recommendations known through the local paper.

8. The baseball team practices at (its, their) school's field on Saturdays.

9. The fundraising committee has a lot on (its, their) agenda.

10. The crowd left the stadium and approached (its, their) parked cars.

For practice making pronouns agree with compound subjects and collective nouns, go to http://www.college.hmco.com/pic/dolphinwritertwo.

Coordination

The Compound Sentence

In previous sections of this Handbook, you worked on mastering the simple sentence, an independent clause. In this section, you will focus on the compound sentence. Learning to use compound sentences correctly will help you elevate the complexity and sophistication of your writing.

Compound Elements

In previous chapters, as you learned about the elements of the basic sentence, you encountered various kinds of compound elements. As you recall, *compound* means more than one. Thus, subjects are compound if there are two or more nouns or pronouns performing the action (active verb), receiving the action (passive verb), or existing in some state of being (linking verb).

  subject   *subject* *verb*

  Jack and his **uncle** *ride* snowmobiles every Saturday.

A verb is compound if the subject performs or receives more than one action:

  subject *verb*   *verb*

  She **polished** the silver and **vacuumed** the floor.

Likewise, direct objects, indirect objects, antecedents of pronouns, and other sentence elements can be compound.

In the next sections, you will see how sentences can be compound, and you will learn to distinguish compound sentences from compound elements in a simple sentence.

EXERCISE 45

In each of the following sentences, circle the two words that form a compound element. Then, on the blank, identify the element as CS (compound subject) or CV (compound verb).

___ **1.** The children cried and ran into the other room.

___ **2.** My brother and I enjoy playing poker.

___ **3.** Dogs and cats are nice pets to have.

___ **4.** We swam and snorkeled in Jamaica.

___ **5.** Mark composes music and sings his own songs.

___ **6.** Luisa builds and paints bird houses.

___ **7.** John and Mary Beth are not speaking right now.

___ **8.** The dog leaped from the boat and swam to shore.

___ **9.** My father and brother are very close.

___ **10.** Music and art are my favorite hobbies.

For practice identifying compound elements in sentences, go to http://www .college.hmco.com/pic/dolphinwritertwo.

Three Kinds of Compound Sentences

Compound sentences contain at least two different independent clauses. An **independent clause** contains a subject and a verb and expresses a complete thought, so it could stand alone as a complete sentence.

    subject verb   *subject   verb*
    Ratings were low, so the network canceled the show.

   subject verb   *subject verb*
   He *proposed* to her; **she**   *said* no.

   subject verb   *subject verb*
   She   *hates* hip-hop music; however, **she**   *went* to the concert anyway.

EXERCISE 46

In each of the following compound sentences, circle the subjects and underline the verbs.

1. Rhonda specializes in pediatrics, but she practices gerontology as well.

2. We went swimming; they went hiking.

3. I got a manicure; my nails looked pretty.

4. The car died, for it was old and unreliable.

5. The plants needed water, so Emilio got the hose.

6. We went out to lunch, and we talked for two hours.

7. James traveled to Paris; he brought back lots of magazines.

8. Your dog needs a rabies shot, or it will lack protection from the disease.

9. The plates are on the table, and the flatware is on the counter.

10. I need your help; I cannot do this alone.

For practice identifying subjects and verbs in compound sentences, go to http://www.college.hmco.com/pic/dolphinwritertwo.

Because it contains two separate independent clauses, a compound sentence can form two complete sentences that could each be written separately:

Ratings were low. The network canceled the show.
He proposed to her. She said no.
She hates hip-hop music. However, she went to the concert anyway.

However, the two independent clauses are combined to form one longer compound sentence because there is some relationship between the two. In the first example, for instance, the first event is the *cause* of the second event, so the clauses can be linked together with a coordinating conjunction (*so*) preceded by a comma to indicate this relationship. We could separate these two independent clauses and write them as two simple sentences, but linking them together increases the sophistication of the writing. It also prevents readers from having to determine on their own whether or how the two simple sentences are related.

There are three ways to form compound sentences. You can join independent clauses with a comma and a coordinating conjunction, with a semicolon followed by a conjunctive adverb, or with only a semicolon.

Independent Clauses Joined by a Coordinating Conjunction

The first way to form a compound sentence is to join two independent clauses with a coordinating conjunction. You know that the conjunctions *and, or, for, but, so, nor,* and *yet* link together words, phrases, clauses, and sentences. These words are known as the *coordinating conjunctions* because they join coordinate, or equal, elements. Two coordinate, independent clauses can be joined with one of these conjunctions preceded by a comma:

subject verb   *subject verb*

    We *stopped* at the bakery, <u>and</u> then we   *went* to the bank.

subject verb   *subject verb*

    I   *want* to have a dog, <u>but</u> I   *know* nothing about animals.

subject verb   *subject verb*

    You *can spend* your gift certificate now, <u>or</u> you *can save* it for something better.

Each of the coordinating conjunctions indicates a certain type of relationship.

Addition:	*and*
Cause or effect:	*for, so*
Contrast:	*but, yet*
Choice or alternative:	*or, nor*

EXERCISE 47

On the blank in each of the following sentences, insert the word *and, or, for, but, so, nor,* or *yet* to indicate the relationship between the two independent clauses.

1. I do not think I should go, ____ I am going to stay home.

2. Fred walks to work, ____ he is in very good shape.

3. Rose loves baseball, ____ her husband finds it boring.

4. We went to the shore, ____ we also went to the spa.

5. He will not exercise, ____ will he eat right.

6. Either you are with us, ____ you are against us.

7. He is not sure of his career goal, ____ he is majoring in business.

8. The rain kept us from cleaning up the backyard, ____ it was far too soggy.

9. I will try my best to get you the singing job, ____ I cannot promise anything.

10. Would you like paper, ____ would you like plastic?

For practice using coordinating conjunctions to indicate relationships, go to http://www.college.hmco.com/pic/dolphinwritertwo.

When you join two independent clauses with a coordinating conjunction, notice that you add a comma *before* (and not after) the conjunction.

Incorrect: The day is rainy and, the streets are wet.
Correct: The day is rainy, and the streets are wet.

You would not, however, use a comma when using a coordinating conjunction to connect two subjects, two verbs, or two other compound elements.

EXERCISE 48

On the blanks provided, write compound sentences that are correctly punctuated.

1. _____ and _____ .
2. _____ so _____ .
3. _____ but _____ .
4. _____ or _____ .
5. _____ for _____ .
6. _____ nor _____ .
7. _____ yet _____ .

For practice writing and punctuating compound sentences with coordinating conjunctions, go to http://www.college.hmco.com/pic/dolphinwritertwo.

Independent Clauses Joined by a Semicolon and Conjunctive Adverb

The second way to join two independent clauses involves using a semicolon followed by a **conjunctive adverb** or transitional phrase. Some of these are

also	moreover
as a result	nevertheless
consequently	next
finally	meanwhile
furthermore	on the other hand
hence	otherwise
however	similarly
in addition	soon

indeed	still
in fact	then
instead	therefore
likewise	thus

He is very smart; **in fact,** he graduated as valedictorian of his class.
The rain was very heavy; **as a result,** the basement flooded.
She has a law degree; **however,** she does not work as an attorney.

In these compound sentences, the semicolon connects the two independent clauses. However, the conjunctive adverb or transitional phrase (which is followed by a comma) clarifies the relationship between the two clauses. (If you ended the first independent clause with a period and began the second sentence with the conjunctive adverb or phrase, you would achieve the same effect.) For example, the adverbs and phrase *as a result, consequently, therefore,* and *thus* all indicate a cause/effect relationship. The adverbs and phrase *however, instead, nevertheless,* and *on the other hand* signal contrast. The adverbs *finally, next,* and *soon* indicate a time order relationship.

Your choice of a conjunctive adverb matters, for you can change the meaning of a sentence by changing just the conjunctive adverb:

They married without knowing each other well; **then,** they divorced ten years later.

In this sentence, the word *then* indicates only a time relationship between the two clauses. Notice how the meaning changes in the next compound sentence:

They married without knowing each other well; **consequently,** they divorced ten years later.

In this sentence, the word *consequently* suggests that their marrying without knowing each other well was the *cause* of the breakup.

EXERCISE 49

On the blank in each of the following sentences, insert one of the conjunctive adverbs or transitional phrases in the list on pages 491–492 to indicate the relationship between the two independent clauses.

1. She wants to compete in the triathlon; _____, she is running and biking every day.

2. We were not able to attend the board meeting; _____, we could not participate in the discussion.

3. The child expected to enjoy the trip; _____, he quickly became homesick.

4. Pedro finally quit smoking; _____, he has begun working out.

5. I would love to have you sing at my party; _____, Jackie will sing!

6. The school is having a casino night to raise money; _____, the church is having a fundraiser, too.

7. We could go now; _____, there is no harm in waiting.

8. Eating a balanced diet is good for your health; _____, eating well helps you manage your weight.

9. Land prices have risen in the past year; _____, property once worth $100,000 is now worth two times that!

10. I could not attend my daughter's piano recital; _____, I did not hear her new song.

For practice using conjunctive adverbs to indicate clause relationships, go *to* http://www.college.hmco.com/pic/dolphinwritertwo.

When you join independent clauses with a semicolon followed by a conjunctive adverb, the semicolon comes *before* the conjunctive adverb and a comma comes *after* it:

Incorrect: The painting is unusual, nevertheless, I like it.
Correct: The painting is unusual**; nevertheless,** I like it.

Do not make the mistake of using a comma in place of the semicolon, or you will create an error called a *comma splice,* which is discussed later in this chapter.

Independent Clauses Joined by a Semicolon

The third way to form a compound sentence is to join independent clauses with just a semicolon:

We have to leave now; it is time for dinner.
He did not want to seem rude; he fibbed about liking her new house.

Notice that when a semicolon joins independent clauses, the second clause begins with a lowercase letter because it is still part of the same sentence.

Before you link two independent clauses with just a semicolon, make sure that the two ideas they express are so closely related that they belong in a single sentence. One clause may show a cause and the other an effect. The two ideas stated in the clauses may be contrasting. There could be a time relationship, and so on. Then consider whether you should provide a conjunctive adverb that more explicitly states the relationship, as discussed in the previous section. Your reader may or may not discern the relationship you mean to suggest, so providing an adverb will remove the guesswork:

> He did not want to seem rude; **therefore,** he fibbed about liking her new house.

Adding the conjunctive adverb *therefore* makes the relationship between the two independent clauses more clear.

Distinguishing Compound Elements from Compound Sentences

At the beginning of this section, you reviewed compound sentence elements such as compound subjects, compound verbs, and compound direct objects. Now that you know how to write compound sentences, you can practice distinguishing them from a basic, or simple, sentence containing a compound element. Knowing the difference will ensure that you punctuate your sentences correctly.

Notice the difference between the following sentences:

> *subject verb*   *verb*
> The **day** *started* out rainy but then *cleared*.

> *subject verb*   *subject verb*
> The **day** *started* out rainy, but then the **sky** *cleared*.

Should the first sentence have a comma after the word *rainy* and before the coordinating conjunction *but*? No, it should not; the first sentence is not a compound sentence. It contains a compound verb: the subject is *day*, and the two verbs are *started* and *cleared*. Because it does not contain two different subject-verb relationships, each in a separate independent clause, we do not add a comma before the conjunction.

EXERCISE 50

For each of the following sentences, write **CS** on the blank if the sentence is compound. Write **CE** on the blank if the sentence contains a compound sentence element but is not a compound sentence. Then add missing punctuation as needed.

___ **1.** Josie and Angelo graduated with honors.

___ **2.** They worked steadily and stopped for only two short breaks.

___ **3.** Sheng studied but did not do very well on the exam.

___ **4.** I asked her and she said yes.

—— **5.** The sun is shining and the flowers are blooming.

—— **6.** He sings well but does not play an instrument.

—— **7.** It might be the right time to move but I still am not convinced.

—— **8.** Joel either jogs or lifts weights every day.

—— **9.** I did the dishes and my son swept the floor.

—— **10.** Either you will do well or you will not do well.

For practice distinguishing and punctuating compound sentences and compound elements, go to http://www.college.hmco.com/pic/dolphinwritertwo.

Avoiding Comma Splices and Run-ons When Writing Compound Sentences

Now that you have learned how to write the three different kinds of compound sentences, you can learn to recognize two serious errors—the comma splice and the run-on sentence—that occur when compound sentences are not correctly punctuated.

The Comma Splice

A **comma splice** occurs when a comma is used where a semicolon should be:

> He is holding a full house, he definitely has the winning hand.
> She made the salad, meanwhile, he got the drinks.

In both of these sentences, only a comma separates the two independent clauses. A comma is appropriate if the clauses are joined with a coordinating conjunction; however, neither of these two includes a conjunction. In the first sentence, the comma must be replaced with a semicolon:

> He is holding a full house; he definitely has the winning hand.

In the second example, which includes the conjunctive adverb *meanwhile*, the first comma must be changed to a semicolon:

> She made the salad; meanwhile, he got the drinks.

You can also correct a comma splice by replacing the incorrect comma with a period and creating two separate sentences. However, the comma error is usually an indication that the two independent clauses are related, so it is often more appropriate to link them in some type of compound sentence.

EXERCISE 51

On the blank before each of the following sentences, write **CS** if the sentence contains a comma splice and **Correct** if it is correct. In those sentences you have labeled **CS**, circle the commas that must be changed to semicolons.

_____ 1. The car is out of gas, it will not start.

_____ 2. The beginning of that movie was interesting, but I lost interest in the story.

_____ 3. The time to make a move is here, so you should make a decision.

_____ 4. The grill is ready, put on the hotdogs.

_____ 5. *Extreme Makeover* is my favorite show, do you watch it?

_____ 6. It is beginning to look like rain, get out your umbrellas!

_____ 7. I buy my plants around the second week of May, that is the best time to buy them.

_____ 8. The garbage needs to go out, for it is very smelly.

_____ 9. I need to change the litter box, and you need to bathe the cat.

_____ 10. The dishwasher needs repair, it is making a weird noise.

For practice identifying and correcting comma splices, go to http://www.college.hmco.com/pic/dolphinwritertwo.

The Run-on Sentence

A **run-on sentence**, which is also known as *a fused* sentence, occurs when there is no punctuation at all between two independent clauses:

We could go sailing we could go skiing.
She would love to visit Madrid she does not have a valid passport.
Lasagna is his favorite food he eats it often.

These three sentences each contain two independent clauses that are run together without any punctuation.

If we want to write them as compound sentences, we can correct them in three ways. First of all, we could simply add a semicolon between the two independent clauses:

We could go sailing; we could go skiing.
She would love to visit Madrid; she does not have a valid passport.
Lasagna is his favorite food; he eats it often.

Or we could add a comma and an appropriate coordinating conjunction:

We could go sailing, **or** we could go skiing.
She would love to visit Madrid, **but** she does not have a valid passport.
Lasagna is his favorite food, **so** he eats it often.

A third way to correct a run-on sentence is to add a semicolon and an appropriate conjunctive adverb or transitional phrase followed by a comma:

We could go sailing; **on the other hand,** we could go skiing.
She would love to visit Madrid; **however,** she does not have a valid passport.
Lasagna is his favorite food; **therefore,** he eats it often.

For a list of conjunctive adverbs, see pages 491–492 of this Handbook.

EXERCISE 52

For each of the following run-on sentences, write three different corrections on the blanks provided. Make sure you add the necessary punctuation to your corrected sentences.

1. She asked for a vacation her boss agreed to give her time off.

_____

_____

_____

2. My house needs to be repainted it looks terrible.

_____

_____

_____

3. Jim's car broke down he needs to buy a new one.

_____

_____

_____

4. She needs a manicure he needs a pedicure.

_____

_____

_____

5. Rafael was sick last week he recovered.

_____

_____

_____

For practice identifying and correcting run-on sentences, go to http://www
.college.hmco.com/pic/dolphinwritertwo.

Subordination

The Complex Sentence

In the previous section, you learned about compound sentences, which link equal related ideas together to make their relationships clearer to readers. This section discusses how to increase the clarity and sophistication of your writing by creating complex sentences, which combine dependent and independent clauses.

Dependent Clauses

As you recall from previous sections of this Handbook, an *independent clause* is a group of words that can stand alone as a separate sentence because it contains both a subject and a verb and expresses a complete thought. A **dependent clause** also contains both a subject and a verb. However, a dependent clause cannot stand alone because it begins with a subordinating conjunction or a relative pronoun (such as *because* or *who*) and consequently does *not* express a complete thought. In order to make sense, it must be attached to an independent clause. Hence a dependent clause *depends* upon an independent clause to complete its meaning. Notice how the following dependent clauses express thoughts that are incomplete.

> Because she did not practice
> Who goes to the coffee shop in the morning
> Unless you plan to be present

However, when these dependent clauses are added to independent clauses, their meaning becomes complete and clear:

> *dependent clause*   *independent clause*
> *Because she did not practice,* her playing sounded terrible.

> *dependent clause*   *independent clause*
> *When you get to the coffee shop,* call me.

> *independent clause*   *dependent clause*
> I will not count on you *unless you plan to be present.*

Combining one or more dependent clauses with an independent clause creates a **complex sentence.**

A **compound-complex sentence** contains two or more independent clauses and at least one dependent clause:

> Before they close the shop tonight, Carol will prepare the bank deposit, and Lola will turn off the lights.

Subordinating Conjunctions

When you learned about compound sentences, you saw that one way to link their independent clauses together is with a *coordinating conjunction.* These conjunctions indicate that both clauses are *coordinate,* or equal. The clauses in a complex sentence, however, are not equal. One of them is dependent on, or subordinate to, the other. Thus, one way that they are linked together is with **subordinating conjunctions,** words that indicate this subordinate relationship. By adding one of the following subordinating conjunctions or phrases to the beginning of a clause, you make it dependent, or subordinate.

after	though
although	unless
as	until
because	so that
before	when
even if	whenever
even though	whereas
if	whether
in order that	while
since	

Notice how adding one of these words to an independent clause instantly creates a dependent clause that requires the addition of an independent clause to complete its meaning:

Independent clause:	We lost the game.
Dependent clause:	**After** we lost the game
Dependent clause:	**Even though** we lost the game
Dependent clause:	**When** we lost the game

These subordinating conjunctions not only point out which idea is subordinate but also indicate the relationship (time order, cause or effect, contrast, and so on) between the two ideas expressed in the dependent and independent clauses.

EXERCISE 53

In each of the following complex sentences, circle the subordinating conjunction and underline the entire dependent clause.

1. When we arrive, I will call you.
2. Because my car is broken, I need to drop it off at the gas station.
3. Manuel turned off the radio because it was giving him a headache.
4. Mindy will stay home unless she finds someone to watch her kids.
5. When you have finished eating, you can watch TV.
6. Whenever you read that poem, think of me.
7. We should go snowboarding even though the snow is man-made.
8. We should not start eating until everyone is served.
9. They will have cookies after they eat dinner.
10. If you decide to leave, let me know.

For practice recognizing subordinating conjunctions and dependent clauses in complex sentences, go to http://www.college.hmco.com/pic/dolphinwritertwo.

Punctuating Dependent Clauses

When a dependent clause that begins with a subordinating conjunction starts a sentence, the dependent clause is followed by a comma:

dependent clause　　　　　*independent clause*
Because she suffers from allergies, she cannot own a rabbit.

dependent clause   *independent clause*
Since she came to work here, the office has become more disorganized.

However, if the dependent clause *follows* the independent clause, you usually do not need a comma.

independent clause   *dependent clause*
She cannot own a rabbit *because she suffers from allergies.*

independent clause   *dependent clause*
The office has become more disorganized *since she came to work here.*

EXERCISE 54

In each of the following sentences, underline the dependent clause and add a comma to the sentence if one is needed. If no comma is needed, write the word COR-RECT beside the sentence.

1. She did not renew her passport until it expired.

2. Although she did not tell him he guessed where she was going anyway.

3. The trees have a lot of buds because we have had so much rain.

4. Even though we lost the state championship we felt like winners anyway.

5. Unless you change your mind I will pick you up at six o'clock.

6. We will wait for you until you get here.

7. Wherever he goes he takes his lucky rabbit's foot.

8. They will not go if you do not.

9. Let Glenn know when you plan to eat dinner.

10. It has been a long time since I last saw you.

For practice punctuating dependent clauses, go to http://www.college .hmco.com/pic/dolphinwritertwo.

Relative Clauses

A **relative clause,** which is also called an *adjective clause,* is a special type of dependent clause. It begins with a relative pronoun, such as *that, which, who,* or *whom,* and is usually found in the middle of a sentence. This type of clause functions in a sentence as an adjective, so like a one-word adjective, it is placed next to the noun or pronoun that it modifies.

> *adjective dependent clause*
>
> The file **that he looked at** is missing. (The clause is an adjective that answers the question *which file?*)

> *adjective dependent clause*
>
> Her paper, **which she wrote in a day,** earned a C. (The clause is an adjective that modifies the word *paper.*)

The relative pronoun often serves as the subject of the relative dependent clause:

> Children **who eat well** benefit from a balanced diet.
> The vase **that fell and broke** was very rare.

However, the relative pronoun can be another element in the relative clause. In the following example, it is the direct object:

> The man **whom you love** sent you a letter.

EXERCISE 55

In each of the following sentences, underline the relative clause.

1. The person whom I admire most is Eleanor Roosevelt.
2. My new car, which is parked across the street, gets good gas mileage.
3. The sandwich that I bought was disgusting.
4. Mr. and Mrs. Morris, who live on Terrace Place, have six children.
5. The tree that I just planted is starting to bud.
6. The person whom you should contact is the principal.
7. The house that has the largest garden is the most beautiful.
8. My brother John, who skateboards, loves outdoor sports.
9. Our oven, which broke last week, is too old to fix.
10. The cake that she made has chocolate icing.

For practice recognizing relative clauses in sentences, go to http://www
.college.hmco.com/pic/dolphinwritertwo.

Punctuating Relative Clauses

You may have noticed that some of the example sentences in this section have
included commas around relative clauses, and some have not. Whether a relative clause is separated from the rest of the sentence by commas depends on
whether the clause is essential or nonessential to the meaning of the sentence. The
nonessential relative clause (also called a *nonrestrictive* clause because it does not
limit the meaning of the sentence) adds information that is not necessary for
knowing which person or thing the writer is discussing:

Mr. Ricardo, *who lives in the mansion,* is very wealthy.

In this sentence, the relative clause *who lives in the mansion* is not essential for
knowing who the subject is. Mr. Ricardo, the subject of the independent clause,
has already been identified, so the relative clause telling where he lives could be
eliminated without any loss of meaning. Therefore, the relative clause is separated
from the rest of the sentence by placing a comma before and a comma after it.

Sometimes, however, a relative clause offers information that is essential for
knowing which person or thing the writer is discussing. These clauses are sometimes called *restrictive* because they limit the possible meaning of the sentence.

The man *who lives in the mansion* is very wealthy.

In this sentence, we would not know which man the writer is discussing without
the information in the relative clause. Therefore, the clause is essential, so it is
not enclosed within commas.

Using That, Which, Who, and Whom Correctly

Writers often confuse the relative pronouns *that, which, who,* and *whom*. They
cannot be used interchangeably, so you will need to learn to distinguish them
from one another.

First of all, the relative pronouns *that* and *which* refer to things and animals; the relative pronouns *who* and *whom* refer to humans.

Incorrect: A woman **that** inspires me is Hillary Rodham Clinton.
Correct: A woman **who** inspires me is Hillary Rodham Clinton.

Next you will need to distinguish between *that* and *which*. *That* begins essential relative clauses; *which* begins *nonessential* relative clauses.

essential relative clause

The foods **that I love the most** are chicken and pasta.

nonessential relative clause

I eat chicken and pasta, **which are my favorite foods,** at least once a week.

Therefore, relative clauses beginning with *that* will not be enclosed in commas. Relative clauses beginning with *which* offer information that is not essential, so they are set off with commas from the rest of the sentence.

Finally, learn the difference between *who* and *whom*. In the section about pronouns, you studied the subjective and objective forms of pronouns. The relative pronoun *who* is the subjective form. Therefore, it is the correct pronoun to use for the subject or word that renames the subject:

subject

The person **who** *gets the most pledges* wins the contest.

As you recall from the previous section about punctuating essential and nonessential relative clauses, you will separate any *who* relative clause that offers nonessential information with commas from the rest of the sentence:

Nancy, *who arrived yesterday,* plans to stay a month.

The relative pronoun *whom* is the objective form. Therefore, it is the appropriate form to use for a direct object, indirect object, or object of a preposition:

direct object

The woman **whom** *the judges chose* cried tears of joy.

Use commas before and after a *whom* relative clause if the information it offers is not essential:

nonessential relative clause

His brother, **whom he loves,** is his best friend.

EXERCISE 56

In each of the following sentences, circle the correct relative pronoun. Use the punctuation in each sentence for clues about the right choice.

1. The teacher (who, whom) gave us the most feedback was Ms. Brennan.

2. An animal (which, that) makes me tremble is the python.

3. My best friend, (who, whom) I see often, lives in Nanuet.

4. *Beaches* is the only movie (that, which) makes her sob.

5. *Beaches,* (that, which) is my favorite movie, makes me sob.

6. The man (who, whom) called said he will be stopping by.

7. The message (that, which) I left you is about the schedule.

8. The person (who, whom) wins the trophy must beat the record.

9. My dog, (that, which) was a gift from my best friend, spends a lot of time on my lap.

10. Her fiancé, (who, whom) she plans to marry next year, is a doctor.

For practice using that, which, who, *and* whom *correctly in sentences, go to* http://www.college.hmco.com/pic/dolphinwritertwo.

EXERCISE 57

Add necessary commas to each of the following sentences. Use the relative pronouns in the sentences as clues. If no commas should be added, write the word CORRECT beside the sentence.

1. The movie that got him thinking was *Philadelphia.*

2. *Toy Story* which is a great movie is Patrick's favorite.

3. Betty McMahon who is my cousin has two children.

4. The baseball team that is his favorite is the Red Sox.

5. His girlfriend was the only one whom he trusted.

6. The sandwich that I ordered was supposed to be tuna.

7. My sandwich which was supposed to be tuna arrived with ham.

8. The package that was supposed to arrive at two arrived at three.

9. People who jog regularly are healthier than people who do not.

10. My driving test which I took on May 1 was very successful.

For practice punctuating sentences with relative clauses, go to http://www
.college.hmco.com/pic/dolphinwritertwo.

Avoiding Sentence Fragments

You learned at the beginning of this section that dependent clauses cannot stand alone. A dependent clause must be attached to an independent clause that completes its meaning. Therefore, if a dependent clause ends with a period, it becomes a type of sentence fragment:

Sentence fragment: Although he loves to exercise.
Sentence fragment: That she plans to revise herself.

In the next sections, you will learn methods for correcting these fragments.

Correcting Adverb Dependent Clause Sentence Fragments

Adverb dependent clause sentence fragments begin with a subordinating conjunction and end, incorrectly, with a period:

Sentence fragment: **Even though** he is a minor.
Sentence fragment: **Because** this hotel does not have any rooms.

This type of fragment can be corrected in one of two ways. First of all, you can simply remove the subordinating conjunction, making the clause independent:

He is a minor.
This hotel does not have any rooms.

However, making this change may alter the meaning of your writing.
The second way to correct a dependent clause fragment is to connect it to the independent clause that completes its meaning. This independent clause is usually the sentence that comes immediately before or after the fragment:

Even though he is a minor, he still has an opinion.
I will have to go to a different hotel *because this hotel does not have any rooms.*

Correcting Relative Clause Sentence Fragments

Relative clause sentence fragments begin with a relative pronoun and end (incorrectly) with a period:

Sentence fragment: **Which** I do not understand.
Sentence fragment: **Who** keeps students engaged.

This type of fragment can be corrected in one of two ways. First of all, you can rewrite the fragment to eliminate the relative pronoun and create an independent clause:

I do not understand the homework assignment.
Mrs. Peavey keeps students engaged.

Notice that you will usually have to change the subject or direct object or add one to those clauses that lack one.

The second way to correct a relative clause fragment is to attach it to the independent clause that completes its meaning. This independent clause is often the sentence that comes immediately before or after the fragment:

I have not done the homework assignment, *which I do not understand.*
Mrs. Peavey is a great teacher *who keeps students engaged.*

EXERCISE 58

On the blanks provided, rewrite each of the following fragments in two different ways so that they are no longer sentence fragments. Add or delete words as necessary to make these fragments parts of complete sentences.

1. That I found.

_____

_____

2. Even though it was expensive.

_____

_____

3. Because she had no money.

_____

_____

4. Who does not know Roger.

_____

_____

5. Which was funny.

_____

_____

For information about avoiding other types of sentence fragments, see The Basic Sentence section of this Handbook.

For practice correcting sentence fragments, go to http://www.college.hmco
.com/pic/dolphinwritertwo.

Parallelism

When a sentence contains either a pair or a series of elements that are equal in meaning or value, those elements must be **parallel**. That is, the elements must be in the same form or have the same structure. Parallelism gives sentences balance, which makes them easier to read and understand. So as you write, you will need to make sure that your words, phrases, and clauses are all parallel.

Parallel Words

A pair or a series of words in a sentence should have the same form or be the same part of speech:

Parallel nouns: **Neighbors, friends,** and **visitors** attended the barbecue.
Parallel adjectives: Her singing was **beautiful, lilting,** and **melodic.**
Parallel adverbs: He dances **gracefully** and **emotionally.**

Can you find the parallelism error in the following sentence?

She enjoys dancing, singing, and boats.

This sentence contains a series of three direct objects. Although all three are nouns, the first two are gerunds, verbals ending in *-ing* that function as nouns. The third item in the series is not a gerund, so the sentence contains an error in parallelism. To correct it, we need to change the form of the third item in the series to a gerund:

She enjoys dancing, singing, and **boating.**

If the series takes the form of adverbs, make sure all of its elements are adverbs. If the series takes the form of adjectives, make sure all of its elements are adjectives, and so on.

In addition, do not mix single-word elements with phrases:

She enjoys dancing, singing, and **to sail in the bay on Saturdays.**

In this series of direct objects, the first two are gerunds, but the last item is an infinitive phrase. Even though an infinitive (another verbal) or an infinitive phrase can also be a noun (as it is here), its form does not match that of the gerunds. Consequently, the sentence contains a parallelism error.

Parallel Phrases

A pair or series of phrases must be parallel as well.

Parallel prepositional phrases:
She looked **in the dresser, under the stove,** and **behind the door.**

Parallel infinitive phrases:
She is determined **to make a lot of money, to get her doctorate,** and **to move to a bigger house.**

Parallel gerund phrases:
Falling down the stairs, getting poison ivy, and **catching the flu** are a few of the things that happened to Sarah this year.

Can you find the parallelism errors in the following sentence?

To get out of debt, cut up your credit cards, paying cash for your purchases, and patient saving for more expensive items.

This sentence offers a list of things to do to get out of debt, but the three things are presented in three different grammatical forms:

cut up your credit cards (verb phrase and direct object)
paying cash for your purchases (gerund phrase)
patient saving for more expensive items (noun phrase)

Because of the parallelism errors, this sentence is difficult to comprehend. To correct it, rewrite the sentence so that all three phrases are in the same form:

To get out of debt, **cut** up your credit cards, **pay** cash for your purchases, and patiently **save** for more expensive items. (verbs)

To get out of debt, begin **cutting** up your credit cards, **paying** cash for your purchases, and patiently **saving** for more expensive items. (gerund phrases)

To get out of debt, you need **the courage** to cut up your credit cards, **the resolve** to pay cash for your purchases, and **the patience** to save for more expensive items. (noun phrases)

Also, avoid combining a series of phrases with a clause:

The week before he planned to propose marriage, he rented a boat, ordered flowers, and the restaurant took his reservation.

In what should be a series of three verbs followed by direct objects, the first two items are verbs and direct objects, but the third item is an independent clause. To correct the parallelism error, rewrite the clause as a verb and direct object:

The week before he planned to propose marriage, he **rented** a boat, **ordered** flowers, and **made** a dinner reservation.

The coordinating conjunctions, especially the words *and*, *or*, and *but*, will often signal the need for parallel construction of the phrases they join. Also, pay attention to parallelism when you write two words or phrases that are joined with pairs of conjunctions, such as *either/or*, *neither/nor*, *not only/but also*, *but/and*, and *not/but*:

The money was *not* **for her** *but* **for him.**
His obligation was *not only* **to himself** *but also* **to his daughter.**

EXERCISE 59

In each of the following sentences, underline the word or phrase that is preventing parallelism.

1. Mike is intelligent, creative, and has determination.
2. When I am sick, I like to read, rest, and taking medicine.
3. Before we go out, make sure you take out the garbage, turn off the lights, and that the door is locked.
4. If you want to become a better cook, watch cooking shows, take a cooking class, and all the right ingredients at the grocery store should be bought.
5. Buying a car, getting my master's degree, and to have a family are three of my goals.
6. We went over the river, through the woods, and grandmother's driveway was reached.
7. She feels great admiration for not only her grandfather and her Uncle Pete.
8. The book was delivered not from Borders, and it did come from Amazon.
9. To adopt a healthy lifestyle, eat right, exercise, and maintaining a good sleep pattern.
10. Jim enjoys playing sports, reading, and sometimes he watches television.

For practice recognizing parallelism errors, go to http://www.college.hmco .com/pic/dolphinwritertwo.

Parallel Clauses

Like words and phrases, clauses must also be parallel. When written in pairs and series, both independent and dependent clauses should have the same structure.

Parallelism and Independent Clauses

When pairs or series of independent clauses express parallel ideas, they must be parallel in structure:

One brother is plump, and the other is slim.

Notice how changing the structure of the second independent clause makes the relationship between the two clauses a little harder to understand:

One brother is plump, and "slim" best describes the other one.

This sentence is not only more difficult to understand, but its lack of balance also causes it to sound cumbersome and awkward.

Now read two more compound sentences that lack parallelism and try to determine how the structure changes:

He broke up with his girlfriend, and the rejection was struggled with by her.
Does absence make the heart grow fonder, or out of sight out of mind?

In the first example, the first independent clause is in the active voice, and the second one is in the passive voice. Notice how much easier it is to understand this sentence when the second clause is also written in the active voice:

He broke up with his girlfriend, and **she struggled** with his rejection.

In the second example, the second clause is not in the question form of the first clause. To make the clauses parallel, we could write:

Does absence make the heart grow fonder, or **is** a person out of sight also out of mind?

The coordinating conjunctions, especially the words *and, or,* and *but,* will often signal the need for the parallel construction of the clauses they join. Also, pay attention to parallelism when you write two independent clauses that are joined with pairs of conjunctions such as *either/or, neither/nor,* or *not only/but also.*

Either **we will reach** the summit of the mountain, *or* **we will die** trying.

Not only **can he** prepare gourmet meals, *but* **he** *also* **can** repair a leaky faucet.

EXERCISE 60

Identify each of the following compound sentences as parallel (P) or not parallel (NP). Write your answers on the blanks provided.

___ **1.** Either she will get her doctorate degree, or writing a novel will be her next pursuit.

___ 2. One brother is chatty, and "quiet" is how we think of the other one.

___ 3. Either we will go to the Blue Pig ice cream store, or we will go to Hoffman's Ice Cream Parlor.

___ 4. He drove into a lake, and damage was done to his truck.

___ 5. She not only knows Spanish; she knows French.

___ 6. Juanita wanted a new job, so she began searching the classified ads.

___ 7. Either we will stay for the entire movie, but we might have to go home in the middle of it.

___ 8. One of my sisters is a dancer, and the other is a violin player.

___ 9. Do you believe in magic, or *realistic* describes you better?

___ 10. Either we will have dinner, or going to Trisha's will be our plan.

For practice recognizing parallelism errors in compound sentences, go to http://www.college.hmco.com/pic/dolphinwritertwo.

Parallelism and Dependent Clauses

In complex and compound-complex sentences, too, a pair or series of dependent clauses should be parallel in structure:

Parallel noun clauses (direct objects):
I hope **that you will come to my party** and **that you will bring me a gift.**

Parallel noun clauses (subjects):
When he was born and **where he lives now** are none of our business.

Parallel adverb clauses:
The murder occurred sometime **after the caterer arrived** but **before he left.**

Many errors in parallelism occur when writers unintentionally mix words, phrases, and/or clauses in pairs or series of elements. The following sentence, for example, is not parallel:

dependent clause   independent clause

He told her **that he loved her,** and **she should run away with him.**

In this sentence, the subject (*he*) says two things, so these two things should be expressed with parallel structure. But they are not: one is in the form of a noun dependent clause, and the other is in the form of an independent clause. To correct this error, we need only to delete the comma after *her* and add the word *that* before the independent clause to make it dependent:

He told her **that** he loved her and **that** she should run away with him.

Can you spot the parallelism errors in the following sentences?

She is a talented golfer and who is also good at bowling.

He was angry about the change and since no one had notified him.

Because she lacked experience and displaying a negative attitude, she was not hired for the job.

The first sentence pairs a noun phrase (*a talented golfer*) with a relative clause (*who is also good at bowling*). To correct it, revise so that the sentence contains two noun phrases:

She is a talented **golfer** and a good **bowler.**

The second sentence pairs a prepositional phrase (*about the change*) with a dependent clause (*since no one had notified him*). To correct it, revise the sentence so that it contains either two prepositional phrases or two dependent clauses:

He was angry **about** the change and **about** the lack of notification. (prepositional phrases)

He was angry **since** the change had been made and **since** no one had notified him. (dependent clauses)

In the third sentence, a dependent clause (*Because she lacked experience*) is paired with a participle phrase (*displaying a negative attitude*). To correct this sentence, rewrite it to include either two dependent clauses or two participle phrases:

Because she lacked experience and **because** she displayed a negative attitude, she was not hired for the job. (dependent clauses)

Lacking experience and **displaying** a negative attitude, she was not hired for the job. (participle phrases)

In addition, you could also revise this sentence to include a compound object of the preposition:

Because of her **lack** of experience and negative **attitude,** she was not hired for the job.

Identify each of the following complex sentences as parallel (**P**) or not parallel (**NP**). Write your answers on the blanks provided.

____ 1. Because it was dark and failing to turn on the lights, I fell down.

____ 2. She is an amazing wife and who is also a fantastic mother.

____ 3. Frank was happy about completing the triathlon and that he finished fifth.

____ 4. Liz is a great writer and who knows grammar inside and out.

____ 5. Annie delighted in decorating the dining room and that it was the right color.

____ 6. Because we are sisters and in addition to having a lot in common, we talk every day.

____ 7. She told me that she could go and getting back in two hours.

____ 8. Because you like music and because I do, too, we should go to the concert together.

____ 9. I try to exercise before I eat breakfast or after I leave work.

____ 10. Because of the rain and there was ice on the roads, our trip was canceled.

For practice recognizing parallelism errors in dependent clauses, go to http://www.college.hmco.com/pic/dolphinwritertwo.

Combining Sentences

To make the necessary connections for your readers, to reduce wordiness, and to increase the overall sophistication of your writing, you will want to vary the length of your sentences. Earlier in this Handbook, you learned to join two independent clauses together in compound sentences to more clearly indicate the relationship between two ideas. In this section, you will learn how to combine two sentences. Combining sentences involves not simply linking but actually *blending* them together. As you revise and edit your writing, experiment with the six different ways to turn one sentence into an element of another sentence.

Use a Compound Subject or Compound Verb

One way to combine sentences is to create a compound subject or a compound verb to blend one sentence into another. For example, look at these two sets of short sentences:

> Jose drives a station wagon. Fred drives one, too.
> Jennifer bought coffee. Then she went to the library.

The first set of sentences can be combined by using a compound subject to blend the information in the second sentence into the first sentence:

subject   *subject*
> **Jose** and **Fred** drive station wagons.

The second set of sentences can be combined by using a compound verb to blend the information in the second sentence into the first sentence:

    verb   *verb*
> Jennifer **bought** coffee and then **went** to the library.

Note that both of these revised sentences are less wordy.

EXERCISE 62

On the blanks provided, combine each of the following pairs of sentences by using a compound subject or a compound verb.

1. Peggy went to the post office. Enrique went, too.

_____

2. Li gets up at six. Jackie gets up at six, too.

_____

3. Marie went skating on the lake. Then she did some ice fishing.

_____

4. Erin picked up her Chinese food. Afterward, she picked up her dry cleaning.

_____

5. Peter enjoys baseball. Fred enjoys baseball, too.

_____

6. Carrie is a marketing manager for the company. Luis is also a marketing manager for the company.

_____

7. Aggie drove to Delaware. Then she went to a crab restaurant.

_____

8. I went to the spa. Later, I had dinner.

_____

9. Alan installed the new television. He hooked it up to the DVD player.

_____

10. The nursery school is on this block. The music school is also on this block.

_____

For practice using a compound subject or compound verb, go to http://www.college.hmco.com/pic/dolphinwritertwo.

Use a Dependent Clause

Another way to combine sentences is to turn one of the sentences into a dependent clause. For example, look at these sets of sentences:

> She did not read the directions. She failed the test.
> The artist had already painted the canvas. He then realized his mistake.

The first set of sentences can be combined by turning the first independent clause into a dependent clause and attaching it to the second independent clause:

dependent clause   _independent clause_

Because she did not read the directions, she failed the test.

The second set of sentences can be combined by turning the second sentence into a dependent clause:

independent clause   _dependent clause_

The artist had already painted the canvas **before he realized his mistake.**

In both new sentences, the information in one of the original sentences becomes a dependent clause for the other original sentence. Notice how the relationship between the two sentences becomes much clearer when they are combined.

EXERCISE 63

On the blanks provided, combine each of the following pairs of sentences by turning one of them into a dependent clause.

1. It was snowing. We did not go to the flea market.

   _____

2. I asked her about her class. She told me all about it.

   _____

3. The show had already begun. They let us in.

   _____

4. We did not respond to that e-mail. We were busy.

   _____

5. Franco will go to the concert. He will go when Jane arrives.

   _____

6. The teenagers moved to our area last summer. The neighborhood has become much noisier.

   _____

   _____

7. He searched the living room for his glasses. She searched the kitchen.

   _____

8. Jennifer had already begun mixing the cake batter. She noticed the missing ingredients.

   _____

   _____

9. There was a thunderstorm on Friday. Rita did not go to the Mets game.

   _____

10. I will keep working here. I will stay until you hire someone else.

    _____

For practice on turning sentences into dependent clauses, go to http://www .college.hmco.com/pic/dolphinwritertwo.

Use a Relative Clause

Sentences can also be combined by turning one of them into a relative (adjective) clause. Read the following two sets of sentences:

> Some people eat fruits and vegetables often. These people are generally healthy.
>
> The play won a Tony Award. I liked it.

The first set of sentences can be combined by turning the first sentence into a relative clause and blending it into the second sentence:

relative clause

> People **who often eat fruits and vegetables** are generally healthy.

The second set of sentences can be combined by turning the second sentence into a relative clause:

relative clause

> The play **that I liked** won a Tony Award.

Notice that the relationships are clearer when the sentences are combined.

EXERCISE 64

On the blanks provided, combine each of the following pairs of sentences by turning one of them into a relative clause.

1. People in some cultures eat a great deal of yogurt. They are healthier.

   _____

2. That singer won a Grammy Award. He is one of Tom's favorites.

   _____

3. The alarm clock went off. We keep it in the bedroom.

   _____

4. My purple dress is my favorite. It is a Pucci.

   _____

5. Rey was at the game. He had on a Yankees shirt.

   _____

6. The book won an Edgar Award. Diana liked it.

   _____

7. The house on the corner will be auctioned. It is fifty years old.

_____

8. The zoo is in downtown San Diego. The zoo is very beautiful.

_____

9. Some people can suffer heart attacks. They are people with clogged arteries.

_____

10. The contestant was disqualified. He was the contestant selected by the judges.

_____

To practice turning sentences into relative clauses, go to http://www.college
.hmco.com/pic/dolphinwritertwo.

Use an Appositive

Sentences can also be combined by turning one of them into an appositive. For example, read the following sentences:

> Renee delivered an interesting speech. She is the valedictorian.
> The coat was a gift from her parents. It was lime green.

The first set of sentences can be combined by turning the second one into an appositive and blending it into the first sentence:

> _appositive_
> Renee, **the valedictorian,** delivered an interesting speech.

The second set of sentences can be combined by turning the first one into an appositive:

> _appositive_
> The coat, **a gift from her parents,** was lime green.

EXERCISE 65

On the blanks provided, combine each of the following pairs of sentences by turning one of them into an appositive.

1. The president of our company gave us a lot of praise. He is a very kind man.

_____

2. Lance Armstrong dated singer Sheryl Crow. He is a great cyclist.

_____

3. Barbara is an alto. She sang a song from _Riverdance._

_____

4. The shoes are uncomfortable. They are high-heeled pumps.

_____

5. Nancy prepared a delicious roast. She is a gourmet chef.

_____

6. The vehicle is stalling out. It is a minivan.

_____

7. The dessert is very creamy. It is a type of mousse.

_____

8. Mr. Wilson was our science teacher. He is now teaching high school.

_____

9. The dog ran toward the woods. It is a miniature Schnauzer.

_____

10. My sister is an editor at a publishing company. She got a promotion at work.

_____

To practice turning sentences into appositives, go to http://www.college .hmco.com/pic/dolphinwritertwo.

Use a Prepositional Phrase

Yet another way to combine sentences is to turn the information in one of them into a prepositional phrase. For example, read these sentences:

The tree had the kite. The kite was stuck.
She heard her favorite song. The radio was playing it.

The first set of sentences can be combined by turning the first sentence into a prepositional phrase and blending it into the second sentence:

prepositional phrase
The kite was stuck **in the tree.**

The second set of sentences can be combined by turning the second sentence into a prepositional phrase:

prepositional phrase
She heard her favorite song **on the radio.**

EXERCISE 66

On the blanks provided, combine each of the following pairs of sentences by turning one of them into a prepositional phrase.

1. The cat was motionless. Its location was the driveway.

_____

2. I saw my favorite vocalist. She performed at the Bijoux.

_____

3. He drove to Ohio. It was snowing.

_____

4. She washed the dirty laundry. She finished at almost noon.

_____

5. Patrick picked up the shoes. They were in the hallway.

_____

6. Maggie drove us to college. We used her van.

_____

7. Donald burned the hamburgers. They were being grilled at the time.

_____

8. I found the scarf. Its location was the closet.

_____

9. John picked up the refrigerator. He picked it up at Atlantic Appliance.

_____

10. Tom laid the tile. He put it in the foyer.

_____

To practice turning sentences into prepositional phrases, go to http://www
.college.hmco.com/pic/dolphinwritertwo.

Use a Participle (-*ed* or -*ing*) Phrase

One last way to combine sentences is to turn one of the sentences into a participle phrase. For example, read the following sets of sentences:

> He was a fugitive. He was wanted in three states.
> She crouched down low. She remained hidden from sight.

The first set of sentences can be combined by turning the second sentence into a participle phrase and blending it with the first sentence:

participle phrase

He was a fugitive **wanted in three states.**

The second set of sentences can be combined by turning the first sentence into a participle phrase:

participle phrase

Crouching down low, she remained hidden from sight.

NOTE: When using this method, beware of creating dangling or misplaced modifiers. Put the participle phrase, which functions as an adjective, next to the noun or pronoun that it modifies.

EXERCISE 67

On the blanks provided, combine each of the following pairs of sentences by turning one of them into a participle phrase.

1. She is an artist. She is working in the Southwest.

_____

2. The dog hid in the grass. It waited for mice.

_____

3. He was a busy college student. He was taking a full course load.

_____

4. She drove erratically. She had an accident.

_____

5. Mary is a great orator. She is wanted for speaking engagements.

_____

6. Bonnie wants to look at the antiques. They are stored in the attic.

_____

7. Rose followed her heart. She rejected the billionaire's marriage proposal.

_____

8. Marlon is a real estate tycoon. He is making huge deals.

_____

9. Maureen is a writer. She is publishing her first novel in the spring.

_____

10. Julio won a medal. He competed in the summer Olympic Games.

_____

To practice turning sentences into participle phrases, go to http://www
.college.hmco.com/pic/dolphinwritertwo.

Mechanics

Punctuation

It is important to use correct punctuation in sentences. The proper punctuation
marks help readers read more easily, and these marks also prevent confusion
and misreading. In this section, you will learn the rules for the major punctuation marks: periods, question marks, exclamation points, commas, semicolons,
colons, apostrophes, and quotation marks.

Periods, Question Marks, and Exclamation Points

Periods, question marks, and exclamation points are all types of end punctuation. That is, they indicate that a sentence has ended.

> I cannot see you.
> Where did you go?
> There you are!

Using a period is the most common way to end a sentence. If a sentence does not
ask a question or present its content with strong emotion, it ends with a period.
The question mark ends a sentence that asks a question, such as _Where are you?_
If a sentence is exclamatory, such as the last sentence in the preceding example,
it ends with an exclamation point. You probably will not use exclamation
points as frequently as you use periods and question marks in your writing, but
if you want to convey severity or excitement in a sentence, an exclamation point

is appropriate. Also use an exclamation point to end a strong interjection: *Yes! What a wonderful idea!*

In addition, a period is used to indicate abbreviations, such as the abbreviations for Doctor (Dr.), Registered Nurse (R.N.), or Mister (Mr.).

EXERCISE 68

In each of the following sentences, supply the necessary end punctuation marks or periods used with abbreviations.

1. Who is Francine

2. Get this woman out of here

3. Do not forget to comb your hair

4. Mr Meyers is my uncle

5. Put that down before it breaks

6. Where do you want to go for lunch, Irene

7. Did you buy a new boat yesterday

8. Dee finished her homework

9. Is Jackie an R N or an M D

10. Do not forget to lock the door

For practice punctuating with periods, question marks, and exclamation points, go to http://www.college.hmco.com/pic/dolphinwritertwo.

Commas

Commas often seem to be tricky punctuation marks. However, there are basically eight rules for comma usage. Learn these eight rules; then, each time you wonder whether or not you should insert a comma, ask yourself if the situation is one of those described here.

Commas separate certain elements in sentences. Use commas to

1. Separate words in a series of three or more words, phrases, or clauses:

> I went to the library and looked through some fiction, nonfiction, and reference books.
>
> The paper blew across the yard, down the street, and into the river.

2. Help connect two independent clauses that are joined by a coordinating conjunction (*and, but, for, nor, yet, or, so*).

> I went to the department store, **but** I forgot to buy stockings.

3. Separate introductory elements, including dependent clauses, and transitional or explanatory words from the main part of the sentence:

> Running down the street, I broke the heel of my shoe.
>
> Because she attended every class, she received an award for perfect attendance.
>
> We will, however, attend the graduation ceremony.

4. Separate an element—such as an appositive, certain relative clauses, or the name of the person being spoken to—that could be removed from the sentence without changing its meaning:

> The play, which is overly long, is difficult to sit through.
> Mrs. Miller, my piano teacher, is very talented.
> I wonder, Elaine, if it is acceptable to take that book without asking.

5. Separate two or more coordinate (equal) adjectives:

> This delicate, colorful shirt looks great on you.

6. Separate the quoted material from the verb introducing it in direct quotations:

> She said, "Please return this book."

7. Separate phrases that indicate contrast:

> I asked her to hand me a cup, not a bowl.

8. Separate mild interjections from the rest of the sentence:

> No, I do not want more cake.

EXERCISE 69

In each of the following sentences, add commas as necessary.

1. Because it is late I will have to ask you to leave.

2. He decided to buy markers pencils and paper.

3. We were going to go out but Juana convinced us to stay in.

4. This music station which is mostly pop is fun to listen to.

5. George my painter will return in three hours.

6. Can you do the job Tom?

7. Tony said "Yes it is wise to go."

8. Jack advised us to run not walk to the sale at Circuit City.

9. Driving down the street Peg discovered that the car's gas tank was nearly empty.

10. Do you need eggs juice or just milk?

For practice punctuating with commas, go to http://www.college.hmco .com/pic/dolphinwritertwo.

Semicolons

There are only two uses of the semicolon in sentences:

1. To link two independent clauses:

> You should give me a ride; I do not have a car.
>
> Greg and Jennifer did not carpool to work; otherwise, she would have been on time.

2. To separate the items in lists that contain internal commas:

> In attendance at the meeting were Mr. Jones, president; Ms. Anderson, vice president; Mr. Lee, treasurer; and Mrs. Lopez, secretary.

EXERCISE 70

In each of the following sentences, add semicolons as necessary.

1. Angela wrote the preface I wrote the endnotes.

2. We visited several cities on our trip, including Houston, Texas Baton Rouge, Lousiana and Biloxi, Mississippi.

3. In the photograph were Samuel, my uncle Rose, my aunt Hannah, my niece and Kenny, my nephew.

4. Do not forget to renew your passport you cannot travel to France without it.

5. The play starts at nine we do not want to miss the opening curtain.

For practice punctuating with semicolons, go to http://www.college.hmco .com/pic/dolphinwritertwo.

Apostrophes

Apostrophes have only three uses.

    1. They form contractions that indicate missing letters:

        do not = don't
        have not = haven't
        there is = there's
        you are = you're

    2. They indicate possession:

        Mrs. Smith's garden
        the girls' mittens
        my brother-in-law's motorcycle

    3. They are used to form plurals of single letters and numerals:

        She earned A's in all of her classes.

        When you are rolling dice, two 1's are called *snake eyes* and two 6's are called *boxcars.*

EXERCISE 71

In each of the following sentences, add apostrophes as necessary.

1. Dont go down that dark alley.

2. Theres nothing like a big piece of chocolate cake.

3. Youre a wonderful friend.

4. Johns children dont have any manners.

5. Paul got all As in his courses.

6. Jims sister is an accountant.

7. Shes having a graduation party.

8. Its going to rain.

9. Sidneys book is going to be a bestseller.

10. The gymnast received 9s from three of the judges.

For practice punctuating with apostrophes, go to http://www.college.hmco
.com/pic/dolphinwritertwo.

Colons

These are two main uses for colons:

1. They introduce a list:

> The executive board of the parent-teacher association at my school
> is composed of the following members: president, vice president, sec-
> retary, and treasurer.

2. They can introduce a direct quotation (in place of a comma):

> Every time I use salt in my cooking, I throw a bit over my right
> shoulder and say: "Once over the shoulder for good luck."

EXERCISE 72

In each of the following sentences, add colons as necessary.

1. The following people will go on the camping trip Nick, Lynn, Nate, and Kerry.

2. When you go to the mall, buy me these things shoes, socks, pants, and shirts.

3. My father always says "Look before you leap."

4. Do not forget to add these things to your list feed the dog, do the laundry,
   and prune the hedges.

5. Before deciding, always ask yourself "What are the pros and cons of each
   choice?"

For practice punctuating with colons, go to http://www.college.hmco.com/pic/dolphinwritertwo.

Quotation Marks

Quotation marks have three main uses in sentences. They are used to

1. Indicate that you are using (quoting) someone else's exact words:

   Someone once said, "Beauty is only skin deep."

2. Indicate that you are using a word in an unusual way or expressing reservation:

   I do not agree with Mayor Elliott's position on the energy "program."

Used in this way, the quotation marks indicate that the writer thinks that "program" is not the correct way to describe the energy situation.

3. Indicate titles of poems, short stories, song titles, and articles:

   I recently read the poem "To a Skylark."

EXERCISE 73

In each of the following sentences, add quotation marks as necessary.

1. Mayor Schmidt said, I cannot support that movement.

2. Have you read the essay My Life?

3. That is not what I would call model behavior.

4. I did not enjoy hearing the song Better Now.

5. The announcer said, Ladies and gentlemen, please take your seats.

For practice punctuating with quotation marks, go to http://www.college.hmco.com/pic/dolphinwritertwo.

Capitalization

It is important to use capital letters properly. To make sure you are capitalizing words correctly, learn the rules in this section.

The Rules of Capitalization

- The first letter of the first word in every sentence is capitalized:

  *A*fter much thought, we decided to sell our house.

- Whenever the pronoun *I* is used in a sentence, it is capitalized, regardless of its placement in a sentence:

  I wanted to go to the awards dinner, but *I* did not have a way to get to the restaurant.

- Proper nouns—those nouns that name specific people, places, and things— are capitalized, as are family relative titles:

  We went to *A*ruba with *A*unt *R*ose, *U*ncle *E*d, and *J*ack.

- Proper adjectives—adjectives formed from proper nouns—are also capitalized:

  The *L*ebanese businesswoman traveled internationally for work.

- Titles that precede names are capitalized, but those that are not followed by names are not capitalized:

  *P*resident Anwar Sadat, the late *p*resident of Egypt, was a great humanitarian.

- Directions that are names of regions are capitalized; compass points (north, south, east, west) are not capitalized.

  The *S*outhwest is a lovely part of the country to visit, as is eastern Utah.

- Capitalize the days of the weeks, the months of the year, and holidays:

  On *F*riday, *D*ecember 31, we will celebrate *N*ew *Y*ear's *D*ay.

- Capitalize the names of countries, nationalities, and specific languages:

  Despite being *B*elgian and speaking *F*rench, Louise speaks fluent *E*nglish.

- Capitalize the major words in the titles of books, articles, and songs:

  The Catcher in the Rye is a wonderful novel.

- Capitalize the names of religions, races, and tribes, such as Jews, African Americans, Hispanics, and Navajos:

  The Catholic church is on Main Street.

- Capitalize names of organizations, such as the Republican Party, the National League, and the Association of Teachers:

  The *D*emocratic *P*arty is known for its fundraising efforts.

■ Capitalize the names of buildings and businesses, such as Shea Stadium, Mount Sinai Hospital, and Bloomingdale's:

> The **W**aldorf **A**storia is a luxurious hotel.

■ Capitalize titles of school courses, such as Anatomy I and English 101:

> My **H**istory 452 course meets on Wednesdays at three o'clock.

■ Capitalize historical periods, such as the Renaissance and the Ice Age, and the names of major conflicts, such as the Civil War:

> **W**orld **W**ar I saw an increase in American casualties.

■ Acronyms—those letters that stand for a longer title—are capitalized:

> The National Rifle Association, or **NRA**, is a strong group in Washington.

EXERCISE 74

In each of the following sentences, circle every word that should begin with a capital letter.

1. we will discuss the novel *siddhartha* on friday.

2. after her husband, president gerald ford, left office, betty ford opened a successful rehabilitation hospital for substance abusers.

3. i love watching television shows about politics.

4. when you eat fried chicken, it is acceptable to pick it up with your fingers.

5. at this time of year, mexico is quite warm.

6. ming, marisa, and alison enjoy going to the gym.

7. we enjoy indian food very much.

8. when pablo visited italy, he toured the murano glass museum.

9. i used to go to san francisco three times a year for pleasure.

10. our congressman is a member of the republican party.

For more practice capitalizing words correctly, go to http://www.college .hmco.com/pic/dolphinwritertwo.

Spelling

The Importance of Correct Spelling

Before you submit anything you have written to someone else, you will need to check it carefully for spelling errors. Readers tend to judge writing that is marred by misspellings as sloppy, careless, or indicative of a lack of knowledge. In order to avoid these kinds of judgments, make sure you have spelled every word in your paper correctly.

You can check spelling in three main ways:

1. *Look up words in a dictionary.* During the proofreading and editing stage of the writing process, comb your paper carefully for words that might be misspelled. If you have the slightest doubt that a word is correctly spelled, look it up.
2. *Use a computer spell-checker to help you locate misspelled words.* Word processing programs such as Microsoft Word will identify possible misspellings for you and even suggest the correct spellings. These programs are not foolproof, but they will help you find more errors so that you can remove them from your paper.
3. *Ask others to proofread your papers.* Ask people you know—relatives, friends, coworkers—who are known to be good spellers to read your draft and circle possible misspellings.

Some Spelling Rules

In addition to using one or more of the three methods for locating spelling errors, you can learn a few rules that will help you improve your spelling.

Forming Plurals

Most words are made plural by adding an *-s* to the end of the word. For example, add an *-s* to *head* to make the plural *heads*. Or add an *-s* to the word *hand* to make the plural *hands*. However, as with many of the rules you have learned so far in this Handbook, there are exceptions to the rules. They are listed as follows:

Nouns that end with -s, -z, -x, -sh, and –ch. To form the plural of a noun that ends in *-s*, *-z*, *-x*, *-sh*, or *-ch*, add *-es*:

pass   pass*es*
buzz   buzz*es*
tax   tax*es*

crash   crash*es*
glitch   glitch*es*

Nouns that end in -o. In most cases, also add *-es* to nouns that end in *o*:

potato   potato*es*
tomato   tomato*es*

There are a few exceptions, such as the word *pianos.*

Words ending in -f or -fe. Words ending in *-f* or *-fe* are made plural in one of three ways. For some, add *-s*, as with other plurals:

belief   belief*s*
chief   chief*s*

For words that end in *–ff* or *-ffe*, add either *-s* or *-es*:

staff   staff*s*
gaffe   gaff*es*
giraffe   giraff*es*

Some words ending in *-f* or *-fe* are made plural with *-ves*:

shelf   shel*ves*
elf   el*ves*
life   li*ves*

Words that are the same whether singular or plural. Some words are the same in both their singular and plural forms:

deer   sheep
elk   fish

EXERCISE 75

For each of the following sentences, write the plural form of the boldfaced word on the blank provided.

1. I am taking four **class.** _____

2. The two girls were dressed as **witch.** _____

3. Rafe caught three **fish.** _____

4. At this company, we have a lot of **chief.** _____

5. The **staff** at each company are responsible for a variety of tasks. _____

Adding Suffixes to Words

-*y* words. Change the final -*y* to -*i* and add -*es* to make words ending in -*y* plural or to change the verb tense:

supply	suppl*ies*	suppl*ied*
cry	cr*ies*	cr*ied*
empty	empt*ies*	empt*ied*

-*e* words. When you add certain suffixes to many words that end in -*e*, you will drop that final -*e* before adding the suffix:

bike	bik*ing*
love	lov*able*
obese	obes*ity*

Doubling a final letter. Double the final letter if (1) it is a consonant, (2) its last two letters are a vowel followed by a consonant, (3) it is a one-syllable word or is accented on the last syllable, or (4) the suffix that you want to add starts with a vowel:

hop	hop*ped*	hop*ping*
rub	rub*bed*	rub*bing*
refer	refer*red*	refer*ring*

-*ally* and -*ly* words. An adjective or other word becomes an adverb when -*ally* or -*ly* is added. If the word ends in -*ic*, add -*ally*, as in *frantically.* Otherwise, add -*ly* to the end of it, as in *lovely.*

EXERCISE 76

Add -*ing* or -*ed*, as appropriate, to the word in parentheses, and write the correct form of the word on the blank provided in each sentence.

1. We love to go _____. (*bike*)

2. We _____ to the end of the road. (*race*)

3. Do you like to go _____? (*shop*)

4. I _____ the spot to get it out. (*rub*)

5. Joe _____ to get there on time. (*try*)

Add *-ally* or *-ly* to the word in parentheses, and write the correct form of the word on the blank provided in each sentence.

6. He searched _____ for his lost son. (*frantic*)

7. That company is _____ sound. (*financial*)

8. John _____ has a penny to his name. (*occasion*)

9. The snow _____ covered the sidewalk. (*partial*)

10. Mark thought about the problem _____. (*logic*)

ie **and** *ei* **Words.** Usually, if we say the old rhyme "*I* before *E* except after *C* or when sounding like *A* as in n**ei**ghbor and w**ei**gh," we can figure out how to spell *-ie* and *-ei* words. Again, there are exceptions to this rule.

> *ie*: science, conscience, species, sufficient
>
> *ei*: seize, either, weird, height, foreign, leisure, counterfeit, forfeit, neither, sleight

EXERCISE 77

In each of the following sentences, circle every word that is misspelled, and write above it the correct spelling. If there are no misspelled words, write "Correct."

1. Your consceince should be your guide.

2. Do you have a sufficeint amount of money?

3. The performance artist was wierd.

4. Niether one of us had any money.

5. What do you do with your leisure time?

6. Either one of us can watch the kids.

7. When the team was late for the game, it had to forfiet.

8. That twenty-dollar bill is a counterfeit.

9. Have you taken any foriegn correspondence courses?

10. The government seized all of the property.

For practice locating spelling errors, go to http://www.college.hmco.com/pic/dolphinwritertwo.

Commonly Confused Words

Here are some commonly confused homonyms (words that sound alike), with their definitions. Study these words to learn the differences in their meanings:

accept	to agree to
except	excluding
adverse	negative
averse	reluctant
advice	counsel
advise	to give an opinion
affect	to influence
effect	result (noun)
allude	to refer to indirectly
elude	to evade
allusion	indirect reference
illusion	false impression
assure	to guarantee
ensure	to guarantee
insure	to cover or underwrite
bare	naked
bear	large animal; to carry
bazaar	festival
bizarre	odd
bored	without interest
board	flat piece of wood; to climb on
breath	mouthful of air
breathe	to take breaths

by	near
buy	to purchase
capitol	building in which a legislature meets
capital	assets; seat of government
cite	to refer to
site	location
sight	ability to see
close	to shut
clothes	apparel
coarse	rough
course	path; unit of study
complement	to balance; to go together
compliment	admiring comment
conscience	moral/ethical principles
conscious	aware
decent	civilized or well mannered
descent	to go down
dissent	to disagree with
defuse	to calm
diffuse	to spread
desert	arid, sandy place
dessert	a sweet served at the end of dinner
devise	to concoct
device	mechanism
disburse	to pay out
disperse	to scatter
dual	twofold
duel	contest between two combatants
dye	to change color
die	to expire
elicit	to draw out
illicit	illegal
envelop	to surround
envelope	cover; packet

fair	balanced
fare	transportation charge
farther	beyond (distance)
further	additional
faze	to put off, disturb
phase	stage
fiscal	relating to money
physical	having to do with the body
for	in favor of; intended for
fore	front
four	a number
formally	officially
formerly	previously
hear	to perceive sound
here	at this time; presently
hole	gap
whole	all together
incidence	occurrence
incident	event
instance	example
its	possessive of *it*
it's	contraction of *it is*
know	to be aware of something
no	rejection
later	afterward
latter	concluding
lead	to show the way; a metallic element
led	showed the way
liable	accountable
libel	written slander
lightening	lessening a load
lightning	electricity related to a storm event
lose	to misplace
loose	unfastened

meat	animal protein
meet	to convene or get together
miner	someone who works underground in a mine
minor	of lesser importance
passed	approved or accepted; gone by
past	history; what went before
patience	endurance or fortitude
patients	people under the care of a doctor
peace	serenity
piece	a segment of something larger
peak	climax
peek	to steal a look
pique	to arouse interest or ire
personal	private
personnel	group of employees
plain	without adornment
plane	flat surface; aeronautical transportation
populace	public
populous	densely populated
pore	small opening; to study
pour	to dispense
pray	to meditate
prey	quarry or victim
precede	to come before
proceed	to go ahead
presence	attendance
presents	gifts
principal	head of a school
principle	belief
quiet	calm; without sound
quite	to a certain extent
rain	precipitation
reign	rule
rein	strap to hold a horse

raise	to lift up
raze	to tear down
right	correct
rite	ritual
write	to put pen to paper
road	street
rode	traveled
root	origin
rout	disorderly retreat; defeat
route	direction
sale	transaction
sail	part of a boat
scene	location
seen	noticed
stationary	not moving
stationery	writing paper and envelopes
than	a conjunction used to indicate an unequal comparison or difference
then	subsequently
their	belonging to them
there	in that place
they're	contraction of *they are*
threw	tossed
through	during; from beginning to end
to	in the direction of
too	also
two	a number
waist	the midsection of the body
waste	garbage; to use up illogically
weak	without strength
week	seven days
weather	climate; to endure
whether	a conjunction used to indicate alternatives
which	a pronoun indicating choice
witch	a woman possessing magical powers

| who's | contraction of *who is* |
| whose | the possessive form of *who* |

| wood | a piece of lumber |
| would | past tense of the verb *will* |

yore	of old
your	the possessive of *you*
you're	contraction of *you are*

EXERCISE 78

In each of the following sentences, circle the word that fits the context of the sentence.

1. (Your, You're) a great teacher.

2. Do you (accept, except) my proposal?

3. He is a (decent, descent, dissent) fellow.

4. When you run the marathon, do not forget to (breath, breathe).

5. I (assure, ensure, insure) you that I always tell the truth.

6. That magician is a master of (allusion, illusion).

7. The cat sees mice as (pray, prey).

8. What time would you like to (meat, meet)?

9. We should just (precede, proceed) with the plan.

10. No gifts, please; your (presents, presence) is enough.

Abbreviations

In some respects, this might be called the era of abbreviations because writers are used to quick e-mails and instant messages with shorthand for common phrases such as "be right back" (brb). No doubt more and more written conversation abbreviations will show up all the time, but in writing paragraphs and essays for college, traditional rules for using abbreviations correctly continue to apply.

What to Abbreviate

Check this table to learn what you do need to abbreviate.

Abbreviate	*Examples*
Titles before and after people's names	Mr., Ms., Mrs., Dr., Jr., Sr., C.P.A., M.D., Ph.D., D.V.M.
Time and date words before and after a number	200 B.C.E., 554 C.E., A.D. 1776, 200 B.C., 5:00 a.m., 12:00 p.m.
Names of organizations, corporations, and certain countries	UK, USA, FBI, NAACP, NCAA, NSA, UNICEF

What Not to Abbreviate

Do Not Abbreviate	*Examples*
Titles before a person's full name	Professor Aguilar, Reverend Smith, Officer Jones, Sergeant Reyes
Days and months	Friday, Wednesday, August, January
Measurements	three pounds, one inch, six feet
States and countries (except when in a mailing address)	Iowa, California, British Columbia, Canada, Nigeria, New Zealand
Course title	English (not Eng), Chemistry 101 (not Chem)

Numbers

Here are some guidelines for when you need to spell out numbers:

When a number appears at the beginning of a sentence, spell it out:

> Eight players showed up for the baseball game.

When a number can be expressed in one or two words, spell it:

> eighteen children
> two thousand years

Use a hyphen with numbers between twenty-one and ninety-nine:

> She turned thirty-two the same day her great-great grandmother would have turned two hundred.

NOTE: On the other hand, use numerals in your writing in the following situations:

When a number cannot be expressed as one or two words	672 redwoods left
Decimals, percents, fractions	5.2, 36 percent, 1/2
Game scores	7–4
Precise sums of money used with a dollar sign	$2.19
Route or road number	Route 12, Interstate 95
Dates (days and years)	June 25, 1959
Chapters, pages, volumes	chapter 6, page 482, volume 32
Addresses	12 Beacon Street, 174 Elm Avenue

Additional Practice for Multilingual Writers

English differs from other languages in certain aspects of grammar and sentence construction. For writers whose native language is not English, this appendix addresses some of those issues.

Countable and Noncountable Nouns

Many nouns in the English language are **countable**. That is, they refer to things—such as dollars, birds, compact discs, and waves—that are separate units. Therefore, they can be counted, and they have both singular and plural forms:

Singular	*Plural*
boat	boats
message	messages
potato chip	potato chips
child	children

Other nouns in English, however, are **noncountable**. They name ideas, emotions, or other things that cannot be divided into separate parts or pieces. Some examples of noncountable nouns follow:

Abstract ideas: honesty, bravery, happiness, patience

Activities: homework, housework, football, surfing, chess, sleeping

Things made up of small particles or grains: oatmeal, salt, sugar, flour, dust

Liquids: blood, soup, paint, coffee, water, milk, gravy, oil

Certain foods: bread, popcorn, butter, cheese, ham, beef, bacon

Gases: air, steam, hydrogen, oxygen, smoke, pollution

Things with individual parts that are thought of as a whole: furniture, garbage, luggage, jewelry, food, clothing, money

Weather and other natural phenomena: snow, rain, thunder, sunshine, fog, gravity

Materials: cotton, glass, concrete, copper, steel, wood

Subjects or fields of study: biology, photography, English, math, computer science

Noncountable nouns do not have a plural form. Adding an –s to the noncountable noun *fun,* for example, is not appropriate. *Fun* does not have a plural form, so *funs* would be incorrect.

Some nouns have both a countable and a noncountable meaning. The context determines which meaning is specific, and therefore countable, or more general, and therefore noncountable.

Countable: She accidentally broke two wine **glasses.**
Noncountable: The window is made of **glass.**

Countable: He was charged with two **crimes.**
Noncountable: **Crime** does not pay.

EXERCISE 1

Write the correct form of the noun in parentheses in each blank.

1. John mowed the _____. (*grass*)

2. Did you happen to pick up our _____? (*mail*)

3. She drank three _____ of coffee. (*cup*)

4. Athletes must be sure to drink enough _____. (*water*)

5. I like both white and wheat _____. (*bread*)

6. For two days this week, they had to walk to school in the _____. (*rain*)

7. She needs a few _____ of cloth to make the skirt. (*yard*)

8. They ate _____ and _____ for dinner. (*chicken, potato*)

9. He likes to watch baseball _____ on television. (*game*)

10. She has acquired much _____ from her college courses. (*knowledge*)

Articles

The is a definite article, a kind of adjective that refers to one or more specific things. It is used before singular and plural countable nouns.

the zoo
the salesclerk
the organizations
the feelings

The can sometimes be used before noncountable nouns if the noun is specifically identified.

She was surprised by **the** patience he displayed.
I was able to find **the** information you need.

A and *an* are indefinite articles that refer to one nonspecific thing. They are used before singular countable nouns.

a teacher
a promise
an ability
an orange

A and *an* are never used before noncountable nouns.

⁂ **EXERCISE 2**

Circle any article that is used incorrectly. If the use of articles in the sentence is correct, write *Correct* on the blank.

1. He is a member of the team. _____

2. She has the patience with young children. _____

3. The police officers showed a courage. _____

4. I will eat a bread with my soup. _____

5. She has not only the beauty but also the intelligence. _____

6. He was in a trouble again. _____

7. I have an advice for you. _____

8. We have an idea for the project. _____

9. His parents gave him the permission to go. _____

10. They are in a love, so they feel the happiness. _____

Order of Verbs in Verb Phrases

There are twelve verb tenses, which are listed and illustrated in the following chart.

SIMPLE TENSES indicate a past, present, or future action.

Present tense	He walks to school every day.
Past tense	He walked to school last year.
Future tense	He will walk to school next year.

PERFECT TENSES indicate that an action was or will be completed before another time or action.

Present perfect tense	He has walked to school every day for the last three years.
Past perfect tense	He had walked to school once or twice in the past.
Future perfect tense	By the time he graduates, he will have walked to school for three years.

PROGRESSIVE TENSES indicate continuing action at a specific time.

Present progressive tense	He is walking to school right now.
Past progressive tense	He was walking to school at 7:30 yesterday.
Future progressive tense	He will be walking to school at 7:30 tomorrow morning.
Present perfect progressive tense	He has been walking to school for twenty minutes now.
Past perfect progressive tense	He had been walking for twenty minutes when he realized that he did not have his backpack.
Future perfect progressive tense	When the clock strikes eight, he will have been walking for thirty minutes.

As you can see from this chart, different combinations of helping (or auxillary) verbs and main verbs allow speakers of English to indicate different times and qualities of verbs. The components of verbs must occur in a specific order:

MODAL* + BASE FORM OF VERB
I must write.
He can write.
They must write.

Has/have/had + PAST PARTICIPLE OF VERB
I have written.
He has written.
They had written.

Is/are/was/were + PRESENT PARTICIPLE (–ING FORM) OF VERB
I am writing.
He is writing.
They are writing.

MODAL + has/have + PAST PARTICIPLE FORM OF VERB
I might have written.
He should have written.
They could have written.

MODAL + be + PRESENT PARTICIPLE OF VERB
I could be writing.
He will be writing.
They may be writing.

MODAL + has/have + been + PRESENT PARTICIPLE OF VERB
I will have been writing.
He must have been writing.
They may have been writing.

---

*The modals are *can, could, may, might, must, will, would, should,* and *shall.*

EXERCISE 3

Fill in the blank with the words in parentheses in the order that correctly expresses the tense.

1. Next week, they _____ a new semester. (*starting be will*)

2. They _____ the trash out this morning. (*have taken must*)

3. She _____ the number. (*have should known*)

4. When he was finally caught, he _____ money for six months. (*stealing been had*)

5. At the end of the month, they _____ for six weeks. (*been will traveling have*)

6. You _____ my ticket. (*bought could have*)

7. I _____ you a package very soon. (*be will sending*)

8. By the time she graduates, she _____ in college for five years. (*have been will*)

9. He _____. (*been dreaming have must*)

10. They _____ tomorrow. (*be may leaving*)

For additional practice using verbs and verb tenses, see the Parts of Speech section of the Handbook.

Verbs with Gerunds and Infinitives

Some verbs are followed by a gerund (a *verbal*, a verb form that functions as another part of speech in a sentence), and others are followed by an infinitive, another verbal. A **gerund** is the *-ing* form of a verb that acts as a noun in a sentence.

> **Dancing** is great exercise.
> She enjoys **reading** and **traveling**.

The following verbs are usually followed by a gerund:

admit	discuss	finish	practice	resist
avoid	dislike	imagine	put off	risk
consider	enjoy	miss	quit	stop
deny	escape	postpone	recall	suggest

You would not write: *He practiced **to hit** the ball*. Instead, you would write: *He practiced **hitting** the ball*.

An **infinitive** is made up of the word *to* plus the base form of a verb. It most often functions as a noun in a sentence (but can also be an adjective or an adverb). The following infinitives (nouns) are direct objects:

He asked her **to dance.**
She likes **to read.**

The following verbs are usually followed by an infinitive acting as a noun (direct object):

afford	fail	mean	offer
agree	forget	need	refuse
appear	hesitate	neglect	remember
begin	hope	plan	start
continue	intend	prefer	try
decide	learn	pretend	wait
expect	like	promise	

You would not write: *She cannot afford **buying** a new car* (gerund phrase). Instead, you would write: *She cannot afford **to buy** a new car*. Notice that gerunds and infinitives can take objects to form gerund or infinitive phrases. When that happens, the whole verbal phrase functions as the sentence element (direct objects in these examples).

EXERCISE 4

Circle the correct word or words for each sentence.

1. She just learned (driving, to drive) a car.

2. Did he offer (paying, to pay) the bill?

3. They recall (visiting, to visit) this place long ago.

4. Do not forget (turning, to turn) off the lights.

5. I hope (graduating, to graduate) in the spring.

6. He dislikes (waiting, to wait) in line.

7. She quit (smoking, to smoke) last month.

8. They decided (going, to go) home.

9. Have you finished (reading, to read) the newspaper?

10. Lee imagined (winning, to win) the race.

Verbs with Prepositions

Prepositions are often used with verbs to express certain meanings. For example, notice how the verb *wait* is paired with different prepositions in the following examples:

> I waited **for** an hour.
> I waited **on** the customers.
> I waited **at** the bus stop.
> I waited **in** the waiting room.

These prepositions are not interchangeable, for they express different meanings. Consult a dictionary when you are unsure of the right preposition to use with a particular verb.

EXERCISE 5

Circle the correct preposition for each sentence.

1. He was not charged (with, for) a crime.

2. He was not charged (with, for) the refill.

3. I do not agree (to, with) you.

4. I did not agree (to, with) their request.

5. She cannot part (with, from) him.

6. She cannot part (with, from) those earrings.

7. Can you wait (in, for) me?

8. Can you wait (in, for) the car?

9. We differ (from, about) one another when it comes to political views.

10. We differ (from, about) the solution to that math problem.

The Prepositions *in, at,* and *on*

For expressions related to time and place, the prepositions *in, at,* and *on* have specific meanings.

Use *in*

- before a month, year, season, century, or period: *in June, in 2003, in spring, in the nineteenth century, in a week*
- before a city, state, country, or continent: *in Seattle, in California, in France, in South America*
- to mean "into" or "inside of": *in the kitchen, in the lake*

Use *at*

- before an actual clock time: *at 5 o'clock*
- before a specific place or address: *at the post office, at 1612 Oak Street*

Use *on*

- before a day or date: *on Thursday, on April 5*
- before holidays: *on Thanksgiving, on Labor Day*
- to mean "supported by," "on top of," or "at a certain place": *on the bench, on the table, on Oak Street*

EXERCISE 6

Circle the correct preposition for each sentence.

1. I will meet you (in, at, on) Friday.
2. I will meet you (in, at, on) the morning.
3. I will meet you (in, at, on) 7:15.
4. The store is (in, at, on) West Avenue.
5. The store is (in, at, on) 202 West Avenue.
6. They jumped (in, on) the lake.

"As Eyes Pan Ground Zero, Words Fail" (Mackson), 221–223
Assertive topic sentences, 338
Assumptions, avoiding, 233
"At Large: Giving Teachers Guns a Simple but Stupid Idea" (Pitts), 389–393
Audience (reader)
    avoiding assumptions about, 233
    considering, in argument, 336–338, 351
    emotional words and, 101
    helping to understand, 286–287, 321
    offending, 342
    orienting to topic, 131–132
    persuading, 287
    stimulating interest of, 128–131
    topic sentence and, 59, 60–61
    traits of active readers, 171–172
    understanding of main idea, 87
Auxiliary (helping) verbs, 424, 442, 445–447

Background information, 131–132
Baker, Russell, 11–13, 16
Barone, Michael, 165–167
Barry, Dave, 376–380
Barry, Vincent, 197
Becker, Anne, 188–189
Bird by Bird (Lamott), 14–15
Body of essay, 126, 135–137, 142–143
Body of paragraph, 61–62
Book citation, 363
Books (library research), 202

Borgenicht, David, 230–231
Brainstorming, 24–25, 31, 139, 194
Branching, 48
Brookner, Anita, 17
Buildings, names of, 531
Bullet points, 230
Businesses, names of, 531
"Bzzzz...Slap!" (Kluger), 83

Call number, 202
Call to action, 137–138, 338–339
"Can E-mail Be Saved from 'Spam'?" (Merline), 175–180
Capitalization, 529–531
Case, of pronouns, 478–480
Causal order organization, 310
Cause/effect, 323
Cause/effect pattern, 65, 66
Cause/effect transitions, 69
Cause/effect writing, 305–319
    developing points in, 312
    essays, 313–317
    ideas and topic sentence, 306–310, 312, 313
    Internet resources, 318–319
    longer passages, 312–313
    organization and transitions, 310–312, 313
    paragraphs, 306–312
    review, 318
    topic ideas, 318–319
Chain reaction of causes/effects, 307
Chicago Manual of Style, 348
Christopherson, Michelle, 197
Citations, in text, 348, 363
Classification, 256–270
    in definition writing, 322

developing, 261
essays, 264–268
Internet resources, 270
longer passages, 262–264
organization and transitions, 259–261
organizing principle for, 257–259
paragraphs, 257–261
review, 269
steps in writing, 268
topic ideas for, 269–270
topic sentence for, 258, 259
Classification pattern, 65, 66
Clauses, 428
    coordinate clauses, 499
    dependent (*See* Dependent clauses)
    independent (*See* Independent clauses)
    parallel, 510–514
    relative (*See* Relative clauses)
    restrictive or nonrestrictive, 503
Clear reference of pronouns, 482–483
Clichés, 102–103
Clustering
    informal outlines and, 48–49, 50
    in prewriting, 25–27
    in writing description, 209–210
Coherence, revising for, 81–85
Cohesiveness, revising for, 79–80
Collective nouns, 417
    agreement of pronouns and, 486–487
    subject-verb agreement and, 476–477
Colons, 528
Combination method note taking, 280
Combined modes of development, 355–369

common combinations,
    356–357
developing details in,
    361–362
essays, 363–367
Internet resources, 369
longer passages, 362–363
organization and
    transitions for, 359–361
paragraphs, 357–362
review, 368
steps in, 367–368
topic ideas, 369
topic sentence and,
    357–359
Combined mode
    paragraphs, 357–362
developing details in,
    361–362
organization and
    transitions, 359–361
topic sentence in,
    357–359
Combined sentences,
    514–523
appositives in, 519–520
compound subject or
    compound verb,
    515–516
dependent clauses in,
    516–517
editing, 95–97
participle phrases in,
    522–523
prepositional phrases in,
    520–521
relative clauses in,
    518–519
Commas, 524–526
adjectives and, 461–462
correcting run-ons, 497
punctuating dependent
    clauses, 500–501
punctuating relative
    clauses, 503, 504
use in compound
    sentences, 494
use in series, 524
Comma splice, 108–109,
    493, 495–496

Common expressions,
    104–105
Commonly confused words
    (homonyms), 536–541
Comparative adjectives,
    422–423, 460–461
Comparative adverbs, 426,
    464
Comparison/contrast,
    286–304
in combined modes of
    development,
    356–357
in definition writing, 323
essays, 295–302
Internet resources, 304
longer passages, 294–295
main idea, 288
organization and
    transitions, 290–293
paragraphs, 288–293
in persuasion, 287,
    288–289
points of comparison,
    288–289, 293
review, 303
steps in writing, 302
topic ideas, 303–304
topic sentence, 288, 290
Comparison/contrast
    pattern, 65, 66
Comparison transitions, 69,
    291
Compass points, 530
Completeness, revising for,
    76–78
Complete subjects,
    432–433
Complex sentences, 97,
    498–507
dependent clauses in,
    498–501
parallelism in, 512
punctuating dependent
    clauses, 500–501
relative clauses in,
    502–505
subordinating
    conjunctions in,
    499–500

Composition
body of essay, 142–143
paragraphs, 62–71, 72
Compound-complex
    sentences, 97, 499, 512
Compound elements,
    494–495
Compound sentences, 97,
    487–498
comma splices, avoiding,
    495–496
compound elements
    contrasted, 494–495
elements of, 487–488
independent clauses in,
    488, 489
kinds of, 488–494
run-ons, avoiding,
    496–498
Compound subjects,
    433–434
agreement of pronouns
    and, 486
in combined sentences,
    515–516
subject-verb agreement
    and, 475–476
Compound verbs, 435,
    515–516
Computers, 71, 110, 115
Concessions, in argument,
    341–343, 352
Conclusion of essay, 126,
    137–138, 144–145
Conjunctions, 427–429
coordinating (See
    Coordinating
    conjunctions)
correlative, 428
as prepositions, 429
subordinating, 428,
    499–500, 506
Conjunctive adverbs,
    425–426
correcting run-ons, 497
independent clauses
    joined by, 491–493
Conlin, Mary Lou,
    200–201
Consequences, 137

Consistency
    of pronouns, 480–481
    in verb tense, 456–457
Contractions, 527
Contradiction, 130
Contrast. *See*
    Comparison/contrast
Contrast phrases, 525
Contrast transitions, 292
Coordinate adjectives, 525
Coordinate clauses, 499
Coordinating conjunctions,
    427–428
    correcting run-ons, 497
    independent clauses
        joined by, 490–491
    joining sentences with,
        95–96
    parallelism and, 510, 511
Coordination. *See*
    Compound sentences
Correlative conjunctions,
    428
Countable nouns, 544, 545,
    546
Countries, 530
Cox, Lynne, 198
Crary, David, 81
Credibility of sources, 249
Critical reading, 180–187
    answering questions,
        181–182
    critical thinking as goal,
        181
    discussions in, 182
    Internet resources, 192
    note taking in, 181,
        182–184
Critical thinking, 165–168,
    181

Dangling modifiers,
    110–112, 467
"The Dating Game: The
    Dangers of Cash-Based
    Courtship" (Morse),
    84–85
Days of week, 530
"The Deeper Truth of Good
    and Evil" (Gellman),
    412–416

Definition, 320–334
    in combined modes of
        development, 357
    determining topic
        sentence, 321–322, 328
    developing details, 327
    essays, 327–332
    generating ideas, 322–324
    Internet resources, 334
    longer passages, 327–328
    organization and
        transitions, 325–326
    paragraphs, 321–327
    review, 333
    steps in, 332
    topic ideas for, 333–334
Definition pattern, 65, 66
"The Deli" (Machin),
    200–201
Demonstrative pronouns,
    419
Dependent clauses, 428
    combined sentences using,
        516–517
    in complex sentences,
        498–501
    parallel, 512–514
    punctuating, 500–501
    sentence fragments,
        505–506
    subordinating conjunctions
        and, 499–500
    turning sentence into, 96
Description, 209–226
    in combined modes of
        development, 356–357
    Internet resources, 226
    longer descriptions and
        essays, 219–223
    main idea and topic
        sentence, 210–212
    organization and
        transitions, 213–215
    paragraphs, 209–215
    prewriting, 209–210
    review, 224–225
    selecting details, 212
    steps in writing, 224
    topic ideas for, 225–226
    using vivid language,
        215–218

Description pattern, 65, 66
Descriptive details, 322, 323
"Design Submission" (Lin),
    219–220
Details
    developing, in combined
        paragraphs, 361–362
    developing, in definition,
        327
    in developing illustration,
        249
    factual or sensory, 199,
        200–201, 215–216,
        219–220
    relevant, in process
        writing, 233–234
    selecting, for description,
        212
    selecting, for narratives,
        195–196
Diagrams, 307, 309, 310,
    313, 317
Dialogue, 199
Diction, 98–103
    emotion, 101–102
    level of formality, 98–99
    originality, 102–103
    specificity of words,
        100–101, 199
Dictionary, use of, 115
Directions, capitalization of,
    530
Directive process, 227–228
Direct objects, 436–437
Direct quotations, 348
    introduced by colons, 528
    as introduction of essay,
        129
    punctuation, 529
    separating with commas,
        525
Discussions, in critical
    reading, 182
Distractions, 21
Division, 271–285
    in combined modes of
        development, 357
    in definition writing, 322
    determining parts and
        main idea, 273
    developing parts, 277

essays, 281–283
Internet resources, 285
longer passages, 277–279
organization and
    transitions, 274–277
paragraphs, 272–277
research, 280
review, 284
steps in writing, 283
topic ideas for, 284–285
topic sentence, 273–274
Division pattern, 65, 66
Dobbs, Lou, 349–350
Dominant impression,
    210–211, 219–220
"Don't LOL, but Texting
    Turns Me Off"
    (Veciana-Suarez),
    408–411
Double final letter, 534
Double negatives, 464–465
Double-spaced manuscript,
    117
"Do You Want to Be a
    Millionaire?" (Pride),
    116
Drafts. *See* Final draft; First
    draft

Editing, 18
    combining sentences,
        95–97
    correcting spelling errors,
        115–116
    for diction, 98–103
    eliminating wordiness,
        103–106
    errors in grammar and
        mechanics, 113–115
    of first draft, 71
    to improve style, 94–106
    major sentence errors,
        106–113
    peer review in, 118–119,
        121–122
    review, 122–123
    revising compared, 75–76
    sentence length, 95
    student demonstrations,
        118–122

types of sentences and,
    97–98
in writing essays,
    152–155
Effects, 357
Embedding sentences, 96
Emotion, 101–102
Emotional evidence, 346,
    352
"Encourage Organ Donors
    with a Little Quid Pro
    Quo" (Reed), 182–184
Encyclopedia citation, 363
Errors
    comma splices, 108–109
    faulty parallelism,
        112–113
    in freewriting, 23
    in grammar and
        mechanics, 113–115,
        116, 124
    misplaced or dangling
        modifiers, 110–112,
        466–467
    parallelism, 508, 509,
        513
    reducing with peer review,
        114–115, 119
    run-on sentences,
        108–109
    sentence fragments,
        106–108
    in sentence structure,
        106–113
    spelling errors, 115–116
    typographical, 118
Essays, 125–157
    argument, 347–351
    body of, 126, 135–137,
        142–143
    cause/effect, 313–317
    classification, 264–268
    combined modes of
        development, 363–367
    comparison/contrast,
        295–302
    conclusion of, 126,
        137–138, 144–145
    definition, 327–332
    description, 219–223

division, 281–283
identifying parts of,
    126–128
illustration, 250–253
Internet resources, 157
introduction of, 126,
    128–134
narrative essays, 200–205
process writing, 235–239
purposes of, 125–138
review, 156
student demonstration,
    138–155
Essential clauses, 503
Evidence, 61–62, 317,
    345–346, 352
Examples
    in definition writing, 322,
        323
    as introduction of essay,
        129
    in writing illustration,
        243, 244–245, 246,
        253–254
Example transitions, 69
Exclamation points,
    523–524
Expert opinion, 321
Explanation, 323

Facts, 129
Factual details
    in description, 215–216,
        219–220
    in narration, 199,
        200–201
Far-to-near pattern,
    219–220
Feedback, 7–10. *See also*
    Peer review
Figurative language,
    216–217
Final draft, 18, 116–118,
    155
First draft
    "big picture" and, 70
    composing on computer,
        71
    of essay, 141–145
    of research paper, 295

revising, 153–155
setting aside, in revising, 85, 88–89
wordiness in, 104
First-person point of view, 480
Fletcher, Winston, 234–235
Formality, level of, 98–99
Formal outlines, 46–47, 274
Format of final draft, 117
Framework for ideas, 36–42
Freewriting, 22–24, 31–32, 139
Fused sentences, 496–498
Future perfect progressive tense, 446
Future perfect tense, 446
Future progressive tense, 446
Future tense, 445–447

Gellman, Marc, 412–416
Gender, 483, 484–485
Gerunds, 450, 549–550
Gibbs, Nancy, 385–389
"The Good-News Generation" (Leo), 281–283
Grammar checks, by computer, 110
Grammatical errors, 113–115, 116, 124
Gray, John, 296–301
Group names, 530
Growing Ideas (Christopherson), 197
Growing Up (Baker), 11

Hannah, Barry, 217
Headings, 172, 230
Helping verbs, 442
Helping (auxiliary) verbs, 424, 445–447
Highbeam Research, 221
Highlighting technique, 76–77, 173–174, 280
"His Politeness Is Her Powerlessness" (Tannen), 242–243
Historical periods, 531

Holidays, 530
Homonyms, 536–541
Hongo, Garrett, 213–214
"How Do I Love Thee" (Trotter), 264–267
"How to Write a Personal Letter" (Keillor), 236–238

"The Ice Storm" (Hannah), 217
Ideas
determining order of, 35–44
formulating, 20
generating, 158–168, 306, 308, 322–324
grouping together, 39–42, 50
idea clusters, 27
modes of development (*See specific modes of development*)
reading and, 158–168
relationships, 46
relevance of, 38–39, 49–50
repetition of, 84–85
Illustration, 242–255
adequate examples, 246
in combined modes of development, 356–357
to develop definition, 327
developing, 249
essays, 250–253
Internet resources, 255
longer passages, 250
main idea and topic sentence, 244
organization and transitions, 246–248
paragraphs, 243–249
relevant examples, 244–245
review, 254
summary, 253–254
topic ideas, 255
Illustration pattern, 65, 66
Illustration transitions, 325, 326

Immediate causes and effects, 307
Implied main idea, 321, 362
Indefinite pronouns, 419, 473–475, 484–486
Indents, 117
Independent clauses, 428, 430, 498
attaching dependent clauses to, 96
in compound sentences, 488, 489
joined by conjunctive adverbs, 491–493
joined by coordinating conjunction, 490–491
joined by semicolon and conjunctive adverb, 491–492
joined by semicolon only, 493–494
joining with commas, 525
linking with semicolons, 526
parallel, 511–512
sentence fragments and, 506, 507
Indirect objects, 437–438
Infinitives, 450, 550
Informal language, 99
Informal outlines, 48–49, 50
Information, kinds of, 131–132, 219–220, 249
Informative process, 228
Intentional plagiarism, 315
Interjections, 429
Internet resources
argument, 354
browsers, 34
classification, 270
combined modes of development, 369
comparison/contrast, 304
critical reading, 192
definition, 334
description, 226
Essay Punch Web site, 157

grammatical errors, 124
illustration, 255
Journal for You, 17
narration, 207
online writing centers, 93
organizing and outlining, 52
outlining, 285
paragraphs, 74
process writing, 241
for research, 221
Interrogative pronouns, 420
Intervening prepositional phrases, 471–472
Introduction of essay, 126, 128–134, 144–145
An Introduction to Physical Science (Shipman et al), 228
Introductory elements, 525
Introductory material, 172
Inverted word order, 472–473
Irregular adjectives, 423, 460
Irregular verbs, 447–450
"It's Not in My Job Description" (Barry), 197
"It's Time to Make Up Your Mind" (Fletcher), 234–235

Jans, Nick, 184–186
Journalists, 27–28

Keillor, Garrison, 236–238
Keller, Helen, 363–367
Key words, repetition of, 84–85
"Kids and Chores" (Pantley), 84
Kluger, Jeffrey, 83
Knowledge, 6–7, 20
"Kubota" (Hongo), 213–214

Lamott, Anne, 14–15
Language, 99, 199–201, 215–218
Languages, capitalization of, 530

Layers of development
completeness and, 76, 78
in paragraphs, 67–68, 72
source material as, 295
Learning, reading for, 165–168
"Learning to Write" (Baker), 11–13
Left-to-right pattern, 213
Leo, John, 251–253, 281–283
"Let Students Have Cell Phones" (Stevenson), 8–9
Level of formality, 98–99
Library of Congress Subject Headings system, 202
Library research, 202
"'Like,' Like, Covers It All" (Skenazy), 399–403
Lin, Maya Ying, 219–220
Linking verbs, 441–443
Lipsyte, Robert, 159–161
Lists, 348, 363, 526, 528
Logical evidence, 345–346, 352
Logical fallacies, 346
Logical organization, 43–44, 50

Machin, Carmen, 200–201
Mackson, Oliver, 221–223
Magazine citation, 363
Main idea, 29–31, 32
cause/effect, 306–308
comparison/contrast, 288
in description, 210–212
in division writing, 273
in illustration, 244
implied, 321, 362
in narrative paragraphs, 193–195
in note taking, 174
in process writing, 229
reader's understanding of, 87
in summarizing, 262
in topic sentence, 55, 62–64
Main idea statements, 30–31, 32

organizing and, 36–37
in writing argument, 351
in writing essays, 139–140
"Many States Rethinking Lock-Up Policies for Criminals" (Crary), 81
Margins, 117
Matheson, Whitney, 381–385
Mechanics, 523–531
capitalization, 529–531
errors in, 113–115, 116, 124
punctuation, 523–529
Merline, John, 175–180
Metaphors, 216, 217
Microsoft Word, 110
Misplaced modifiers, 110–112, 466–467
"Mr. Fix-It and the Home-Improvement Committee" (Gray), 296–301
"MLA Formatting and Style Guide" (Purdue), 348, 363
MLA (Modern Language Association) style, 348, 363
Modern Language Association (MLA) style, 348, 363
Modifiers, 457–469
adjectives (*See* Adjectives)
adverbs (*See* Adverbs)
misplaced or dangling, 110–112, 466–467
overuse of, 468–469
in simple sentences, 438–439
writing better sentences, 468–469
Months of year, 530
Morse, Anne, 84–85
"Most Divorced Dads Deserve to See Their Kids" (Schultz), 403–407
"Mother Tongue" (Tan), 370–375

Multilingual writers, practice for, 544–553
   articles, 546–547
   countable and noncountable nouns, 544–545, 546
   gerunds and infinitives, verbs with, 549–551
   prepositions, verbs with, 551
   prepositions *in, at,* and *on,* 552–553
   unnecessary repetition of subjects, 553
   verb phrases, order of verbs in, 547–549
"Municipal Solid Waste in the United States" (EPA), 277–279
Myths about outlining, 44–46

Names of regions, 530
Narration, 193–208
   combined modes of development, 356–357
   in definition writing, 33, 322
   Internet resources, 207
   longer narratives and essays, 200–205
   main idea and topic sentence, 193–195, 200–201
   organization and transitions, 196–198
   review, 205
   selecting details, 195–196
   steps in writing, 205
   topic ideas for, 206
   using vivid language, 199–200
   writing narrative paragraphs, 193–198
Narration pattern, 65, 66
Narrative organization, 213, 249
Narrative transitions, 275
Nationalities, 530
Natural organization, 42–44

Near-to-far pattern, 213
Newsweek magazine, 221
The New York Times, 221
Noncountable nouns, 544–545, 546
"No Need to Stew: A Few Tips to Cope with Life's Annoyances" (Urbina), 394–398
Nonessential clauses, 503
Nonprint sources for research, 236
Nonrestrictive clauses, 503
"Not All in the Family" (Salerno), 168–170
Note card note taking, 280
Note taking (annotating), 280
   in active reading, 174–180
   in critical reading, 181, 182–184
Noun appositives, 478–479
Noun phrases, 439–440
Nouns, 417–418
   antecedents, 482
   appositives, 439–440, 478–479
   collective nouns, 417, 476–477, 486–487
   countable and noncountable, 544–545, 546
   forming plurals of, 532–533
   proper nouns, 417, 477, 530
   relative clause as, 502
   singular, ending in -s, 476
   subject-verb agreement, 476–477
Number, agreement of pronouns in, 484, 485
Numbers
   as organizational markers, 230–231
   spelling out, 542–543

Oates, Joyce Carol, 215–216
Objective case of pronouns, 479

Objects
   direct objects, 436–437
   indirect objects, 437–438
   of prepositions, subjects and, 434–435
Opposing arguments, 341–343, 352
Order of importance organization, 43–44, 81–82, 275, 310
Order of presentation, 35–44, 274–275
Organization, 18, 35–44, 81–84
   argument, 343–345, 352
   ascending/descending order, 259–260
   causal order, 310
   cause/effect writing, 310–312
   classification paragraphs, 257–261
   combined paragraphs, 359–361
   common strategies for, 64–66
   comparison/contrast, 290–293
   of definition, 325–326
   of description, 213–215
   determining framework, 36–42
   division, 274–277
   in narrative paragraphs, 196–198
   natural versus logical order, 42–44, 50
   by order of importance, 81–82
   point-by-point, 291–293
   of process paragraphs, 230–233
   returning to, 70
   review, 51–52
   size order, 259
   spatial order, 82–83, 275
   student demonstration, 49–50
   time order, 81, 275, 310
   using research in, 191
   whole-by-whole, 290–291

in writing essays,
140–141
in writing illustration,
246–248
Organizational markers,
230–231
Organizational skills, 146
Organizations,
capitalization of, 530
Originality of word choices,
102–103
"Our Energy Conundrum"
(Zuckerman), 314–316
Outlines, 44, 64–66, 174
Outlining, 18, 44–51
in cause/effect writing,
317
combined modes of
development and, 359
formal outlines, 46–47,
274
informal outlines, 48–49,
50
Internet resources, 52,
285
myths about, 44–46
PowerPoint presentations
and, 45
review, 51–52
student demonstration,
49–50
in writing essays,
140–141, 142
Outside-to-inside pattern,
213

"Pain Gains" (Verghese),
161–164
Pantley, Elizabeth, 84
Paragraphs, 53–74
argument, 336–346
body of, 61–62
cause/effect, 306–312
classification, 257–261
combined paragraphs,
357–362
comparison/contrast,
288–293
composing, 62–71, 72
definition, 321–327
descriptive, 209–215

division, 272–277
essays compared,
125–126
form of, 54
illustration, 243–249
Internet resources, 74
layers of development,
67–68, 72
narrative, 193–198
number of sentences in,
77, 79
organization strategies,
64–66
outlines, 66
prewriting for, 32–33
process paragraphs,
229–234
purpose of, 53, 59,
60–61
review, 73
student demonstration,
71–72, 118–122
tips for composing,
70–71, 72
topic sentence of, 54–63
transition words and
phrases, 68–70, 72
Parallel clauses, 510–514
dependent clauses,
512–514
independent clauses,
511–512
Parallelism, 508–514
clauses, 510–514
errors, 112–113, 508,
509, 513
phrases, 509–510
words, 508
Paraphrasing, 262, 329, 348
"Parenting for the Long
Haul: Success in High
School May Not Carry
into Adulthood"
(Becker), 188–189
Partial quotation, 348
Participle phrases,
459–460, 522–523
Participles, 450–451
Parts of speech, 417–430.
*See also individual
parts of speech*

adjectives (*See* Adjectives)
adverbs (*See* Adverbs)
conjunctions, 427–429,
499–500, 506
interjections, 429
nouns (*See* Nouns)
prepositions (*See*
Preposition(s))
pronouns (*See* Pronouns)
verbs (*See* Verb(s))
Passive verbs, 441–443
Passive voice, 452–453
Past participle, 447,
448–449
Past perfect progressive
tense, 446
Past perfect tense, 446
Past progressive tense, 446
Past tense, 423, 443–444,
445, 448–449
Patterns Plus (Conlin),
200–201
Peer review
in editing phase,
118–119, 121–122
in evaluating draft of
essay, 146–152
as feedback, 85–87,
89–91
reducing errors with,
114–115, 119
role in revising, 85–90
Peer reviewers, qualities of,
88
Peer review sheets, 85–87,
89, 91
Perfect verb tenses, 547
Periodicals, 202
Periods, 523–524
Personal pronouns, 419
Personification, 216, 217
Persuasion
argument, 335, 338–339
comparison/contrast, 287,
288–289
Photocopy/highlight note
taking, 280
Photographs, 27
Phrases
adjective phrases, 421
as adjectives, 458–459

as adverbs, 463–464
analyzing, 77
helping verbs in, 424
noun phrases, 418, 439–440
parallel, 509–510
participle, 459–460, 522–523
prepositional (*See* Prepositional phrases)
separating with commas, 525
verbal, 432
verb phrases, 424, 547–549
Pitts, Leonard, Jr., 389–393
Piven, Joshua, 230–231
Place, 552–553
Plagiarism, 315
"PLEASE! Turn Off Cell Phone During Funeral" (Long), 98
Plurals
with apostrophes, 527
forming, 532–534
pronouns, 474, 486
subjects, verb tense and, 443
Point-by-point organization pattern, 291–293
Point of view, 480–481
Points of comparison
in cause/effect writing, 312
in comparison/contrast writing, 288–289, 293
in longer passages, 294–295
Possession, 527
Possessive case of pronouns, 480
PowerPoint presentations, 45
Practice, opportunity for, 7–10
Prediction, 137
Preposition(s), 426–427
conjunctions as, 428, 429
in, at, and *on,* 552–553
objects of, subjects and, 434–435
verbs with, 551

Prepositional phrases, 426, 427
as adverbs, 425, 463–464
avoiding sentence fragments, 459–460
combined sentences using, 520–521
intervening, 471–472
Present perfect progressive tense, 446
Present perfect tense, 446
Present perfect tense verbs, 547
Present progressive tense, 446
Present tense, 423, 443, 445, 448–449
Previewing text, 172–173
Prewriting, 18–34
asking questions, 27–29
brainstorming, 24–25, 31, 139, 194
clustering, 25–27
description, 209–210
freewriting, 22–24
to generate ideas, 306, 308, 323–324
organizing and, 36–38
returning to, 70
review, 33–34
selecting details for narratives, 195–196
student demonstration, 31–33
talking, 21–22
topic to main idea, 29–31
using research in, 191
in writing essays, 139–140
Pride, William M., 116
Process paragraphs, 229–234
developing, 233–234
main idea and topic sentence, 229
organization and transitions, 230–233
Process pattern, 65, 66
Process writing, 227–241
directive process, 227–228

essays, 235–239
informative process, 228
Internet resources, 241
longer passages, 234–235
paragraphs, 229–234
review, 239–240
summary, 239
topic ideas, 240–241
Progressive verb tenses, 547
"Proms Equalize High School Lives" (Welsh), 56–57
Pronouns, 419–421
agreement, 483–487
capitalization, 530
case of, 478–480
clear reference, 482–483
consistency, 480–481
demonstrative pronouns, 419
indefinite, 419, 473–475, 484–486
interrogative pronouns, 420
personal pronouns, 419
proper, capitalization of, 530
relative pronouns, 420, 502, 503–505
unnecessary repetition of subjects, 553
Proofreading, 94
for spelling errors, 115, 116
for typographical errors, 118
in writing essays, 152, 153–155
Proper adjectives, 530
Proper nouns, 417, 477, 530
Proper pronouns, 530
Punctuation, 523–529
of adjectives, 461–462, 525
apostrophes, 527–528
colons, 528
commas (*See* Commas)
periods, question marks, and exclamation points, 523–524

quotation marks, 529
relative clauses, 503
semicolons, 491–494,
    497, 526–527

Question(s)
    answering, in critical
        reading, 181–182
    asking, 27–29
    in conclusion of essay,
        138
    formulating, in active
        reading, 173
    as introduction of essay,
        130
Question marks, 523–524
Quotation marks, 529

Races and tribes, 530
The Reader's Guide to
    Periodical Literature,
    202
Reading
    active reading (*See* Active
        reading)
    critical reading (*See*
        Critical reading)
Reading journal, 187–190
Reading Selections. *See*
    individual titles and
    authors
Reading/writing connection,
    158–192
    active reading, 171–180
    critical reading, 180–187
    ideas, 158–164
    improving writing skills,
        168–171
    learning and critical
        thinking, 165–168, 181
    review, 192
    use of reading journal,
        187–190
Redundant expressions, 105
Reed, Ishmael, 243
Reed, Lawrence W.,
    182–184
Reference works, in library,
    202

Relative clauses
    combined sentences using,
        518–519
    in complex sentences,
        502–505
    essential or nonessential,
        503
    punctuating, 503
    sentence fragments,
        506–507
Relative pronouns, 420,
    502, 503–505
Relevance
    of ideas, 38–39, 49–50
    of topic, 130
Relevant details
    examples, in illustration,
        244–245
    in process writing,
        233–234
    supporting reasons,
        340–341, 352
Religions, 530
Remote causes and effects,
    307
Rereading, 70
Research, 221, 292
Research writing, 191
    first draft of research
        paper, 295
    in library, 202
    note-taking methods, 280
    plagiarism, 315
    source material, 221, 236,
        249, 329, 348
    summarizing, 262
    using outlining, 47
    using questions, 28
    Works Cited list, 348,
        363
Reservation, indicating, 529
Restatement, 262
Restrictive clauses, 503
Revision, 18, 75–93
    for coherence, 81–85
    for cohesiveness, 79–80
    for completeness, 76–78
    drafts of essays, 146–152
    editing compared, 75–76

first draft, 85, 88–89,
    153–155
organization and, 81–84
peer review in, 85–90
repetition and, 84–85
review, 92–93
student demonstration,
    88–90
Run-on sentences, 108–109,
    496–498

Salerno, Steve, 168–170
School courses, 531
Schultz, Connie, 403–407
Search engines, 221
Second-person point of
    view, 480–481
Self-expression, opportunity
    for, 4
Semicolons, 526–527
    correcting run-ons, 496,
        497
    independent clauses
        joined by, 491–494
Sensory details (information)
    in description, 215–216,
        219–220
    in narration, 199,
        200–201
Sentence(s), 106, 430–487
    avoiding fragments,
        440–441, 451–452
    capitalization, 530
    combined, 95–97,
        514–523
    complex, 97, 498–507,
        512
    compound, 97, 487–498
    compound-complex, 97,
        499, 512
    improving, 468–469
    major errors in, 106–113
    modifiers, 457–469
    number of, in paragraphs,
        77, 79
    pronouns and pronoun
        agreement, 478–487
    simple sentences,
        430–440

subject-verb agreement, 469–478

topic sentences (*See* Topic Sentences)

types of, 97–98

verbs (*See* Verb(s); Verb tenses)

Sentence fragments, 57, 106–108

avoiding, 440–441, 451–452

dependent clauses, 505–506

participle or prepositional phrases, 459–460

relative clause, 506–507

Sentence length, 95

Series, 524

Shipman, James T., 228

Similes, 216, 217

Simple sentences, 97, 430–440

appositives in, 439–440

direct objects, 436–437

indirect objects in, 437–438

modifiers, 438–439

subjects of, 430–435

verbs, 435–436

Simple subjects, 432–433

Simple verb tenses, 547

Singular nouns ending in -*s*, 476

Singular pronouns, 474, 486

Size order organization, 259

Skenazy, Lenore, 399–403

Source material, 249, 329, 348

Spatial order organization, 82–83, 275

Spatial transitions, 213–214, 215, 218–220

Specific ideas, 58–59

Specific thesis statement, 142

Specific words, 100–101, 199, 216

Spelling, 532–543

abbreviations, 541–542

adding suffixes, 534–536

computer spell-checkers, 110, 115

forming plurals, 532–534

homonyms, 536–541

identifying and correcting errors, 110, 115–116

importance of, 532

numbers, 542–543

rules for, 532–536

Statistics, 129

Stevenson, Jamie, 8–9

"Stone Skipping 101" (Walker), 227–228

Storytelling. *See* Narration

Striking, 71

Strong verbs, 454–456

Student demonstrations

editing paragraphs, 118–122

essays, 138–155

freewriting, 31–32

organizing and outlining, 49–50

paragraphs, 71–72

prewriting, 31–33

revising, 88–90

"Student Problems Begin at Home: Public Schools Struggle to Fulfill Rearing Roles Abandoned by Parents" (Jans), 184–186

Style

APA style, 348

editing to improve, 94–106

MLA style, 348, 363

Subject(s), 430–435

complete, 432–433

compound, 433–434, 475–476, 486, 515–516

locations of, 431–432

objects of prepositions and, 434–435

passive voice and, 452

simple, 432–433

singular or plural, verb tense and, 443

unnecessary repetition of, 553

Subjective case of pronouns, 478, 479

Subject-verb agreement, 469–478

basics of, 469–470

collective nouns, 476–477

compound subjects and, 475–476

indefinite pronouns and, 473–475

intervening prepositional phrases, 471–472

inverted word order, 472–473

singular nouns ending in -*s*, 476

titles and proper nouns, 477

tricky issues in, 470–478

Subordinating conjunctions, 428, 499–500, 506

Subordination. *See* Complex sentences

Suffixes, adding, 534–536

Summaries, 174, 253–254, 262

"The Summer of All Fears" (Piven and Borgenicht), 230–231

Superlative adjectives, 422–423, 460–461

Superlative adverbs, 426, 464

Supporting points, 262, 340–341, 352

"Swimming to Antarctica" (Cox), 198

"Taking It Off the Streets" (Leo), 251–253

"A Tale of Two Nations" (Barone), 165–167

Talking, in prewriting, 21–22

Tan, Amy, 370–375
Tannen, Deborah, 242–243
"A Thanksgiving Feast in Aburi" (Angelou), 203–205
That/which confusion, 503–504
Thesis of essay, 125
Thesis statement
  finding, in active reading, 172
  first draft, 141–142
  in introduction to essay, 132–134
"They All Just Went Away" (Oates), 215–216
Thinking skills, 5–6, 165–168, 181
Third-person point of view, 481
Thought chains, 25–27
"Three Days to See" (Keller), 363–367
Timed writing, 24
Time magazine, 221
Time order expressions, 552–553
Time order organization, 81, 275, 310
Time order transitions, 68, 196–197, 230, 232–233
Titles, 477, 529, 530
"To Err Is Wrong" (von Oech), 250
Topic
  finding, 20, 23, 24–25
  narrowing, 20, 23
  orienting audience to, 131–132
  prewriting and, 29–31
  relevance of, explaining, 130
Topic ideas
  in cause/effect writing, 318–319
  for classification, 269–270

combined development, 369
comparison/contrast, 303–304
  for definition, 333–334
  for description, 225–226
  for division, 284–285
  for illustration, 255
  for narration, 206
  process writing, 240–241
  for writing argument, 353–354
Topic sentences, 54–61
  audience and, 59, 60–61
  cause/effect writing, 308, 309–310, 312, 313
  characteristics of, 57–61
  in classification, 258, 259
  cohesiveness and, 79
  combined development, 357–359
  comparison/contrast, 288, 290
  composition and, 70
  in definition writing, 321–322, 328
  in description, 210–212
  division, 273–274
  in illustration, 244
  main idea and, 55, 62–64
  in narratives, 193–195, 200–201
  organization pattern and, 65, 66
  persuasive, in argument, 338–339
  in process writing, 229
  revising, 87
"To Reach for the Stars" (Dobbs), 349–350
Transitions, 69
  argument, 343–345
  cause/effect writing, 310–312, 313
  classification paragraphs, 259–261
  combined development and, 359–361

comparison/contrast, 290–293
definition, 325–326
description, 213–215
division, 275–277
illustration, 247, 248
in narrative paragraphs, 196–198, 275
organization and, 81–84
in paragraphs, 68–70, 72
process paragraphs, 230–233
spatial, 213–214, 215, 218–220
time order transitions, 68, 196–197, 230, 232–233
Trotter, Robert J., 264–267
Types of sentences, 97–98
Typographical errors, 118

Underlining, 173–174
Understanding, expanding, 5–6
Unintentional plagiarism, 315
Urbina, Ian, 394–398
U.S. News and World Report, 221
USA Today, 221

Vague terms, 100–101, 242
Veciana-Suarez, Ana, 408–411
Verb(s), 423–424, 430
  active verbs, 199, 200–201, 441–443
  agreement (*See* Subject-verb agreement)
  auxiliary (helping), 424, 442, 445–447
  compound, 435, 515–516
  with gerunds or infinitives, 549–551
  irregular verbs, 447–450
  linking, 441–443
  order of, in verb phrases, 547–549

passive, 441–443
passive versus active
voice, 452–453
past participle, 447,
448–449
with prepositions, 551
in simple sentences,
435–436, 441–457
strong versus weak verbs,
454–456
Verbal(s), 418, 432,
450–451
Verbal phrases, 432
Verb phrases, 424, 547–549
Verb tenses, 443–450
chart of, 446
consistency in, 456–457
future tense, 445–447
past tense, 423, 443–444,
445, 448–449
present tense, 423, 443,
448–449
simple, perfect, or
progressive, 547
Verghese, Abraham,
161–164
Visual aids, 172
Vivid language, 199–200,
215–218
active verbs, 199,
200–201, 441–443

factual and sensory
details, 199, 200–201
specific words, 199
Voice, passive versus active,
452–453
von Oech, Roger, 250

Walker, Cameron, 227–228
Weak verbs, 454–456
Web site citation, 363
"What Is Terrorism?",
328–332
"What Makes a True Sports
Hero?" (Lipsyte),
159–161
"What's the Matter with
Moviegoers?"
(Matheson), 381–385
Whole-by-whole
organization pattern,
290–291
Who/whom confusion, 504
"Winning the War on
Drugs" (Barry),
376–380
Word(s)
commonly confused
(homonyms), 536–541
originality of choices,
102–103
parallel, 508

repetition of key words,
84–85
specificity of, 100–101,
199, 216
transition words, 68–70,
72
Wordiness, 103–106
Word order, inverted,
472–473
Word processing programs,
71
Works Cited list, 348, 363
Writer's block, 19, 20
Writing, 1–17
expectations and
attitudes, 2–3
improving skills,
168–171
increasing knowledge
about, 6–7
learning from others,
11–15
as opportunity, 4–6
as process, 18–19, 191

Zuckerman, Mortimer B.,
314–316

Rhetorical Index

Narration

"Learning to Write,"
p. 11 (Chapter 1)
"Not All in the Family,"
p. 168 (Chapter 8)
Coffeehouse scene,
p. 197 (Chapter 9)
Love of swimming,
p. 198 (Chapter 9)
Gang members in a
store, p. 200
(Chapter 9)
"A Thanksgiving Feast
in Aburi," p. 203
(Chapter 9)

Description

Run-down playground,
p. 80 (Chapter 5)
14-year-old girl, p. 83
(Chapter 5)
Nursing home parking
lot, p. 213
(Chapter 10)
Home movie, p. 215
(Chapter 10)
Condemned property,
p. 215 (Chapter 10)
Ice storm, p. 217
(Chapter 10)

"Maya Ying Lin's
Design Submission
to the Vietnam
Veterans Memorial
Competition,"
p. 219 (Chapter 10)
"As Eyes Pan Ground
Zero, Words Fail,"
p. 221 (Chapter 10)

Process

From *Bird by Bird*,
p. 14 (Chapter 1)
Mosquitoes, p. 83
(Chapter 5)
Improving test
performance, p. 145
(Chapter 7)
Skipping stones, p. 227
(Chapter 11)
Earthquakes, p. 228
(Chapter 11)
Shark attacks, p. 230
(Chapter 11)
Vaccines, p. 232
(Chapter 11)
Conquering
procrastination,
p. 234 (Chapter 11)
"How to Write a
Personal Letter,"
p. 236 (Chapter 11)

Illustration

Young man on a train,
p. 56 (Chapter 4)
Prom dresses, p. 56
(Chapter 4)
Welfare recipient, p. 62
(Chapter 4)
"What Makes a True
Sports Hero?"
p. 159 (Chapter 8)
Indirectness in Japanese
culture, p. 242
(Chapter 12)
Puritans' mean streak,
p. 243 (Chapter 12)
Founding Fathers,
p. 248 (Chapter 12)
Fear of failure, p. 250
(Chapter 12)
"Taking It Off the
Streets," p. 251
(Chapter 12)
"No Need to Stew,"
p. 394 (Reading
Selections)
"'Like,' Like, Covers It
All," p. 399
(Reading Selections)
"Don't LOL, but
Texting Turns Me
Off," p. 408
(Reading Selections)

"The Deeper Truth of Good and Evil," p. 412 (Reading Selections)

Classification

Kinds of annoying drivers, p. 76 (Chapter 5)
Psychological stressors, p. 256 (Chapter 13)
Types of language, p. 257 (Chapter 13)
Kinds of domestic violence, p. 261 (Chapter 13)
"How Do I Love Thee?" p. 264 (Chapter 13)
"Mother Tongue," p. 370 (Reading Selections)
"What's the Matter with Moviegoers?" p. 381 (Reading Selections)

Division

Parts of the brain, p. 371 (Chapter 14)
Branches of U.S. government, p. 272 (Chapter 14)
Parts of a budget, p. 376 (Chapter 14)
Analysis of garbage, p. 277 (Chapter 14)

"The Good-News Generation," p. 281 (Chapter 14)

Comparison/Contrast

Camping versus staying in a hotel, p. 77 (Chapter 5)
Child-rearing now and in the past, p. 80 (Chapter 5)
Paper grocery bags versus plastic grocery bags, p. 80 (Chapter 5)
Courtship versus dating, p. 84 (Chapter 5)
"A Tale of Two Nations," p. 165 (Chapter 8)
Studying alone versus studying with a group, p. 286 (Chapter 15)
SAT versus ACT, p. 287 (Chapter 15)
American English versus British English, p. 293 (Chapter 15)
American workers versus German workers, p. 294 (Chapter 15)
"Mr. Fix-It and the Home-Improvement Committee," p. 296 (Chapter 15)

"The Deeper Truth of Good and Evil," p. 412 (Reading Selections)

Cause/Effect

Younger workers, p. 56 (Chapter 4)
Benefits of yoga p. 77 (Chapter 5)
Children and chores, p. 84 (Chapter 5)
Courtship, p. 84 (Chapter 5)
"What Makes a True Sports Hero?" p. 159 (Chapter 8)
"Pain Gains," p. 161 (Chapter 8)
"Can E-mail Be Saved From Spam?" p. 175 (Chapter 8)
"Student Problems Begin at Home," p. 184 (Chapter 8)
Reasons young men postpone marrying, p. 305 (Chapter 16)
Effects of Internet access, p. 306 (Chapter 16)
Effects of social phobia, p. 311 (Chapter 16)
Effects of working more hours, p. 312 (Chapter 16)
"Our Energy Conundrum," p. 314 (Chapter 16)

Spammers, p. 344
(Chapter 18)
"Don't LOL, but
Texting Turns Me
Off," p. 408
(Reading Selections)

Definition

Psychological stressors,
p. 256 (Chapter 13)
Love, p. 320
(Chapter 17)
Retronym, p. 321
(Chapter 17)
Blog, p. 326
(Chapter 17)
Hero, p. 327
(Chapter 17)
"What is Terrorism?"
p. 328 (Chapter 17)

Argument

"Let Students Have Cell
Phones" (student
essay), p. 8
(Chapter 1)

Chickens as pets, p. 55
(Chapter 4)
"Do You Want to Be a
Millionaire?" p. 116
(Chapter 6)
"The Best Job I Have
Ever Had" (student
essay), p. 126
(Chapter 7)
"Satellite or Cable?"
(student essay),
p. 127 (Chapter 7)
"Encourage Organ
Donors with a Little
Quid Pro Quo,"
p. 182 (Chapter 8)
Homeschooling, p. 335
(Chapter 18)
Spammers, p. 344
(Chapter 18)
National test for
teachers, p. 345
(Chapter 18)
"To Reach for the
Stars," p. 349
(Chapter 18)
"And On the Seventh
Day We Rested,"
p. 385 (Reading
Selections)

"Giving Teachers Guns
a Simple but Stupid
Idea," p. 389
(Reading Selections)
"Most Divorced Dads
Deserve to See Their
Kids," p. 403
(Reading Selections)

Combination of Rhetorical Modes

"Be Proactive About
Studying," p. 69
(Chapter 4)
Organ donation, p. 355
(Chapter 19)
Walt Disney World
Magic Kingdom,
p. 361 (Chapter 19)
Noisy lake, p. 362
(Chapter 19)
"Three Days to See,"
p. 363 (Chapter 19)
"Winning the War on
Drugs," p. 376
(Reading Selections)